Clashing Views
on Controversial
Educational Issues

7th edition

Edited, Selected, and with Introductions by

James Wm. Noll
University of Maryland

The Dushkin Publishing Group, Inc.

For Stephanie and Sonja

Photo Acknowledgments

Part 1   Buildings/The Dushkin Publishing Group
Part 2   The Apple® Macintosh® Classic® personal computer

Manufactured in the United States of America

Seventh Edition, First Printing

Library of Congress Cataloging-in-Publication Data

Main entry under title:
    Taking sides: clashing views on controversial educational issues
      1. Education. I. Noll, James Wm., *comp.*

                          370.9
ISBN: 1–56134–124–X   92–74288

 Printed on Recycled Paper

The Dushkin Publishing Group, Inc.
Sluice Dock, Guilford, CT 06437

PREFACE

Controversy is the basis of change and, hopefully, improvement. Its lack signifies the presence of complacency, the authoritarian limitation of viewpoint expression, or the absence of realistic alternatives to the existing circumstances. An articulate presentation of a point of view on a controversial matter breathes new life into abiding human and social concerns. Controversy prompts reexamination and, perhaps, renewal.

Education is controversial. Arguments over the most appropriate aims, the most propitious means, and the most effective control have raged over the centuries. Particularly in the United States, where the systematic effort to provide education has been more democratically dispersed and more varied than elsewhere, educational issues have been contentiously debated. Philosophers, psychologists, sociologists, professional educators, lobbyists, government officials, school boards, local pressure groups, taxpayers, parents, and students have all voiced their views.

This book aims to present opposing or sharply varying viewpoints on issues, both fundamental and of current concern, in the field of education. Those that address fundamental issues, such as the purposes of education, the control of schooling, the moral development of the young, and the equalization of opportunity, are taken from the works of prominent and seminal thinkers whose ideas are much discussed.

With the background provided by the examination of arguments on fundamental issues, the student is better prepared to analyze specific issues currently undergoing heated debate. These include "choice" plans for schools, home schooling, preventing urban dropout, cultural literacy, multicultural education, discipline, tracking, mainstreaming, bilingual education, and sex education.

I have made every effort to select views from a wide range of thinkers—philosophers, psychologists, sociologists, professional educators, political leaders, historians, researchers, and gadflies.

Each issue is accompanied by an *introduction*, which sets the stage for debate, and each issue concludes with a *postscript* that summarizes the debate, considers other views on the issue, and suggests additional readings. By combining the material in this volume with the informational background provided by a good introductory textbook, the student should be prepared to address the actual problems confronting the schools today.

My hope is that the students will find challenges in the material presented here—provocations that will inspire them to better understand the roots of educational controversy, to attain a greater awareness of possible alternatives in dealing with the various issues, and to stretch their personal powers of

i

creative thinking in the search for more promising resolutions of the problems.

Changes to this edition This seventh edition represents a considerable revision. There are eight completely new issues: *Will Reforming School Funding Remove "Savage Inequalities"?* (Issue 7); *Should National Goals Guide School Performance?* (Issue 8); *Can "Choice" Lead the Way to Educational Reform?* (Issue 9); *Will the "Edison Project" Prompt Major Reforms?* (Issue 10); *Do Black Students Need an Afrocentric Curriculum?* (Issue 14); *Should Bilingual Education Programs Be Abandoned?* (Issue 15); *Do "Discipline Programs" Promote Ethical Behavior?* (Issue 18); and *Should Schools of Education Be Abolished?* (Issue 20). In addition, modifications in the pairings have been made in *Is Home Schooling a Viable Alternative?* (Issue 11); *Should Literacy Be Based on Traditional Culture?* (Issue 13); and *Is Mainstreaming Beneficial to All?* (Issue 17) in order to update the position. Although Issue 15 is new, the YES reading has been retained from an issue that appeared in the previous edition, because of its effectiveness. In all, there are 18 new selections.

A word to the instructor An *Instructor's Manual With Test Questions* (multiple-choice and essay) is available through the publisher for the instructor using *Taking Sides* in the classroom. A general guidebook, called *Using Taking Sides in the Classroom*, which discusses methods and techniques for integrating the pro-con approach into any classroom setting, is also available.

Acknowledgments I am thankful for the kind and efficient assistance given to me by Marguerite L. Egan, program manager, and the staff at The Dushkin Publishing Group. I was also greatly assisted in my work by the suggestions from the many users of *Taking Sides* who responded to a questionnaire sent by the publisher. Their comments have enhanced the quality of this edition of the book and are reflected in the new issues as well as the issues that have been retained. Special thanks go to those who responded with specific suggestions for the seventh edition:

Shirley L. Adams
University of Scranton

Edward V. Bell
William Paterson College

Deron Robert Boyles
Georgia State University

Christopher J. Campisano
Trenton State College

Joseph F. Coleman
Gwynedd-Mercy College

Thomas H. Cuppett
Lake-Sumter Community College

Clifford H. Edwards
Brigham Young University

Samuel T. Harris
Wright State University

Herbert N. Hoffman
Adelphi University

Jessica C. Kimmel
Incarnate Word College

Katherine Glass Kirkpatrick
Birmingham Southern College

Harry J. Klein
La Salle University

Ida R. Margolis
Stockton State College

Thomas S. Nagel
San Diego State University

Albert L. Nelson
Kansas Wesleyan University

Gail Rittenbach
Walla Walla College

Richard W. Robison
Manchester College

Leo R. Sandy
Rivier College

Donald S. Seckinger
University of Wyoming

Frank J. Sottile
University of Scranton

Nancy H. Vick
Longwood College

James Wm. Noll
University of Maryland

CONTENTS IN BRIEF

CONTENTS

Noted philosopher John Dewey suggests a reconsideration of the traditional approaches to schooling, giving fuller attention to the social development of the learner and the quality of his or her total experience. Robert M. Hutchins, former chancellor of the University of Chicago, argues for a liberal arts education geared to the development of intellectual powers.

Writer and editor Clifton Fadiman argues for standardized subject matter, which rescues the learner from triviality and capriciousness. Educator John Holt feels that an imposed curriculum damages the individual and usurps a basic human right to select one's own path of development.

Noted psychologist and proponent of behaviorism B. F. Skinner critiques the concept of "inner freedom" and links learning and motivation to the influence of external forces. Noted psychologist and educator Carl R. Rogers offers the "humanistic" alternative to behaviorism, insisting on the reality of subjective forces in human motivation.

Professor of education Lawrence Kohlberg outlines his theory that, following Dewey and Piaget, links values to cognitive growth. Professor of education Edward A. Wynne feels that the schools, under the influence of Kohlberg and others, have abandoned our educational traditions.

Professor of education R. Freeman Butts warns that current efforts to redefine the relationship between religion and schooling are eroding the Constitution's intent. Professor of political science Robert L. Cord offers a more accommodating interpretation of this intent.

Mortimer J. Adler, director of the Institute for Philosophical Research, contends that equality of educational opportunity can be attained in qualitative terms by establishing uniform curricular objectives for all. Former public schools superintendent Floretta Dukes McKenzie points out Adler's faulty assumptions about the learning process and his lack of attention to the realities of contemporary society.

Sociology professor Ruth Sidel examines Jonathan Kozol's controversial book *Savage Inequalities* and finds his argument for the equalization of funding compelling. Journalist Peter Schrag argues that Kozol's analysis is sometimes simplistic and often impractical.

Hudson Institute scholar Denis P. Doyle lauds "America 2000" as a history-making initiative in federal policy. Evans Clinchy, a scholar at the Institute for Responsive Education, finds a major internal contradiction in the document and calls for serious rethinking.

Political science researchers John E. Chubb and Terry M. Moe, authors of the much-discussed *Politics, Markets, and America's Schools,* make the case for choice as a means of true reform. Frances C. Fowler of Miami University in Oxford, Ohio, analyzes the premises underlying the proposals of Chubb and Moe and finds an antidemocratic tone.

Geoffrey Morris, executive editor of *National Review,* describes and lauds Chris Whittle's new plan for a nationwide network of for-profit, private secondary schools. Social activist Jonathan Kozol sees the plan, called the Edison Project, as corporate exploitation and a threat to public schooling.

David Guterson, a public school teacher, explains why he and his wife educate their own children at home. Jennie F. Rakestraw and Donald A. Rakestraw, assistant professors at Georgia Southern College, examine the history and legal status of home schooling and raise questions about the balance of power between parents and society.

Professor of education and former school superintendent Larry Cuban offers some basic assumptions and specific guidelines for dealing with the urban dropout problem. Paul Woodring, an emeritus professor of educational psychology, attacks the conventional wisdom and turns his attention outside the school.

Professor of English E. D. Hirsch, Jr., insists that higher levels of literacy must be achieved through a renewed emphasis on traditional information and a common culture. Professor of education James A. Banks argues that the nation's demographic makeup necessitates a curriculum reshaped along multicultural lines.

Black studies professor Molefi Kete Asante puts forth his argument for providing black students with an Afrocentric frame of reference, which will also enhance their self-esteem. Noted historian Arthur M. Schlesinger, Jr., documents his concerns about the recent spread of Afrocentric programs, the multiculturalization of the curriculum, and the use of history as therapy.

History of education professor Diane Ravitch finds inadequate evidence of success in bilingual education programs and expresses concern over the effort's politicization. Donaldo Macedo, an associate professor of linguistics, deplores the incessant attack on bilingual education by Ravitch and other conservatives and explores pedagogical and political implications of abandoning such programs.

Associate professor Jeannie Oakes argues that tracking exaggerates initial differences among students and contributes to mediocre schooling for many who are placed in middle or lower tracks. Charles Nevi, the director of curriculum and instruction for the Puyallup School District, feels that tracking accommodates individual differences while making "high-status knowledge" available to all.

Dean of education Dean C. Corrigan traces the roots of the Education for All Handicapped Children Act and concludes that mainstreaming can restore a sense of social purpose to the schools. Susan Ohanian, a free-lance writer and former teacher, provides case study evidence of dysfunctions in the execution of the federal mandate for mainstreaming.

Lee Canter, developer of the Assertive Discipline program, argues for the value of a positive approach to behavior management. John F. Covaleskie of Syracuse University criticizes the behavioral approach and claims that it fails to shape character.

Professor of education Kevin Ryan argues for movement toward a firmer moral grounding of sex education programs. Peter Scales, a leading advocate of sexuality education, feels that current objections to these programs are unwarranted.

Researcher Rita Kramer reports on her nationwide observations of teacher training institutions, concluding that they are not doing what they should do. School of education dean Donald J. Stedman feels that these programs are necessary and can be retooled to reach maximum effectiveness.

INTRODUCTION

Ways of Thinking About Educational Issues
James Wm. Noll

CULTURAL AND SOCIAL DYNAMICS

Concern about the quality of education has been expressed by philosophers, politicians, and parents for centuries. There has been a perpetual and unresolved debate regarding the definition of education, the relationship between school and society, the distribution of decision-making power in educational matters, and the means for improving all aspects of the educational enterprise.

In recent decades the growing influence of thinking drawn from the humanities and the behavioral and social sciences has brought about the development of interpretive, normative, and critical perspectives, which have sharpened the focus on educational concerns. These perspectives have allowed scholars and researchers to closely examine the contextual variables, value orientations, and philosophical and political assumptions that shape both the status quo and reform efforts.

The study of education involves the application of many perspectives to the analysis of "what is and how it got that way" and "what can be and how we can get there." Central to such study are the prevailing philosophical assumptions, theories, and visions that find their way into real-life educational situations. The application situation, with its attendant political pressures, sociocultural differences, community expectations, parental influence, and professional problems, provides a testing ground for contending theories and ideals.

This "testing ground" image applies only insofar as the status quo is malleable enough to allow the examination and trial of alternative views. Historically, institutionalized education has been characteristically rigid. As a "testing ground" of ideas it has often lacked an orientation encouraging innovation and futuristic thinking. Its political grounding has usually been conservative.

As social psychologist Allen Wheelis points out in *Quest for Identity*, social institutions by definition tend toward solidification and protectionism. His depiction of the dialectical development of civilizations centers on the tension between the security and authoritarianism of "institutional processes" and the dynamism and change-orientation of "instrumental processes."

Similarly, the "lonely crowd" theory of Riesman, Glazer, and Denny portrays a civilizational drift from a traditional imposed and authoritarian value structure to a socialized and internalized ethic to a contemporary situation of value fragmentation. Having cracked, or at least called into question, many of the institutional rigidities of church, school, and home, people in technologically advanced societies face three basic possibilities: learning to live with diversity and change, sliding into a new form of institutional rigidity, or reverting to traditional authoritarianism.

The field of education seems to graphically illustrate these observations. Educational practices are primarily tradition-bound. The twentieth-century reform movement, spurred by the ideas of John Dewey, A. S. Neill, and a host of critics who campaigned for change in the 1960s, challenged the structural rigidity of schooling. The current situation is one of contending forces: those who wish to continue the struggle for true reform, those who demand a return to a more traditional or "basic" model, and those who are shaping a new form of procedural conformity around the tenets of behaviorism and competency-based approaches.

We are left with the abiding questions: What is an "educated" person? What should be the primary purpose of organized education? Who should control the decisions influencing the educational process? Should the schools follow society or lead it toward change? Should schooling be compulsory?

Long-standing forces have molded a wide variety of responses to these fundamental questions. The religious impetus, nationalistic fervor, philosophical ideas, the march of science and technology, varied interpretations of "societal needs," and the desire to use the schools as a means for social reform have been historically influential. In recent times other factors have emerged to contribute to the complexity of the search for answers—social class differences, demographic shifts, increasing bureaucratization, the growth of the textbook industry, the changing financial base for schooling, teacher unionization, and strengthening of parental and community pressure groups.

The struggle to find the most appropriate answers to these questions now involves, as in the past, an interplay of societal aims, educational purposes, and individual intentions. Moral development, the quest for wisdom, citizenship training, socioeconomic improvement, mental discipline, the rational control of life, job preparation, liberation of the individual, freedom of inquiry—these and many others continue to be topics of discourse on education.

A detailed historical perspective on these questions and topics may be gained by reading the several interpretations of noted scholars in the field. R. Freeman Butts has written a brief but effective summary portrayal in "Search for Freedom—The Story of American Education," *NEA Journal* (March 1960). A partial listing of other sources includes: R. Freeman Butts and Lawrence Cremin, *A History of Education in American Culture*; S. E. Frost, Jr., *Historical and Philosophical Foundations of Western Education*; Harry Good and Edwin

Teller, *A History of Education*; Adolphe Meyer, *An Educational History of the American People*; Robert L. Church and Michael W. Sedlak, *Education in the United States: An Interpretive History*; Merle Curti, *The Social Ideas of American Educators*; Henry J. Perkinson, *The Imperfect Panacea: American Faith in Education, 1865–1965*; Clarence Karier, *Man, Society, and Education*; V. T. Thayer, *Formative Ideas in American Education*; Frank P. Besag and Jack L. Nelson, *The Foundations of Education: Stasis and Change*; H. Warren Button and Eugene F. Provenzo, Jr., *History of Education and Culture in America*; and David Tyack and Elisabeth Hansot, *Managers of Virtue: Public School Leadership in America, 1820–1980*.

These and other historical accounts of the development of schooling demonstrate the continuing need to address educational questions in terms of cultural and social dynamics. A careful analysis of contemporary education demands attention not only to the historical interpretation of developmental influences but also to the philosophical forces that define formal education and the social and cultural factors that form the basis of informal education.

EXAMINING VIEWPOINTS

In his book *A New Public Education*, Seymour Itzkoff examines the interplay between informal and formal education, concluding that economic and technological expansion have pulled people away from the informal culture by placing a premium on success in formal education. This has brought about a reactive search for less artificial educational contexts within the informal cultural community, which recognizes the impact of individual personality in shaping educational experiences.

This search for a reconstructed philosophical base for education has produced a barrage of critical commentary. Those who seek radical change in education characterize the present schools as mindless, manipulative, factory-like, bureaucratic institutions that offer little sense of community, pay scant attention to personal meaning, fail to achieve curricular integration, and maintain a psychological atmosphere of competitiveness, tension, fear, and alienation. Others deplore the ideological movement away from the formal organization of education, fearing an abandonment of standards, a dilution of the curriculum, an erosion of intellectual and behavioral discipline, and a decline in adult and institutional authority.

Students of education (whether prospective teachers, practicing professionals, or interested laypeople) must examine closely the assumptions and values underlying alternative positions in order to clarify their own viewpoints. This tri-level task may best be organized around the basic themes of purpose, power, and reform. These themes offer access to the theoretical grounding of actions in the field of education, to the political grounding of such actions, and to the future orientation of action decisions.

A general model for the examination of positions on educational issues includes the following dimensions: identification of the viewpoint, recognition of the stated or implied assumptions underlying the viewpoint, analysis of the validity of the supporting argument, and evaluation of the conclusions and action-suggestions of the originator of the position. The stated or implied assumptions may be derived from a philosophical or religious orientation, from scientific theory, from social or personal values, or from accumulated experience. Acceptance by the reader of an author's assumptions opens the way for a receptive attitude regarding the specific viewpoint expressed and its implications for action. The argument offered in justification of the viewpoint may be based on logic, common experience, controlled experiments, information and data, legal precedents, emotional appeals, and/or a host of other persuasive devices.

Holding the basic model in mind, readers of the positions presented in this volume (or anywhere else, for that matter) can examine the constituent elements of arguments—basic assumptions, viewpoint statements, supporting evidence, conclusions, and suggestions for action. The careful reader will accept or reject the individual elements of the total position. One might see reasonableness in a viewpoint and its justification but be unable to accept the assumptions on which it is based. Or one might accept the flow of argument from assumptions to viewpoint to evidence but find illogic or impracticality in the stated conclusions and suggestions for action. In any event, the reader's personal view is tested and honed through the process of analyzing the views of others.

PHILOSOPHICAL CONSIDERATIONS

Historically, organized education has been initiated and instituted to serve many purposes—spiritual salvation, political socialization, moral uplift, societal stability, social mobility, mental discipline, vocational efficiency, and social reform, among others. The various purposes have usually reflected the dominant philosophical conception of human nature and the prevailing assumptions about the relationship between the individual and society. At any given time, competing conceptions may vie for dominance—social conceptions, economic conceptions, conceptions that emphasize spirituality, or conceptions that stress the uniqueness and dignity of the individual, for example.

These considerations of human nature and individual-society relationships are grounded in philosophical assumptions, and these assumptions find their way to such practical domains as schooling. In Western civilization there has been an identifiable (but far from consistent and clear-cut) historical trend in the basic assumptions about reality, knowledge, values, and the human condition. This trend, made manifest in the philosophical positions of idealism, realism, pragmatism, and existentialism, has involved a shift in emphasis from the spiritual world to nature to human behavior to the social individual to the free individual, and from eternal ideas to fixed natural laws to social interaction to the inner person.

The idealist tradition, which dominated much of philosophical and educational thought until the eighteenth and nineteenth centuries, separates the changing, imperfect material world and the permanent, perfect spiritual or mental world. As Plato saw it, for example, human beings and all other physical entities are particular manifestations of an ideal reality which, in material existence, humans can never fully know. The purpose of education is to bring us closer to the absolute ideals, pure forms, and universal standards that exist spiritually by awakening and strengthening our rational powers. For Plato, a curriculum based on mathematics, logic, and music would serve this purpose, especially in the training of leaders whose rationality must exert control over emotionality and baser instincts.

Against this tradition, which shaped the liberal arts curriculum in schools for centuries, the realism of Aristotle, with its finding of the "forms" of things *within* the material world, brought an emphasis on scientific investigation and on environmental factors in the development of human potential. This fundamental view has influenced two philosophical movements in education: "naturalism," based on following or gently assisting nature (as in the approaches of John Amos Comenius, Jean-Jacques Rousseau, and Johann Heinrich Pestalozzi), and "scientific realism," based on uncovering the natural laws of human behavior and shaping the educational environment to maximize their effectiveness (as in the approaches of John Locke, Johann Friedrich Herbart, and Edward Thorndike).

In the twentieth century, two philosophical forces (pragmatism and existentialism) have challenged these traditions. Each has moved primary attention away from fixed spiritual or natural influences and toward the individual as shaper of knowledge and values. The pragmatic position, articulated in America by Charles Sanders Peirce, William James, and John Dewey, turns from metaphysical abstractions toward concrete results of action. In a world of change and relativity, human beings must forge their own truths and values as they interact with their environments and each other. The European-based philosophy of existentialism, emerging from such thinkers as Gabriel Marcel, Martin Buber, Martin Heidegger, and Jean-Paul Sartre, has more recently influenced education here. Existentialism places the burdens of freedom, choice, and responsibility squarely on the individual, viewing the current encroachment of external forces and the tendency of people to "escape from freedom" as a serious diminishment of our human possibilities.

All of these basic philosophical views and many of their countless variations are operative today and provide the grounding of most of the positions on contemporary educational issues, including those presented in this book. The conservative and "liberal arts" tradition, emphasizing the humanities, the cultural heritage, and moral standards, can be easily detected in the words of Robert M. Hutchins (Issue 1), Clifton Fadiman (Issue 2), Edward A.

Wynne (Issue 4), Mortimer J. Adler (Issue 6), and E. D. Hirsch, Jr. (Issue 13). The progressive, experimental approach, concentrating on critical intelligence, sociopsychological factors, and social adjustment, is found in the ideas of John Dewey (Issue 1), John Holt (Issue 2), Lawrence Kohlberg (Issue 4), and James A. Banks (Issue 13). Modern behaviorism, taking cues from the earlier scientific realism, finds its way into education through the views of B. F. Skinner (Issue 3), while existentialist concerns regarding human subjectivity, self-actualization, and authenticity are aired by Carl R. Rogers (Issue 3) and, perhaps, David Guterson (Issue 11).

And so these many theoretical slants contend for recognition and acceptance as we continue the search for broad purposes in education and as we attempt to create curricula, methodologies, and learning environments that fulfill our stated purposes. This is carried out, of course, in the real world of the public schools in which social, political, and economic forces often predominate.

POWER AND CONTROL

Plato, in the fourth century B.C., found existing education manipulative and confining and, in the *Republic*, described a meritocratic approach designed to nurture intellectual powers so as to form and sustain a rational society. Reform-oriented as Plato's suggestions were, he nevertheless insisted on certain restrictions and controls so that his particular version of the "ideal" could be met.

The ways and means of education have been fertile grounds for power struggles throughout history. Many educational efforts have been initiated by religious bodies, often creating a conflict situation when secular authorities have moved into the field. Schools have usually been seen as repositories of culture and social values and, as such, have been overseen by the more conservative forces in society. To others, bent on social reform, the schools have been treated as a spawning ground for change. Given these basic political forces, conflict is inevitable.

When one speaks of the control of education, the range of influence is indeed wide. Political influences, governmental actions, court decisions, professional militancy, parental power, and student assertion all contribute to the phenomenon of control. And the domain of control is equally broad—school finances, curriculum, instructional means and objectives, teacher certification, accountability, student discipline, censorship of school materials, determination of access and opportunity, and determination of inclusion and exclusion.

The general topic of power and control leads to a multitude of questions: Who should make policy decisions? Must the schools be puppets of the government? Can the schools function in the vanguard of social change? Can cultural indoctrination be avoided? Can the schools lead the way to full social integration? Can the effects of social class be eradicated? Can and should the schools teach values? Dealing with such questions is complicated by the increasing power of the federal government in educational matters. Congressional legislation has broadened substantially from the early land grants and aid to agricultural and vocational programs to more recent laws covering aid to federally impacted areas, school construction aid, student loans and fellowships, support for several academic areas of the curriculum, work-study programs, compensatory education, employment opportunities for youth, adult education, aid to libraries, teacher preparation, educational research, career education, education of the handicapped, and equal opportunity for females. This proliferation of areas of influence has caused the federal administrative bureaucracy to blossom from its meager beginnings in 1867 into a cabinet-level Department of Education in 1979.

State legislatures and state departments of education have also grown in power, handling greater percentages of school appropriations and controlling basic curricular decisions, attendance laws, accreditation, research, etc. Local school boards, once the sole authorities in policy-making, now share the role with higher governmental echelons as the financial support sources shift away from the local scene. Simultaneously, strengthened teacher organizations and increasingly vocal pressure groups at the local, state, and national levels have forced a widening of the base for policy decisions.

SOME CONCLUDING REMARKS

The schools often seem to be either facing backward or to be completely absorbed in the tribulations of the present, lacking a vision of possible futures that might guide current decisions. The present is inescapable, obviously, and certainly the historical and philosophical underpinnings of the present situation must be understood, but true improvement often requires a break with conventionality—a surge toward a desired future.

The radical reform critique of government-sponsored compulsory schooling has depicted organized education as a form of cultural or political imprisonment that traps young people in an artificial and mainly irrelevant environment and rewards conformity and docility while inhibiting curiosity and creativity. Constructive reform ideas that have come from this critique include the creation of "open" classrooms, the de-emphasis of external motivators, the diversification of educational experience, and the building of a true sense of "community" within the instructional environment.

Starting with Francis Wayland Parker's schools in Quincy, Massachusetts, and John Dewey's laboratory school at the University of Chicago around the turn of the current century, the campaign to make schools into more productive and humane places has been relentless. The duplication of A. S. Neill's Summerhill model in the free school movement in the 1960s, the open classroom/open space trends of recent years, the several curricular variations on applications of "humanistic" ideals, and the emergence of schools without walls, storefront schools, and street academies in a number of urban areas testify to the desire to reform the present system or to build alternatives to it.

The progressive education movement, the development of "life adjustment" goals and curricula, and the "whole person" theories of educational psychology moved the schools toward an expanded concept of schooling that embraced new subject matters and new approaches to discipline during the first half of this century. Since the 1950s, however, pressure for a return to a narrower concept of schooling as intellectual training has sparked new waves of debate. Out of this situation have come attempts by educators and academicians to design new curricular approaches in the basic subject matter areas, efforts by private foundations to stimulate organizational innovations and to improve the training of teachers, and federal government support of the community school model and the career educational curriculum. Yet, criticism of the schools abounds. The schools, according to many who use their services, remain too factorylike, too age-segregated, and too custodial. Alternative paths are still sought—paths that would allow action-learning, work-study, and a diversity of ways to achieve success.

H. G. Wells has told us that human history becomes more and more a race between education and catastrophe. What is needed in order to win this race is the generation of new ideas regarding cultural change, human relationships, ethical norms, the uses of technology, and the quality of life. These new ideas, of course, may be old ideas newly applied. One could do worse, in thinking through the problem of improving the quality of education, than to turn to the third-century philosopher Plotinus, who called for an education directed to "the outer, the inner, and the whole." For Plotinus, "the outer" represented the public person, or the socioeconomic dimension of the total human being; "the inner" reflected the subjective dimension, the uniquely experiencing individual, or the "I"; and "the whole" signified the universe of meaning and relatedness, or the realm of human, natural, and spiritual connectedness. It would seem that education must address all of these dimensions if it is to truly help people in the lifelong struggle to shape a meaningful existence. If educational experiences can be improved in these directions, the end result might be people who are not just filling space, filling time, or filling a social role, but who are capable of saying something worthwhile in their lives.

PART 1

Fundamental Issues

The issues discussed in this section are fundamental to any inquiry into education. The answers to the questions raised explore diverse views of human nature, educational aims, moral development, religion, equality of opportunity, and political influence as they relate to shaping educational policy.

Should Schooling Be Based on Social Experiences?

Should Schools Determine What Is Learned?

Should Behaviorism Shape Educational Practices?

Should Values Be Developed Rather Than Transmitted?

Is Church-State Separation Being Threatened?

Does a Common Curriculum Promote Equality?

Will Reforming School Funding Remove "Savage Inequalities"?

Should National Goals Guide School Performance?

ISSUE 1

Should Schooling Be Based on Social Experiences?

YES: John Dewey, from *Experience and Education* (Macmillan, 1938)

NO: Robert M. Hutchins, from *The Conflict in Education* (Harper & Row, 1953)

ISSUE SUMMARY

YES: Philosopher John Dewey suggests a reconsideration of traditional approaches to schooling, giving fuller attention to the social development of the learner and the quality of his or her total experience.
NO: Noted educator and one-time chancellor of the University of Chicago Robert M. Hutchins argues for a liberal arts education geared to the development of intellectual powers.

Throughout history, organized education has served many purposes—the transmission of tradition, knowledge, and skills; the acculturation and socialization of the young; the building and preserving of political-economic systems; the provision of opportunity for social mobility; the enhancement of the quality of life; and the cultivation of individual potential, among others. At any given time, schools pursue a number of such goals, but the elucidation of a primary or overriding goal, which gives focus to all others, has been a source of continuous contention.

Schooling in America has been extended in the last 100 years to vast numbers of young people, and during this time the argument over aims has gained momentum. At the turn of the century, John Dewey was raising serious questions about the efficacy of the prevailing approach to schooling. He believed that schooling was often arid, pedantic, and detached from the real lives of children and youths. In establishing his laboratory school at the University of Chicago, Dewey hoped to demonstrate that experiences provided by schools could be meaningful extensions of the normal social activities of learners, having as their primary aim the full experiential growth of the individual.

In order to accomplish this, Dewey sought to bring the learner into an active and intimate relationship with the subject matter. The problem-solving or inquiry approach that he and his colleagues at Columbia University in New York City devised became the cornerstone of the "new education"—the progressive education movement.

In 1938, Dewey himself (as expressed in his article that follows) sounded a note of caution to progressive educators who may have abandoned too completely the traditional disciplines in their attempt to link schooling with the needs and interests of the learners. Having spawned an educational revolution, Dewey, in his later years, emerges as more of a compromiser.

In that same year, William C. Bagley, in "An Essentialists' Platform for the Advancement of American Education," harshly criticized what he felt were anti-intellectual excesses promulgated by progressivism. In the 1950s and 1960s this theme was elaborated on by other academics, among them Robert M. Hutchins, Hyman Rickover, Arthur Bestor, and Max Rafferty, who demanded a return to intellectual discipline, higher standards, and moral guidance.

Hutchins's critique of Dewey's pragmatic philosophy was perhaps the best reasoned. He felt that the emphasis on immediate needs and desires of students and the focus on change and relativism detracted from the development of the intellectual skills needed for the realization of human potential.

In the following selections, John Dewey charts the necessary shift from the abstractness and isolation of traditional schooling to the concreteness and vitality of the newer concept. Robert M. Hutchins dissects the assumptions underlying Dewey's position and puts forth his own theory based on the premise that human nature is constant and functions the same in every society.

YES   John Dewey

EXPERIENCE AND EDUCATION

Mankind likes to think in terms of extreme opposites. It is given to formulating its beliefs in terms of *Either-Ors*, between which it recognizes no intermediate possibilities. When forced to recognize that the extremes cannot be acted upon, it is still inclined to hold that they are all right in theory but that when it comes to practical matters circumstances compel us to compromise. Educational philosophy is no exception. The history of educational theory is marked by opposition between the idea that education is development from within and that it is formation from without; that it is based upon natural endowments and that education is a process of overcoming natural inclination and substituting in its place habits acquired under external pressure.

At present, the opposition, so far as practical affairs of the school are concerned, tends to take the form of contrast between traditional and progressive education. If the underlying ideas of the former are formulated broadly, without the qualifications required for accurate statement, they are found to be about as follows: The subject-matter of education consists of bodies of information and of skills that have been worked out in the past; therefore, the chief business of the school is to transmit them to the new generation. In the past, there have also been developed standards and rules of conduct; moral training consists of forming habits of action in conformity with these rules and standards. Finally, the general pattern of school organization (by which I mean the relations of pupils to one another and to the teachers) constitutes the school as a kind of institution sharply marked off from other social institutions. Call up in imagination the ordinary schoolroom, its time schedules, schemes of classification, of examination and promotion, of rules of order, and I think you will grasp what is meant by "pattern of organization." If then you contrast this scene with what goes on in the family, for example, you will appreciate what is meant by the school being a kind of institution sharply marked off from any other form of social organization.

From John Dewey, *Experience and Education* (Macmillan, 1938). Copyright © 1938 by Kappa Delta Pi, an international honor society in education. Reprinted by permission.

The three characteristics just mentioned fix the aims and methods of instruction and discipline. The main purpose or objective is to prepare the young for future responsibilities and for success in life, by means of acquisition of the organized bodies of information and prepared forms of skill which comprehend the material of instruction. Since the subject-matter as well as standards of proper conduct are handed down from the past, the attitude of pupils must, upon the whole, be one of docility, receptivity, and obedience. Books, especially textbooks, are the chief representatives of the lore and wisdom of the past, while teachers are the organs through which pupils are brought into effective connection with the material. Teachers are the agents through which knowledge and skills are communicated and rules of conduct enforced.

I have not made this brief summary for the purpose of criticizing the underlying philosophy. The rise of what is called new education and progressive schools is of itself a product of discontent with traditional education. In effect it is a criticism of the latter. When the implied criticism is made explicit it reads somewhat as follows: The traditional scheme is, in essence, one of imposition from above and from outside. It imposes adult standards, subject-matter, and methods upon those who are only growing slowly toward maturity. The gap is so great that the required subject-matter, the methods of learning and of behaving are foreign to the existing capacities of the young. They are beyond the reach of the experience the young learners already possess. Consequently, they must be imposed; even though good teachers will use devices of art to cover up the imposition so as to relieve it of obviously brutal features.

But the gulf between the mature or adult products and the experience and abilities of the young is so wide that the very situation forbids much active participation by pupils in the development of what is taught. Theirs is to do—and learn, as it was the part of the six hundred to do and die. Learning here means acquisition of what already is incorporated in books and in the heads of the elders. Moreover, that which is taught is thought of as essentially static. It is taught as a finished product, with little regard either to the ways in which it was originally built up or to changes that will surely occur in the future. It is to a large extent the cultural product of societies that assumed the future would be much like the past, and yet it is used as educational food in a society where change is the rule, not the exception.

If one attempts to formulate the philosophy of education implicit in the practices of the new education, we may, I think, discover certain common principles amid the variety of progressive schools now existing. To imposition from above is opposed expression and cultivation of individuality; to external discipline is opposed free activity; to learning from texts and teachers, learning through experience; to acquisition of isolated skills and techniques by drill, is opposed acquisition of them as mean of attaining ends which make direct vital appeal; to preparation for a more or less remote future is opposed making the most of the opportunities of present life; to static aims and materials is opposed acquaintance with a changing world.

Now, all principles by themselves are abstract. They become concrete only in the consequences which result from their application. Just because the principles set forth are so fundamental and far-reaching, everything depends upon the interpretation given them as they are put into practice in the school and the home. It is at this point that the reference made earlier to *Either-Or* philosophies becomes peculiarly pertinent. The general philosophy of the new education may be sound, and yet the difference in abstract principles will not decide the way in which the moral and intellectual preference involved shall be worked out in practice. There is always the danger in a new movement that in rejecting the aims and methods of that which it would supplant, it may develop its principles negatively rather than positively and constructively. Then it takes its clew in practice from that which is rejected instead of from the constructive development its own philosophy.

I take it that the fundamental unity of the newer philosophy is found in the idea that there is an intimate and necessary relation between the processes of actual experience and education. If this be true, then a positive and constructive development of its own basic idea depends upon having a correct idea of experience. Take, for example, the question of organized subject-matter. . . . The problem for progressive education is: What is the place and meaning of subject-matter and of organization *within* experience? How does subject-matter function? Is there anything inherent in experience which tends towards progressive organization of its contents? What results follow when the materials of experience are not progressively organized? A philosophy which proceeds on the basis of rejection, of sheer opposition, will neglect these questions. It will tend to suppose that because the old education was based on ready-made organization, therefore it suffices to reject the principle of organization *in toto*, in-

stead of striving to discover what it means and how it is to be attained on the basis of experience. We might go through all the points of difference between the new and the old education and reach similar conclusions. When external control is rejected, the problem becomes that of finding the factors of control that are inherent within experience. When external authority is rejected, it does not follow that all authority should be rejected, but rather that there is need to search for a more effective source of authority. Because the older education imposed the knowledge, methods, and the rules of conduct of the mature person upon the young, it does not follow, except upon the basis of the extreme *Either-Or* philosophy, that the knowledge and skill of the mature person has no directive value for the experience of the immature. On the contrary, basing education upon personal experience may mean more multiplied and more intimate contacts between the mature and the immature than ever existed in the traditional school, and consequently more, rather than less, guidance by others. The problem, then, is: how these contacts can be established without violating the principle of learning through personal experience. The solution of this problem requires a well thought-out philosophy of the social factors that operate in the constitution of individual experience.

What is indicated in the foregoing remarks is that the general principles of the new education do not of themselves solve any of the problems of the actual or practical conduct and management of progressive schools. Rather, they set new problems which have to be worked out on the basis of a new philosophy of experience. The problems are not even recognized, to say nothing of being solved, when it is assumed that it suffices to reject the ideas and practices of the old education and then go to the opposite extreme. Yet I am sure that you will appreciate what is meant when I say that many of the newer schools tend to make little or nothing of organized subject-matter of study; to proceed as if any form of direction and guidance by adults were an invasion of individual freedom, and as if the idea that education should be concerned with the present and future meant that acquaintance with the past has little or no role to play in education. Without pressing these defects to the point of exaggeration, they at least illustrate what is meant by a theory and practice of education which proceeds negatively or by reaction against what has been current in education rather than by a positive and constructive development of purposes, methods, and subject-matter on the foundation of a theory of experience and its educational potentialities.

It is not too much to say that an educational philosophy which professes to be based on the idea of freedom may become as dogmatic as ever was the traditional education which is reacted against. For any theory and set of practices is dogmatic which is not based upon critical examination of its own underlying principles. Let us say that the new education emphasizes the freedom of the learner. Very well. A problem is now set. What does freedom mean and what are the conditions under which it is capable of realization? Let us say that the kind of external imposition which was so common in the traditional school limited rather than promoted the intellectual and moral development of the young. Again, very well. Recognition of this serious defect sets a problem. Just what is the role of the teacher and of books in pro-

moting the educational development of the immature? Admit that traditional education employed as the subject-matter for study facts and ideas so bound up with the past as to give little help in dealing with the issues of the present and future. Very well. Now we have the problem of discovering the connection which actually exists *within* experience between the achievements of the past and the issues of the present. We have the problem of ascertaining how acquaintance with the past may be translated into a potent instrumentality for dealing effectively with the future. We may reject knowledge of the past as the *end* of education and thereby only emphasize its importance as a *means*. When we do that we have a problem that is new in the story of education: How shall the young become acquainted with the past in such a way that the acquaintance is a potent agent in appreciation of the living present? . . .

In short, the point I am making is that rejection of the philosophy and practice of traditional education sets a new type of difficult educational problem for those who believe in the new type of education. We shall operate blindly and in confusion until we recognize this fact; until we thoroughly appreciate that departure from the old solves no problems. What is said in the following pages is, accordingly, intended to indicate some of the main problems with which the newer education is confronted and to suggest the main lines along which their solution is to be sought. I assume that amid all uncertainties there is one permanent frame of reference: namely, the organic connection between education and personal experience; or, that the new philosophy of education is committed to some kind of empirical and experimental philosophy. But experience and experiment are not self-explanatory ideas. Rather, their meaning is part of the problem to be explored. To know the meaning of empiricism we need to understand what experience is.

The belief that all genuine education comes about through experience does not mean that all experiences are genuinely or equally educative. Experience and education cannot be directly equated to each other. For some experiences are miseducative. Any experience is miseducative that has the effect of arresting or distorting the growth of further experience. An experience may be such as to engender callousness; it may produce lack of sensitivity and of responsiveness. Then the possibilities of having richer experience in the future are restricted. Again, a given experience may increase a person's automatic skill in a particular direction and yet tend to land him in a groove or rut; the effect again is to narrow the field of further experience. An experience may be immediately enjoyable and yet promote the formation of a slack and careless attitude; this attitude then operates to modify the quality of subsequent experiences so as to prevent a person from getting out of them what they have to give. Again, experiences may be so disconnected from one another that, while each is agreeable or even exciting in itself, they are not linked cumulatively to one another. Energy is then dissipated and a person becomes scatter-brained. Each experience may be lively, vivid, and "interesting," and yet their disconnectedness may artificially generate dispersive, disintegrated, centrifugal habits. The consequence of formation of such habits is inability to control future experiences. They are then taken, either by way of enjoyment or of discontent and revolt, just as they come. Under such circumstances, it is idle to talk of self-control.

Traditional education offers a plethora of examples of experiences of the kinds just mentioned. It is a great mistake to suppose, even tacitly, that the traditional schoolroom was not a place in which pupils had experiences. Yet this is tacitly assumed when progressive education as a plan of learning by experience is placed in sharp opposition to the old. The proper line of attack is that the experiences which were had, by pupils and teachers alike, were largely of a wrong kind. How many students, for example, were rendered callous to ideas, and how many lost the impetus to learn because of the way in which learning was experienced by them? How many acquired special skills by means of automatic drill so that their power of judgment and capacity to act intelligently in new situations was limited? How many came to associate the learning process with ennui and boredom? How many found what they did learn so foreign to the situations of life outside the school as to give them no power of control over the latter? How many came to associate books with dull drudgery, so that they were "conditioned" to all but flashy reading matter?

If I ask these questions, it is not for the sake of wholesale condemnation of the old education. It is for quite another purpose. It is to emphasize the fact, first, that young people in traditional schools do have experiences; and, secondly, that the trouble is not the absence of experiences, but their defective and wrong character—wrong and defective from the standpoint of connection with further experience. The positive side of this point is even more important in connection with progressive education. It is not enough to insist upon the necessity of experience, nor even of activity in experience. Everything depends upon the *quality* of the experience which is had. The quality of an experience has two aspects. There is an immediate aspect of agreeableness or disagreeableness, and there is its influence upon later experiences. The first is obvious and easy to judge. The *effect* of an experience is not borne on its face. It sets a problem to the educator. It is his business to arrange for the kind of experiences which, while they do not repel the student, but rather engage his activities are, nevertheless, more than immediately enjoyable since they promote having desirable future experiences. Just as no man lives or dies to himself, so no experience lives or dies to itself. Wholly independent of desire or intent, every experience lives on in further experiences. Hence the central problem of an education based upon experience is to select the kind of present experiences that live fruitfully and creatively in subsequent experiences.

. . . Here I wish simply to emphasize the importance of this principle [of the continuity of experience] for the philosophy of educative experience. A philosophy of education, like my theory, has to be stated in words, in symbols. But so far as it is more than verbal it is a plan for conducting education. Like any plan, it must be framed with reference to what is to be done and how it is to be done. The more definitely and sincerely it is held that education is a development within, by, and for experience, the more important it is that there shall be clear conceptions of what experience is. Unless experience is so conceived that the result is a plan for deciding upon subject-matter, upon methods of instruction and discipline, and upon material equipment and social

organization of the school, it is wholly in the air. It is reduced to a form of words which may be emotionally stirring but for which any other set of words might equally well be substituted unless they indicate operations to be initiated and executed. Just because traditional education was a matter of routine in which the plans and programs were handed down from the past, it does not follow that progressive education is a matter of planless improvisation.

The traditional school could get along without any consistently developed philosophy of education. About all it required in that line was a set of abstract words like culture, discipline, our great cultural heritage, etc., actual guidance being derived not from them but from custom and established routines. Just because progressive schools cannot rely upon established traditions and institutional habits, they must either proceed more or less haphazardly or be directed by ideas which, when they are made articulate and coherent, form a philosophy of education. Revolt against the kind of organization characteristic of the traditional school constitutes a demand for a kind of organization based upon ideas. I think that only slight acquaintance with the history of education is needed to prove that educational reformers and innovators alone have felt the need for a philosophy of education. Those who adhered to the established system needed merely a few fine-sounding words to justify existing practices. The real work was done by habits which were so fixed as to be institutional. The lesson for progressive education is that it requires in an urgent degree, a degree more pressing than was incumbent upon former innovators, a philosophy of education based upon a philosophy of experience.

I remarked incidentally that the philosophy in question is, to paraphrase the saying of Lincoln about democracy, one of education of, by, and for experience. No one of these words, *of*, *by*, or *for*, names anything which is self-evident. Each of them is a challenge to discover and put into operation a principle of order and organization which follows from understanding what education experience signifies.

It is, accordingly, a much more difficult task to work out the kinds of materials, of methods, and of social relationships that are appropriate to the new education than is the case with traditional education. I think many of the difficulties experienced in the conduct of progressive schools and many of the criticisms leveled against them arise from this source. The difficulties are aggravated and the criticisms are increased when it is supposed that the new education is somehow easier than the old. This belief is, I imagine, more or less current. Perhaps it illustrates again the *Either-Or* philosophy, springing from the idea that about all which is required is *not* to do what is done in traditional schools.

I admit gladly that the new education is *simpler* in principle than the old. It is in harmony with principles of growth, while there is very much which is artificial in the old selection and arrangement of subjects and methods, and artificiality always leads to unnecessary complexity. But the easy and the simple are not identical. To discover what is really simple and to act upon the discovery is an exceedingly difficult task. After the artificial and complex is once institutionally established and ingrained in custom and routine, it is easier to walk in the paths that have been beaten than it is, after taking a new point of view, to work out

what is practically involved in the new point of view. The old Ptolemaic astronomical system was more complicated with its cycles and epicycles than the Copernican system. But until organization of actual astronomical phenomena on the ground of the latter principle had been effected the easiest course was to follow the line of least resistance provided by the old intellectual habit. So we come back to the idea that a coherent *theory* of experience, affording positive direction to selection and organization of appropriate educational methods and materials, is required by the attempt to give new direction to the work of the schools. The process is a slow and arduous one. It is a matter of growth, and there are many obstacles which tend to obstruct growth and to deflect it into wrong lines.

. . . [W]e must escape from the tendency to think of organization in terms of the *kind* of organization, whether of content (or subject-matter), or of methods and social relations, that mark traditional education. I think that a good deal of the current opposition to the idea of organization is due to the fact that it is so hard to get away from the picture of the studies of the old school. The moment "organization" is mentioned imagination goes almost automatically to the kind of organization that is familiar, and in revolting against that we are led to shrink from the very idea of any organization. On the other hand, educational reactionaries, who are now gathering force, use the absence of adequate intellectual and moral organization in the newer type of school as proof not only of the need of organization, but to identify any and every kind of organization with that instituted before the rise of experimental science. Failure to develop a conception of organization upon the empirical and experimental basis gives reactionaries a too easy victory. But the fact that the empirical sciences now offer the best type of intellectual organization which can be found in any field shows that there is no reason why we, who call ourselves empiricists, should be "pushovers" in the matter of order and organization.

NO
Robert M. Hutchins

THE BASIS OF EDUCATION

The obvious failures of the doctrines of adaptation, immediate needs, social reform, and of the doctrine that we need no doctrine at all may suggest to us that we require a better definition of education. Let us concede that every society must have some system that attempts to adapt the young to their social and political environment. If the society is bad, in the sense, for example, in which the Nazi state was bad, the system will aim at the same bad ends. To the extent that it makes men bad in order that they may be tractable subjects of a bad state, the system may help to achieve the social ideals of the society. It may be what the society wants; it may even be what the society needs, if it is to perpetuate its form and accomplish its aims. In pragmatic terms, in terms of success in the society, it may be a "good" system.

But it seems to me clearer to say that, though it may be a system of training, or instruction, or adaptation, or meeting immediate needs, it is not a system of education. It seems clearer to say that the purpose of education is to improve men. Any system that tries to make them bad is not education, but something else. If, for example, democracy is the best form of society, a system that adapts the young to it will be an educational system. If despotism is a bad form of society, a system that adapts the young to it will not be an educational system, and the better it succeeds in adapting them the less educational it will be.

Every man has a function as a man. The function of a citizen or a subject may vary from society to society, and the system of training, or adaptation, or instruction, or meeting immediate needs may vary with it. But the function of a man as man is the same in every age and in every society, since it results from his nature as a man. The aim of an educational system is the same in every age and in every society where such a system can exist: it is to improve man as man.

If we are going to talk about improving men and societies, we have to believe that there is some difference between good and bad. This difference must not be, as the positivists think it is, merely conventional. We cannot tell this difference by any examination of the effectiveness of a given program as the pragmatists propose; the time required to estimate these effects is usually too long and the complexity of society is always too great for us to say that the consequences of a given program are altogether clear. We cannot discover the difference between good and bad by going to the laboratory, for men and societies are not laboratory animals. If we believe that there is no truth, there is no knowledge, and there are no values except those which are validated by laboratory experiment, we cannot talk about the improvement of men and societies, for we can have no standard of judging anything that takes place among men or in societies.

Society is to be improved, not by forcing a program of social reform down its throat, through the schools, or otherwise, but by the improvement of the individuals who compose it. As Plato said, "Governments reflect human nature. States are not made out of stone or wood, but out of the characters of their citizens: these turn the scale and draw everything after them." The individual is the heart of society. . . .

Man is by nature free, and he is by nature social. To use his freedom rightly he needs discipline. To live in society he needs the moral virtues. Good moral and intellectual habits are required for the fullest development of the nature of man.

To develop fully as a social, political animal man needs participation in his own government. A benevolent despotism will not do. You cannot expect the slave to show the virtues of the free man unless you first set him free. Only democracy, in which all men rule and are ruled in turn for the good life of the whole community, can be an absolutely good form of government. . . .

Education deals with the development of the intellectual powers of men. Their moral and spiritual powers are the sphere of the family and the church. All three agencies must work in harmony; for, though a man has three aspects, he is still one man. But the schools cannot take over the role of the family and the church without promoting the atrophy of those institutions and failing in the task that is proper to the schools.

We cannot talk about the intellectual powers of men, though we can talk about training them, or amusing them, or adapting them, and meeting their immediate needs, unless our philosophy in general tells us that there is knowledge and that there is a difference between true and false. We must believe, too, that there are other means of obtaining knowledge than scientific experimentation. If knowledge can be sought only in the laboratory, many fields in which we thought we had knowledge will offer us nothing but opinion or superstition, and we shall be forced to conclude that we cannot know anything about the most important aspects of man and society. If we are to set about developing the intellectual powers of man through having them acquire knowledge of the most important subjects, we have to begin with the proposition that experimentation and empirical data will be of only limited use to us, contrary to the convictions of many American social scientists, and that philosophy, history, literature, and art give us knowledge, and significant knowledge, on the most significant issues.

If the object of education is the improvement of men, then any system of education that is without values is a contradiction in terms. A system that seeks bad values is bad. A system that denies the existence of values denies the possibility of education. Relativism, scientism, skepticism, and anti-intellectualism, the four horsemen of the philosophical apocalypse, have produced that chaos in education which will end in the disintegration of the West.

The prime object of education is to know what is good for man. It is to know the goods in their order. There is a hierarchy of values. The task of education is to help us understand it, establish it, and live by it. This Aristotle had in mind when he said: "It is not the possessions but the desires of men that must be equalized, and this is impossible unless they have a sufficient education according to the nature of things."

Such an education is far removed from the triviality of that produced by the doctrines of adaptation, of immediate needs, of social reform, or of the doctrine of no doctrine at all. Such an education will not adapt the young to a bad environment, but it will encourage them to make it good. It will not overlook immediate needs, but it will place these needs in their proper relationship to more distant, less tangible, and more important goods. It will be the only effective means of reforming society.

This is the education appropriate to free men. It is liberal education. If all men are to be free, all men must have this education. It makes no difference how they are to earn their living or what their special interests or aptitudes may be. They can learn to make a living, and they can develop their special interests and aptitudes, after they have laid the foundation of free and responsible manhood through liberal education. It will not do to say that they are incapable of such education. This claim is made by those who are too indolent or unconvinced to make the effort to give such education to the masses.

Nor will it do to say that there is not enough time to give everybody a liberal education before he becomes a specialist. In America, at least, the waste and frivolity of the educational system are so great that it would be possible through getting rid of them to give every citizen a liberal education and make him a qualified specialist, too, in less time than is now consumed in turning out uneducated specialists.

A liberal education aims to develop the powers of understanding and judgment. It is impossible that too many people can be educated in this sense, because there cannot be too many people with understanding and judgment. We hear a great deal today about the dangers that will come upon us through the frustration of educated people who have got educated in the expectation that education will get them a better job, and who then fail to get it. But surely this depends on the representations that are made to the young about what education is. If we allow them to believe that education will get them better jobs and encourage them to get educated with this end in view, they are entitled to a sense of frustration if, when they have got the education, they do not get the jobs. But, if we say that they should be educated in order to be men, and that everybody, whether he is ditch-digger or a bank president, should have this education because he is a man, then the ditch-digger may still feel frustrated, but not because of his education.

Nor is it possible for a person to have too much liberal education, because it is impossible to have too much understanding and judgment. But it is possible to undertake too much in the name of liberal education in youth. The object of liberal education in youth is not to teach the young all they will ever need to know. It is to give them the habits, ideas, and techniques that they need to continue to educate themselves. Thus the object of formal institutional liberal education in youth is to prepare the young to educate themselves throughout their lives.

I would remind you of the impossibility of learning to understand and judge many of the most important things in youth. The judgment and understanding of practical affairs can amount to little in the absence of experience with practical affairs. Subjects that cannot be understood without experience should not be taught to those who are without experience. Or, if these subjects are taught to those who are without experience, it should be clear that these subjects can be taught only by way of introduction and that their value to the student depends on his continuing to study them as he acquires experience. The tragedy in America is that economics, ethics, politics, history, and literature are studied in youth, and seldom studied again. Therefore the graduates of American universities seldom understand them.

This pedagogical principle, that subjects requiring experience can be learned only by the experienced, leads to the conclusion that the most important branch of education is the education of adults. We sometimes seem to think of education as something like the mumps, measles, whooping cough, or chicken pox. If a person has had education in childhood, he need not, in fact he cannot, have it again. But the pedagogical principle that the most important things can be learned only in mature life is supported by a sound philosophy in general. Men are rational animals. They achieve their terrestrial felicity by the use of reason. And this means that they have to use it for their entire lives. To say that they should learn only in childhood would mean that they were human only in childhood.

And it would mean that they were unfit to be citizens of a republic. A republic, a true *res publica*, can maintain justice, peace, freedom, and order only by the exercise of intelligence. When we speak of the consent of the governed, we mean, since men are not angels who seek the truth intuitively and do not have to learn it, that every act of assent on the part of the governed is a product of learning. A republic is really a common educational life in process. So Montesquieu said that, whereas the principle of a monarchy was honor, and the principle of a tyranny was fear, the principle of a republic was education.

Hence the ideal republic is the republic of learning. It is the utopia by which all actual political republics are measured. The goal toward which we started with the Athenians twenty-five centuries ago is an unlimited republic of learning and a worldwide political republic mutually supporting each other.

All men are capable of learning. Learning does not stop as long as a man lives, unless his learning power atrophies because he does not use it. Political freedom cannot endure unless it is accompanied by provision for the unlimited acquisition of knowledge. Truth is not long retained in human affairs without continual learning and relearning. Peace is unlikely unless there are continuous, unlimited opportunities for learning and unless men continuously avail themselves of them. The world of law and justice for which we yearn, the worldwide political republic, cannot be realized without the worldwide republic of learning. The civilization we seek willbe achieved when all men are citizens of the world republic of law and justice and of the republic of learning all their lives long.

POSTSCRIPT

Should Schooling Be Based on Social Experiences?

Intellectual training versus social-emotional-mental growth—the argument between Dewey and Hutchins reflects a historical debate that flows from the ideas of Plato and Aristotle and which continues today. The positions put forth by Clifton Fadiman and John Holt in Issue 2, "Should Schools Determine What Is Learned?" reflect this continuing debate, as do some of the other selections in this volume. Psychologists, sociologists, curriculum and instruction specialists, and popular critics have joined philosophers in commenting on this central concern.

Followers of Dewey contend that training the mental powers cannot be isolated from other factors of development and, indeed, can be enhanced by attention to the concrete social situations in which learning occurs. Critics of Dewey worry that the expansion of effort into the social and emotional realm only detracts from the intellectual mission that is schooling's unique province.

Was the progressive education movement ruinous, or did it lay the foundation for the education of the future? A reasonably even-handed appraisal can be found in Lawrence Cremin's *The Transformation of the School* (1961). The free school movement of the 1960s, at least partly derived from progressivism, is analyzed in Allen Graubard's *Free the Children* (1973) and Jonathan Kozol's *Free Schools* (1972).

Other sources that represent a wide spectrum of views regarding primary goals for education include Paul Nash's *Models of Man* (1968); Edward J. Power's *Evolution of Educational Doctrine* (1969); Arthur Pearl's *The Atrocity of Education* (1972); Stephen K. Bailey's *The Purposes of Education* (1976); *Doctrines of the Great Educators* (1979) by Robert R. Rusk and James Scotland; Mortimer J. Adler's *The Paideia Proposal* (1982); John I. Goodlad's *A Place Called School* (1984); Theodore R. Sizer's *Horace's Compromise* (1984); and *Horace's School* (1992).

Among the best of recent explorations of philosophical alternatives are Gerald L. Gutek's *Philosophical and Ideological Perspectives on Education* (1988); Edward J. Power's *Philosophy of Education: Studies in Philosophies, Schooling, and Educational Policies* (1990); and *Philosophical Foundations of Education* (1990) by Howard Ozmon and Samuel Craver.

Questions that must be addressed include: Can the "either/or" polarities of this basic argument be overcome? Is the articulation of overarching general aims essential to the charting of a productive and worthwhile educational experience? And how can the classroom teacher relate to general philosophical aims?

ISSUE 2

Should Schools Determine What Is Learned?

YES: Clifton Fadiman, from "The Case for Basic Education," in James D. Koerner, ed., *The Case for Basic Education* (Council for Basic Education, 1959)

NO: John Holt, from *Escape from Childhood* (E. P. Dutton, 1974)

ISSUE SUMMARY

YES: Writer and editor Clifton Fadiman argues that standardized subject matter rescues the learner from triviality and capriciousness and sets the stage for successful and meaningful interaction in the world.

NO: Educator John Holt feels that an imposed curriculum damages the individual and usurps a basic human right to select one's own path of development.

Controversy over the content of education has been particularly keen since the 1950s. The pendulum has swung from learner-centered progressive education to an emphasis on structured intellectual discipline to calls for radical reform in the direction of "openness" to the recent rally to go "back to basics."

The conservative viewpoint, articulated by such writers as Robert M. Hutchins, Clifton Fadiman, Jacques Barzun, Arthur Bestor, and James Koerner, arises from concerns about the drift toward informalism and the decline in academic achievement in recent decades. Taking philosophical cues from Plato's contention that certain subject matters have universal qualities that prompt mental and characterological development, the "basics" advocates argue against incidental learning, student choice, and diminution of structure and standards. Jacques Barzun summarizes the viewpoint succinctly: "Nonsense is at the heart of those proposals that would replace definable subject matters with vague activities copied from 'life' or with courses organized around 'problems' or 'attitudes.' "

The reform viewpoint, represented by John Holt, Paul Goodman, Ivan Illich, Charles Silberman, Edgar Friedenberg, and others, portrays the typical traditional school as a mindless, indifferent, social institution dedicated to producing fear, docility, and conformity. In such an atmosphere, the viewpoint holds, learners either become alienated from the established curriculum or learn to play the school "game" and thus achieve a hollow success.

Taking cues from the ideas of John Dewey and A. S. Neill, the "radical reformers" have given rise to a flurry of alternatives to regular schooling during recent decades. Among these are free schools, which follow the Summerhill model; urban storefront schools, which attempt to develop a true sense of "community"; "schools without walls," which follow the Philadelphia Parkway Program model; "commonwealth" schools, in which students, parents, and teachers share responsibility; and various "humanistic education" projects within regular school systems, which emphasize students' self-concept development and choice-making ability.

The utilitarian tradition that has descended from Benjamin Franklin, Horace Mann, and Herbert Spencer, Dewey's theory of active experiencing, and Neill's insistence on free and natural development support the reform position. The ideology rejects the factory model of schooling with its rigidly set curriculum, its neglect of individual differences, its social engineering function, and its pervasive formalism. "Basics" advocates, on the other hand, express deep concern over the erosion of authority and the watering down of demands upon students, which result from the reform ideology.

In the following pairing, Clifton Fadiman argues the case for basic education, emphasizing prescribed studies, drawing on his own experience of schooling, and demonstrating the meaningfulness of "old-fashioned" education. In opposition, John Holt goes beyond his earlier concerns about the oppressiveness of the school curriculum to propose complete freedom for the learner to determine all aspects of his or her educational development.

YES

Clifton Fadiman

THE CASE FOR BASIC EDUCATION

The present educational controversy, like all crucial controversies, has its roots in philosophy. One's attitude toward the proposals advanced in this book depends on one's conception of man. It depends on one's view of his nature, his powers, and his reason for existence.

If, consciously or unconsciously, one takes the position that his nature is essentially animal; that his powers lie largely in the area of social and biological adaptation; and that his reason for existence is either unknowable or (should he advance one) a form of self-delusion—then the case for basic education, and consequently for education itself, falls to the ground. By the same token the case for physical, social, and vocational training becomes irrefutable.

On the other hand, if one takes the position that man's nature is both animal *and* rational; that his powers lie not only in the area of adaptation but also in that of creation; and that his reason for existence is somehow bound up with the fullest possible evolution of his mental and spiritual capacities— then the case for basic education, and consequently for education itself, is established; and further discussion becomes a matter, however interesting and important, of detail.

A crisis period is not necessarily marked by disaster or violence or even revolutionary change. It is marked by the absence of any general, tacit adherence to an agreed-upon system of values. It is in such a crisis period that we live. Of the two positions briefly outlined above, a minority adheres to the first. Another minority adheres to the second. But most of us waver between the two or have never reflected on either. Our present educational system quite properly mirrors this uncertainty of the majority. It mirrors our own mental chaos. There is nothing else it *can* do, for ours is a democratic society, and all our institutions are representative.

Now neither of the positions is logically demonstrable, though some have tried to bend them to logic, as well as to propaganda. They are faiths. The scholars whose essays comprise this book deal explicitly with questions of curriculum. Implicitly, however, they are proclaiming the faith by which they

From Clifton Fadiman, "The Case for Basic Education," in James D. Koerner, ed., *The Case for Basic Education* (Council for Basic Education, 1959). Copyright © 1959 by The Council for Basic Education, 725 15th Street, NW, Washington, DC 20005. Reprinted by permission.

live. Furthermore, they are proclaiming that this is the faith by which Western civilization lives.

Because all faiths are attackable, everything they say can be attacked. Indeed everything they say may be wrong. But the attack can only be sustained by the proclamation of an opposing faith. And if they are wrong, they are wrong only in the sense that no faith can be "proved" right.

Thus the *Metaphysics* of Aristotle opens with the well-known statement: "All men by nature desire to know." This is not a statement of fact in the sense that "All men are born with lungs" is a statement of fact. It is not statistically checkable. It is not a self-evident truth. Cursory observation of many men seems to give it the lie. Depending on whether we prefer the language of logic or the language of emotion we may call it either an assumption or a declaration of faith. If the assumption is denied, or the declaration countered by an opposing declaration, this book, as well as education itself, becomes an irrelevancy. But in that case the cultural fruits of civilization also become an irrelevancy, because they would appear to flow, not from some blind process of unending adaptation, but from Aristotle's proposition. Any doubt cast on that proposition also casts doubt on the permanent value of culture.

It may be that the proposition *is* untenable. Perhaps all men do not by nature desire to know. We can then fall back on a second line of defense. We can say that at least men have acted *as if* they did so desire. Aristotle's dictum may be an illusion. But it looks like a creative illusion.

He has another dictum. He tells us that man is a social animal. Put the two statements together. Were man not a social animal but an anarchic animal, his desire to know would have both its origin and its terminus located in himself. But, as he is a social and not an anarchic animal, he socializes and finally systematizes his desire to know. This socialization and systematization are what we mean by education. The main, though not the only, instrument of education is an odd invention, only three thousand years old, called the school. The primary job of the school is the efficient transmission and continual reappraisal of what we call tradition. Tradition is the mechanism by which all past men teach all future men.

Now arises the question: If all men by nature desire to know, and if that desire is best gratified by education and the transmission of tradition, what should be the character of that education and the content of that tradition? At once a vast, teeming chaos faces us: apparently men desire to know and transmit all kinds of matters, from how to tie a four-in-hand to the attributes of the Godhead.

Obviously this chaos cannot be taught. Hence in the past men have imposed upon it form, order, and hierarchy. They have selected certain areas of knowledge as the ones that, to the exclusion of others, both *can* and *should* be taught.

The structure of this hierarchy is not a matter of accident. Nor is it a matter of preference. The teacher may not teach only what happens to interest him. Nor may the student choose to be taught only what happens to interest him. The criteria of choice are many and far from immutable. But there is an essential one. Basic education concerns itself with those matters which, once learned, enable the student to learn all the other matters whether trivial or complex, that cannot properly be the subjects of elementary and secondary schooling. In other words, both logic and experience suggest that certain subjects have generative power and others do not have generative power. When we have learned to tie a four-in-hand, the subject is exhausted. It is self-terminating. Our knowledge is of no value for the acquisition of further knowledge. But once we have learned to read we can decipher instructions for the tieing of a four-in-hand. Once we have learned to listen and observe, we can learn from someone else how to tie a four-in-hand.

It has, up to our time, been the general experience of men that certain subjects and not others possess this generative power. Among these subjects are those that deal with language, whether or not one's own; forms, figures and numbers; the laws of nature; the past; and the shape and behavior of our common home, the earth. Apparently these master or generative subjects endow one with the ability to learn the minor or self-terminating subjects. They also endow one, of course, with the ability to learn the higher, more complex developments of the master subjects themselves.

To the question, "Just what are these master subjects?" the contributors to this book supply a specific answer. It happens to be a traditional answer. That is, these are, more or less, with modifications in each epoch, the subjects that Western civilization has up to recent times considered basic. That they are traditional is not an argument in their favor. The contributors believe that they are sanctioned not only by use and wont but by their intrinsic value.

The word *intrinsic* is troublesome. Is it possible that, as the environment changes, the number and names of the basic subjects must also change? At a certain time, our own for example, is it possible that driver-education is more basic than his-

tory? Many of us think so, or act as if we thought so. Again I would suggest that if we do think so, or act as if we thought so, it is not because we wish to lower the accident rate (though that is what we say) but because we unconsciously conceive of man primarily as an adaptive animal and not as a rational soul. For if he is primarily the first, then at the present moment in our human career driver-education *is* basic; but if he is primarily the second it is, though desirable, not basic.

I think the authors of this book would concede that with the environmental changes the relative importance of the basic subjects will also change. It is obvious that a post-Newtonian world must accord more attention to the mathematical and physical sciences than did the pre-Newtonian world. But *some* science has at all times been taught. Similarly in a hundred years the American high school student may be universally offered Russian rather than French or German. But this does not affect the principle that *some* systematic instruction in *some* leading foreign language will remain a basic necessity.

In other words, however their forms may be modified, a core of basic or generative subjects exists. This core is not lightly to be abandoned, for once it is abandoned we have lost the primary tools which enable us to make any kind of machine we wish. Other subjects may seem transiently attractive or of obvious utility. It is pleasant to square-dance, for instance and it is useful to know how to cook. Yet we cannot afford to be seduced by such "subjects." Hard though it may be, we must jettison them in favor of the basic subject matters. And there is no time for an eclectic mixture: only a few years are available in which [to] educe, to educate the rational soul. We cannot afford bypaths. We cannot afford pleasure. All education, Aristotle tells us, is accompanied by pain. Basic education is inescapably so accompanied, as well as by that magnificent pleasure that comes of stretching, rather than tickling, the mind.

I have briefly outlined the standard case for basic education insofar as it rests on an unchanging philosophic faith or view of human nature. But there is a more urgent, though less fundamental, argument still to be advanced. In sum it is this: while basic education is *always* a necessity, it is peculiarly so in our own time. . . .

I am a very lucky man, for I believe that my generation was just about the last one to receive an undiluted basic education. As this is written, I am fifty-four years old. Thus I received my secondary school education from 1916 to 1920. Though I was not well educated by European standards, I was very well educated by present-day American ones. . . .

My high school was part of the New York City system. It had no amenities. Its playground was asphalt and about the size of two large drawing rooms. It looked like a barracks. It made no provision for dramatics or square dancing. It didn't even have a psychiatrist—perhaps because we didn't need one. The students were all from what is known as the "underprivileged"—or what we used to call poor—class. Today this class is depended on to provide the largest quota of juvenile delinquents. During my four years in high school there was one scandalous case in which a student stole a pair of rubbers.

Academically my school was neither very good nor very bad. The same was true of me. As the area of elective subjects was strictly limited. I received approximately the same education my fellows did. (Unfortunately Latin was not compulsory: I had to learn it—badly—by myself later on.) Here is what—in addition to the standard minors of drawing, music, art and gym—I was taught some forty years ago:

Four years of English, including rigorous drill in composition, formal grammar and public speaking.

Four years of German.

Three years of French.

Three or four years (I am not sure which) of history, including classical, European and American, plus a no-nonsense factual course in civics. . . .

One year of physics.

One year of biology.

Three years of mathematics, through trigonometry.

That, or its near equivalent, was the standard high school curriculum in New York forty years ago. That was all I learned, all any of us learned, all all of us learned. All these subjects can be, and often are, better taught today—when they are taught at all on this scale. However, I was taught French and German well enough so that in later years I made part of my living as a translator. I was taught rhetoric and composition well enough to make it possible for me to become a practicing journalist. I was taught public speaking well enough to enable me to replace my lower-class accent with at least a passable one; and I learned also the rudiments of enunciation, placing, pitch, and proper breathing so that in after years I found it not too difficult to get odd jobs as a public lecturer and radio-and-television handyman.

I adduce these practical arguments only to explode them. They may seem important to the life-adjuster. They are not important to me. One can make a living without French. One can even make a living without a knowledge of spelling. And it is perfectly possible to rise to high estate without any control whatsoever over the English language.

What *is* important about this old-fashioned basic education (itself merely a continuation and sophistication of the basic education then taught in the primary schools) is not that it prepared me for life or showed me how to get along with my fellow men. Its importance to me and, I believe, to most of my fellow students, irrespective of their later careers, is twofold:

(1) It furnished me with a foundation on which later on, within the limits of my abilities, I could erect any intellectual structure I fancied. It gave me the wherewithal for the self-education that should be every man's concern to the hour of his death.

(2) It precluded my ever becoming Lost.

In drawing the distinction between generative and self-terminating subjects we have already discussed (1).

I want now to explain (2) because the explanation should help to make clear why in our time basic education is needed not only in principle but as a kind of emergency measure. . . .

Considered as a well-rounded American I am an extremely inferior product. I am a poor mechanic. I play no games beyond a little poorish tennis and I haven't played that for five years. I swim, type, dance and drive raggedly, though, with respect to the last, I hope non-dangerously. I have had to learn about sex and marriage without benefit of classroom instruction. I would like to be well-rounded and I admire those who

are. But it is too late. I take no pleasure in my inferiorities but I accept the fact that I must live with them.

I feel inferior. Well and good. It seems to hurt nobody. But, though I feel inferior, I do not feel Lost. I have not felt lost since being graduated from high school. I do not expect ever to feel lost. This is not because I am wise, for I am not. It is not because I am learned, for I am not. It is not because I have mastered the art of getting along with my peers, for I do not know the first thing about it. I am often terrified by the world I live in, often horrified, usually unequal to its challenges. But I am not lost in it.

I know how I came to be an American citizen in 1959; what large general movements of history produced me; what my capacities and limitations are; what truly interests me; and how valuable or valueless these interests are. My tastes are fallible but not so fallible that I am easily seduced by the vulgar and transitory—though often enough I am unequal to a proper appreciation of the noble and the permanent. In a word, like tens of millions of others in this regard, I feel at home in the world. I am at times scared but I can truthfully say that I am not bewildered.

I do not owe this to any superiority of nature. I owe it, I sincerely believe, to the conventional basic education I received beginning about a half century ago. It taught me how to read, write, speak, calculate, and listen. It taught me the elements of reasoning and it put me on to the necessary business of drawing abstract conclusions from particular instances. It taught me how to locate myself in time and space and to survey the present in the light of an imperfect but ever-functioning knowledge of the past. It provided me with great models by which to judge my own lesser performances. And it gave me the ability to investigate for myself anything that interested me, provided my mind was equal to it. . . .

The average high school graduate today is just as intelligent as my fellow students were. He is just as educable. But he is Lost, in greater or lesser degree.

By that I mean he feels little relation to the whole world in time and space, and only the most formal relation to his own country. He may "succeed," he may become a good, law-abiding citizen, he may produce other good, law-abiding citizens, and on the whole he may live a pleasant—that is, not painful—life. Yet during most of that life, and particularly after his fortieth year or so, he will feel vaguely disconnected, rootless, purposeless. Like the very plague he will shun any searching questions as to his own worth, his own identity. He will die after having lived a fractional life.

Is this what he really wants? Perhaps it is. It all comes round again to what was said at the opening of these remarks. Again it depends on one's particular vision of man. If we see our youngster as an animal whose main function is biological and social adaptation on virtually a day-to-day basis, then his fractional life is not fractional at all. It is total. But in that case our school curriculum should reflect our viewpoint. It should include the rudiments of reading so that our high school graduate may decipher highway markers, lavatory signs, and perhaps the headlines of some undemanding newspaper. It should include a large number of electives, changing every year, that may be of use to him in job hunting. And primarily it should include as much play and sport as possible, for these are the proper activities of animals, and our boy is an animal.

Yet the doubt persists. Is this really what he wants? And once again the answer depends on our faith. For example, the "Rockefeller Report" on Education (published in 1958 and called The Pursuit of Excellence) did not issue, except indirectly, from surveys, analyses, polls or statistical abstracts. It issued from faith. The following sentences do not comprise a scientific conclusion. They are an expression of faith, like the Lord's Prayer:

"What most people, young or old, want is not merely security or comfort or luxury—although they are glad enough to have these. They want meaning in their lives. If their era and their culture and their leaders do not or cannot offer them great meanings, great objectives, great convictions, then they will settle for shallow and trivial meanings."

There is no compulsion to believe this. If we do not believe it, and unqualifiedly, there is no case for basic education. Which means that, except for the superior intellect, there is no case for traditional education at all. In that event we should at once start to overhaul our school system in the light of a conception of man that sees him as a continually adjusting, pleasure-seeking, pain-avoiding animal.

But if we do believe it, and unqualifiedly, then the proposals contained [here] might at least be considered as guidelines, subject to discussion and modification.

The root of our trouble does not lie in an unbalanced curriculum, or in an inadequate emphasis on any one subject, or in poor teaching methods, or in insufficient facilities, or in underpaid instructors. It lies in the circumstance that

somehow the average high school graduate does not know who he is, where he
is, or how he got there. It lies in the fact
that naturally enough he "will settle for
shallow and trivial meanings."

NO

John Holt

ESCAPE FROM CHILDHOOD

Young people should have the right to control and direct their own learning, that is, to decide what they want to learn, and when, where, how, how much, how fast, and with what help they want to learn it. To be still more specific, I want them to have the right to decide if, when, how much, and by whom they want to be *taught* and the right to decide whether they want to learn in a school and if so which one and for how much of the time.

No human right, except the right to life itself, is more fundamental than this. A person's freedom of learning is part of his freedom of thought, even more basic than his freedom of speech. If we take from someone his right to decide what he will be curious about, we destroy his freedom of thought. We say, in effect, you must think not about what interests and concerns *you*, but about what interests and concerns *us*.

We might call this the right of curiosity, the right to ask whatever questions are most important to us. As adults, we assume that we have the right to decide what does or does not interest us, what we will look into and what we will leave alone. We take this right for granted, cannot imagine that it might be taken away from us. Indeed, as far as I know, it has never been written into any body of law. Even the writers of our Constitution did not mention it. They thought it was enough to guarantee citizens the freedom of speech and the freedom to spread their ideas as widely as they wished and could. It did not occur to them that even the most tyrannical government would try to control people's minds, what they thought and knew. That idea was to come later, under the benevolent guise of compulsory universal education.

This right to each of us to control our own learning is now in danger. When we put into our laws the highly authoritarian notion that someone should and could decide what all young people were to learn and, beyond that, could do whatever might seem necessary (which now includes dosing them with drugs) to compel them to learn it, we took a long step down a very steep and dangerous path. The requirement that a child go to school, for about six hours a day, 180 days a year, for about ten years, whether or not he learns anything there, whether or not he already knows it or could learn it faster or better somewhere else, is such gross violation of civil liberties that few adults would stand for it. But the child who resists is treated as a criminal. With this requirement we created an industry, an army of people whose whole work was to tell young people what they had to learn and to try to make them learn it. Some of these people, wanting to exercise even more power over others, to be even more "helpful," or simply because the industry is not growing fast enough to hold all the people who want to get into it, are now beginning to say, "If it is good for children for us to decide what they shall learn and to make them learn it, why wouldn't it be good for everyone? If compulsory education is a good thing, how can there be too much of it? Why should we allow anyone, of any age, to decide that he has had enough of it? Why should we allow older people, any more than young, not to know what we know when their ignorance may have bad consequences for all of us? Why should we not *make* them know what they *ought* to know?"

They are beginning to talk, as one man did on a nationwide TV show, about "womb-to-tomb" schooling. If hours of homework every night are good for the young, why wouldn't they be good for us all—they would keep us away from the TV set and other frivolous pursuits. Some group of experts, somewhere, would be glad to decide what we all ought to know and then every so often check up on us to make sure we knew it—with, of course, appropriate penalties if we did not.

I am very serious in saying that I think this is coming unless we prepare against it and take steps to prevent it. The right I ask for the young is a right that I want to preserve for the rest of us, the right *to decide what goes into our minds*. This is much more than the right to decide whether or when or how much to go to school or what school you want to go to. That right is important, but it is only part of a much larger and more fundamental right, which I might call the right to Learn, as opposed to being Educated, *i.e.,* made to learn what someone else thinks would be good for you. It is not just compulsory schooling but compulsory Education that I oppose and want to do away with.

That children might have the control of their own learning, including the right to decide if, when, how much, and where they wanted to go to school, frightens and angers many people. They ask me, "Are you saying that if the parents wanted the child to go to school, and the child didn't want to go, that he wouldn't have to go? Are you saying that if the parents wanted the child to go to one school, and the child wanted to go to another, that the child would have the right to decide?" Yes, that is what I say. Some people ask, "If school wasn't compulsory, wouldn't many parents take their children out of school to exploit their labors in one way or another?" Such questions are often both snobbish and hypocritical. The questioner assumes and implies (though rarely says) that these bad parents are people poorer and less schooled than he. Also, though he appears to be defending the right of children to go to school, what he really is defending is the right of the state to compel them to go whether they want to or not. What he wants, in short, is that children should be in school, not that they should have any choice about going.

But saying that children should have the right to choose to go or not to go to school does not mean that the ideas and wishes of the parents would have no weight. Unless he is estranged from his parents and rebelling against them, a child cares very much about what they think and want. Most of the time, he doesn't want to anger or worry or disappoint them. Right now, in families where the parents feel that they have some choice about their children's schooling, there is much bargaining about schools. Such parents, when their children are little, often ask them whether they want to go to nursery school or kindergarten. Or they may take them to school for a while to try it out. Or, if they have a choice of schools, they may take them to several to see which they think they will like the best. Later, they care whether the child likes his school. If he does not, they try to do something about it, get him out of it, find a school he will like.

I know some parents who for years had a running bargain with their children. "If on a given day you just can't stand the thought of school, you don't feel well, you are afraid of something that may happen, you have something of your own that you very much want to do—well, you can stay home." Needless to say, the schools, with their supporting experts, fight it with all their might— Don't Give into Your Child, Make Him Go to School, He's Got to Learn. Some parents, when their own plans make it possible for them to take an interesting trip, take their children with them. They don't ask the schools' permission, they just go. If the child doesn't want to make the trip and would rather stay in school, they work out a way for him to do that. Some parents, when their child is frightened, unhappy, and suffering in school, as many children are, just take him out. Hal Bennett, in his excellent book *No*

More Public School, talks about ways to do this.

A friend of mine told me that when her boy was in third grade, he had a bad teacher, bullying, contemptuous, sarcastic, cruel. Many of the class switched to another section, but this eight-year-old, being tough, defiant, and stubborn, hung on. One day—his parents did not learn this until about two years later—having had enough of the teacher's meanness, he just got up from his desk and without saying a word, walked out of the room and went home. But for all his toughness and resiliency of spirit, the experience was hard on him. He grew more timid and quarrelsome, less outgoing and confident. He lost his ordinary good humor. Even his handwriting began to go to pieces—it was much worse in the spring of the school year than in the previous fall. One spring day he sat at breakfast, eating his cereal. After a while he stopped eating and sat silently thinking about the day ahead. His eyes filled up with tears, and two big ones slowly rolled down his cheeks. His mother, who ordinarily stays out of the school life of her children, saw this and knew what it was about. "Listen," she said to him, "we don't have to go on with this. If you've had enough of that teacher, if she's making school so bad for you that you don't want to go any more, I'll be perfectly happy just to pull you right out. We can manage it. Just say the word." He was horrified and indignant. "No!" he said, "I couldn't do that." "Okay," she said, "whatever you want is fine. Just let me know." And so they left it. He had decided that he was going to tough it out, and he did. But I am sure knowing that he had the support of his mother and the chance to give it up if it got too much for him gave him the strength he needed to go on.

To say that children should have the right to control and direct their own learning, to go to school or not as they choose, does not mean that the law would forbid the parents to express an opinion or wish or strong desire on the matter. It only means that if their natural authority is not strong enough the parents can't call in the cops to make the child do what they are not able to persuade him to do. And the law may say that there is no limit to the amount of pressure or coercion the parents can apply to the child to deny him a choice that he has a legal right to make.

When I urge that children should control their learning, there is one argument that people bring up so often that I feel I must anticipate and meet it here. It says that schools are a place where children can for a while be protected against the bad influences of the world outside, particularly from its greed, dishonesty, and commercialism. It says that in school children may have a glimpse of a higher way of life, of people acting from other and better motives than greed and fear. People say, "We know that society is bad enough as it is and that children go out into the larger world as soon as they wanted, they would be tempted and corrupted just that much sooner."

They seem to believe that schools are better, more honorable places than the world outside—what a friend of mine at Harvard once called "museums of virtue." Or that people in school, both children and adults, act from higher and better motives than people outside. In this they are mistaken. There are, of course, some good schools. But on the whole, far from being the opposite of, or an antidote to, the world outside, with all its envy, fear, greed, and obsessive competitiveness, the schools are very much like it. If anything, they are worse, a terrible, abstract, simplified caricature of it. In the world outside the school, some work, at least, is done honestly and well, for its own sake, not just to get ahead of others; people are not everywhere and always being set in competition against each other; people are not (or not yet) in every minute of their lives subject to the arbitrary, irrevocable orders and judgement of others. But in most schools, a student is every minute doing what others tell him, subject to their judgement, in situations in which he can only win at the expense of other students.

This is a harsh judgement. Let me say again, as I have before, that schools are worse than most of the people in them and that many of these people do many harmful things they would rather not do, and a great many other harmful things that they do not even see as harmful. The whole of school is much worse than the sum of its parts. There are very few people in the U.S. today (or perhaps anywhere, any time) in *any* occupation, who could be trusted with the kind of power that schools give most teachers over their students. Schools seem to me among the most anti-democratic, most authoritarian, most destructive, and most dangerous institutions of modern society. No other institution does more harm or more lasting harm to more people or destroys so much of their curiosity, independence, trust, dignity, and sense of identity and worth. Even quite kindly schools are inhibited and corrupted by the knowledge of children and teachers alike that they are *performing* for the judgement and approval of others—the children for the teachers; the teachers for the parents, supervisors, school board, or the state. No one is ever free from feeling that he is being judged all the time, or soon may be. Even after the best class experiences teachers must ask themselves, "Were we right to do that? Can we prove we were right? Will it get us in trouble?"

What corrupts the school, and makes it so much worse than most of the people in it, or than they would like it to be, is its power—just as their powerlessness corrupts the students. The school is corrupted by the endless anxious demand of the parents to know how their child is doing—meaning is he ahead of the other kids—and their demand that he be kept ahead. Schools do not protect children from the badness of the world outside. They are at least as bad as the world outside, and the harm they do to the children in their power creates much of the badness of the world outside. The sickness of the modern world is in many ways a school-induced sickness. It is in school that most people learn to expect and accept that some expert can always place them in some sort of rank or hierarchy. It is in school that we meet, become used to, and learn to believe in the totally controlled society. We do not learn much science, but we learn to worship "scientists" and to believe that anything we might conceivably need or want can only come, and someday will come, from them. The school is the closest we have yet been able to come to Huxley's *Brave New World*, with its alphas and betas, deltas and epsilons—and now it even has its soma. Everyone, including children, should have the right to say "No!" to it.

POSTSCRIPT

Should Schools Determine What Is Learned?

The free/open school movement values small, personalized educational settings in which students engage in activities that have personal meaning. One of the movement's ideological assumptions, emanating from the philosophy of Jean-Jacques Rousseau, is that, given a reasonably unrestrictive atmosphere, the learner will pursue avenues of creative and intellectual self-development. This confidence in self-motivation is the cornerstone of Holt's advocacy of freedom for the learner, a position he elaborates upon in his books *Instead of Education* (1988) and *Teach Your Own* (1982). The argument has gained some potency with recent developments in home-based computer-assisted instruction.

Writers in the field of curriculum theory have been struggling in the past decade to design approaches that can accomplish Holt's goals within the school context. Volumes of articles and essays enunciating this new direction include *Curriculum Theorizing: The Reconceptualists* (1975) edited by William Pinar and *Curriculum and the Cultural Revolution* (1972) edited by David E. Purpel and Maurice Belanger. These books present a general view that stands for greater emphasis on self-fulfillment, personal liberty, diversity, pluralism, and social justice. A 1975 publication of the Association for Supervision and Curriculum Development, *Schools in Search of Meaning*, edited by James B. Macdonald and Esther Zaret, pursues similar ideological paths toward curricular reform.

A culmination of the Fadiman appraisal of the value of tightly organized schooling and the need for curricular clarity and certainty can be seen in the 1982 publication by the Institute for Philosophical Research of *The Paideia Proposal: An Educational Manifesto*. Written by Mortimer J. Adler, on behalf of a group of distinguished scholars and practitioners, the book charts the essential ingredients of an approach to schooling that aims at instilling in all students the general aspects of culture that will enable them to lead civilized lives. The proposal advocates a uniform course of study built around the acquisition of organized knowledge, the development of learning skills, and the understanding of ideas and values. The Institute for Philosophical Research's 1988 yearbook, *Content of the Curriculum*, edited by Ronald S. Brandt, seems to present a compromise portrait of a revitalized traditional curriculum.

Two recent and extremely provocative books address the linked problems of curriculum imposition and student freedom of thought: John Taylor Gatto's *Dumbing Us Down: The Hidden Curriculum of Compulsory Schooling* (1992) and Lewis J. Perelman's *School's Out: Hyper-learning, the New Technology, and the End of Education* (1992). Gatto, a New York City Teacher of the Year, also expressed his views in a powerful article in *New Age Journal* (September/October 1990) titled "Our Children Are Dying in Our Schools."

ISSUE 3

Should Behaviorism Shape Educational Practices?

YES: B. F. Skinner, from *Beyond Freedom and Dignity* (Bantam Books, 1972)

NO: Carl R. Rogers, from *Freedom to Learn* (Merrill, 1983)

ISSUE SUMMARY

YES: B. F. Skinner, influential proponent of behaviorism and professor of psychology, critiques the concept of "inner freedom" and links learning and motivation to the influence of external forces.

NO: Professor of psychology and psychiatry Carl R. Rogers offers the "humanistic" alternative to behaviorism, insisting on the reality of subjective forces in human motivation.

Intimately enmeshed with considerations of aims and purposes and determination of curricular elements are the psychological base that affects the total setting in which learning takes place and the basic means of motivating learners. Historically, the atmosphere of schooling has often been characterized by harsh discipline, regimentation, and restriction. The prison metaphor often used by critics in describing school conditions rings true all too often.

Although calls to make schools pleasant have been sounded frequently, they have seldomly been heeded. Roman rhetorician Marcus Fabius Quintilian (ca. A.D. 35–ca. 100) advocated a constructive and enjoyable learning atmosphere. John Amos Comenius in the seventeenth century suggested a gardening metaphor in which learners were given kindly nurturance. Johann Heinrich Pestalozzi established a model school in the nineteenth century that replaced authoritarianism with love and respect.

Yet school as an institution retains the stigma of authoritarian control—attendance is compelled, social and psychological punishment is meted out, and the decision-making freedom of students is limited and often curtailed. These practices lead to rather obvious conclusions: either the prevailing belief is that young people are naturally evil and wild and therefore must be tamed in a restricting environment, or that schooling as such is so unpalatable that people must be forced and cajoled to reap its benefits—or both.

Certainly philosopher John Dewey (1895–1952) was concerned about this circumstance, citing at one time the superintendent of his native Burlington,

Vermont, school district as admitting that the schools were a source of "grief and mortification" and were "unworthy of patronage." Dewey rejected both the need for "taming" and the defeatist attitude that the school environment must remain unappealing. He hoped to create a motivational atmosphere that would engage learners in real problem-solving activities, thereby sustaining curiosity, creativity, and attachment. The rewards were to flow from the sense of accomplishment and freedom, which was to be achieved through the disciplined actions necessary to solve the problem at hand.

More recent treatment of the allied issues of freedom, control, and motivation has come from the two major camps in the field of educational psychology: the behaviorists (rooted in the early twentieth-century theories of Pavlov, Thorndike, and Watson) and the humanists (emanating from the Gestalt and field theory psychologies developed in Europe and America earlier in this century).

B. F. Skinner has been the dominant force in translating behaviorism into recommendations for school practices. The humanistic viewpoint has been championed by Carl R. Rogers, Abraham Maslow, Fritz Perls, Rollo May, and Erich Fromm, most of whom ground their psychological theories in the philosophical assumptions of existentialism and phenomenology.

Skinner believes that "inner" states are merely convenient myths, that motives and behaviors are shaped by environmental factors. These shaping forces, however, need not be negative, nor must they operate in an uncontrolled manner. Our present understanding of human behavior allows us the freedom to shape the environmental forces, which in turn shape us. With this power, Skinner contends, we can replace aversive controls in schooling with positive reinforcements that heighten the students' motivation level and make learning more efficient. Skinner deals with the problem of freedom and control in the selection that follows.

Carl R. Rogers, representing humanistic psychology, critiques Skinner's behaviorist approach and sets forth his argument supporting the reality of freedom as an inner human state that is the wellspring of responsibility, will, and commitment.

YES

B. F. Skinner

FREEDOM THROUGH CONTROL

Almost all living things act to free themselves from harmful contacts. A kind of freedom is achieved by the relatively simple forms of behavior called reflexes. A person sneezes and frees his respiratory passages from irritating substances. He vomits and frees his stomach from indigestible or poisonous food. He pulls back his hand and frees it from a sharp or hot object. More elaborate forms of behavior have similar effects. When confined, people struggle ("in rage") and break free. When in danger they flee from or attack its source. Behavior of this kind presumably evolved because of its survival value; it is as much a part of what we call the human genetic endowment as breathing, sweating, or digesting food. And through conditioning similar behavior may be acquired with respect to novel objects which could have played no role in evolution. These are no doubt minor instances of the struggle to be free, but they are significant. We do not attribute them to any love of freedom; they are simply forms of behavior which have proved useful in reducing various threats to the individual and hence to the species in the course of evolution.

A much more important role is played by behavior which weakens harmful stimuli in another way. It is not acquired in the form of conditioned reflexes, but as the product of a different process called operant conditioning. When a bit of behavior is followed by a certain kind of consequence, it is more likely to occur again, and a consequence having this effect is called a reinforcer. Food, for example, is a reinforcer to a hungry organism; anything the organism does that is followed by the receipt of food is more likely to be done again whenever the organism is hungry. Some stimuli are called negative reinforcers; any response which reduces the intensity of such a stimulus—or ends it—is more likely to be emitted when the stimulus recurs. Thus, if a person escapes from a hot sun when he moves under cover, he is more likely to move under cover when the sun is again hot. The reduction in temperature reinforces the behavior it is "contingent upon"—that is, the behavior it follows. Operant conditioning also occurs when a person simply avoids a hot sun—when, roughly speaking, he escapes from the *threat* of a hot sun.

Negative reinforcers are called aversive in the sense that they are the things organisms "turn away from." The term suggests a spatial separation—moving or running away from something—but the essential relation is temporal. In a standard apparatus used to study the process in the laboratory, an arbitrary response simply weakens an aversive stimulus or brings it to an end. A great deal of physical technology is the result of this kind of struggle for freedom. Over the centuries, in erratic ways, men have constructed a world in which they are relatively free of many kinds of threatening or harmful stimuli—extremes of temperature, sources of infection, hard labor, danger, and even those minor aversive stimuli called discomfort.

Escape and avoidance play a much more important role in the struggle for freedom when the aversive conditions are generated by other people. Other people can be aversive without, so to speak, trying; they can be rude, dangerous, contagious, or annoying, and one escapes from them or avoids them accordingly. They may also be "intentionally" aversive—that is, they may treat other people aversively because of what follows. Thus, a slave driver induces a slave to work by whipping him when he stops; by resuming work the slave escapes from the whipping (and incidentally reinforces the slave driver's behavior in using the whip). A parent nags a child until the child performs a task; by performing the task the child escapes nagging (and reinforces the parent's behavior). The blackmailer threatens exposure unless the victim pays; by paying, the victim escapes from the threat (and reinforces the practice). A teacher threatens corporal punishment or failure until his students pay attention; by pay-

ing attention the students escape from the threat of punishment (and reinforce the teacher for threatening it). In one form or another intentional aversive control is the pattern of most social coordination—in ethics, religion, government, economics, education, psychotherapy, and family life.

A person escapes from or avoids aversive treatment by behaving in ways which reinforce those who treated him aversively until he did so, but he may escape in other ways. For example, he may simply move out of range. A person may escape from slavery, emigrate or defect from a government, desert from an army, become an apostate from a religion, play truant, leave home, or drop out of a culture as a hobo, hermit, or hippie. Such behavior is as much a product of the aversive conditions as the behavior the conditions were designed to evoke. The latter can be guaranteed only by sharpening the contingencies or by using stronger aversive stimuli.

Another anomalous mode of escape is to attack those who arrange aversive conditions and weaken or destroy their power. We may attack those who crowd us or annoy us, as we attack the weeds in our garden, but again the struggle for freedom is mainly directed toward intentional controllers—toward those who treat others aversively in order to induce them to behave in particular ways. Thus, a child may stand up to his parents, a citizen may overthrow a government, a communicant may reform a religion, a student may attack a teacher or vandalize a school, and a dropout may work to destroy a culture.

It is possible that man's genetic endowment supports this kind of struggle for freedom: when treated aversively people tend to act aggressively or to be reinforced by signs of having worked aggressive damage. Both tendencies should have had evolutionary advantages, and they can easily be demonstrated. If two organisms which have been coexisting peacefully receive painful shocks, they immediately exhibit characteristic patterns of aggression toward each other. The aggressive behavior is not necessarily directed toward the actual source of stimulation; it may be "displaced" toward any convenient person or object. Vandalism and riots are often forms of undirected or misdirected aggression. An organism which has received a painful shock will also, if possible, act to gain access to another organism toward which it can act aggressively. The extent to which human aggression exemplifies innate tendencies is not clear, and many of the ways in which people attack and thus weaken or destroy the power of intentional controllers are quite obviously learned.

What we may call the "literature of freedom" has been designed to induce people to escape from or attack those who act to control them aversively. The content of the literature is the philosophy of freedom, but philosophies are among those inner causes which need to be scrutinized. We say that a person behaves in a given way because he possesses a philosophy, but we infer the philosophy from the behavior and therefore cannot use it in any satisfactory way as an explanation, at least until it is in turn explained. The literature of freedom, on the other hand, has a simple objective status. It consists of books, pamphlets, manifestoes, speeches, and other verbal products, designed to induce people to act to free themselves from various kinds of intentional control. It does not impart a philosophy of freedom; it induces people to act.

The literature often emphasizes the aversive conditions under which people live, perhaps by contrasting them with conditions in a freer world. It thus makes the conditions more aversive, "increasing the misery" of those it is trying to rescue. It also identifies those from whom one is to escape or those whose power is to be weakened through attack. Characteristic villains of the literature are tyrants, priests, generals, capitalists, martinet teachers, and domineering parents.

The literature also prescribes modes of action. It has not been much concerned with escape, possibly because advice has not been needed; instead, it has emphasized how controlling power may be weakened or destroyed. Tyrants are to be overthrown, ostracized, or assassinated. The legitimacy of a government is to be questioned. The ability of a religious agency to mediate supernatural sanctions is to be challenged. Strikes and boycotts are to be organized to weaken the economic power which supports aversive practices. The argument is strengthened by exhorting people to act, describing likely results, reviewing successful instances on the model of the advertising testimonial, and so on.

The would-be controllers do not, of course, remain inactive. Governments make escape impossible by banning travel or severely punishing or incarcerating defectors. They keep weapons and other sources of power out of the hands of revolutionaries. They destroy the written literature of freedom and imprison or kill those who carry it orally. If the struggle for freedom is to succeed, it must then be intensified.

The importance of the literature of freedom can scarcely be questioned. Without help or guidance people submit to aversive conditions in the most surprising way. This is true even when the aversive conditions are part of the natural environment. Darwin observed, for example, that the Fuegians seemed to make no effort to protect themselves from the cold; they wore only scant clothing and made little use of it against the weather. And one of the most striking things about the struggle for freedom from intentional control is how often it has been lacking. Many people have submitted to the most obvious religious, governmental, and economic controls for centuries, striking for freedom only sporadically, if at all. The literature of freedom has made an essential contribution to the elimination of many aversive practices in government, religion, education, family life, and the production of goods.

The contributions of the literature of freedom, however, are not usually described in these terms. Some traditional theories could conceivably be said to define freedom as the absence of aversive control, but the emphasis has been on how the condition *feels*. Other traditional theories could conceivably be said to define freedom as a person's condition when he is behaving under nonaversive control, but the emphasis has been upon a state of mind associated with doing what one wants. According to John Stuart Mill, "Liberty consists in doing what one desires." The literature of freedom has been important in changing practice (it has changed practices whenever it has had any effect whatsoever), but it has nevertheless defined its task as the changing of states of mind and feelings. Freedom is a "possession." A person escapes from or destroys the power of a controller in order to feel free, and once he feels free and can do what he desires, no further action is recommended and none is prescribed by the literature of freedom, except perhaps eternal vigilance lest control be resumed.

The feeling of freedom becomes an unreliable guide to action as soon as would-be controllers turn to nonaversive measures, as they are likely to do to avoid the problems raised when the controllee escapes or attacks. Nonaversive measures are not as conspicuous as aversive and are likely to be acquired more slowly, but they have obvious advantages which promote their use. Productive labor, for example, was once the result of punishment: the slave worked to avoid the consequences of not working. Wages exemplify a different principle; a person is paid when he behaves in a given way so that he will continue to behave in that way. Although it has long been recognized that rewards have useful effects, wage systems have evolved slowly. In the nineteenth century it was believed that an industrial society required a hungry labor force; wages would be effective only if the hungry worker could exchange them for food. By making labor less aversive—for instance, by shortening hours and improving conditions—it has been possible to get men to work for lesser rewards. Until recently teaching was almost entirely aversive: the student studies to escape the consequences of not studying, but nonaversive techniques are gradually being discovered and used. The skillful parent learns to reward a child for good behavior rather than punish him for bad. Religious agencies move from the threat of hellfire to an emphasis on God's love, and governments turn from aversive sanctions to various kinds of inducements. . . . What the layman calls a reward is a "positive reinforcer," the effects of which have been exhaustively studied in the experimental analysis of operant behavior. The effects are not as easily recognized as those of aversive contingencies because they tend to be deferred, and applications have therefore been delayed, but techniques as powerful as the older aversive techniques are now available. . . .

The literature of freedom has never come to grips with techniques of control which do not generate escape or counterattack because it has dealt with the problem in terms of states of mind and feelings. In his book *Sovereignty*, Bertrand de Jouvenel quotes two important figures in that literature. According to Leibnitz, "Liberty consists in the power to do what one wants to do," and according to Voltaire, "When I can do what I want to do, there is my liberty for me." But both writers add a concluding phrase: Leibnitz, " . . . or in the power to want what can be got," and Voltaire, more candidly, " . . . but I can't help wanting what I do want." Jouvenel relegates these comments to a footnote, saying that the power to want is a matter of "interior liberty" (the freedom of the inner man!) which falls outside the "gambit of freedom."

A person wants something if he acts to get it when the occasion arises. A person who says "I want something to eat" will presumably eat when something becomes available. If he says "I want to get warm," he will presumably move into a warm place when he can. These acts have been reinforced in the past by whatever was wanted. What a person *feels* when he feels himself wanting something depends upon the circumstances. Food is reinforcing only in a state of deprivation, and a person who wants something to eat may feel parts of that state—for example, hunger pangs. A person who wants to get warm presumably feels cold. Conditions associated with a high probability of responding may also

be felt, together with aspects of the present occasion which are similar to those of past occasions upon which behavior has been reinforced. Wanting is not, however, a feeling, nor is a feeling the reason a person acts to get what he wants. Certain contingencies have raised the probability of behavior and at the same time have created conditions which may be felt. Freedom is a matter of contingencies of reinforcement, not of the feelings the contingencies generate. The distinction is particularly important when the contingencies do not generate escape or counterattack. . . .

The literature of freedom has encouraged escape from or attack upon all controllers. It has done so by making any indication of control aversive. Those who manipulate human behavior are said to be evil men, necessarily bent on exploitation. Control is clearly the opposite of freedom, and if freedom is good, control must be bad. What is overlooked is control which does not have aversive consequences at any time. Many social practices essential to the welfare of the species involve the control of one person by another, and no one can suppress them who has any concern for human achievements. . . . [I]n order to maintain the position that all control is wrong, it has been necessary to disguise or conceal the nature of useful practices, to prefer weak practices just because they can be disguised or concealed, and—a most extraordinary result indeed!—to perpetuate punitive measures.

The problem is to be free men, not from control, but from certain kinds of control, and it can be solved only if our analysis takes all consequences into account. How people feel about control, before or after the literature of freedom has worked on their feelings, does not lead to useful distinctions.

Were it not for the unwarranted generalization that all control is wrong, we should deal with the social environment as simply as we deal with the nonsocial. Although technology has freed men from certain aversive features of the environment, it has not freed them from the environment. We accept the fact that we depend upon the world around us, and we simply change the nature of the dependency. In the same way, to make the social environment as free as possible of aversive stimuli, we do not need to destroy that environment or escape from it; we need to redesign it.

Man's struggle for freedom is not due to a will to be free, but to certain behavioral processes characteristic of the human organism, the chief effect of which is the avoidance of or escape from so-called "aversive" features of the environment. Physical and biological technologies have been mainly concerned with natural aversive stimuli; the struggle for freedom is concerned with stimuli intentionally arranged by other people. The literature of freedom has identified the other people and has proposed ways of escaping from them or weakening or destroying their power. It has been successful in reducing the aversive stimuli used in intentional control, but it has made the mistake of defining freedom in terms of states of mind or feelings, and it has therefore not been able to deal effectively with techniques of control which do not breed escape or revolt but nevertheless have aversive consequences. It has been forced to brand all control as wrong and to misrepresent many of the advantages to be gained from a social environment. It is unprepared for the next step, which is not to free men from control but to analyze and change the kinds of control to which they are exposed.

NO

Carl R. Rogers

FREEDOM AND COMMITMENT

One of the deepest issues in modern life, in modern man, is the question as to whether the concept of personal freedom has any meaning whatsoever in our present-day scientific world. The growing ability of the behavioral scientist to predict and to control behavior has brought the issue sharply to the fore. If we accept the logical positivism and strictly behavioristic emphases which are predominant in the American psychological scene, there is not even room for discussion. . . .

But if we step outside the narrowness of the behavioral sciences, this question is not only *an* issue, it is one of the primary issues which define modern man. Friedman in his book (1963, p. 251) makes his topic "the problematic of modern man—the alienation, the divided nature, the unresolved tension between personal freedom and psychological compulsion which follows on 'the death of God'." The issues of personal freedom and personal commitment have become very sharp indeed in a world in which man feels unsupported by a supernatural religion, and experiences keenly the division between his awareness and those elements of his dynamic functioning of which he is unaware. If he is to wrest any meaning from a universe which for all he knows may be indifferent, he must arrive at some stance which he can hold in regard to these timeless uncertainties.

So, writing as both a behavioral scientist and as one profoundly concerned with the human, the personal, the phenomenological and the intangible, I should like to contribute what I can to this continuing dialogue regarding the meaning of and the possibility of freedom.

MAN IS UNFREE

. . . In the minds of most behavioral scientists, man is not free, nor can he as a free man commit himself to some purpose, since he is controlled by factors

Excerpted from Carl R. Rogers, *Freedom to Learn for the 80s* (Merrill, 1983). Copyright © 1983 by Bell & Howell Company. Reprinted by permission of Merrill, an imprint of Macmillan Publishing Company.

outside of himself. Therefore, neither freedom nor commitment is even a possible concept to modern behavioral science as it is usually understood.

To show that I am not exaggerating, let me quote a statement from Dr. B. F. Skinner of Harvard, who is one of the most consistent advocates of a strictly behavioristic psychology. He says,

> The hypothesis that man is not free is essential to the application of scientific method to the study of human behavior. The free inner man who is held responsible for his behavior is only a prescientific substitute for the kinds of causes which are discovered in the course of scientific analysis. All these alternative causes lie *outside* the individual (1953, p.477).

This view is shared by many psychologists and others who feel, as does Dr. Skinner, that all the effective causes of behavior lie outside of the individual and that it is only through the external stimulus that behavior takes place. The scientific description of behavior avoids anything that partakes in any way of freedom. For example, Dr. Skinner (1964, pp. 90–91) describes an experiment in which a pigeon was conditioned to turn in a clockwise direction. The behavior of the pigeon was "shaped up" by rewarding any movement that approximated a clockwise turn until, increasingly, the bird was turning round and round in a steady movement. This is what is known as operant conditioning. Students who had watched the demonstration were asked to write an account of what they had seen. Their responses included the following ideas: that the pigeon was conditioned to *expect* reinforcement for the right kind of behavior; that the pigeon *hoped* that something would bring the food back again; that the pigeon *observed* that a certain behavior seemed to produce a particular result; that the pigeon *felt* that food would be given it because of its action; that the bird came to *associate* his action with the clock of the food dispenser. Skinner ridicules these statements because they all go beyond the observed behavior in using such words as *expect, hope, observe, felt,* and *associate.* The whole explanation from his point of view is that the bird was reinforced when it emitted a given kind of behavior; the pigeon walked around until the food container again appeared; a certain behavior produced a given result; food was given to the pigeon when it acted in a given way; the click of the food dispenser was related in time to the bird's action. These statements describe the pigeon's behavior from a scientific point of view.

Skinner goes on to point out that the students were undoubtedly reporting what they would have expected, felt and hoped under similar circumstances. But he then makes the case that there is no more reality to such ideas in the human being than there is in the pigeon, that it is only because such words have been reinforced by the verbal community in which the individual has developed, that such terms are used. He discusses the fact that the verbal community which conditioned them to use such terms saw no more of their behavior than they had seen of the pigeon's. In other words the internal events, if they indeed exist, have no scientific significance.

As to the methods used for changing the behavior of the pigeon, many people besides Dr. Skinner feel that through such positive reinforcement human behavior as well as animal behavior can be "shaped up" and controlled. In his book *Walden Two,* Skinner says,

Now that we know how positive reinforcement works and how negative doesn't, we can be more deliberate and hence more successful in our cultural design. We can achieve a sort of control under which the controlled, though they are following a code much more scrupulously than was ever the case under the old system, nevertheless *feel free*. They are doing what they want to do, not what they are forced to do. That's the source of the tremendous power of positive reinforcement—there is no restraint and no revolt. By a careful cultural design we control not the final behavior but the *inclination* to behave—the motives, the desires, the wishes. The curious thing is that in that case *the question of freedom never arises* (1948, p. 218).

. . . I think it is clear from all of this that man is a machine—a complex machine, to be sure, but one which is increasingly subject to scientific control. Whether behavior will be managed through operant conditioning as in *Walden Two* or whether we will be "shaped up" by the unplanned forms of conditioning implied in social pressure, or whether we will be controlled by electrodes in the brain, it seems quite clear that science is making out of man an object and that the purpose of such science is not only understanding and prediction but control. Thus it would seem to be quite clear that there could be no concept so foreign to the facts as that man is free. Man is a machine, man is unfree, man cannot commit himself in any meaningful sense; he is simply controlled by planned or unplanned forces outside of himself.

MAN IS FREE

I am impressed by the scientific advances illustrated in the examples I have given. I regard them as a great tribute to the ingenuity, insight, and persistence of the individuals making the investigations. They have added enormously to our knowledge. Yet for me they leave something very important unsaid. Let me try to illustrate this, first from my experience in therapy.

I think of a young man classed as schizophrenic with whom I had been working for a long time in a state hospital. He was a very inarticulate man, and during one hour he made a few remarks about individuals who had recently left the hospital; then he remained silent for almost forty minutes. When he got up to go, he mumbled almost under his breath, "If some of *them* can do it, maybe I can too." That was all—not a dramatic statement, not uttered with force and vigor, yet a statement of choice by this young man to work toward his own improvement and eventual release from the hospital. It is not too surprising that about eight months after that statement he was out of the hospital. I believe this experience of responsible choice is one of the deepest aspects of psychotherapy and one of the elements which most solidly underlies personality change.

I think of another young person, this time a young woman graduate student, who was deeply disturbed and on the borderline of a psychotic break. Yet after a number of interviews in which she talked very critically about all of the people who had failed to give her what she needed, she finally concluded: "Well, with that sort of a foundation, it's really up to *me*. I mean it seems to be really apparent to me that I can't depend on someone else to *give* me an education." And then she added very softly: "I'll really have to get it myself." She goes on to explore this experience of important and responsible choice. She finds it a frightening experience, and yet one which gives her a feeling of strength. A force seems to surge up within her which is big and strong, and yet she also feels very much alone and sort of cut off from support. She adds: "I am going to begin to do more things that I know I should do." And she did.

I could add many other examples. One young fellow talking about the way in which his whole life had been distorted and spoiled by his parents finally comes to the conclusion that, "Maybe now that I *see* that, it's up to *me*." . . .

For those of you [who] have seen the film *David and Lisa*—and I hope that you have had that rich experience—I can illustrate exactly what I have been discussing. David, the adolescent schizophrenic, goes into a panic if he is touched by anyone. He feels that "touching kills," and he is deathly afraid of it, and afraid of the closeness in human relationships which touching implies. Yet toward the close of the film he makes a bold and positive choice of the kind I have been describing. He has been trying to be of help to Lisa, the girl who is out of touch with reality. He tries to help at first in an intellectually contemptuous way, then increasingly in a warmer and more personal way. Finally, in a highly dramatic movement, he says to her, "Lisa, take my hand." He *chooses*, with obvious conflict and fear, to leave behind the safety of his untouchableness, and to venture into the world of real human relationships where he is literally and figuratively in *touch* with another. You are an unusual person if the film does not grow a bit misty at this point.

Perhaps a behaviorist could try to account for the reaching out of his hand by saying that it was the result of intermit-

tent reinforcement of partial movements. I find such an explanation both inaccurate and inadequate. It is the *meaning* of the *decision* which is essential to understanding the act.

What I am trying to suggest in all of this is that I would be at a loss to explain the positive change which can occur in psychotherapy if I had to omit the importance of the sense of free and responsible choice on the part of my clients. I believe that this experience of freedom to choose is one of the deepest elements underlying change.

THE MEANING OF FREEDOM

Considering the scientific advances which I have mentioned, how can we even speak of freedom? In what sense is a client free? In what sense are any of us free? What possible definition of freedom can there be in the modern world? Let me attempt such a definition.

In the first place, the freedom that I am talking about is essentially an inner thing, something which exists in the living person quite aside from any of the outward choices of alternatives which we so often think of as constituting freedom. I am speaking of the kind of freedom which Viktor Frankl vividly describes in his experience of the concentration camp, when everything—possessions, status, identity—was taken from the prisoners. But even months and years in such an environment showed only "that everything can be taken from a man but one thing: the last of the human freedoms—to choose one's own attitude in any given set of circumstances, to choose one's own way" (1959, p. 65). It is this inner, subjective, existential freedom which I have observed. It is the realization that "I can live myself, here and now, by my own choice." It is the quality of courage which enables a person to step into the uncertainty of the unknown as he chooses himself. It is the discovery of meaning from within oneself, meaning which comes from listening, sensitively and openly to the complexities of what one is experiencing. It is the burden of being responsible for the self one chooses to be. It is the recognition of a person that he is an emerging process, not a static end product. The individual who is thus deeply and courageously thinking his own thoughts, becoming his own uniqueness, responsibly choosing himself, may be fortunate in having hundreds of objective outer alternatives from which to choose, or he may be unfortunate in having none. But his freedom exists regardless. So we are first of all speaking of something which exists within the individual, something phenomenological rather than external, but nonetheless to be prized.

The second point in defining this experience of freedom is that it exists not as a contradiction of the picture of the psychological universe as a sequence of cause and effect, but as a complement to such a universe. Freedom rightly understood is a fulfillment by the person of the ordered sequence of his life. The free man moves out voluntarily, freely, responsibly, to play his significant part in a world whose determined events move through him and through his spontaneous choice and will.

I see this freedom of which I am speaking, then, as existing in a different *dimension* than the determined sequence of cause and effect. I regard it as a freedom which exists in the subjective person, a freedom which he courageously uses to live his potentialities. The fact that this type of freedom seems completely irrec-

oncilable with the behaviorist's picture of man is something which I will discuss a bit later. . . .

THE EMERGENCE OF COMMITMENT

I have spoken thus far primarily about freedom. What about commitment? Certainly the disease of our age is lack of purpose, lack of meaning, lack of commitment on the part of individuals. Is there anything which I can say in regard to this?

It is clear to me that in therapy, as indicated in the examples that I have given, commitment to purpose and to meaning in life is one of the significant elements of change. It is only when the person decides, "I am someone; I am someone worth being: I am committed to being myself," that change becomes possible.

At a very interesting symposium at Rice University recently, Dr. Sigmund Koch sketched the revolution which is taking place in science, literature and the arts, in which a sense of commitment is again becoming evident after a long period in which that emphasis has been absent.

Part of what he meant by that may be illustrated by talking about Dr. Michael Polanyi, the philosopher of science, formerly a physicist, who has been presenting his notions about what science basically is. In his book, *Personal Knowledge*, Polanyi makes it clear that even scientific knowledge is personal knowledge, committed knowledge. We cannot rest comfortably on the belief that scientific knowledge is impersonal and "out there," that it has nothing to do with the individual who has discovered it. Instead, every aspect of science is pervaded by disciplined personal commitment, and Polanyi makes the case very persuasively that the whole attempt to divorce science from the person is a completely unrealistic one. I think I am stating his belief correctly when I say that in his judgment logical positivism and all the current structure of science cannot save us from the fact that all knowing is uncertain, involves risk, and is grasped and comprehended only through the deep, personal commitment of a disciplined search.

Perhaps a brief quotation will give something of the flavor of his thinking. Speaking of great scientists, he says:

So we see that both Kepler and Einstein approached nature with intellectual passions and with beliefs inherent in these passions, which led them to their triumphs and misguided them to their errors. These passions and beliefs were theirs, personally, even universally. I believe that they were competent to follow these impulses, even though they risked being misled by them. And again, what I accept of their work today, I accept personally, guided by passions and beliefs similar to theirs, holding in my turn that my impulses are valid, universally, even though I must admit the possibility that they may be mistaken (1959, p.145).

Thus we see that a modern philosopher of science believes that deep personal commitment is the only possible basis on which science can firmly stand. This is a far cry indeed from the logical positivism of twenty or thirty years ago, which placed knowledge far out in impersonal space.

Let me say a bit more about what I mean by commitment in the psychological sense. I think it is easy to give this word a much too shallow meaning, indicating that the individual has, simply by conscious choice, committed himself to one course of action or another. I think the meaning goes far

deeper than that. Commitment is a total organismic direction involving not only the conscious mind but the whole direction of the organism as well.

In my judgment, commitment is something that one *discovers* within oneself. It is a trust of one's total reaction rather than of one's mind only. It has much to do with creativity. Einstein's explanation of how he moved toward his formulation of relativity without any clear knowledge of his goal is an excellent example of what I mean by the sense of commitment based on a total organismic reaction. He says:

"During all those years there was a feeling of direction, of going straight toward something concrete. It is, of course, very hard to express that feeling in words but it was decidedly the case and clearly to be distinguished from later considerations about the rational form of the solution" (quoted in Wertheimer, 1945, p. 183-184).

Thus commitment is more than a decision. It is the functioning of an individual who is searching for the directions which are emerging within himself. Kierkegaard has said, "The truth exists only in the process of becoming, in the process of appropriation" (1941, p.72). It is this individual creation of a tentative personal truth through action which is the essence of commitment.

Man is most successful in such a commitment when he is functioning as an integrated, whole, unified individual. The more that he is functioning in this total manner the more confidence he has in the directions which he unconsciously chooses. He feels a trust in his experiencing, of which, even if he is fortunate, he has only partial glimpses in his awareness.

Thought of in the sense in which I am describing it, it is clear that commitment is an achievement. It is the kind of purposeful and meaningful direction which is only gradually achieved by the individual who has come increasingly to live closely in relationship with his own experiencing—a relationship in which his unconscious tendencies are as much respected as are his conscious choices. This is the kind of commitment toward which I believe individuals can move. It is an important aspect of living in a fully functioning way.

THE IRRECONCILABLE CONTRADICTION

I trust it will be very clear that I have given two sharply divergent and irreconcilably contradictory points of view. On the one hand, modern psychological science and many other forces in modern life as well, hold the view that man is unfree, that he is controlled, that words such as purpose, choice, commitment have no significant meaning, that man is nothing but an object which we can more fully understand and more fully control. Enormous strides have been and are being made in implementing this perspective. It would seem heretical indeed to question this view.

Yet, as Polanyi has pointed out in another of his writings (1957), the dogmas of science can be in error. He says:

In the days when an idea could be silenced by showing that it was contrary to religion, theology was the greatest single source of fallacies. Today, when any human thought can be discredited by branding it as unscientific, the power previously exercised by theology has passed over to science; hence science has become in its turn the greatest single source of error.

So I am emboldened to say that over against this view of man as unfree, as an object, is the evidence from therapy, from subjective living, and from objective research as well, that personal freedom and responsibility have a crucial significance, that one cannot live a complete life without such personal freedom and responsibility, and that self-understanding and responsible choice make a sharp and measurable difference in the behavior of the individual. In this context, commitment does have meaning. Commitment is the emerging and changing total direction of the individual, based on a close and acceptant relationship between the person and all of the trends in his life, conscious and unconscious. Unless, as individuals and as a society, we can make constructive use of this capacity for freedom and commitment, mankind, it seems to me, is set on a collision course with fate. . . .

A part of modern living is to face the paradox that, viewed from one perspective, man is a complex machine. We are every day moving toward a more precise understanding and a more precise control of this objective mechanism which we call man. On the other hand, in another significant dimension of his existence, man is subjectively free; his personal choice and responsibility account for the shape of his life; he is in fact the architect of himself. A truly crucial part of his existence is the discovery of his own meaningful commitment to life with all of his being.

POSTSCRIPT

Should Behaviorism Shape Educational Practices?

The freedom-determinism or freedom-control argument has raged in philosophical, political, and psychological circles down through the ages. Is freedom of choice and action a central, perhaps *the* central, characteristic of being human? Or is freedom only an illusion, a refusal to acknowledge the external shaping of all human actions?

Moving the debate into the field of education, John Dewey depicts a developmental freedom that is acquired through improving one's ability to cope with problems. A. S. Neill (*Summerhill: A Radical Approach to Child Rearing*), who advanced the ideas of early twentieth-century progressive educators and the establishment of free schools, sees a more natural inborn freedom in human beings, which must be protected and allowed to flourish. B. F. Skinner refuses to recognize this "inner autonomous man" but sees freedom resulting from the scientific reshaping of the environment that influences us. Skinner ends *Beyond Freedom and Dignity* with the challenging statement, "We have not yet seen what man can make of man."

Just as Skinner has struggled to remove the stigma from the word *control*, arguing that it is the true gateway to freedom, John Holt, in *Freedom and Beyond* (1972), points out that freedom and free activities are not "unstructured"—indeed, that the structure of an open classroom is vastly more complicated than the structure of a traditional classroom.

If both of these views have validity, then we are in a position, as Dewey counselled, to go beyond either-or polemics on these matters and build a more constructive educational atmosphere. Jerome S. Bruner has consistently suggested ways in which free inquiry and subject matter structure can be effectively blended. Arthur W. Combs, in journal articles and in a report titled *Humanistic Education: Objectives and Assessment* (1978), has helped to bridge the ideological gap between humanists and behaviorists by demonstrating that subjective outcomes can be assessed by direct or modified behavioral techniques.

Other perspectives on the learning atmosphere in schools may be found in William Glasser's *Control Theory in the Classroom* (1986) and *The Quality School* (1990) and in Howard Gardner's *The Unschooled Mind: How Children Think and How Schools Should Teach* (1991).

B. F. Skinner's death in 1990 prompted a number of evaluations, among them "Skinner's Stimulus: The Legacy of Behaviorism's Grand Designer," Jeff Meade, *Teacher* (November/December 1990); "The Life and Contributions of Burrhus Frederic Skinner," Robert P. Hawkins, *Education and Treatment of Children* (August 1990); and Fred S. Keller, "Burrhus Frederic Skinner (1904–1990) (A Thank You)," *Journal of Applied Behavior Analysis* (Winter 1990).

ISSUE 4

Should Values Be Developed Rather Than Transmitted?

YES: Lawrence Kohlberg, from "The Cognitive-Developmental Approach to Moral Education," *Phi Delta Kappan* (June 1975)

NO: Edward A. Wynne, from "The Great Tradition in Education: Transmitting Moral Values," *Educational Leadership* (December 1985/January 1986)

ISSUE SUMMARY

YES: Professor of education Lawrence Kohlberg outlines his theory that, in the tradition of Dewey and Piaget, links value development to cognitive growth.
NO: Professor of education Edward A. Wynne feels that, under the influence of Kohlberg and others, schools have abandoned educational traditions by failing to teach specific moral values.

Do schools have a moral purpose? Can virtue be taught? Should the shaping of character take precedence over the training of the intellect? Is the person possessing a highly developed rationality automatically ethical? Are contemporary schools limited to teaching a secularized morality? Should the schools cease meddling in value-charged matters?

Much of the history of education chronicles how philosophers, theorists, education officials, and the general public have responded to the questions above. In almost all countries, and certainly in early America, the didactic teaching of moral values, often those of a particular religious interpretation, was central to the process of education.

Although the direct connection between religion and schooling has faded, the image of the teacher as a value model persists, and the ethical dimension of everyday activities and human relations insinuates itself into the school atmosphere regardless of any curricular neglect of moral controversy. Normative discourse inundates the educational environment; school is a world of "rights" and "wrongs" and "oughts" and "don'ts."

At present, we must try to define and delineate the moral intentions of public education. Storms of controversy rage over the instructional use of value-laden materials and over methodological approaches that seem to some people to be value-destructive. Localized explosions regarding textbooks, entire curricula, and films bear witness to the volatility of the moral dimension of education.

Additional problems emerge from the attempt to delineate the school's role: Can school efforts supplement the efforts of home and church? Can the schools avoid representing a "middle-class morality," which disregards the cultural base of minority group values? Should the schools do battle against the value-manipulation forces of the mass media and the popular culture?

In the 1960s and 1970s a number of approaches to these problems emerged. Lawrence Kohlberg fashioned strategies that link ethical growth to levels of cognitive maturity, tracing a range of moral stages from punishment avoidance to recognition of universal principles. This approach employs discussion of moral dilemmas that demand increasingly sophisticated types of moral reasoning.

Another approach popularized during this period was values clarification, developed and refined by Louis Raths, Merrill Harmin, Sidney Simon, and Howard Kirschenbaum. This moral education program attempts to assist learners in understanding their own attitudes, preferences, and values, as well as those of others, placing emphasis on feelings, emotions, sensitivity, and shared perceptions.

Recent years have seen the marketing of a wide range of materials and games slanted toward moral development objectives. Some of these have been criticized as superficial, others as bordering on the psychoanalytical. With or without prepackaged aids, can teachers navigate the waters of moral education in an organized and effective manner?

Edward A. Wynne, who deplores the tendency for schools to avoid the direct transmission of moral values, thinks that teachers can once again fulfill this role. Wynne agrees with former secretary of education William J. Bennett's call for "moral literacy" through clear articulation of cultural ideals and, if necessary, indoctrination.

YES

Lawrence Kohlberg

THE COGNITIVE-DEVELOPMENTAL
APPROACH TO MORAL EDUCATION

The cognitive-developmental approach was fully stated for the first time by John Dewey. The approach is called *cognitive* because it recognizes that moral education, like intellectual education, has its basis in stimulating the *active thinking* of the child about moral issues and decisions. It is called developmental because it sees the aims of moral education as movement through moral stages. According to Dewey:

> The aim of education is growth or *development*, both intellectual and moral. Ethical and psychological principles can aid the school in the *greatest of all constructions—the building of a free and powerful character*. Only knowledge of the *order and connection of the stages in psychological development can insure this*. Education is the work of *supplying the conditions* which will enable the psychological functions to mature in the freest and fullest manner.

Dewey postulated three levels of moral development: 1) the *pre-moral* or *preconventional* level "of behavior motivated by biological and social impulses with results for morals," 2) the *conventional* level of behavior "in which the individual accepts with little critical reflection the standards of his group," and 3) the *autonomous* level of behavior in which "conduct is guided by the individual thinking and judging for himself whether a purpose is good, and does not accept the standard of his group without reflection."[1]

Dewey's thinking about moral stages was theoretical. Building upon his prior studies of cognitive stages, Jean Piaget made the first effort to define stages of moral reasoning in children through actual interviews and through observations of children (in games with rules). Using this interview material, Piaget defined the pre-moral, the conventional, and the autonomous levels as follows: 1) the *pre-moral stage*, where there is no sense of obligation to rules; 2) the *heteronomous stage*, where the right was literal obedience to rules and an equation of obligation with submission to power and punishment (roughly ages 4–8); and 3) the *autonomous stage*, where the purpose and consequences of following rules are considered and obligation is based on reciprocity and exchange (roughly ages 8–12).[2]

In 1955 I started to redefine and validate (through longitudinal and cross-cultural study) the Dewey-Piaget levels and stages. The resulting stages are presented in Table 1.

We claim to have validated the stages defined in Table 1. The notion that stages can be *validated* by longitudinal study implies that stages have definite empirical characteristics. The concept of stages (as used by Piaget and myself) implies the following characteristics:

1. Stages are "structured wholes," or organized systems of thought. Individuals are *consistent* in level of moral judgment.

2. Stages form an *invariant sequence*. Under all conditions except extreme trauma, movement is always forward, never backward. Individuals never skip stages; movement is always to the next stage up.

3. Stages are "hierarchical integrations." Thinking at a higher stage includes or comprehends within it lower-stage thinking. There is a tendency to function at or prefer the highest stage available.

Each of these characteristics has been demonstrated for moral stages. Stages are defined by responses to a set of verbal moral dilemmas classified according to an elaborate scoring scheme. Validating studies include:

1. A 20-year study of 50 Chicago-area boys, middle- and working-class. Initially interviewed at ages 10–16, they have been reinterviewed at three-year intervals thereafter.

2. A small, six-year longitudinal study of Turkish villages and city boys of the same age.

3. A variety of other cross-sectional studies in Canada, Britain, Israel, Taiwan, Yucatán, Honduras, and India.

With regard to the structured whole or consistency criterion, we have found that more than 50% of an individual's thinking is always at one stage, with the remainder at the next adjacent stage (which he is leaving or which he is moving into).

With regard to invariant sequence, our longitudinal results have been presented in the *American Journal of Orthopsychiatry*, and indicate that on every retest individuals were either at the same stage as three years earlier or had moved up. This was true in Turkey as well as in the United States.

With regard to the hierarchical integration criterion, it has been demonstrated that adolescents exposed to written statements at each of the six stages comprehend or correctly put in their own words all statements at or below their own stage but fail to comprehend any statements more than one stage above their own. Some individuals comprehend the next stage above their own; some do not. Adolescents prefer (or rank as best) the highest stage they can comprehend.

To understand moral stages, it is important to clarify their relations to stage of logic or intelligence, on the one hand, and to moral behavior on the other. Maturity of moral judgment is not highly correlated with IQ or verbal intelligence (correlations are only in the 30s, accounting for 10% of the variance). Cognitive development, in the stage sense, however, is more important for moral development than such correlations suggest. Piaget has found that after the child learns to speak there are three major stages of reasoning: the intuitive, the concrete operational, and the formal operational. At around age 7, the child enters the stage of concrete logical thought: he can make logical inferences, classify,

(continued on p. 55)

Table 1

Definition of Moral Stages

I. Preconventional level

At this level, the child is responsive to cultural rules and labels of good and bad, right or wrong, but interprets these labels either in terms of the physical or the hedonistic consequences of action (punishment, reward, exchange of favors) or in terms of the physical power of those who enunciate the rules and labels. The level is divided into the following two stages:

Stage 1: *The punishment-and-obedience orientation.* The physical consequences of action determine its goodness or badness, regardless of the human meaning or value of these consequences. Avoidance of punishment and unquestioning deference to power are valued in their own right, not in terms of respect for an underlying moral order supported by punishment and authority (the latter being Stage 4).

Stage 2: *The instrumental-relativist orientation.* Right action consists of that which instrumentally satisfies one's own needs and occasionally the needs of others. Human relations are viewed in terms like those of the marketplace. Elements of fairness, of reciprocity, and of equal sharing are present, but they are always interpreted in a physical, pragmatic way. Reciprocity is a matter of "you scratch my back and I'll scratch yours," not of loyalty, gratitude, or justice.

II. Conventional level

At this level, maintaining the expectations of the individual's family, group, or nation is perceived as valuable in its own right, regardless of immediate and obvious consequences. The attitude is not only one of *conformity* to personal expectations and social order, but of loyalty to it, of actively *maintaining*, supporting, and justifying the order, and of identifying with the person or group involved in it. At this level, there are the following two stages:

Stage 3: *The interpersonal concordance or "good boy-nice girl" orientation.* Good behavior is that which pleases or helps others and is approved by them. There is much conformity to stereotypical images of what is majority or "natural" behavior. Behavior is frequently judged by intention—"he means well" becomes important for the first time. One earns approval by being "nice."

Stage 4: *The "law and order" orientation.* There is orientation toward authority, fixed rules, and the maintenance of the social order. Right behavior consists of doing one's duty, showing respect for authority, and maintaining the given social order for its own sake.

III. Postconventional, autonomous, or principled level

At this level, there is a clear effort to define moral values and principles that have validity and application apart from the authority of the groups or persons holding these principles and apart from the individual's own identification with these groups. This level also has two stages:

Stage 5: *The social-contract, legalistic orientation*, generally with utilitarian overtones. Right action tends to be defined in terms of general individual rights and standards which have been critically examined and agreed upon by the whole society. There is a clear awareness of the relativism of personal values and opinions and a corresponding emphasis upon procedural rules for reaching consensus. Aside from what is constitutionally and democratically agreed upon, the right is a matter of personal "values" and "opinion." The result is an emphasis upon the "legal point of view," but with an emphasis upon the possibility of changing law in terms of rational considerations of social utility (rather than freezing it in terms of Stage 4 "law and order"). Outside the legal realm, free agreement and contract is the binding element of obligation. This is the "official" morality of the American government and constitution.

Stage 6: *The universal-ethical-principle orientation.* Right is defined by the decision of conscience in accord with self-chosen *ethical principles* appealing to logical comprehensiveness, universality, and consistency. These principles are abstract and ethical (the Golden Rule, the categorical imperative); they are not concrete moral rules like the Ten Commandments. At heart, these are universal principles of *justice*, of the *reciprocity* and *equality* of human *rights*, and of respect for the dignity of human beings as *individual persons* ("From Is to Ought," pp. 164, 165).

—Reprinted from *The Journal of Philosophy*, October 25, 1973.

and handle quantitative relations about concrete things. In adolescence individuals usually enter the stage of formal operations. At this stage they can reason abstractly, i.e., consider all possibilities, form hypotheses, deduce implications from hypotheses, and test them against reality.[3]

Since moral reasoning clearly is reasoning, advanced moral reasoning depends upon advanced logical reasoning: a person's logical stage puts a certain ceiling on the moral stage he can attain. A person whose logical stage is only concrete operational is limited to the preconventional moral stages (Stages 1 and 2). A person whose logical stage is only partially formal operational is limited to the conventional moral stages (Stages 3 and 4). While logical development is necessary for moral development and sets limits to it, most individuals are higher in logical stage than they are in moral stage. As an example, over 50% of late adolescents and adults are capable of full formal reasoning, but only 10% of these adults (all formal operational) display principled (Stages 5 and 6) moral reasoning.

The moral stages are *structures of moral judgment* or *moral reasoning*. *Structures* of moral judgment must be distinguished from the *content* of moral judgment. As an example, we cite responses to a dilemma used in our various studies to identify moral stage. The dilemma raises the issue of stealing a drug to save a dying woman. The inventor of the drug is selling it for 10 times what it costs him to make it. The woman's husband cannot raise the money, and the seller refuses to lower the price or wait for payment. What should the husband do?

The choice endorsed by a subject (steal, don't steal) is called the *content* of his moral judgment in the situation. His reasoning about the choice defines the

structure of his moral judgment. This reasoning centers on the following 10 universal moral values or issues of concern to persons in these moral dilemmas:

1. Punishment
2. Property
3. Roles and concerns of affection
4. Roles and concerns of authority
5. Law
6. Life
7. Liberty
8. Distributive justice
9. Truth
10. Sex

A moral choice involves choosing between two (or more) of these values as they *conflict* in concrete situations of choice.

The stage or structure of a person's moral judgment defines; 1) *what* he finds valuable in each of these moral issues (life, law), i.e., how he defines the value, and 2) *why* he finds it valuable, i.e., the reasons he gives for valuing it. As an example, at Stage 1 life is valued in terms of the power or possessions of the person involved; at Stage 2, for its usefulness in satisfying the needs of the individual in question or others; at Stage 3, in terms of the individual's relations with others and their valuation of him; at Stage 4, in terms of social or religious law. Only at Stages 5 and 6 is each life seen as inherently worthwhile, aside from other consideration.

MORAL JUDGMENT VS. MORAL ACTION

Having clarified the nature of stages of moral *judgment*, we must consider the relation of moral judgment to moral *action*. If logical reasoning is a necessary but not sufficient condition for mature moral judgment, mature moral judgment is a necessary but not sufficient condition for mature moral action. One cannot follow moral principles if one does not understand (or believe in) moral principles. However, one can reason in terms of principles and not live up to these principles. As an example, Richard Krebs and I found that only 15% of students showing some principled thinking cheated as compared to 55% of conventional subjects and 70% of preconventional subjects. Nevertheless, 15% of the principled subjects did cheat, suggesting that factors additional to moral judgment are necessary for principled moral reasoning to be translated into "moral action." Partly, these factors include the situation and its pressures. Partly, what happens depends upon the individual's motives and emotions. Partly, what the individual does depends upon a general sense of will, purpose, or "ego strength." As an example of the role of will or ego strength in moral behavior, we may cite the study of Krebs: Slightly more than half of his conventional subjects cheated. These subjects were also divided by a measure of attention/will. Only 26% of the "strong-willed" conventional subjects cheated; however, 74% of the "weak-willed" subjects cheated.

If maturity of moral reasoning is only one factor in moral behavior, why does the cognitive-developmental approach to moral education focus so heavily upon moral reasoning? For the following reasons:

1. Moral judgment, while only one factor in moral behavior, is the single most important or influential factor yet discovered in moral behavior.

2. While other factors influence moral behavior, moral judgment is the only distinctively *moral* factor in moral behavior. To illustrate, we noted that the Krebs study indicated that "strong-willed" conventional stage subjects resisted cheating more than "weak-willed" subjects. For those at a preconventional level of moral reasoning, however, "will" had an opposite effect. "Strong-willed" Stages 1 and 2 subjects cheated more, not less, than "weak-willed" subjects, i.e., they had the "courage of their (amoral) convictions" that it was worthwhile to cheat. "Will," then, is an important factor in moral behavior, but it is not distinctively moral; it becomes moral only when informed by mature moral judgment.

3. Moral judgment change is long-range or irreversible; a higher stage is never lost. Moral behavior as such is largely situational and reversible or "loseable" in new situations.

AIMS OF MORAL AND CIVIC EDUCATION

Moral psychology describes what moral development is, as studied empirically. Moral education must also consider moral philosophy, which strives to tell us what moral development ideally *ought to be*. Psychology finds an invariant sequence of moral stages; moral philosophy must be invoked to answer whether a later stage is a better stage. The "stage" of senescence and death follows the "stage" of adulthood, but that does not mean that senescence and death are better. Our claim that the latest or principled stages of moral reasoning are morally better stages, then, must rest on consid erations of moral philosophy.

The tradition of moral philosophy to which we appeal is the liberal and ra tional tradition, in particular the "for malistic" or "deonotological" tradition running from Immanuel Kant to John Rawls. Central to this tradition is the claim that an adequate morality is *principled*, i.e., that it makes judgments in terms of *universal* principles applicable to all mankind. *Principles* are to be distinguished from *rules*. Conventional morality is grounded on rules, primarily "thou shalt nots" such as are represented by the Ten Commandments, prescriptions of kinds of actions. Principles are, rather, universal guides to making a moral decision. An example is Kant's "categorical imperative," formulated in two ways. The first is the maxim of respect for human personality, "Act always toward the other as an end, not as a means." The second is the maxim of universalization, "Choose only as you would be willing to have everyone choose in your situation." Principles like that of Kant's state the formal conditions of a moral choice or action. In the dilemma in which a woman is dying because a druggist refuses to release his drug for less than the stated price, the druggist is not acting morally, though he is not violating the ordinary moral rules (he is not actually stealing or murdering). But he is violating principles: He is treating the woman simply as a means to his ends of profit, and he is not choosing as he would wish anyone to choose (if the druggist were in the dying woman's place, he would not want a druggist to choose as he is choosing). Under most circumstances, choice in terms of conventional moral rules and choice in terms of principles coincide. Ordinarily, principles dictate not stealing (avoiding stealing is implied by acting in terms of a regard for others as ends and in terms of what one would want everyone to do). In a situation where stealing is the only means to save a life, however, principles contradict the ordinary rules and would dictate stealing. Unlike rules which are supported by social authority,

principles are freely chosen by the individual because of their intrinsic moral validity.[4]

The conception that a moral choice is a choice made in terms of moral principles is related to the claim of liberal moral philosophy that moral principles are ultimately principles of justice. In essence, moral conflicts are conflicts between the claims of persons, and principles for resolving these claims are principles of justice, "for giving each his due." Central to justice are the demands of *liberty, equality*, and *reciprocity*. At every moral stage, there is a concern for justice. The most damning statement a school child can make about a teacher is that "he's not fair." At each higher stage, however, the conception of justice is reorganized. At Stage 1, justice is punishing the bad in terms of "an eye for an eye and a tooth for a tooth." At Stage 2, it is exchanging favors and goods in an equal manner. At Stages 3 and 4, it is treating people as they desire in terms of the conventional rules. At Stage 5, it is recognized that all rules and laws flow from justice, from a social contract between the governors and the governed designed to protect the equal rights of all. At Stage 6, personally chosen moral principles are also principles of justice, the principles any member of a society would choose for that society if he did not know what his position was to be in the society and in which he might be the least advantaged. Principles chosen from this point of view are, first, the maximum liberty compatible with the like liberty of others and, second, no inequalities of goods and respect which are not to the benefit of all, including the least advantaged.

As an example of stage progression in the orientation of justice, we may take judgments about capital punishment.

Capital punishment is only firmly rejected at the two principled stages, when the notion of justice as vengeance or retribution is abandoned. At the sixth stage, capital punishment is not condoned even if it may have some useful deterrent effect in promoting law and order. This is because it is not a punishment we would choose for a society if we assumed we had as much chance of being born into the position of a criminal or murderer as being born into the position of a law abider.

Why are decisions based on universal principles of justice better decisions? Because they are decisions on which all moral men could agree. When decisions are based on conventional moral rules, men will disagree, since they adhere to conflicting systems of rules dependent on culture and social position. Throughout history men have killed one another in the name of conflicting moral rules and values, most recently in Vietnam and the Middle East. Truly moral or just resolutions of conflicts require principles which are, or can be, universalizable.

ALTERNATIVE APPROACHES

We have given a philosophic rationale for stage advance as the aim of moral education. Given this rationale, the developmental approach to moral education can avoid the problems inherent in the other two major approaches to moral education. The first alternative approach is that of indoctrinative moral education, the preaching and imposition of the rules and values of the teacher and his culture on the child. In America, when this indoctrinative approach has been developed in a systematic manner, it has usually been termed "character education."

Moral values, in the character education approach, are preached or taught in terms of what may be called the "bag of virtues." In the classic studies of character by Hugh Hartshorne and Mark May, the virtues chosen were honesty, service, and self-control. It is easy to get superficial consensus on such a bag of virtues— until one examines in detail the list of virtues involved and the details of their definition. Is the Hartshorne and May bag more adequate than the Boy Scout bag (a Scout should be honest, loyal, reverent, clean, brave, etc.)? When one turns to the details of defining each virtue, one finds equal uncertainty or difficulty in reaching consensus. Does honesty mean one should not steal to save a life? Does it mean that a student should not help another student with his homework?

Character education and other forms of indoctrinative moral education have aimed at teaching universal values (it is assumed that honesty or service are desirable traits for all men in all societies), but the detailed definitions used are relative; they are defined by the opinions of the teacher and the conventional culture and rest on the authority of the teacher for their justification. In this sense character education is close to the unreflective valuings by teachers which constitute the hidden curriculum of the school.[5] Because of the current unpopularity of indoctrinative approaches to moral education, a family of approaches called "values clarification" has become appealing to teachers. Values clarification takes the first step implied by a rational approach to moral education: the eliciting of the child's own judgment or opinion about issues or situations in which values conflict, rather than imposing the teacher's opinion on him. Values clarification, however, does not attempt to go further than eliciting awareness of values; it is assumed that becoming more self-aware about one's values is an end in itself. Fundamentally, the definition of the end of values education as self-awareness derives from a belief in ethical relativity held by many value-clarifiers. As stated by Peter Engel, "One must contrast value clarification and value inculcation. Value clarification implies the principle that in the consideration of values there is no single correct answer." Within these premises of "no correct answer," children are to discuss moral dilemmas in such a way as to reveal different values and discuss their value differences with each other. The teacher is to stress that "our values are different," not that one value is more adequate than others. If this program is systematically followed, students will themselves become relativists, believing there is no "right" moral answer. For instance, a student caught cheating might argue that he did nothing wrong, since his own hierarchy of values, which may be different from that of the teacher, made it right for him to cheat.

Like values clarification, the cognitive-developmental approach to moral education stresses open or Socratic peer discussion of value dilemmas. Such discussion, however, has an aim: stimulation of movement to the next stage of moral reasoning. Like values clarification, the developmental approach opposes indoctrination. Stimulation of movement to the next stage of reasoning is not indoctrinative, for the following reasons:

1. Change is in the way of reasoning rather than in the particular beliefs involved.

2. Students in a class are at different stages; the aim is to aid movement at each to the next stage, not convergence on a common pattern.

3. The teacher's own opinion is neither stressed nor invoked as authoritative. It enters in only as one of many opinions, hopefully one of those at a next higher stage.

4. The notion that some judgments are more adequate than others is communicated. Fundamentally, however, this means that the student is encouraged to articulate a position which seems most adequate to him and to judge the adequacy of the reasoning of others.

In addition to having more definite aims than values clarification, the moral development approach restricts value education to that which is moral or, more specifically, to justice. This is for two reasons. First, it is not clear that the whole realm of personal, political, and religious values is a realm which is non-relative, i.e., in which there are universals and a direction of development. Second, it is not clear that the public school has a right or mandate to develop values in general.[6] In our view, value education in the public schools should be restricted to that which the school has the right and mandate to develop: an awareness of justice, or of the rights of others in our constitutional system. While the Bill of Rights prohibits the teaching of religious beliefs, or of specific value systems, it does not prohibit the teaching of the awareness of rights and principles of justice fundamental to the Constitution itself.

When moral education is recognized as centered in justice and differentiated from value education or affective education, it becomes apparent that moral and civic education are much the same thing. This equation, taken for granted by the classic philosophers of education from

Plato and Aristotle to Dewey, is basic to our claim that a concern for moral education is central to the educational objectives of social studies.

NOTES

1. These levels correspond roughly to our three major levels: the preconventional, the conventional, and the principled. Similar levels were propounded by William McDougall, Leonard Hobhouse, and James Mark Baldwin.

2. Piaget's stages correspond to our first three stages; Stage 0 (pre-moral), Stage 1 (heteronomous), and Stage 2 (instrumental reciprocity).

3. Many adolescents and adults only partially attain the stage of formal operations. They do consider all the actual relations of one thing to another at the same time, but they do not consider all possibilities and form abstract hypotheses. A few do not advance this far, remaining "concrete operational."

4. Not all freely chosen values or rules are principles, however. Hitler chose the "rule," "exterminate the enemies of the Aryan race," but such a rule is not a universalizable principle.

5. As an example of the "hidden curriculum," we may cite a second-grade classroom. My son came home from this classroom one day saying he did not want to be "one of the bad boys." Asked "Who are the bad boys?" he replied, "The ones who don't put their books back and get yelled at."

6. Restriction of deliberate value education to the moral may be clarified by our example of the second-grade teacher who made tidying up of books a matter of moral indoctrination. Tidiness is a value, but it is not a moral value. Cheating is a moral issue, intrinsically one of fairness. It involves issues of violation of trust and taking advantage. Failing to tidy the room may under certain conditions be an issue of fairness, when it puts an undue burden on others. If it is handled by the teacher as a matter of cooperation among the group in this sense, it is a legitimate focus of deliberate moral education. If it is not, it simply represents the arbitrary imposition of the teacher's values on the child.

NO

Edward A. Wynne

THE GREAT TRADITION IN EDUCATION: TRANSMITTING MORAL VALUES

Within the recent past, American education substantially disassociated itself from what may be called the great tradition in education: the deliberate transmission of moral values to students. Despite this separation, many education reforms are being considered or are under way to increase the academic demands made on students. These reforms can be generally helpful; however, unless they are sensitive to the implications of our break with the great tradition, their effect on student conduct and morality may be transitory or even harmful. To understand the significance of the great tradition, we must engage in a form of consciousness-raising by enriching our understanding of the past and by understanding the misperceptions that pervade contemporary education.

The transmission of moral values has been the dominant educational concern of most cultures throughout history. Most educational systems have been simultaneously concerned with the transmission of cognitive knowledge—skills, information, and techniques of intellectual analysis—but these admittedly important educational aims, have rarely been given priority over moral education. The current policies in American education that give secondary priority to transmitting morality represent a sharp fracture with the great tradition.

Our break with the past is especially significant in view of the increase since the early 1950s of youth disorder: suicide, homicide, and out-of-wedlock births. Patterns revealed by statistics coincide with popular conceptions about these behaviors. For instance, in 16 of the past 17 Gallup Polls on education, pupil discipline has been the most frequent criticism leveled against public schools. One may wonder if better discipline codes and more homework are adequate remedies for our current school problems, or whether these dysfunctions are more profound and should be treated with more sensitive and complex remedies. Although literacy and student diligence are unquestionably worthy of pursuit, they are only a part of the process of communicating serious morality. If we want to improve the ways

From Edward A. Wynne, "The Great Tradition in Education: Transmitting Moral Values," *Educational Leadership*, vol. 43, no. 4 (December 1985/January 1986), pp. 4–9. Copyright © 1985 by The Association for Supervision and Curriculum Development. Reprinted by permission. All rights reserved.

we are now transmitting morality, it makes sense to recall the way morality was transmitted before youth disorder became such a distressing issue.

SOME DEFINITIONS

The term "moral values" is ambiguous and requires some definition. It signifies the specific values that particular cultures generally hold in regard. Such values vary among cultures; during World War II, a Japanese who loved his homeland was likely to be hostile to Americans, and vice versa. Value conflicts along national or ethnic lines are common, although most cultures treat the characteristic we call "patriotism" as a moral value, and treat "treason" with opprobrium. Comparable patterns of value govern interpersonal relations in cultures: beliefs about proper family conduct or the nature of reciprocal relationships. Such beliefs are laden with strong moral components.

In sum, common "moral values" are the vital common beliefs that shape human relations in each culture. Often these values—as in the Ten Commandments—have what is popularly called a religious base. Whether their base is religious, traditional, or secular, however, such values are expected to be widely affirmed under most circumstances.

The term "educational systems" also is somewhat obscure. Contemporary Americans naturally think in terms of formal public or private schools and colleges. But for most history, and all prehistory, formal agencies were a minute part of children's and adolescents' education. In traditional cultures, education was largely transmitted by various formal and informal nonschool agencies: nuclear and extended families; religious institutions; "societies" for the young organized and monitored by adults. In addition, the complex incidental life of preindustrial rural and urban societies, and the demands of work in and out of the family socialized young persons into adult life. Many of these agencies still play important educational roles in contemporary America; nonetheless, in the modern period, the gradual replacement of such agencies by schools has been a strong trend.

TRANSMITTING MORAL VALUES

Whether the dominant educational system has been formal or informal, the transmission of moral values has persistently played a central role. This role has been necessary and universal for two reasons.

1. Human beings are uniquely adaptable animals and live in nearly all climates and in diverse cultural systems. But, as the anthropologist Yehudi Cohen (1964) put it, "No society allows for the random and promiscuous expression of emotions to just anyone. Rather, one may communicate those feelings, either verbally, physically, or materially, to certain people." Because our means of communicating emotions are socially specific, slow maturing young persons must be socialized gradually to the right—or moral—practices appropriate to their special environment.

2. Without effective moral formation, the human propensity for selfishness—or simply the advancement of self-interest—can destructively affect adult institutions. Thus, moral formation is necessary to cultivate our inherent, but moderate, propensity for disinterested sacrifice. The institutions of any persisting society must be organized to ensure

that people's "unselfish genes" are adequately reinforced.

The general modes of moral formation have remained relatively stable throughout all cultures. To be sure, social class and sex-related differences have influenced the quantity and nature of moral formation delivered to the young; for instance, in many environments, limited resources have restricted the extent and intensity of the education provided to lower-class youths. Furthermore, the substance of the moral training transmitted to older youths has varied among cultures: according to Plato, Socrates was put to death because the Athenians disapproved of the moral training he was offering to Athenian young men. But such variations do not lessen the strength of the general model. Despite his affection for Socrates, Plato, in *The Republic* (circa 390 B.C.) emphasized the importance of constraining the learning influences on children and youths, to ensure appropriate moral outcomes.

Although secular and church-related educators have disputed the *means* of moral formation since the nineteenth century both, until comparatively recently, have agreed on their programs' behavioral *ends*. Children should be moral: honest, diligent, obedient, and patriotic. Thus, after the American Revolution, deists and secularists such as Thomas Jefferson and John Adams felt democracy would fail unless citizens acquired an unusually high degree of self-discipline and public spiritedness. They termed this medley of values "republican virtue." After the revolution, many of the original 13 states framed constitutions with provisions such as " . . . no government can be preserved to any people, but by a firm adherence to justice, moderation, temperance, frugality,

and virtue."[1] The founders believed that popular education would be a means of developing such precious traits. As the social historians David J. And Sheila Rothman have written, "The business of schools [in our early history] was not reading and writing but citizenship, not education but social control." The term "social control" may have a pejorative sound to our modern ears, but it simply and correctly means that schools were concerned with affecting conduct, rather than transmitting information or affecting states of mind.

CHARACTERISTICS OF THE GREAT TRADITION

Although issues in moral formation posed some conflicts in traditional societies, there were great areas of congruence around the great tradition of transmitting moral values. Documents generated in historical societies as well as ethnographic studies of many ancient and primitive cultures reveal through anecdote and insight the principles that characterize the tradition. Since the principles are too often ignored in contemporary education, we should consider them in some detail.

• *The tradition was concerned with good habits of conduct as contrasted with moral concepts or moral rationales.* Thus, the tradition emphasized visible courtesy and deference. In the moral mandate, "Honor thy father and mother," the act of *honoring* can be seen. It is easier to observe people *honoring* their parents than *loving* them. Loving, a state of mind, usually must be inferred.

• *The tradition focused on day-to-day moral issues: telling the truth in the face of evident temptation, being polite, or obeying legitimate authority.* It assumed that most moral challenges arose in mundane situations, and that people were often prone to act improperly.

• *The great tradition assumed that no single agency in society had the sole responsibility for moral education.* The varieties of moral problems confronting adults and youths were innumerable. Thus, youths had to be taught to practice morality in many environments. One agency, for example, the nuclear family or the neighborhood, might be deficient, so considerable redundancy was needed. In other words, there could be no neutrality about educating the young in morality: youth-serving agencies were either actively promoral or indifferent.

• *The tradition assumed that moral conduct, especially of the young, needed persistent and pervasive reinforcement.* To advance this end, literature, proverbs, legends, drama, ritual, and folk tales were used for cautionary purposes. Systems of symbolic and real rewards were developed and sustained: schools used ribbons, awards, and other signs of moral merit; noneducational agencies used praise and criticism as well as many symbolic forms of recognition.

• *The tradition saw an important relationship between the advancement of moral learning and the suppression of wrong conduct.* Wrong acts, especially in the presence of the young, were to be aggressively punished, as punishment not only suppressed bad examples, but also corrected particular wrongdoers. The tradition also developed concepts such as "scandal," a public, immoral act that also lowered the prestige of a person or institution. Conversely, since secret immoral acts were less likely to confuse or misdirect innocent persons, they received less disapproval.

• *The tradition was not hostile to the intellectual analysis of moral problems.*

Adults recognized that life occasionally generates moral dilemmas. In the Jewish religious tradition, learned men were expected to analyze and debate Talmudic moral issues. Other cultures have displayed similar patterns. But such analyses typically relied on a strong foundation of habit-oriented, mundane moral instruction and practice. Instruction in exegetical analysis commenced only after the selected neophyte had undergone long periods of testing, memorized large portions of semididactic classics, and displayed appropriate deference to exegetical experts.

• *The great tradition assumed that the most important and complex moral values were transmitted through persistent and intimate person-to-person interaction.* In many cases, adult mentors were assigned to develop close and significant relationship with particular youths. The youths might serve as apprentices to such persons, or the mentors might accept significant responsibilities for a young relative. In either case, constructive moral shaping required a comparatively high level of engagement.

• *The tradition usually treated "learners," who were sometimes students, as members of vital groups, such as teams, classes, or clubs.* These groups were important reference points for communicating values, among them, group loyalty, and the diverse incidents of group life provided occasions for object lessons. The emphasis on collective life contrasts sharply with the individualism that pervades contemporary American education, and which is often mistaken for "humanism."

• *The tradition had a pessimistic opinion about the perfectibility of human beings, and about the feasibility or value of breaking with previous socialization patterns.* The tradition did not contend that whatever "is" is necessarily right, but it did assume that the persistence of certain conduct over hundreds of years suggested that careful deliberation should precede any modification or rejection.

As schooling spread, the tendency was to present the formal curriculum in a manner consistent with the tradition, and thus to focus on the transmission of correct habits and values. We should not assume that the interjection of moral concern was necessarily cumbersome. The famous *McGuffey's Reader* series featured stories and essays by substantial writers, such as Walter Scott and Charles Dickens. The literary quality of such writings was appropriate to the age of the student. Significantly, both the materials and their authors supported the development of certain desired traits.

CHARACTER EDUCATION

The most recent efflorescence of the great tradition in America can be found in the "character education" movement in our public schools between 1880 and about 1930. That movement attempted to make public schools more efficient transmitters of appropriate moral values.

The efforts to foster character education assumed schools had to operate from a purely secular basis, which posed special challenges for moral formation. Whereas some earlier education reformers had semisecular sympathies, in previous eras their impact had been tempered by the proreligious forces concurrently affecting schools. Before 1900, for example, probably 15-25 percent of American elementary and secondary school pupils attended either private or public schools that were explicitly religious; another 25-50 percent attended public schools that were tacitly religious. For example,

they used readings from the *King James Bible*.

The character education movement articulated numerous traditional moral aims: promptness, truthfulness, courtesy, and obedience. The movement strove to develop elementary and secondary school programs to foster such conduct. It emphasized techniques such as appropriately structured materials in history and literature; school clubs and other extracurricular activities; rigorous pupil discipline codes; and daily flag salutes and frequent assemblies. Many relatively elaborate character education plans were designed and disseminated to schools and school districts. Often the plans were adopted through the mandate of state legislatures or state boards of education. Some modern authorities, such as James Q. Wilson (1973), have perceived a strong relationship between the character education movement and the relatively high levels of youth order in America during the nineteenth century.

AN UNFAVORABLE EVALUATION

From the first, the supporters of character education emphasized rational organization and research. Despite such attempts, much of the research was superficial. Nonetheless, the research persisted because of the importance attributed to character, and gradually its quality improved. During the mid-1920s, researchers led by Hugh Hartschorne and Mark A. May concluded that the relationship between pupil good conduct and the application of formal character education approach was slight. Good conduct appeared to be relatively situation-specific: a person might routinely act correctly in one situation and incorrectly in another slightly different one. A person could cheat on exams, for example, but not steal money from the class fund. This situational specificity meant that good character was not a unified trait that could be cultivated by any single approach.

Despite this research, character education was never formally abandoned. Few educators or researchers have ever said publicly that schools should *not* be concerned with the morality or character of their pupils. Indeed, recent research and statistical reanalysis of earlier data has contended that Hartschorne and May's findings were excessively negative. Still, their research was a turning point in the relationship between American public education and the great tradition of moral values. Before the research many schools were fully concerned with carrying forward that tradition, and the intellectual forces affecting schools were in sympathy with such efforts. Even after the 1930s, many schools still reflexively maintained their former commitment to moral formation; the prevailing intellectual climate among researchers and academics, however, was indifferent or hostile to such efforts. Gradually, a disjunction arose between what some educators and many parents thought was appropriate (and what some of them applied), and what was favored by a smaller, more formally trained group of experts.

Ironically, the research findings of Hartschorne and May did not refute conflict with the major intellectual themes of the great tradition. The tradition emphasized that moral formation was complex. To be effective, it had to be incremental, diverse, pervasive, persistent, and rigorous. Essentially, it relied on probabilistic principles: the more frequent and more diverse techniques applied, the more

likely that more youths would be properly formed; but even if all techniques were applied, some youths would be "missed." Given such principles, it logically follows that the measured long-term effect of any limited program of "moral instruction" would be minute.

The Hartschorne and May findings demonstrated that American expectations for character education were unrealistic, a proposition not inconsistent with expectations we seem to have for *any* education technique. This does not mean that education's effects are inconsequential, but that Americans often approach education from a semi-utopian perspective. We have trouble realizing that many things happen slowly, and that not all problems are solvable.

NEW APPROACHES TO MORAL INSTRUCTION

During the 1930s, 1940s, and 1950s, there was little intellectual or research concern with moral formation in America. Schools continued to be engaged in moral instruction, both deliberately or incidentally, but the in-school process relied on momentum stimulated by earlier perspectives. In other words, moral instruction went on, but without substantial intellectual underpinning.

Since the 1960s, a number of different—perhaps more scientific—approaches to moral instruction have evolved. Many of these approaches have been described by the term "moral education." Among these have been values clarification, identified with Louis L. Raths and Sidney B. Simon, and the moral development approach identified with Lawrence Kohlberg and his colleagues. Despite the variations among contemporary approaches, almost all the more recent techniques have had certain common elements. Their developers were not school teachers, ministers, or education administrators, but college professors who sought to emphasize the scientific base for their efforts. But, most important, the approaches disavowed the great tradition's persistent concern with affecting *conduct*. The moral dilemmas used in some exercises were highly abstract and probably would never arise in real life. Their aim was to cause students to feel or reason in particular ways rather than to practice right conduct immediately.

The developers of the new systems were conscious of Hartschorne and May's research. They recognized the difficulty of shaping conduct and presumably felt that shaping patterns of reasoning was more feasible. Furthermore, many of the moral education approaches were designed as curriculum materials that could be taught through lectures and class discussion. Such designs facilitated their adoption by teachers and schools. Had the approaches aimed to pervasively affect pupil day-to-day conduct, they would have been more difficult to disseminate. Finally, both the researchers and the proponents of the new approaches felt it was morally unjustifiable to apply the vital pressures needed to actually shape pupil's conduct, feeling such pressures would constitute "indoctrination." On the other hand, methods of moral reasoning apparently might be taught as routine school subjects with the tacit consent of the pupils involved.

The anti-indoctrination stance central to the new approaches invites amplification. Obviously, the great tradition regarded the issue of indoctrination as a specious question. Proponents of the great tradition say, "Of course indoctrination happens. It is ridiculous to be-lieve children are capable of objectively assessing most of the beliefs and values they must absorb to be effective adults. They must learn a certain body of 'doctrine' to function on a day-to-day basis in society. There is good and bad doctrine, and thus things must be weighed and assessed. But such assessment is largely the responsibility of parents and other appropriate adults."

It is hard to articulate fairly the position of the anti-indoctrinators. Although they are against indoctrination, they provide no clear answer as to how children are given many real choices in a relatively immutable world necessarily maintained by adults. The anti-indoctrinators also do not say what adults are to do when children's value choices and resulting potential conduct are clearly harmful to them or others. After all, punishments for bad value choices are, in effect, forms of indoctrination. And the idea of presenting pupils with any particular approach to moral education in a school is inherently indoctrinative: the pupils are not allowed to refuse to come to school, or to hear seriously the pros and cons articulated by sympathetic spokespersons (or critics) for moral education or to freely choose among various approaches to them. Providing such choices is antithetical to the operation of any school.

To consider another perspective, the secular nature of the typical public school obviously indoctrinates pupils against practicing religion in that environment, although most religions contend that some religious practices of a public nature are inextricably related to day-to-day life. This "reality" of separating religion and public education is understandable. However, it is disingenuous to call this policy nonindoctrinative. Thus, it is specious to talk about student choices. The point is that, *on the whole, school is and should and must be inherently indoctrinative.* The only significant questions are: Will the indoctrination be overt or covert, and what will be indoctrinated?

The great tradition has never died. Many administrators and teachers in public and private schools have continued practices consistent with its principles. Given the increased support from academics and intellectuals, . . . these principles deserve widespread professional support.

NOTE

1. The Virginia Constitution.

REFERENCES

Cohen, Y. *The Transition from Childhood to Adolescence.* Chicago: Aldine, 1964.

Hartschorne, H., and May, M. A. *Studies in Deceit, Studies in Service and Self-Control,* and *Studies in the Organization of Character.* New York: Macmillan, 1928, 1929, 1930.

Klapp. O. *The Collective Search for Identity.* New York: Holt, Rinehart, and Winston, 1969.

Meyers, E. *Education in the Perspective of History.* New York: Harper & Row, 1960.

Rothman, D. J., and Rothman, S. M. *Sources of American Social Tradition.* New York: Basic, 1975.

Wilkinson, R. *Governing Elites.* New York: Oxford University Press, 1969.

Wilson, J. Q. "Crime and American Culture." *The Public Interest* 70 (Winter 1973): 22–48.

Wynne, E. A. *Looking at Schools.* Lexington, MA.: Heath/Lexington, 1980.

Yulish, S. M. *The Search for a Civic Religion,* Lanham, Md.: University Press of America, 1980.

POSTSCRIPT

Should Values Be Developed Rather Than Transmitted?

One of the questions concerning school-developed morality is whether or not the system effectively transmits the desired values. According to Philip W. Jackson, in "The School as Moral Instructor: Deliberate Efforts and Unintentional Consequences," *The World and I* (March 1988), schools generally respond to societal problems by creating extra courses to specifically address them. He cites such examples as driver education for traffic safety problems and sexuality education in response to the rising rate of teenage pregnancies. Jackson supports this reaction as a logical curricular solution, but he feels that gauging the effectiveness of such courses is impossible.

In addition to not knowing if students are learning the desired material, Jackson wonders what moral signals students may pick up that are not intentionally taught. Do day-to-day school routines arbitrarily transmit undesired morals? Again, there is little evidence to base an answer on.

For a full view of the educational problems and alternatives bearing on the values domain, one must sample widely. Some sources that may help clarify this difficult area are Abraham Maslow's *New Knowledge in Human Values* (1959); Milton Rokeach's *The Nature of Human Values* (1973); and a collection of essays presented by Robert Coles in *The Moral Life of Children* (1986).

Other sources that may be illuminating are Philip Phenix's "The Moral Imperative in Contemporary American Education," *Perspectives on Education* (Winter 1969), and John Dewey's *Moral Principles in Education* (1911).

Of more recent vintage are Thomas Lickona's practical guidebook *Raising Good Children* (1983); John A. Howard's article "Re-opening the Books on Ethics: The Role of Education in a Free Society," *American Education* (October 1984); and Jerome Kagan's chapter "Establishing a Morality" in his book *The Nature of the Child* (1984). The December 1985/January 1986 issue of *Educational Leadership* is devoted to the schools' role in the development of character. Harold Howe II offers some challenging ideas in his article "Can Schools Teach Values?" *Teachers College Record* (Fall 1987). Additional books on the topic are *Theories of Moral Development* (1985) by John Martin Rich and Joseph DeVitts; *Schools and Meaning: Essays on the Moral Nature of Schooling* (1985) edited by David E. Purpel and H. Svi Shapiro; and *No Ladder to the Sky: Education and Morality* (1987) by Gabriel Moran.

Thomas Likona's book *Education for Character: How Our Schools Can Teach Respect and Responsibility* (1991) and William K. Kilpatrick's *Why Johnny Can't Tell Right from Wrong: Moral Illiteracy and the Case for Character Education* (1992) offer further insights into the issue.

ISSUE 5

Is Church-State Separation Being Threatened?

YES: R. Freeman Butts, from "A History and Civics Lesson for All of Us," *Educational Leadership* (May 1987)

NO: Robert L. Cord, from "Church-State Separation and the Public Schools: A Re-evaluation," *Educational Leadership* (May 1987)

ISSUE SUMMARY

YES: Professor emeritus of education R. Freeman Butts warns that current efforts to redefine the relationship between religion and schooling are eroding the Constitution's intent.
NO: Professor of political science Robert L. Cord offers a more accommodating interpretation of this intent, one that allows for the school practices that Butts condemns as unconstitutional.

The religious grounding of early schooling in America certainly cannot be denied. Nor can the history of religious influences on the conduct of our governmental functions and our school practices. In the nineteenth century, however, protests against the prevailing Protestant influence in the public schools were lodged by Catholics, Jews, nonbelievers, and other groups, giving rise to a number of issues that revolve around interpretations of the "establishment of religion" and the "free exercise of religion" clauses of the Constitution.

Twentieth-century U.S. Supreme Court cases, such as *Cochran* (1930), *Everson* (1947), *McCollum* (1948), *Zorach* (1952), *Engel* (1962), and *Murray* (1963), attempted to clarify the relationship between religion and schooling. Most of these decisions bolstered the separation of church and state position. Only recently has a countermovement, led in some quarters by the Moral Majority organization of Reverend Jerry Falwell, sought to sway public and legal opinion toward an emphasis on the "free exercise" clause and toward viewing the influence of secular humanism in the schools as "an establishment of religion."

At both the legislative and judicial levels, attempts were made in the 1980s to secure an official place in public education for voluntary prayer, moments of silent meditation, and creationism in the science curriculum. Censorship of textbooks and other school materials, access to facilities by religious groups, and the right of parents to withdraw their children from instruction deemed to be morally offensive and damaging have also been promoted. Humanists (who may be either religious or nonreligious) find a good deal of distortion in these recent attacks on the "secularization" of schooling, and they argue that the materials used in the schools are consistent with the historical goals of character development while also being in tune with the realities of the present times.

John Buchanan of People for the American Way argues that public schools are places where young people of differing backgrounds and beliefs can come together and learn tolerance. He and others worry that parental veto power will undermine decision-making and impair school effectiveness. Bill Keith of the Creation Science Legal Defense Fund contends that a parent's liberty with regard to a child's education is a fundamental right, an enduring American tradition.

Resolution of the philosophical questions regarding the content and conduct of public education has become increasingly politicized. Who should control the school curriculum and its materials—school boards, professional educators, community groups, the federal or state governments, parents, or students? Should censorship boards operate at the local, state, or national level—or none of the above? Where does the line get drawn between benevolent intervention and thought control? Can schools be value-neutral?

In the articles presented here, R. Freeman Butts makes the case that legal and historical scholarship points to the broader, separatist, and secular meaning of the First Amendment, which controls the answers to many of these questions. Robert L. Cord bases his argument for a more accommodating interpretation on his findings in primary historical sources and on the actions of the framers of the Constitution.

YES

R. Freeman Butts

A HISTORY AND CIVICS LESSON
FOR ALL OF US

As chairman of the Commission on the Bicentennial of the U.S. Constitution, former Chief Justice Warren E. Burger urges that the occasion provide "a history and civics lesson for all of us." I heartily agree, but the lesson will depend on which version of history you read—and believe.

From May 1982, when President Reagan advocated adoption of a constitutional amendment to permit organized prayer in public schools, Congress has been bitterly divided during the repeated efforts to pass legislation aimed either at amending the Constitution or stripping the Supreme Court and other federal courts of jurisdiction to decide cases about prayers in the public schools. Similar controversies have arisen over efforts of the Reagan administration to promote vouchers and tuition tax credits to give financial aid to parents choosing to send their children to private religious schools.

SCHOOL/RELIGION CONTROVERSIES

I would like to remind educators that the present controversies have a long history, and the way we understand that history makes a difference in our policy judgments. A watershed debate occurred, for example, in 1947 when the Supreme Court spelled out the meaning of the part of the First Amendment which reads, "Congress shall make no law respecting an establishment of religion." The occasion was a challenge to a New Jersey law giving tax money to Catholic parents to send their children by bus to parochial schools. The Court split 5-4 in that case, *Everson* v. *Board of Education,* on whether this practice was, in effect, "an establishment of religion" and thus unconstitutional, but there was no disagreement on the principle. Justice Hugo Black wrote for the majority.

> The "establishment of religion" clause of the First Amendment means at least this: Neither a state nor the Federal Government can pass laws which aid one religion, aid all religions, or prefer one religion over another. . . . No tax in

From R. Freeman Butts, "A History and Civics Lesson for All of Us," *Educational Leadership,* vol. 44, no. 8 (May 1987), pp. 21–25. Copyright © 1987 by The Association for Supervision and Curriculum Development. Reprinted by permission. All rights reserved.

any amount, large or small, can be levied to support any religious activities or institutions, whatever they may be called, or whatever form they may adopt to teach or practice religion. . . . In the words of Jefferson, the clause against establishment of religion by law was intended to erect "a wall of separation between Church and State."[1]

The *Everson* majority accepted this broad principle, but decided, nevertheless, that bus fares were merely welfare aid to parents and children and not aid to the religious schools themselves. The 1948 *McCollum* case prohibited released time for religious instruction in the public schools of Champaign, Illinois, because it violated the *Everson* principle.

These two cases set off a thunderous denunciation of the Supreme Court and calls for impeachment of the justices. They also sent historians of education scurrying to original sources to see how valid this broad and liberal interpretation was.

ESTABLISHMENT PRINCIPLE

The two books at that time that gave most attention to the establishment principle as it related to education were James M. O'Neill's *Religion and Education Under the Constitution*[2] and my own, *The American Tradition in Religion and Education*.[3] O'Neill found the Court's interpretation appalling; I found it basically true to Madison and the majority of the framers of the First Amendment. My book was cited in 1971 in the concurring opinions of Justices Brennan, Douglas, and Black in *Lemon* v. *Kurtzman*.[4] Chief Justice Burger summarized for a unanimous court the accumulated precedents since *Everson* and listed three tests of constitutional state action in education: a secular purpose; neither advancement

nor inhibition of religion; and no excessive government entanglement with religion.

With that decision, I concluded that my views of the framers' intentions had been pretty well accepted: namely, that "an establishment of religion" in the 1780s was "a multiple establishment" whereby public aid could go to several churches, and that this is what the majority of framers, particularly Madison, intended to prohibit in the First Amendment.

Indeed, single religious establishments had existed in nine of the early colonies, but by 1789 when the First Congress drafted the First Amendment, religious diversity had become such a powerful political force that seven states, which included the vast majority of Americans, had either disestablished their churches or had never established any. Only six state constitutions still permitted "an establishment of religion," and all six provided tax funds for several churches, not just one.[5] Naturally, some representatives and senators from those states did not want their multiple establishment threatened by a Bill of Rights in the new federal government. But Madison did.

Madison had prevented just such a multiple establishment in Virginia in 1785 and 1786 and managed instead the passage of Jefferson's powerful Statute for Religious Freedom. In his speech of 8 June 1789, when he introduced his Bill of Rights proposals in the House, he made a double-barreled approach to religious freedom. He proposed (1) to prohibit Congress from establishing religion on a national basis, and (2) to prohibit the states from infringing "equal rights of conscience."

After considerable discussion and some changes of language, the House of Representatives approved both of Madison's proposals and sent them to the Senate. The Senate, however, did not approve the prohibition on the states. Furthermore, a minority in the Senate made three attempts to narrow the wording of the First Amendment to prohibit Congress from establishing a single church or giving preference to one religious sect or denomination. The majority, however, rejected all such attempts to narrow Madison's proposal, and the Senate finally accepted the wording of Madison's conference committee. This was then finally adopted by both houses. Madison's broad and liberal interpretation of the establishment clause as applied to Congress had won.[6]

Neither Madison nor the majority of framers intended for government to disdain religion. They intended that republican government guarantee equal rights of conscience to all persons, but it took some 150 years before Madison's views were applied specifically to the states through the Fourteenth Amendment. That is what the Supreme Court did in *Everson*.

FRAMERS' INTENTIONS REDEFINED

But today, "a jurisprudence of original intention" has revived the debates of the 1940s and 1950s, expounding much the same views as those of O'Neill namely that "the framers" intended only to prohibit Congress from establishing a single national church, but would permit aid to all religions on a nonpreferential basis and would even permit the states to establish a single church if they wished. These arguments are now being resurrected or reincarnated (to use the secular meaning of those terms) with even more sophisticated scholarship by such au-

thors as Walter Berns of Georgetown University, Michael Malbin of the American Enterprise Institute, and Robert L. Cord of Northeastern University.[7]

Their works have been cited in legal briefs in several state actions and in at least one federal district court decision, while an increasingly vigorous campaign has been launched by conservative members of Congress and the Reagan administration to appeal to the history of "original intention."

These efforts reached a crescendo of confrontation in summer and fall of 1985, following two Supreme Court decisions. In *Wallace* v. *Jaffree* on 4 June 1985, the Court reversed Federal Judge W. Brevard Hand's decision that Alabama's laws providing for prayer in the public schools were, indeed, permissible and did not violate the First Amendment's prohibition against "an establishment of religion." Relying in part on Cord's version of history, Judge Hand argued that the Supreme Court had long erred in its reading of the original intention of the framers of the First Amendment. He said that they intended solely to prevent the federal government from establishing a single national church such as the Church of England; therefore, the Congress could aid all churches if it did not give preference to any one; that a state was free to establish a state religion if it chose to do so and, thus, could require or permit prayers in its public schools.

The Supreme Court reversed this decision (6-3), and Justice John Paul Stevens, writing for the Court, rebuked Judge Hand by referring to his "newly discovered historical evidence" as a "remarkable conclusion" wholly at odds with the firmly established constitutional provision that "the several States have no greater power to restrain the individual freedoms protected by the First Amendment than does the Congress of the United States." Justice Stevens emphasized that the Court had confirmed and endorsed time and time again the principle of incorporation, by which the Fourteenth Amendment imposes the same limitations on the states that it imposes on Congress regarding protection of civil liberties guaranteed by the First Amendment and the original Bill of Rights.[8]

However, the confrontations between these views of history were not over. In his long dissenting opinion in *Jaffree*, Associate Justice William H. Rehnquist, now Chief Justice, reasserted an "accommodationist" view of church and state relations. Relying on O'Neill's and Cord's version of history, he argued that the "wall of separation between church and state" is a metaphor based on bad history and that the *Everson* principle "should be frankly and explicitly abandoned." Justice Byron R. White's dissent also supported such "a basic reconsideration of our precedents."

Soon after, on 1 July 1985, the Supreme Court ruled in *Aguilar v. Fenton* (5-4) that the practices of New York City and Grand Rapids, Michigan, in sending public school teachers to private religious schools to teach remedial and enhancement programs for disadvantaged children, were also unconstitutional. Justice William J. Brennan, delivering the Court's opinion, cited the *Everson* principle that the state should remain neutral and not become entangled with churches in administering schools. Dissents were written by the Chief Justice and Justices Sandra Day O'Connor, White, and Rehnquist.[9]

These Supreme Court decisions were greeted with some surprise and considerable elation by liberals and with dis-

may by conservatives. Attorney General Edwin Meese III quickly and forcefully responded on 10 July 1985 in a speech before the American Bar Association. He explicitly criticized the Court's decisions on religion and education as a misreading of history and commended Justice Rehnquist's call for overruling *Everson*. Secretary of Education William Bennett echoed the complaint that the Supreme Court was misreading history. And, then, in October 1985 Justices Brennan and Stevens both gave speeches sharply criticizing the Attorney General's campaign for a "jurisprudence of original intention."

In addition, the White House, the Attorney General, the Justice Department, the Secretary of Education, the former Republican majority of the Senate Judiciary Committee, the new Chief Justice, and the conservative justices of the Supreme Court, by public statements are now ranged against the liberal and centrist members of the Supreme Court and such notable constitutional scholars as Laurence Tribe of Harvard, Herman Schwartz of American University, A. E. Dick Howard of the University of Virginia, and Leonard W. Levy of the Claremont Graduate School. They all appeal to history, but whose version of history do you read—and believe?

All in all, I think it fair to say that the predominant stream of constitutional, legal, and historical scholarship points to the broader, separatist, and secular meaning of the First Amendment against the narrower, cooperationist, or accommodationist meaning. A nonspecialist cannot encompass the vast literature on this subject, but a valuable and readily available source of evidence is the recently published book by Leonard Levy, professor of humanities and chairman of the Claremont University Graduate Faculty of History. He is editor of the *Encyclopedia of the American Constitution* and the author of a dozen books devoted mostly to the Bill of Rights.

In his book on the First Amendment's establishment clause Levy concludes, and I fully agree, that the meaning of "an establishment of religion" is as follows:

> After the American Revolution seven of the fourteen states that comprised the Union in 1791 authorized establishments of religion by law. Not one state maintained a single or preferential establishment of religion. An establishment of religion meant to those who framed and ratified the First Amendment what it meant in those seven states, and in all seven it meant public support of religion on a nonpreferential basis. It was specifically this support on a nonpreferential basis that the establishment clause of the First Amendment sought to forbid.[10]

Acceptance of a narrow, accommodationist view of the history of the establishment clause must not be allowed to be turned into public policies that serve to increase public support for religious schools in any form: vouchers, tax credits, or aid for extremes of "parental choice." They must not be allowed to increase the role of religion in public schools by organized prayer, teaching of Creationism, censorship of textbooks on the basis of their "secular humanism," or "opting out" of required studies in citizenship on the grounds that they offend any sincerely held religious belief, as ruled by Federal District Judge Thomas Hull in Greeneville, Tennessee, in October 1986.[11]

These practices not only violate good public policy, but they also vitiate the thrust toward separation of church and state which, with minor exceptions, marked the entire careers of Madison and Jefferson. William Lee Miller, professor of religious studies at the University of Virginia, wrote the following succinct summary of their views:

> Did "religious freedom" for Jefferson and Madison extend to atheists? Yes. To agnostics, unbelievers, and pagans? Yes. To heretics and blasphemers and the sacrilegious? Yes. To the Jew and the Gentile, the Christian and Mohametan, the Hindoo, and infidel of every denomination? Yes. To people who want freedom *from* religion? Yes. To people who want freedom *against* religion? Yes. . . .
>
> Did this liberty of belief for Jefferson and Madison entail separation of church and state? Yes. A ban on tax aid to religion? Yes. On state help to religion? Yes. Even religion-in-general? Yes. Even if it were extended without any favoritism among religious groups? Yes. The completely voluntary way in religion? Yes.
>
> Did all the founders agree with Jefferson and Madison? Certainly not. Otherwise there wouldn't have been a fight.[12]

The fight not only continues, but seems to be intensifying on many fronts. So, it behooves educators to study these issues in depth, to consider the best historical scholarship available, and to judge present issues of religion and education accordingly.

NOTES

1. *Everson v. Board of Education*, 330 U.S. 1 (1947). Black was joined by Chief Justice Vinson and Justices Douglas, Murphy, and Reed.
2. James M. O'Neill, *Religion and Education Under the Constitution* (New York: Harper, 1949). O'Neill was chairman of the department of speech at Queens College, New York. See also Wilfrid Parsons, S.J., *The First Freedom: Considerations on Church and State in the United States* (New York: Declan X. McMullen, 1948).

3. R. Freeman Butts, *The American Tradition in Religion and Education* (Boston: Beacon Press, 1950). I was professor of education at Teachers College, Columbia University, teaching courses in the history of education. See O'Neill's review of my book in *America*, 9 September 1950, pp. 579–583. See also Leo Pfeffer, *Church, State, and Freedom* (Boston: Beacon Press, 1953) for views similar to mine.

4. *Lemon* v. *Kurtzman*, 403 U.S. 602 (1971). The law struck down in Pennsylvania would have paid part of the salaries of private school teachers of nonreligious subjects.

5. Those six states were Massachusetts, Connecticut, New Hampshire, Maryland, South Carolina, and Georgia.

6. R. Freeman Butts, *Religion, Education, and the First Amendment: The Appeal to History* (Washington, D.C.: People for the American Way, 1985),35. R. Freeman Butts, "James Madison, the Bill of Rights, and Education," *Teachers College Record* 60, 3 (December 1958): 123–128.

7. Walter Berns, *The First Amendment and the Future of American Democracy* (New York: Basic Books, 1976). Michael J. Malbin, *Religion and Politics: The Intentions of the Authors of the First Amendment* (Washington, D.C.: American Enterprise Institute, 1978). Robert L. Cord, *Separation of Church and State: Historical Fact and Current Fiction* (New York: Lambeth Press, 1982) with a Foreword by William F. Buckley, Jr.

8. *Wallace* v. *Jaffree*, 105 S.Ct. 2479 (1985).

9. *Aguilar* v. *Felton*, 105 S.Ct. 3232 (1985).

10. Leonard W. Levy, *The Establishment Clause: Religion and the First Amendment* (New York: Macmillan, 1986), p. xvi.

11. *Mozert* v. *Hawkins*, U.S. District Court for Eastern District of Tennessee, 24 October 1986.

12. *The Washington Post National Weekly Edition*, 13 October 1986, pp. 23–24.

NO

Robert L. Cord

CHURCH-STATE SEPARATION AND THE PUBLIC SCHOOLS: A RE-EVALUATION

For four decades—since the *Everson* v. *Board of Education*[1] decision in 1947—a volatile national debate has raged about the meaning and scope of the First Amendment's establishment clause that mandates separation of church and state. Many of the U.S. Supreme Court's decisions about this matter involve education; therefore, their importance is great to school administrators and teachers who establish and execute policy.

Because of the vagueness of Supreme Court decision making in this important area of constitutional law, public school educators have been accused of violating the First Amendment by allowing or disallowing, for example, the posting of the Ten Commandments, a meeting on school property of a student religious club, or a moment of silent meditation and/or prayer. Today even the very textbooks that students read have become a subject of litigation by parents against a school system, a controversy most likely to end before the Supreme Court.

As this national debate rages, most scholars generally agree that the Founding Fathers' intentions regarding church-state separation are still extremely relevant and important. While the framers of the Constitution and the First Amendment could not foresee many twentieth century problems— especially those growing from advanced technology—many church-state concerns that they addressed in 1787 and 1789 are similar to those we face today.

CONSTITUTION'S WORDS NOT TRIVIAL

Further, if a nation, such as the United States, proclaims that its written Constitution protects individual liberties and truly provides legal restrictions on the actions of government, the words of that organic law—and the principles derived from them—cannot be treated as irrelevant trivia by those who temporarily govern. That is the surest single way to undo constitutional government, for constitutional government requires that the general power of government be defined and limited by law *in fact* as well as in theory.[2]

Published in 1979 to the praise of many respected constitutional scholars, the encyclopedic *Congressional Quarterly's Guide to the U.S. Supreme Court* provided the following meaning of the establishment clause.

The two men most responsible for its inclusion in the Bill of Rights construed the clause *absolutely*. Thomas Jefferson and James Madison thought that the prohibition of establishment meant that a presidential proclamation of Thanksgiving Day was just as improper as a tax exemption for churches.[3]

Despite this authoritative statement, the historical facts are that, as President, James Madison issued at least four Thanksgiving Day proclamations—9 July 1812, 23 July 1813, 16 November 1814, and 4 March 1815.[4] If Madison interpreted the establishment clause absolutely, he violated both his oath of office and the very instruments of government that he helped write and labored to have ratified.[5]

Similarly, if President Thomas Jefferson construed the establishment clause absolutely, he also violated his oath of office, his principles, and the Constitution when, in 1802, he signed into federal law tax exemption for the churches in Alexandria County, Virginia.[6]

Since Jefferson and Madison held the concept of separation of church and state most dear, in my judgment, neither man—as president or in any other public office under the federal Constitution—was an absolutist and neither violated his understanding of the First Amendment's establishment clause. For me, it therefore logically follows that President Madison did not think issuing Thanksgiving Day Proclamations violated the constitutional doctrine of church-state separation, and that President Jefferson held the same view about tax exemption for churches.

Whoever wrote the paragraph quoted from the prestigious *Guide to the U.S. Supreme Court,* I assume, did not intend to deceive, but evidently did not check primary historical sources, was ignorant of Madison's and Jefferson's actions when each was president, and mistakenly relied on inadequate secondary historical writings considered authoritative, as no doubt the paragraph from the *Guide* is, too. This indicates that much misunderstanding and/or misinformation exists about the meaning of the constitutional concept of separation of church and state.

In that context, I examine ideas critical of my writing published in a monograph—*Religion, Education, and the First Amendment: The Appeal to History*—by the eminent scholar, R. Freeman Butts. There he characterized my book, *Separation of Church and State: Historical Fact and Current Fiction,* as a manifestation of some "conservative counterreformation," the purpose of which is "to attack once again the [U.S. Supreme] Court's adherence to the principle of separation between church and state" by characterizing that principle as a "myth" or a "fiction" or merely "rhetoric."[7] The very first paragraph of my book refutes this erroneous characterization.

Separation of Church and State is probably the most distinctive concept that the American constitutional system has contributed to the body of political ideas. In 1791, when the First Amendment's prohibition that "Congress shall make no law respecting an establishment of religion" was added to the United States Constitution, no other country had provided so carefully to prevent the combination of the power of religion with the power of the national government.[8]

While primary historical sources exist that substantiate the Founding Fathers' commitment to church-state separation, other primary sources convince me that much of what the United States Supreme Court and noted scholars have written about it is historically untenable and, in many instances, sheer fiction at odds with the words and actions of the statesmen who placed that very principle in our Constitution.

ABSOLUTE SEPARATION V. "NO PREFERENCE" DOCTRINE

In the 40-year-old *Everson* case the Supreme Court justices, while splitting 5-4 over the immediate issue, were unanimous in proclaiming that the purpose of the establishment clause—and the intention of its framers in the First Congress—was to create a "high and impregnable" wall of separation between church and state.[9]

Unlike the *Everson* Court, Professor Butts, and all "absolute separationist" scholars, I think the full weight of historical evidence—especially the documented public words and deeds of the First Amendment's framers, including James Madison and our early presidents and Congresses—indicates that they embraced a far narrower concept of church-state separation. In my judgment, they interpreted the First Amendment as prohibiting Congress from (1) creating a national religion or establishment, and (2) placing any one religion, religious sect, or religious tradition in a legally preferred position.[10]

Simply put, the framers of the establishment clause sought to preclude discriminatory government religious partisanship, not nondiscriminatory government accommodation or, in some instances, government collaboration with religion. When this "no religious preference" interpretation of the establishment clause is substituted for the Supreme Court's "high and impregnable wall" interpretation, it is easier to understand many historical documents at odds with the absolutists' position. They substantiate that all our early Congresses, including the one that proposed to the states what subsequently became the First Amendment, and all our early presidents, including Jefferson and Madison, in one way or another used sectarian means to achieve constitutional secular ends.

EVERSON CASE

In the *Everson* case, writing the Court's opinion, Justice Black sought to bolster his "high and impregnable wall" dictum with appeals to some carefully chosen actions of Madison, Jefferson, the Virginia Legislature of 1786, and the framers of the First Amendment. Omitted from all of the *Everson* opinions are any historical facts that run counter to that theory. In his writings, I think Professor Butts employs a similar technique of "history by omission." By this I mean that he fails to address indisputable historical facts that are irreconcilable with his absolute separationist views. A few examples will substantiate this extremely important point.

Mentioning Madison's successful Virginia battle against the "Bill Establishing a Provision for Teachers of the Christian Religion" and "Jefferson's historic statute for religious freedom in 1786,"[11] Professor Butts does not explain away Jefferson's Virginia "Bill for Punishing Disturbers of Religious Worship and Sabbath Breakers," which was introduced by Madison in the Virginia Assembly in

1785 and became law in 1786.[12] Further, while he emphasizes Madison's role in introducing and guiding the Bill of Rights through the First Congress,[13] Professor Butts does not explain why the "absolutist" Madison served as one of six members of a Congressional Committee which, without recorded dissent, recommended the establishment of a Congressional Chaplain System. Adopting the Committee's recommendation, the First Congress voted a $500 annual salary from public funds for a Senate chaplain and a like amount for a House chaplain, both of whom were to offer public prayers in Congress.[14]

Nor does Professor Butts explain why, as an absolute separationist, James Madison would, as president, issue discretionary proclamations of Thanksgiving, calling for a day "to be set apart for the devout purposes of rendering the Sovereign of the Universe and the Benefactor of Man [identified earlier in the proclamation by Madison as "Almighty God"] the public homage due to His holy attributes. . . ."[15]

Unexplained also is why Professor Butts' absolute separationist version of Thomas Jefferson would, as president, conclude a treaty with Kaskaskia Indians which, in part, called for the United States to build them a Roman Catholic Church and pay their priest, and subsequently would urge Congress to appropriate public funds to carry out the terms of the treaty.[16] An understanding of what the framers of our Constitution thought about church-state separation would also be furthered if we had explanations of why Presidents Washington, John Adams, and Jefferson apparently did not think they were breaching the "high and impregnable" wall when they signed into law Congressional bills that,

in effect, purchased with enormous grants of federal land, in controlling trusts, the services of the "Society of the United Brethren for propagating the Gospel among the Heathen" to minister to the needs of Christian and other Indians in the Ohio Territory.[17] Like the majority of the Supreme Court, Professor Butts does not comment on these historical documents and events.

When all the historical evidence is considered, I think it relatively clear that the establishment clause was designed to prevent Congress from either establishing a national religion or from putting any one religion, religious sect, or religious tradition into a legally preferred position. In *Everson*, the Supreme Court interpreted the Fourteenth Amendment as prohibiting state legislatures, or their instrumentalities such as school boards, from doing likewise. As a result, the interpretation of the establishment clause by Supreme Court decisions governs the permissible range of both state and federal legislative authority.

Professor Butts thinks my definition of an "establishment of religion" too narrow, and the prohibition which I think the framers intended "plausible but false."[18] Plausible because in the sixteenth and seventeenth centuries, establishments in Europe and in the early American colonies usually meant the establishment of a single church. False because Professor Butts contends that, by the end of the eighteenth century, in America the term "establishment of religion" had taken on a different meaning.

His argument is that "the idea of a single church as constituting 'an establishment of religion' was no longer embedded in the legal framework of any American state when the First Amendment was being debated in Congress in the summer of 1789." Adding that in all of the states that still retained establishments, "multiple establishments were the rule," Professor Butts concludes that "the founders and the framers could not have been ignorant of this fact; they knew very well that this is what the majority in the First Congress intended to prohibit at the federal level."[19]

BUTTS' ARGUMENT UNTENABLE

This argument is simply untenable when considered with the primary historical record. Professor Butts virtually ignored the documents most crucial to an understanding of what the religion clauses were designed to prohibit at the federal level—the suggested constitutional amendments from the various State Ratifying Conventions. Those documents show that they feared, among other things, that important individual rights might be infringed by the powerful new national legislature authorized by the adoption of the federal Constitution.

Their amendments indicate that the states feared interference with the individual's right of conscience and an exclusive religious establishment, *not a multiple national establishment*, as Professor Butts wants us to believe. Typical was the Maryland Ratifying Convention's proposed amendment stating "that there will be no national religion established by law; but that all persons be equally entitled to protection in their religious liberty."[20]

The Virginia Ratifying Convention proposed a "Declaration of Bill of Rights" as amendments to the Constitution that was echoed by North Carolina, Rhode Island, and New York Conventions. Virginia's Article Twenty, adopted 27 June 1788, stated:

That religion, or the duty which we owe to our Creator, and the manner of discharging it, can be directed only by reason and conviction, not by force or violence; and therefore all men have an equal, natural, and unalienable right to the free exercise of religion, according to the dictates of conscience, and that no particular religious sect or society ought to be favored or established, by law, in preference to others.[21]

STATES WANTED NONPREFERENCE

In short, when it came to religious establishments, the State Ratifying Conventions proposed "nonpreference" amendments.

With these proposals in mind, it is easier to understand the wording of Madison's original religion amendment: "The Civil rights of none shall be abridged on account of religious belief or worship, nor shall any national religion be established, nor shall the full and equal rights of Conscience be in any manner, or on any pretext, infringed."[22] Madison wanted the Constitution to forbid the federal government from interfering with the rights of conscience or establish an exclusive national religion—not religions—and the record said so.

The "nonpreference" interpretation is further bolstered by Madison's original wording of his own establishment clause and his later interpretation on the floor of the House of Representatives of the intended prohibitions of the amendment. On 15 August 1789, using virtually the same words employed by the petitioning State Ratifying Conventions,

Mr. Madison said, he apprehended the meaning of the words to be, that Congress should not establish a religion, and enforce the legal observation of it by law, nor compel men to worship

God in any manner contrary to their conscience. Whether the words are necessary or not, he did not mean to say, but . . . he thought it as well expressed as the nature of the language would admit.[23]

Further, the House record indicates that Madison said that "he believed that the people feared one sect might obtain a preeminence, or two combine together, and establish a religion to which they would compel others to conform."[24] Certainly Madison's statements from the record of the First Congress and the other primary documents mentioned here run contrary to the "multiple establishment" thesis.

IMPLICATIONS FOR THE PUBLIC SCHOOLS

Professionals in education may wonder appropriately what the impact would be on public education should the U.S. Supreme Court now choose to reverse some of its major rulings and adopt the narrower interpretation of church-state separation which I believe was intended and embraced by the First Amendment's framers.

First, the establishment clause would continue to prohibit Congress and individual states from creating, in Madison's words, "a national religion."

Second, in keeping with the framers' intent, the establishment clause's "no preference" doctrine, applied directly to the federal government and to the states by the Fourteenth Amendment, would constitutionally preclude all governmental entities from placing any one religion, religious sect, or religious tradition into a preferred legal status. As a consequence, in public schools, the recitation of the Lord's Prayer or readings taken solely from the New Testament would continue to be unconstitutional because they place the Christian religion in a preferred position.

Similarly, the posting of the Ten Commandments only or reading only from the Old Testament would place the Judeo-Christian tradition in an unconstitutionally favored religious status. However, unendorsed readings or postings from many writings considered sacred by various religions, such as the Book of Mormon, the interpretative writings of Mary Baker Eddy, the Bible, the Koran, the Analects of Confucius, would be constitutional. A decision to teach only "creationism" or Genesis would be unconstitutional, while a course in cosmology, exploring a full range of beliefs about the origin of life or the nature of the universe—religious, areligious, or nonreligious—would not violate the First Amendment any more than would a course on comparative religions without teacher endorsement.

In all circumstances where the state is pursuing a valid educational goal, and is religiously nonpartisan in doing so, the professional leadership of the educational unit would decide, as in any other policy, whether such an activity was educationally appropriate or desirable. This would be the case whether the educational unit was a school, a school district, or an entire state educational system. Consequently, adherence to the "no preference" doctrine would return many policy decisions to the appropriate educational authorities, elected or appointed, and reduce the all too frequent present pattern of government by judiciary.

Third, although the First Amendment's free exercise of religion clause would not be contracted by the "no preference" principle, that interpretation would, in some instances, expand the individual's free exercise of religion and other First Amendment rights. This would happen where "equal access" is currently denied public school students.

EQUAL ACCESS ACT

The Equal Access Act of 1984 (Public Law 98-377) prohibits public high schools receiving federal aid from preventing voluntary student groups, including religious ones, from meeting in school facilities before and after class hours or during a club period, if other extracurricular groups have access.[25] The constitutionality of refusing "equal access" to voluntary student religious organizations was litigated in the lower courts[26] before reaching the U.S. Supreme Court in *Bender* v. *Williamsport* in March 1986.[27]

In deciding equal access cases, the lower federal courts applied the Supreme Court's "three part *Lemon*" test to determine whether the establishment clause had been violated. Under this test, first described in *Lemon* v. *Kurtzman*, the Supreme Court held that in order to pass constitutional muster under the establishment clause, the challenged governmental policy or activity must (1) have a secular purpose, (2) be one that has a principal or primary effect which neither advances nor inhibits religion, and (3) not foster an excessive government entanglement with religion.[28]

The "no preference" doctrine, on the other hand, would provide a relatively clearer and easier-to-apply test. Alleged violations would be measured by two simple questions: (1) Is the governmental action within the constitutional power of the acting public body? and (2) Does the governmental action elevate any one religion, religious sect, or religious tradition into a preferred legal status? Either a

"no" to the first question or a "yes" to the second would make the policy unconstitutional.

Unlike the *Lemon* interpretation, the "no preference" interpretation poses less danger to a student's individual First and Fourteenth Amendment liberty. The Third U.S. Circuit Court's decision in *Bender* v. *Williamsport* illustrates this point. There the court held that it was constitutional for a school board to refuse to permit a student-initiated nondenominational prayer club to meet during the regularly scheduled activity period in a public school room.[29] As I see it, that decision subordinated three First Amendment freedoms—free exercise of religion, freedom of speech, and voluntary assembly—to one misinterpreted First Amendment guarantee. Under the "no preference" doctrine, equal access would be guaranteed to *all* religious or, for that matter, irreligious student groups under the same conditions that apply to any other voluntary student group.

Application of the "no preference" interpretation also avoids enormous dangers to an "open society" possible under the *Lemon* test. Can we not see that a court which can hold today that a classroom could not be used by a voluntary religious student group because that use may have as its primary effect the advancement of religion, can tomorrow, by the same logic, bar meeting rooms to students who want to discuss atheism or a book negative about religion, such as Bertrand Russell's *Why I Am Not a Christian*, because the primary effect there might be said to inhibit religion? By the use of *Lemon's* "primary effect" test, books about religion or those said to be irreligious can be removed from public school libraries. Is C. S. Lewis' *The Screwtape Letters* safe? And what about *Inherit the Wind,* or Darwin's *Origin of the Species?* Are we so frightened of ourselves that we are willing to disallow, in our institutions of learning, scrutinization of ultimate issues and values because of fear about where an open marketplace of ideas may eventually take the nation?

Finally, while some actions such as an uncoerced moment of silence for meditation and/or prayer in a public schoolroom[30] or the teaching of educationally deprived students from low-income families for several hours each week in a parochial school by public school teachers, recently held unconstitutional,[31] would be constitutional under the "no preference" interpretation, that does not mean they would automatically become educational policy. In all public educational entities, large or small, what would become policy would be up to the legally empowered decision makers in each of those entities.

NOTES

1. 330 U.S. 1 (1947).

2. Charles H. McIlwain, *Constitutionalism: Ancient and Modern,* rev. ed. (Ithaca, N.Y.: Great Seal Books, 1958), 19-22.

3. *Congressional Quarterly's Guide to the United States Supreme Court* (Washington, D.C.: Congressional Quarterly, Inc., 1979), 461. Emphasis added. The First Amendment has two religion clauses, the "establishment" clause and the "free exercise" clause. U.S. Constitution Amendment I: "Congress shall make no law respecting an establishment of religion, or prohibiting the free exercise thereof. . . ."

4. These proclamations, in their entirety, are published in James D. Richardson, *A Contemplation of the Messages and Papers of the Presidents, 1789-1897,* vol. I (Washington, D.C.: Bureau of National Literature and Art, 1901), 34-35; and Robert L. Cord, *Separation of Church and State: Historical Fact and Current Fiction* (Grand Rapids, Michigan: Baker Book House, 1988), 257-260.

5. After he had left the presidency, and toward the end of his life, Madison wrote a document commonly known as the "Detached Memoranda," which was first published as recently as 1946 in *William and Mary Quarterly* 3 (1946): 534. In it Madison *does* say that Thanksgiving Day proclamations are unconstitutional, as are chaplains in Congress. In light of his actions in public office, these were obviously not his views as a congressman and president. For a fuller discussion of Madison's "Detached Memoranda," see Cord, *Separation,* 29-36.

6. *2 Statutes at Large* 194, Seventh Congress, Sess. 1, Chap. 52. Jefferson *did* believe Thanksgiving Proclamation violated the First Amendment and, unlike Washington, John Adams, and James Madison, declined to issue them.

7. R. Freeman Butts, *Religion, Education, and the First Amendment: The Appeal to History* (Washington, D.C.: People for the American Way, 1986), 9. Butts, an educational historian, is William F. Russell Professor Emeritus, Teachers College, Columbia University; Senior Fellow of the Kettering Foundation; and Visiting Scholar at the Hoover Institution, Stanford University.

8. Cord, *Separation,* XIII.

9. For an extensive critique of the *Everson* case and its interpretation of the establishment clause, see Cord, *Separation,* 103-133.

10. For in-depth study of the "no preference" principle, see Robert L. Cord, "Church-State Separation: Restoring the 'No Preference' Doctrine of the First Amendment," *Harvard Journal of Law & Public Policy* 9 (1986): 129.

11. Butts, *Religion,* 18.

12. Cord, *Separation,* 215-218.

13. Butts, *Religion,* 18-21.

14. Cord, *Separation,* 22-26.

15. Quoted from President Madison's "Proclamation" of "the 9th day of July A.D. 1812." This proclamation is republished in its entirety in Cord, *Separation,* 257.

16. For the entire text of the treaty, see Ibid., 261-263.

17. The full texts of these laws are republished in Cord, 263-270.

18. Butts, *Religion,* 16.

19. Ibid., 18.

20. Jonathan Elliott, *Debates on the Federal Constitution,* vol. II (Philadelphia: J.B. Lippincott Co., 1901), 553.

21. Ibid., vol. III, 659.

22. *Annals of the Congress of the United States, The Debates and Proceedings in the Congress of the United States,* vol. I, Compiled from Authentic Materials, by Joseph Gales, Senior (Washington, D.C.: Gales and Seaton, 1834), 434.

23. Ibid., 730.

24. Ibid., 731.

25. *Congressional Quarterly Weekly Report*, vols. 42, p. 1545, 1854; 43, p. 1807.

26. *Brandon* v. *Board of Education*, 635 F. 2nd 971 (2d Cir. 1980); *cert. denied*, 454 U.S. 1123 (1981); *Lubbock Civil Liberties Union* v. *Lubbock Independent School District*, 669 F. 2d 1038 (5th Cir. 1982), *cert. denied*, 459 U.S. 1155 (1983).

27. *Bender* v. *Williamsport*, 475 U.S. 534, 89 L.Ed. 2d 501 (1986). While the Third Circuit Court dealt with the "equal access" question, the Supreme Court did not reach that constitutional issue because one of the parties to the suit in the Circuit Court lacked standing and, therefore, that Court should have dismissed the case for want of jurisdiction. Ibid., 516.

28. *Lemon* v. *Kurtzman*, 403 U.S. 602, 612, 613 (1971).

29. *Bender* v. *Williamsport*, 741 F. 2d 538, 541 (3rd Cir. 1984).

30. In *Wallace* v. *Jaffree*, 105 S. Ct. 2479 (1985), the U.S. Supreme Court held such a law unconstitutional.

31. In *Grand Rapids* v. *Ball*, 473 U.S. 373, 87 L.Ed. 2d 267 (1985) and *Aguilar* v. *Felton*, 473 U.S. 402, 87 L.Ed. 2d 290 (1985), the Supreme Court held similar programs unconstitutional.

POSTSCRIPT

Is Church-State Separation Being Threatened?

If the Constitution is indeed a document that attempts to guarantee the protection of minority opinions from a possibly oppressive majority, can it be applied equally to all parties in any value-laden dispute such as those involving the relationship of church and state? An exhaustive review of historical cases dealing with manifestations of this basic problem may be found in Martha McCarthy's article "Religion and Public Schools," in the August 1985 issue of the *Harvard Educational Review*.

An extremely wide variety of articles is available on this volatile area of concern, including "Stepchildren of the Moral Majority," Daniel Yankelovich, *Psychology Today* (November 1981); "The Crusade to Ban Books," Stephen Arons, *Saturday Review* (June 1981); "Textbook Censorship and Secular Humanism in Perspective," Franklin Parker, *Religion and Public Education* (Summer 1988); Rod Farmer's "Toward a Definition of Secular Humanism," *Contemporary Education* (Spring 1987); Mel and Norma Gabler's "Moral Relativism on the Ropes," *Communication Education* (October 1987); and Donald Vandenberg's "Education and the Religious," *Teachers College Record* (Fall 1987).

Three other provocative sources of insights are these: Thomas W. Goodhue's "What Should Public Schools Say About Religion?" *Education Week* (April 23, 1986); "How Prayer and Public Schooling Can Coexist," Eugene W. Kelly, Jr., *Education Week* (November 12, 1986); and Edward A. Wynne's "The Case for Censorship to Protect the Young," *Issues in Education* (Winter 1985).

Other excellent sources are these: Warren A. Nord, "The Place of Religion in the World of Public School Textbooks," and Mark G. Yudof, "Religion, Textbooks, and the Public Schools," both in *The Educational Forum* (Spring 1990), and James Davison Hunter's "Modern Pluralism and the First Amendment," *The Brookings Review* (Spring 1990).

Four recent books explore aspects of the issue: *The Rights of Religious Persons in Public Education* (1991) by John W. Whitehead; *Religious Fundamentalism and American Education: The Battle for the Public Schools* (1990) by Eugene F. Provenzo, Jr.; *A Standard for Repair: The Establishment of Religion Clause of the U.S. Constitution* (1992) by Jeremy Gunn; and *Why We Still Need Public Schools: Church/State Relations and Visions of Democracy* (1992) edited by Art Must, Jr.

In the end, the main problem is one of finding an appropriate balance between the two First Amendment clauses within the context of public schooling and making that balance palatable and realizable at the local school level.

ISSUE 6

Does a Common Curriculum Promote Equality?

YES: Mortimer J. Adler, from "The Paideia Proposal: Rediscovering the Essence of Education," *The American School Board Journal* (July 1982)

NO: Floretta Dukes McKenzie, from "The Yellow Brick Road of Education," *Harvard Educational Review* (November 1983)

ISSUE SUMMARY

YES: Mortimer J. Adler, director of the Institute of Philosophical Research, contends that equality of educational opportunity can be attained in qualitative terms by establishing uniform curricular objectives for all.

NO: Former superintendent of public schools Floretta Dukes McKenzie, in a critique of *The Paideia Proposal,* points out Adler's faulty assumptions about the learning process and his lack of attention to the realities of contemporary society.

Quality and equality have been dominant themes in discourse about education in recent decades. Equality of educational opportunity has been dealt with through judicial and legislative means, which have served to break down existing barriers and to provide new means of access and support for groups previously excluded or discriminated against.

Only in recent years has concern been expressed about making qualitative factors in the educational services available to increasing numbers of students. This has gone hand in hand with an accelerated concern for quality and excellence in general. The question for the 1990s is: Can quality and equity be gained simultaneously and, if so, how?

The search for academic excellence pervades most of the thinking contained in recent reports on schooling in this country: the Carnegie Foundation report on high schools; John I. Goodlad's eight-year study of schooling; the Twentieth Century Fund's report on education policy; the College Board's Project Equality; Theodore Sizer's study of high schools; the Action for Excellence plan of the Education Commission of the States; and, of course, Nation at Risk recommendations of the National Commission for Excellence in Education.

It was philosopher Mortimer J. Adler, however, who brought the questions of quality and equality together in a most provocative manner in his educational manifesto *The Paideia Proposal* and subsequent elaborations. Drawing on principles developed some decades back with his University of Chicago colleague Robert M. Hutchins, Adler, as spokesman for the members of the Paideia Group, outlines a plan for providing the same essential schooling for all students regardless of background. This common schooling is to be based on the development of thinking skills, the acquisition of necessary organized information, and the sustenance of intellectual inquiry.

It is Adler's position that we may as well abandon our hope of developing a truly democratic society if we cannot, through our educational institutions, bring all of our citizens to levels of understanding and performance that will ensure thoughtful participation in the processes of government. What we need desperately, the Paideia Group contends, is a renewal of the ancient Greek concept of *paideia*, a community of contributing individuals held together by a sense of common culture and productive intellectual discourse.

The Adler proposal has been widely discussed since its release. Although some critics have attacked the philosophical assumptions that undergird the document, more have raised serious questions regarding the practicality and feasibility of the changes that would be necessitated by widespread adoption of the proposal. Could teachers qualified to carry out the various aspects of the program be found or developed? Would "nonacademic" students be more inclined to drop away from the rigorous intellectual training implied by the proposal? Would students and parents be willing to alter their prevailing view of the schools as an occupational preparation agency?

In the articles that follow, Mortimer J. Adler summarizes the thinking that went into the Paideia Group's proposals for educational reform. Floretta Dukes McKenzie examines and refutes both the theoretical and practical aspects of the Adler position.

YES

Mortimer J. Adler

THE PAIDEIA PROPOSAL

In the first 80 years of this century, we have met the obligation imposed on us by the principle of equal educational opportunity, but only in a quantitative sense. Now, as we approach the end of the century, we must achieve equality in qualitative terms.

This means a completely one-track system of schooling. It means, at the basic level, giving all the young the same kind of schooling, whether or not they are college bound.

We are aware that children, although equal in their common humanity and fundamental human rights, are unequal as individuals, differing in their capacity to learn. In addition, the homes and environments from which they come to school are unequal—either predisposing the child for schooling or doing the opposite.

Consequently, the Paideia Proposal, faithful to the principle of equal educational opportunity, includes the suggestion that inequalities due to environmental factors must be overcome by some form of preschool preparation—at least one year for all and two or even three for some. We know that to make such preschool tutelage compulsory at the public expense would be tantamount to increasing the duration of compulsory schooling from 12 years to 13, 14, or 15 years. Nevertheless, we think that this preschool adjunct to the 12 years of compulsory basic schooling is so important that some way must be found to make it available for all and to see that all use it to advantage.

THE ESSENTIALS OF BASIC SCHOOLING

The objectives of basic schooling should be the same for the whole school population. In our current two-track or multitrack system, the learning objectives are not the same for all. And even when the objectives aimed at those on the upper track are correct, the course of study now provided does not adequately realize these correct objectives. On all tracks in our current system, we fail to cultivate proficiency in the common tasks of learning, and we especially fail to develop sufficiently the indispensable skills of learning.

From Mortimer J. Adler, "The Paideia Proposal: Rediscovering the Essence of Education," *The American School Board Journal* (July 1982). Copyright © 1982 by The National School Boards Association. Reprinted by permission. All rights reserved.

The uniform objectives of basic schooling should be threefold. They should correspond to three aspects of the common future to which all the children are destined: (1) Our society provides all children ample opportunity for personal development. Given such opportunity, each individual is under a moral obligation to make the most of himself and his life. Basic schooling must facilitate this accomplishment. (2) All the children will become, when of age, full-fledged citizens with suffrage and other political responsibilities. Basic schooling must do everything it can to make them good citizens, able to perform the duties of citizenship with all the trained intelligence that each is able to achieve. (3) When they are grown, all (or certainly most) of the children will engage in some form of work to earn a living. Basic schooling must prepare them for earning a living, but not by training them for this or that specific job while they are still in school.

To achieve these three objectives, the character of basic schooling must be general and liberal. It should have a single, required, 12-year course of study for all, with no electives except one—an elective choice with regard to a second language, to be selected from such modern languages as French, German, Italian, Spanish, Russian, and Chinese. The elimination of all electives, with this one exception, excludes what *should* be excluded—all forms of specialization, including particularized job training.

In its final form, the Paideia Proposal will detail this required course of study, but I will summarize the curriculum here in its bare outline. It consists of three main columns of teaching and learning, running through the 12 years and progressing, of course, from the simple to the more complex, from the less difficult to the more difficult, as the students grow older. Understand: The three columns (see chart on next page) represent three distinct modes of teaching and learning. They do not represent a series of courses. A specific course or class may employ more than one mode of teaching and learning, but all three modes are essential to the overall course of study.

The first column is devoted to acquiring knowledge in three subject areas: (A) language, literature, and the fine arts; (B) mathematics and natural science; (C) history, geography, and social studies.

The second column is devoted to developing the intellectual skills of learning. These include all the language skills necessary for thought and communication—the skills of reading, writing, speaking, listening. They also include mathematical and scientific skills; the skills of observing, measuring, estimating, and calculating; and skills in the use of the computer and of other scientific instruments. Together, these skills make it possible to think clearly and critically. They once were called the liberal arts—the intellectual skills indispensable to being competent as a learner.

The third column is devoted to enlarging the understanding of ideas and values. The materials of the third column are books (*not* textbooks), and other products of human artistry. These materials include books of every variety—historical, scientific, and philosophical as well as poems, stories, and essays—and also individual pieces of music, visual art, dramatic productions, dance productions, film or television productions. Music and works of visual art can be used in seminars in which ideas are discussed; but as with poetry and fiction, they also are to be experienced aesthetically, to be

The Paideia Curriculum

	Column One	Column Two	Column Three
Goals	Acquisition of Organized Knowledge	Development of Intellectual Skills and Skills of Learning	Improved Understanding of Ideas and Values
	by means of	*by means of*	*by means of*
Means	Didactic Instruction, Lecturing, and Textbooks	Coaching, Exercises, Supervised Practice	Maieutic or Socratic Questioning and Active Participation
	in these three subject areas	*in these operations*	*in these activities*
Subject Areas, Operations, and Activities	Language, Literature, and Fine Arts; Mathematics and Natural Science; History, Geography, and Social Studies	Reading, Writing, Speaking, Listening, Calculating, Problem Solving, Observing, Measuring, Estimating, Exercising Critical Judgment	Discussion of Books (Not Textbooks) and Other Works of Art; Involvement in Music, Drama, and Visual Arts

The three columns do not correspond to separate courses, nor is one kind of teaching and learning necessarily confined to any one class.

enjoyed and admired for their excellence. In this connection, exercises in the composition of poetry, music, and visual works and in the production of dramatic works should be used to develop the appreciation of excellence.

The three columns represent three different kinds of learning on the part of the student and three different kinds of instruction on the part of teachers.

In the first column, the students are engaged in acquiring information and organized knowledge about nature, man, and human society. The method of instruction here, using textbooks and manuals, is didactic. The teacher lectures, invites responses from the students, monitors the acquisition of knowledge, and tests that acquisition in various ways.

In the second column, the students are engaged in developing habits of performance, which is all that is involved in the development of an art or skill. Art,

skill, or technique is nothing more than a cultivated, habitual ability to do a certain kind of thing well, whether that is swimming and dancing, or reading and writing. Here, students are acquiring linguistic, mathematical, scientific, and historical *know-how* in contrast to what they acquire in the first column, which is *know-that* with respect to language, literature, and the fine arts, mathematics and science, history, geography, and social studies. Here, the method of instruction cannot be didactic or monitorial; it cannot be dependent on textbooks. It must be coaching, the same kind used in the gym to develop bodily skills; only here it is used by a different kind of coach in the classroom to develop intellectual skills.

In the third column, students are engaged in a process of enlightenment, the process whereby they develop their understanding of the basic and controlling ideas in all fields of subject matter and come to appreciate better all the human values embodied in works of art. Here, students move progressively from understanding less to understanding more— understanding better what they already know and appreciating more what they already have experienced. Here, the method of instruction cannot be either didactic or coaching. It must be the Socratic, or maieutic, method of questioning and discussing. It should not occur in any ordinary classroom with the students sitting in rows and the teacher in front of the class, but in a seminar room, with the students sitting around a table and the teacher sitting with them as an equal, even though a little older and wiser.

Of these three main elements in the required curriculum, the third column is completely innovative. Nothing like this is done in our schools, and because it is completely absent from the ordinary curriculum of basic schooling, the students never have the experience of having their minds addressed in a challenging way or of being asked to think about the important ideas, to express their thoughts to defend their opinions in a reasonable fashion.

The only thing that is innovative about the second column is the insistence that the method of instruction here must be coaching carried on either with one student at a time or with very small groups of students. Nothing else can be effective in the development of a skill, be it bodily or intellectual. The absence of such individualized coaching in our schools explains why most of the students cannot read well, write well, speak well, listen well, or perform well any of the other basic intellectual operations.

The three columns are closely interconnected and integrated, but the middle column—the one concerned with linguistic, mathematical, and scientific skills—is central. It both supports and is supported by the other two columns. All the intellectual skills with which it is concerned must be exercised in the study of the three basic subject-matters and in acquiring knowledge about them, and these intellectual skills must be exercised in the seminars devoted to the discussion of books and other things.

In addition to the three main columns in the curriculum, ascending through the 12 years of basic schooling, there are three adjuncts: One is 12 years of physical training, accompanied by instruction in bodily care and hygiene. The second, running through something less than 12 years, is the development of basic manual skills, such as cooking, sewing, carpentry, and the operation of all kinds of machines. The third, reserved for the last year or two, is an introduction to the whole world of work—the range of occupations in which human beings earn their livings. This is not particularized job training. It is the very opposite. It aims at a broad understanding of what is involved in working for a living and of the various ways in which that can be done. If, at the end of 12 years, students wish training for specific jobs, they should get that in two-year community or junior colleges, or on the job itself, or in technical institutes of one sort or another.

Everything that has not been specifically mentioned as occupying the time of the school day should be reserved for after-hours and have the status of extra-curricular activities.

Please, note: The required course of study just described is as important for what it *displaces* as for what it introduces. It displaces a multitude of elective courses, especially those offered in our secondary schools, most of which make little or no contribution to general, liberal education. It eliminates all narrowly specialized job training, which now abounds in our schools. It throws out of the curriculum and into the category of optional extracurricular activities a variety of things that have little or no educational value.

If it did not call for all these displacements, there would not be enough time in the school day or year to accomplish everything that is essential to the general, liberal learning that must be the content of basic schooling.

THE QUINTESSENTIAL ELEMENT

So far, I have set forth the bare essentials of the Paideia Proposal with regard to basic schooling. I have not yet mentioned the quintessential element—the *sine qua non*—without which nothing else can possibly come to fruition, no matter how sound it might be in principle. The heart of the matter is the quality of learning and the quality of teaching that occupies the school day, not to mention the quality of the homework after school.

First, the learning must be active. It must use the whole mind, not just the memory. It must be learning by discovery, in which the student, never the teacher, is the primary agent. Learning by discovery, which is the only genuine learning, may be either unaided or aided. It is unaided only for geniuses. For most students, discovery must be aided.

Here is where teachers come in—as aids in the process of learning by discovery not as knowers who attempt to put the knowledge they have into the minds of their students. The quality of the teaching, in short, depends crucially upon how the teacher conceives his role in the process of learning, and that must be as an aid to the student's process of discovery.

I am prepared for the questions that must be agitating you by now: How and where will we get the teachers who can perform as teachers should? How will we be able to staff the program with teachers so trained that they will be competent to provide the quality of instruction required for the quality of learning desired?

The first part of our answer to these questions is negative: We *cannot* get the teachers we need for the Paideia program from schools of education *as they are now constituted*. As teachers are now trained for teaching, they simply will not do. The ideal—an impracticable ideal—would be to ask for teachers who are, themselves, truly educated human beings. But truly educated human beings are too rare. Even if we could draft all who are now alive, there still would be far too few to staff our schools.

Well, then, what can we look for? Look for teachers who are actively engaged in the process of *becoming* educated human beings, who are themselves deeply motivated to develop their own minds. Assuming this is not too much to ask for the present, how should teachers be schooled and trained in the future? First, they should have the same kind of basic schooling that is recommended in the Paideia Proposal. Second, they should have additional schooling, at the college and even the university level, in which the same kind of general, liberal learning is carried on at advanced levels—more deeply, broadly, and intensively than it can be done in the first 12 years of schooling. Third, they must be given something analogous to the clinical experience in the training of physicians. They must engage in practice-teaching under supervision, which is another way of saying that they must be *coached* in the arts of teaching, not just given didactic instruction in educational psychology and in pedagogy. Finally, and most important of all, they must learn how to teach well by being exposed to the performances of those who are masters of the arts involved in teaching.

It is by watching a good teacher at work that they will be able to perceive what is involved in the process of assisting others to learn by discovery. Perceiving it, they must then try to emulate what they observe, and through this process, they slowly will become good teachers themselves.

The Paideia Proposal recognizes the need for three different kinds of institutions at the collegiate level: The two-year community or junior college should offer a wide choice of electives that give students some training in one or another specialized field, mainly those fields of study that have something to do with earning a living. The four-year college also should offer a wide variety of electives, to be chosen by students who aim at the various professional or technical occupations that require advanced study. Those elective majors chosen by students should be accompanied, for all students, by one required minor, in which the kind of general and liberal learning that was begun at the level of basic schooling is continued at a higher level in the four years of college. And we should have still a third type of collegiate institution—a four-year college in which general, liberal learning at a higher level constitutes a required course of study that is to be taken by all students. *It is this third type of college, by the way, that should be attended by all who plan to become teachers in our basic schools.*

At the university level, there should be a continuation of general, liberal learning at a still higher level to accompany intensive specialization in this or that field of science or scholarship, this or that learned profession. Our insistence on the continuation of general, liberal learning at all the higher levels of schooling stems from our concern with the worst cultural disease that is rampant in our society— *the barbarism of specialization.*

There is no question that our technologically advanced industrial society needs specialists of all sorts. There is no question that the advancement of knowledge in all fields of science and scholarship, and in all the learned professions, needs intense specialization. But for the sake of preserving and enhancing our cultural traditions, as well as for the health of science and scholarship, we need specialists who also are generalists—generally cultivated human beings, not just good plumbers. We need truly educated human beings who can perform their special tasks better precisely because they have general cultivation as well as intensely specialized training.

Changes indeed are needed in higher education, but those improvements cannot reasonably be expected unless improvement in basic schooling makes that possible.

THE FUTURE OF
OUR FREE INSTITUTIONS

I already have declared as emphatically as I know how that the quality of human life in our society depends on the quality of the schooling we give our young people, both basic and advanced. But a marked elevation in the quality of human life is not the only reason improving the quality of schooling is so necessary—not the only reason we must move heaven and earth to stop the deterioration of our schools and turn them in the opposite direction. The other reason is to safeguard the future of our free institutions.

They cannot prosper, they may not even survive, unless we do something to rescue our schools from their current deplorable deterioration. Democracy, in the full sense of that term, came into existence only in this century and only in a few countries on earth, among which the United States is an outstanding example. But democracy came into existence in this century only in its initial conditions, all of which hold out promises for the future that remain to be fulfilled. Unless we do something about improving the quality of basic schooling for all and the quality of advanced schooling for some, there is little chance that those promises ever will be fulfilled. And if they are not, our free institutions are doomed to decay and wither away.

We face many insistently urgent problems. Our prosperity and even our survival depend on the solution of those problems—the threat of nuclear war, the exhaustion of essential resources and of supplies of energy, the pollution or spoilage of the environment, the spiraling of inflation accompanied by the spread of unemployment.

To solve these problems, we need resourceful and innovative leadership. For that to arise and be effective, an educated populace is needed. Trained intelligence—not only on the part of leaders, but also on the part of followers—holds the key to the solution of the problems our society faces. Achieving peace, prosperity, and plenty could put us on the threshold of an early paradise. But a much better educational system than now exists also is needed, for that alone can carry us across the threshold. Without it, a poorly schooled population will not be able to put to good use the opportunities afforded by the achievement of the general welfare. Those who are not schooled to enjoy society can only despoil its institutions and corrupt themselves.

NO

Floretta Dukes McKenzie

THE YELLOW BRICK ROAD
OF EDUCATION

Like Dorothy in *The Wizard of Oz*, educators hold a vision that somewhere—perhaps over the rainbow—a place exists that is free from all the knotty and nagging problems of everyday life. For teachers and school administrators, this "Oz" includes classrooms of endlessly inquisitive and motivated youngsters; instructors with a bottomless reservoir of energy, dedication, and talent; and schools free from yearly political haggles over funds needed to buy the texts, hire staff, and heat buildings. Frontline educators—classroom teachers, principals, and the like—as well as researchers and theorists, work toward the attainment of such an educational paradise. However, as evidenced in *The Paideia Proposal*, a fundamental difference in perspective distinguishes the practitioners' and the academicians' approaches to educational improvement.

To extend *The Wizard of Oz* analogy a bit further, Mortimer Adler regards the educational Oz as Dorothy viewed the Emerald City. Disgruntled with the problems at Aunt Em's farm, Dorothy believed in a better place; she could envision and describe it but lacked a way to get there. Speaking for the Paideia Group—primarily comprising noted college presidents, "think tankers," and foundation officials—Adler also complains about the "present deplorable condition" of schooling and depicts an idyllic state of education, yet offers little direction for reaching it.

On the other hand, far too many educators in the daily business of schooling have lost the excitement and hope Oz offered to Dorothy. After many trials and tribulations, Dorothy discovers that the Wizard is really an illusion; she longs to return to Kansas and is content to face farm life without the wonders of technicolor. Practicing educators, perhaps hardened over the years by too many trips down a yellow brick road of so-called "educational reform," likewise no longer believe in miracles. They frequently rely on teaching children in perhaps outmoded but familiar ways, viewing educa-

From Floretta Dukes McKenzie, "The Yellow Brick Road of Education," *Harvard Educational Review,* vol. 53, no. 4 (November 1983), pp. 389–392. Copyright © 1983 by the President and Fellows of Harvard College. Reprinted by permission. All rights reserved.

tional excellence as something that only a few schools can attain.

As the *Proposal* accurately points out, this disparaging attitude toward educational prospects is a tragic problem which contributes to the debilitating notion that public schooling can make only limited improvements in children's lives. Ironically, however, the *Proposal* itself, with its wholesale condemnation of present educational practices, further erodes the public confidence vital to any attempts at educational reform, particularly one that would prove as costly as the *Proposal*.

The Paideia Proposal claims that U.S. education has only won "half the battle—the quantitative half" of the goal to provide equal educational opportunity to all. Currently, 75 percent of all students graduate from high school compared to only 55 percent as recently as 1950. Although the number of years a child spends in school is not a reliable measure of the quality of education that child has received, this increase indicates more than a mere tally of the classroom hours students are logging in. A number of economists have estimated that between 25 to 50 percent of the increase in the Gross National Product in the last twenty years is due to the increased educational level of the work force.[1] This cannot be attributed simply to the amount of time students spend sitting in schools; it is an indication that schools have succeeded to a commendable degree in teaching meaningful, life-enhancing skills to the young.

Minimizing this country's tremendous gains in providing access to education, as the *Proposal* does, is a serious flaw in any analysis of U.S. education. It is specifically this commitment to educational access which led to the rich diversity in teaching strategies that is essential to meeting the schooling needs of an equally diverse student population.

Educators should not be lured into the popular but mistaken belief that the national emphasis on educational access has not been accompanied by significant improvements in quality. The *Proposal* contends, without offering any supporting evidence, that "basic schooling in America does not now achieve the fundamental objective of opening the doors to the world of learning and providing the guidelines for exploring it." The *Proposal* goes further to suggest—again without examples or data—that U.S. education "used to do so for those who completed high school at the beginning of this century."

One of the few long-range studies of reading achievement indicates that, in 1944, Indiana's sixth- and tenth-grade students did not read as well as their counterparts did in 1976. Clearly, reading is a vital key to opening those doors to the world of learning, and if this ability among students has increased over time, the *Proposal's* claim that education was better in the "good old days" is highly suspect. As the Indiana study indicates, even though access to education has increased greatly, our schools are educating our youth to a much higher standard than they were able to do with only 30 to 40 percent of the student population four decades ago.[2]

Although *The Paideia Proposal's* failure to acknowledge education's accomplishments undermines the basis of the manifesto's suggested reforms, it is not the work's most serious flaw. The *Proposal* reflects assumptions about the learning process that disregard what educators have come to know through years of practice and research. Granted, all children are educable, innately possessing curiosity and an interest in learning. Although educators know this, they must work vigorously to ensure that this idea is incorporated into practice at all times for all children. The *Proposal*, however, makes a quantum conceptual leap by presuming that this belief in children's educability dictates a uniformity in instruction.

"The best education for the best is the best education for all" should not be the guiding principle for instruction, as the *Proposal* contends. As almost any teacher can testify, the methods which work well with the brightest and most eager students do not necessarily spark the interest of children who, for whatever reason, are not achieving as well. This belief, that what is best for the best is best for all, is a dangerously elitist tenet which may destroy the potential of countless young minds. Granted, as the *Proposal* suggests, students need clear direction as to what is expected of them, and the schools must do a better job in this arena. However, contrary to the *Proposal*, higher expectations of students do not necessarily translate into higher student achievement.

All children do not learn in the same fashion, for there is great variety in ways of acquiring and integrating information. Therefore, in almost all cases, rigid prescriptions for instruction invariably fail. Many teachers already have, and many more teachers need, competence in that comprehensive range of instructional strategies—such as didactic, coaching, and Socratic methods—that the *Proposal* details. However, such skills are needed to better meet students' varying levels of instructional needs rather than to reach the suggested single-track core curriculum. Although the *Proposal* decries teachers' narrow repertoire of instructional skills, it is silent on a definitive means of better equipping teachers with such abilities.

Like its questionable assumptions about children's learning processes, the *Proposal's* suppositions concerning the composition of an ideal curriculum are out of touch with both education's proven knowledge base and the realities of contemporary society. As the *Proposal* indicates, "to live well in the fullest human sense involves learning as well as earning." But the key words in this phrase, which the *Proposal* subsequently disregards, are "as well as." By vehemently urging the elimination of almost all vocational training in basic schooling, the Paideia Group has chosen to overlook the very real need and growing demand for students in a technological society to be trained in specific skill areas. Ideally, such well-trained students would also possess the ability and desire for continued learning throughout their lives, which the *Proposal* accurately identifies as the major goal of education. But this goal will not be within students' grasp simply by disposing of specific career training.

Furthermore, the age-old complaint from U.S. business and industry has been that schools—including colleges—let students graduate who lack not only necessary general skills but also specific skills for employment. Historically, U.S. employers have only reluctantly taken on the role of providing the technical training for generally-educated new employees. The *Proposal* apparently overlooks the facts that vocational education arose out of a societal demand for career-trained graduates, that this demand is increasing with the expanding new technologies, and that the business sector will resist taking the responsibility for specific skill training.

Necessary vocational education, the *Proposal* contends, can be obtained after the first twelve years of schooling at either four-year or community colleges. Such postponement of entry into the work force is economically unfeasible for countless young people. The *Proposal* ignores today's reality that post-secondary education is increasingly an expense that fewer and fewer families can bear.

The *Proposal's* failure to recognize career training in schools as a development born, in part, of a strong societal demand highlights one of its other shortcomings: a naive treatment of education's political and economic circumstances. Undoubtedly, superintendents and administrators would eagerly endorse the *Proposal's* call for a debureaucratization of schools. The business of schooling is learning and teaching; however, given the requirements of democracy and the structure for financing public education, schools are also political institutions. Over the last few decades, demands for schools to assume the roles and functions once the sole province of home, church, and government has heavily contributed to the politicization of education. The *Proposal's* simplistic solution to this problem is to hand over greater control to local school principals. Giving principals more authority over the selection and dismissal of school staff and the discipline of students might be a wise and productive change for some school districts, but such actions would do little to remove education from the political sphere.

In today's world, the partner to politics is economics. The *Proposal* admits that, to be successful, its implementation will require higher teacher salaries, better teacher training, smaller class sizes, individual student coaching, more remedial education, and publicly funded preschool for one- to three-year-olds. Yet, despite a national and local climate that favors sharp reductions in educational support, the *Proposal* makes no suggestions for financing the costs of its remedies.

A local example hints at the magnitude of the Paideia price tag. In the District of Columbia public school system, the cost of reducing class size by just one student per class is $4 million a year. To provide preschool classes for only one-third of the 18,000 three- and four-year-olds in the city, the school district's budget would have to be increased by $16 million each year.

Speculation and discussion on needed improvements in U.S. education are healthy and beneficial. Such exercises, however, must not only name the desired destinations but must also consider if the routes to those goals are compatible with existing knowledge based on practice and research. The *Proposal* is very strong on detailing what should be but ignores the reality of what already is. The *Proposal* cites increased parental involvement in education and decreased disruptive student behavior as vital to securing quality education for all. These are not issues which schools heretofore have overlooked; they are the time-worn problems with which educators grapple daily. The *Proposal* does not venture a single idea—tried or untried—on how to resolve these and many other longstanding problems.

The *Proposal* forthrightly communicates to the public some often neglected messages which probably cannot be broadcast too loudly or too frequently: quality education is the key to quality living; the survival of our democratic society depends on the existence of an educated electorate; and education is the gateway to equality for all people. *The Paideia Proposal* is as strong as Dorothy's determination to return to Kansas; as a constructive plan of action for educational improvement, it is as specious as the Wizard's magic powers.

NOTES

1. Harold Hodgkinson, "What's Still Right With Education," *Phi Delta Kappan*, 64 (1982), 233.

2. These statistics came from Harold Hodgkinson, a former director of the National Institute for Education, delivered in a presentation to the Executive Council of the District of Columbia Public Schools, April 1983.

POSTSCRIPT

Does a Common Curriculum Promote Equality?

Throughout most of the history of formal, institutionalized education, the tendency has been to expand the curriculum to meet the needs of a growing constituency. In twentieth-century America the public schools have added great numbers of courses and functions to its original set of obligations to serve the needs of young people and the needs of society in general. Educational reform has often been thought of as an addition process.

Some critics see this general tendency as the primary contributing factor in what is seen as a fragmented, shallow, and purposeless system of schooling. Adler's call for a unified curricular and methodological approach that is clearly focused on the development of the mind has its roots in earlier works: Albert Lynd's *Quackery in the Public Schools;* Arthur Bestor's *Educational Wastelands;* Mortimer Smith's *The Diminished Mind;* Admiral Hyman Rickover's *Swiss Schools and Ours;* James Koerner's *The Miseducation of American Teachers;* and Paul Copperman's *The Literacy Hoax.*

The basic question is: Is this line of criticism of public education valid, and are the ideas suggested for reform right and workable? McKenzie does not think so, and a number of other writers in the November 1983 issue of the *Harvard Educational Review* join her. Of special interest are "The Peter Pan Proposal," by Ronald Gwiazda, and "Education, Democracy, and Social Conflict," by Martin Carnoy.

The debate about the appropriateness of curricular commonality was fueled by former secretary of education William Bennett's recommendations

102

for a prototypical elementary school and high school, put forth during the final year of his tenure in his book *James Madison Elementary School: A Curriculum for American Students*. *What Do Our 17-Year-Olds Know?* (1987) by Diane Ravitch and Chester Finn, Jr., also added to the controversy. Two widely discussed works that directly reflect *paideia* concerns are *The Closing of the American Mind* (1987) by Allan Bloom and *Cultural Literacy: What Every American Needs to Know* (1987) by E. D. Hirsch, Jr.

The general problem of identifying the components of a common curriculum is treated more specifically in Issue 13, "Should Literacy Be Based on Traditional Culture?" and Issue 14, "Do Black Students Need an Afrocentric Curriculum?"

ISSUE 7

Will Reforming School Funding Remove "Savage Inequalities"?

YES: Ruth Sidel, from "Separate and Unequal," *The Nation* (November 18, 1991)

NO: Peter Schrag, from "Savage Equalities: The Case Against Jonathan Kozol," *The New Republic* (December 16, 1991)

ISSUE SUMMARY

YES: Sociology professor Ruth Sidel examines Jonathan Kozol's controversial book *Savage Inequalities* and finds his argument for the equalization of funding compelling.
NO: Journalist Peter Schrag argues that Kozol's analysis is sometimes simplistic and often impractical.

Ever since the landmark school desegregation decision of the U.S. Supreme Court in 1954 and the civil rights legislation of the mid-1960s, the issue of equal opportunity has occupied a dominant position in discourse on education. Governmental actions such as redistricting, forced busing, and the establishment of magnet schools have met with some success in equalizing educational opportunities for all school-age children. But it has become increasingly obvious that these efforts have had only a mild impact on the wide disparity in funding between schools in affluent areas as opposed to those in poverty-stricken areas.

About 20 years ago the courts dealt with a number of cases involving inequities in funding, among them *Hobson v. Hansen* (1971), *Serrano v. Priest* (1971), and *San Antonio v. Rodriguez* (1973). In the last of these, the Supreme Court found that inequities did exist but that they did not violate the equal protection clause of the Fourteenth Amendment since no one was *completely* deprived of educational opportunity. This ruling turned the matter back to the individual states, and, indeed, some 16 years later the Texas court ruled that the Rodriguez children were unconstitutionally denied the right to equal educational opportunity by virtue of their residence in a tax-poor district in San Antonio.

Some states have moved to close the gaps among their school districts' per-pupil expenditures, some by providing a guaranteed base for all, others by giving rewards for increased local tax-raising efforts, and one, Hawaii, by providing full state funding for all public schools. Among the states themselves, of course, wide disparities exist. Figures for 1991–92 show a range in per-pupil spending from New Jersey's high average of $9,246 to Mississippi's low average of $3,183.

In 1991 Jonathan Kozol graphically portrayed the results of prevailing funding practices in his book *Savage Inequalities: Children in America's Schools*. The impact of Kozol's guided tour of dilapidated schools and disheartened students and teachers in East St. Louis, Chicago, New York, Camden, San Antonio, and Washington, D.C., has brought the public to a new level of concern. In addition, two studies, William Julius Wilson's *The Truly Disadvantaged* (1987) and Mike Rose's *Lives on the Boundary* (1989), and two insider's descriptions, Samuel G. Freedman's *Small Victories* (1990) and Emily Sachar's *Shut Up and Let the Lady Teach* (1990), give further evidence of the deterioration of poverty-area schools. As early as 1967 Kozol described his personal experiences in an inner-city school in Boston in another high-impact book, *Death at an Early Age*.

In *Savage Inequalities* Kozol contends that the reforms of the 1980s have had little or no effect on the quality of schools in poor districts. "None of the national reports I saw made even passing reference to inequality or segregation," he states. Efforts to bring about greater equity have been thwarted by taxpayer revolts, the general economic downturn of recent years, and the still-prevailing attitude that putting more money into poor districts will not change anything, that money is not the answer. Kozol contends that policy decisions are often steered by a "conservative anxiety" that equity leads to "leveling," that democratizing opportunity will drag the best schools down to "a sullen norm, a mediocre middle ground of uniformity."

The selections that follow are reactions to Jonathan Kozol's book and its recommendations for action. Ruth Sidel agrees with Kozol's call for an intensive effort to finance the education of every child in America equitably and sees this effort as one step toward developing a just society. Peter Schrag, while acknowledging the emotional impact of Kozol's descriptions, argues that equalization of spending is not the solution. He further suggests that such attempts may even have unintended negative consequences.

YES   Ruth Sidel

SEPARATE AND UNEQUAL

In his latest book, *Savage Inequalities: Children in America's Schools*, Jonathan Kozol describes the city of East St. Louis, Illinois: 98 percent black, with no obstetric services, no regular garbage collection and few jobs. East St. Louis is located in easily flooded lowlands called the Bottoms. Raw sewage flows into basements, playgrounds and backyards all over the city. Lead levels are "astronomical" and fumes from nearby chemical plants poison the air. Premature births and infant mortality rates are extraordinarily high and the majority of children are underimmunized. The U.S. Department of Housing and Urban Development has described East St. Louis, where 75 percent of the population receives some form of public assistance, as "the most distressed small city in America." The *St. Louis Post–Dispatch* describes it as "America's Soweto."

The schools of East St. Louis mirror these horrendous conditions: In 1989 both the Martin Luther King Junior High School and the East St. Louis Senior High School had to be closed after sewage flowed into the kitchen and from the toilets. The same week more than 500 school employees were laid off. The remaining teachers face constant shortages of chalk and paper, the sports facilities are in tatters and the science labs are thirty to fifty years out of date. One teacher states, "I have done without so much for so long that if I were assigned to a suburban school I'm not sure I'd recognize what they were doing. We are utterly cut off."

East St. Louis sets the tone for this moving, often shocking, always heartbreaking book. After his searing depiction of schools there, Kozol goes on to describe inferior, underfinanced, often physically dangerous schools in poor communities and lavish, state-of-the-art, incredibly affluent schools in and around Chicago, New York, the Camden–Cherry Hill area of New Jersey and Washington, D.C. Kozol's special skill is the ability to weave together detailed descriptions of facilities, analyses of the financial situation in each school and district and, above all, interviews with teachers, students and administrators in which he seems to uncover the heart of what they are thinking and feeling. Using these techniques he brings the reader with him during his two-year investigation of schools in some thirty neighborhoods across the country.

What startled Kozol most, and will be indelibly stamped on anyone who reads this important book, is the "remarkable degree of racial segregation that persisted almost everywhere," particularly outside the Deep South. Most of the urban schools he visited were 95 to 99 percent nonwhite and, what is perhaps even more disturbing, few people in positions of power were interested in addressing the issue of segregation. As Kozol states, "The dual society, at least in public education, seems in general to be unquestioned."

NOT ONLY IS THE U.S. PUBLIC EDUCATION system virtually separate but it is grossly unequal. Kozol describes conditions in many of the Chicago schools: a shortage of teachers (on an average morning 5,700 children in 190 classrooms have no teacher); a shortage of supplies (chemistry labs without beakers, water or bunsen burners; playgrounds and gyms without rudimentary equipment; toilets without toilet paper); and a system that long ago gave up on its students ("If a kid comes in not reading," according to one Chicago high school English teacher, "he goes out not reading").

Kozol points out that poor children in some of the worst inner-city schools often start their education with "faith and optimism, and they often seem to thrive during the first few years." But by the third grade their teachers see signs of failure, by the fourth grade the children themselves see failure looming and by fifth or sixth grade many are skipping school; as Kozol states, the route from truanting to dropping out is "direct and swift."

In contrast, the principal of the New Trier High School in Winnetka, Illinois, states confidently, "Our goal is for students to be successful." The school, situated on twenty-seven suburban acres, offers Latin and six other foreign languages; the senior English class is reading Nietzsche, Darwin, Plato, Freud and Goethe. In addition to seven gyms and an Olympic-size swimming pool, New Trier operates a television station. Every freshman is assigned a faculty adviser who counsels roughly two dozen students. At Du Sable, a high school in nearby Chicago, each guidance counselor advises 420 students.

The conditions are duplicated in and around each city Kozol visited. In New York City two schools barely fifteen minutes apart by car reveal the same patterns. Public School 261 in the North Bronx is located in what was once a roller-skating rink. No sign identifies the building as a school; the building has no windows. Four kindergartens and a sixth-grade class of Spanish-speaking children share one room. One full-time and one part-time counselor are available to work with the 1,300 children, 90 percent of whom are black or Latino. Textbooks are scarce and students must often share those that are available.

In the same school district, just a few miles to the west, P.S. 24 is situated in the Riverdale section of the Bronx, a residential area with parks, libraries, large cooperative apartment buildings and many beautiful, expensive homes. The school serves 825 children from kindergarten through the sixth grade. Kozol describes essentially three groupings within the school: one for special classes for the mentally retarded, in which most of the students are poor and black or Latino; one for mainstream students, the vast majority of whom are white and Asian; and a third track for "gifted" students. As Kozol observes, the fourth-grade gifted class is "humming with excitement." The class, according to the teacher, emphasizes "critical thinking, reasoning and logic." The students were at that time writing a new Bill of Rights, examining a concept their personal experience clearly helps them to understand.

Report after report has shown that the poorest districts in New York receive significantly lower allocations than the wealthier districts and that per-pupil expenditures within the city of New York ($5,500 in 1987) are dramatically lower than comparable expenditures in the affluent suburbs surrounding the city (more than $11,000 in some of the affluent communities on Long Island). The same differentials exist, of course, in all the metropolitan areas Kozol examines. The per-pupil expenditure was, for example, $5,500 in the late 1980s in Chicago secondary schools, compared with $8,500 to $9,000 in the highest-spending northern suburbs. But the ultimate meaning of these savage inequalities is their impact on the lives, feelings and self-image of the children themselves. The children movingly speak of the enormous discrepancies between schools for the affluent and schools for the poor, between schools for white children and schools for children of color. A 14-year-old girl states, "We have a school in East St. Louis named for Dr. King. The school is full of sewer water and the doors are locked with chains. Every student in that school is black. It's like a terrible joke on history." A Latino boy from a high school in the South Bronx says, "People on the outside may think that we don't know what it is like for other students, but we *visit* other schools and we have eyes and

we have brains. You cannot hide the differences. You see it and compare." Or an eleventh grader from Camden, New Jersey: "So long as there are no white children in our school, we're going to be cheated. That's America. That's how it is." The children in these schools may not acquire the skills so necessary for living in a postindustrial society, but they certainly learn the explicit meaning of living in a profoundly racist and classist society. Moreover, the children in affluent neighborhoods also absorb the message of living in a grossly unequal society in which individual success is the highest good. Students in the affluent New York City suburb of Rye for the most part oppose busing, suggest a "separate but equal" solution to the problems of inequity in education and offer a blame-the-victim analysis of differences in educational opportunity. When Kozol asks about the possibility of raising taxes in order to equalize educational opportunities one student succinctly summarizes the ideology of the 1980s and the 1990s: "I don't see how that benefits me."

ULTIMATELY, KOZOL ADDRESSES THE CENtral issue of educational equity in a country that prides itself on equal opportunity. As he points out, funding education, particularly during a time of federal cutbacks to human services and extreme reluctance to raise taxes, is a zero-sum game. Additional money for Chicago schools is likely to mean less money for Winnetka students. Improved facilities for students in the rest of the Bronx will, in all likelihood, mean fewer resources for students in Riverdale. Since 1989, when the Texas Supreme Court struck down the old school-financing system based primarily on property taxes, Texas political leaders have searched for a method of attaining school equity. Currently, the so-called Robin Hood plan is in effect there, which takes property-tax money from rich districts and distributes it among poorer districts. Predictably, rich districts complain they will be reduced to mediocrity while poor ones claim they still do not have the resources they need. But the Robin Hood plan may appear elsewhere as well, as lawsuits challenging school financing are under way in twenty-two other states.

The issue is not likely to disappear. The publication of *Savage Inequalities* will insure that the injustice and incredible shortsightedness of American educational policy are vividly and compassionately brought to the forefront of the public's consciousness and the agenda of policy-makers. As with his earlier books, particularly *Death at an Early Age* and *Rachel and Her Children*, Jonathan Kozol movingly and persuasively documents the devastating inequities in American society and provides information and insight that will help move the country toward a more humane educational policy.

But, as Kozol clearly recognizes, a more humane educational policy is not enough. Until the millions of American children who currently live in poverty have an adequate standard of living, until the millions of American children who are hungry have enough to eat, until the millions of homeless children have an adequate place to live, and until all children have first-rate health care, we will not begin to develop a just society. The awareness, discussion and, it is to be hoped, action engendered by *Savage Inequalities* will move us closer to that achievable goal.

NO

Peter Schrag

SAVAGE EQUALITIES

It's almost twenty-five years since the publication of Jonathan Kozol's *Death at an Early Age*, which recounted his eight months as a teacher in a rundown Boston ghetto school. Kozol was fired by the then notorious Boston School Committee for reading Langston Hughes's poem "Ballad of a Landlord" to his fourth-grade class—not part of the syllabus, the school committee said— and instantly became a major voice in the movement for school equity and integration of the late 1960s and early 1970s.

Kozol has never strayed far from that theme and has now returned to it with a book called *Savage Inequalities* that's gotten a respectful, even glowing, reception. Just before it came out, *Publishers Weekly* carried an unprecedented open letter on its cover, where it has never run anything but advertising, to tell George Bush to read this "startling and disturbing" new book. *Savage Inequalities* has made Kozol once again the most visible left-wing critic of American education and the star witness in a movement, now spreading to more than a dozen states—among them Alabama, Alaska, Idaho, Illinois, Indiana, Minnesota, Missouri, New Hampshire, North Dakota, South Dakota, Tennessee—to get court orders to equalize per-pupil spending between public schools in rich and poor communities.

It's a moving book—about filthy schools where roofs leak and halls are flooded each time it rains, where three or four classes have to share a gym or cafeteria because there aren't enough rooms, where teachers have outdated textbooks or none at all. It's also a reminder that a lot of those kids really want to learn, aren't on drugs, and understand that this is a society that treats white suburban children a lot better than it treats black inner-city kids. Given the thin gruel that the Bush administration has served up to deal with the nation's horrendous school problems—roughly equal parts school "choice," testing, and that old conservative favorite "more money's not the answer"—it's not surprising that Kozol is getting attention.

The rationale of the equalizers is simple: unequal spending among schools denies children equal protection of the laws. A poor community with a weak tax base simply can't spend as much on each child's education as a wealthy one, even if it raises rates to the breaking point, and that's patently unfair.

But is equalization of all spending—which, in addition to increasing the spending in poor districts, means capping the spending of affluent or motivated districts—really the solution? Consider California, the only major state where equalization has been thoroughly tried. (Texas and New Jersey are now starting down the same path but haven't gotten beyond the political acrimony and administrative chaos to be fair tests.) The results have been a wondrous illustration of the law of unintended consequences.

The most obvious of those consequences is that equalization sharply reduced local incentives to raise school taxes. After the California Supreme Court ruled, in *Serrano v. Priest* (1976), that the old funding system was unconstitutional, the legislature agreed to bring per-pupil spending in virtually all of the state's districts to within $100 (later revised to $200) of the state average. It proposed to do that not by requiring the rich districts to spend less, something that would have been academically unseemly and politically impossible, but by directing additional state money to the poor districts. Yet since the funding formula also reduced state funding one dollar for each dollar that districts might have raised in additional local property taxes, it eliminated much of the rationale and motivation for local efforts to improve the schools. (The exceptions to the formula were a few oil-rich districts that get no state aid.)

School equalization might have taken decades to achieve had it not been for the fortuitous passage of Proposition 13 in 1978. By slashing and capping local property tax revenues, Prop 13 shifted the burden of school funding to state income and sales taxes, which made equalization a lot easier to realize. But because of 13, and perhaps because of *Serrano* as well, the state's spending on schools has also slipped precipitately—from sixth or seventh in the nation to twenty-fifth or twenty-sixth. California now spends less per child than any other major industrial state, and less than the national average. As one state education official said recently, it is much harder to motivate people to pay more taxes for education when they can't see the results right down the street.

Kozol has a lot of numbers dramatizing the inequities in spending between, for example, Camden and Princeton, New Jersey; Chicago and suburban New Trier High School; and New York City and suburban Manhasset (Long Island). But he doesn't point out that the $7,299 New York City spent on each child in 1989–90 was nearly double what most of the fanciest California suburbs got to spend that same year. California now spends roughly $5,100 a year per student. The national average is $5,500. The university town of Davis, where I live, and which sends as many of its graduates to college as New Trier, would kill to get $6,000 per student, let alone $7,000.

With the power to appropriate funds having shifted from local boards to the state government, it is no longer possible to know who is responsible for the financial problems of the local schools—the board that allocates the funds and overspends or mismanages them or the governor and legislature that fail to pony up enough to begin with. The same goes for responsibility for the construction of new schools, now so incomprehensibly divided between state and local agencies that almost no one understands the system.

Moreover, since school boards no longer have anything to do with setting tax rates, the interest of local business groups and taxpayer organizations in the schools— or in running people for the board—has sharply declined, leaving more and more districts in the control of the only well-financed group that's really interested in school affairs: the teachers' union. The Los Angeles school board, which runs the largest system in the state, is now controlled by people who got the lion's share of their election campaign support from UTLA, the United Teachers of Los Angeles. As fiscal control moves to the state, the moderate citizens' groups that once were the backbone of local government and local schools are less and less involved.

It shouldn't be surprising, then, that the union-dominated Los Angeles board awarded huge raises to its teachers three years ago—the average increase was roughly 27 percent over three years—and is now in deep financial trouble. And though it stands out in its generosity to employees, it's hardly alone. Two other large districts, Oakland and Richmond, are in such financial trouble from general mismanagement that they were taken over by state-appointed trustees; two dozen others teeter on the verge of bankruptcy. One-third of all the state's districts, according to state Controller Gray Davis, are spending more money than they take in.

MANY OF THOSE PROBLEMS ARE ATTRIBUTable to the state's generally dismal fiscal situation, but not all of them. District after district has been overly generous in setting pay scales, counting on state appropriations it didn't get. Most of the extra money that was supposed to go toward improving the inner-city schools also went directly into increasing teacher and administrative salaries even while programs have been cut to the bone. No state in the country has as large a gap between what it pays its school employees and what it spends on everything else. California is fifth in the nation in teachers salaries and dead last—meaning worst—in class size: many classes are now running well over thirty children, even in elementary schools. We also have leaky roofs and rotting buildings, but we have them in the suburbs as well as in the inner cities.

Kozol says, correctly, that poor children are trapped in awful inner-city schools, while the middle class has choices. But he refuses to give poor children the chance to escape to better public schools, through choice. He's also too simplistic in blaming the comparatively poor performance of our schools on money alone. No country has ever done, or even tried, what this country is now trying: to take such a diverse population of children— 20 percent of them from below the poverty level, many of them speaking little English, many from one-parent or no-parent families (all problems George Bush's education "program" ignore[d])— and educate each child at least through the twelfth grade for a high-tech culture. Under the circumstances, our schools are doing better than one might expect—as well at least as we did two decades ago. And given also what we've learned about the schools' external problems— poverty, broken families, teenage pregnancies, drugs, lack of health care, lack of child care—the first place to spend (and equalize) new money on children may not be in the K–12 school program, but on broader social problems.

Although Kozol acknowledges that equalization has been problematic in California, his support for the idea remains undiminished. Of course, Proposition 13 and fiscal mismanagement exacerbated the problems here. But the fact remains that equalization—any way you formulate it—tends to destroy local accountability and erode the supports and sense of mission that make strong schools possible.

POSTSCRIPT

Will Reforming School Funding Remove "Savage Inequalities"?

In a recent interview ("On Savage Inequalities: A Conversation With Jonathan Kozol," Marge Scherer, *Educational Leadership*, December 1992/January 1993), Kozol made his priorities very clear: "We've got to distinguish between injustice and inconvenience. Before we deal with an affluent child's existential angst, let's deal with the kid in Chicago who had not had a permanent teacher for the past five years." This gets at the crux of the matter; in a static and unjust economy Robin Hood is elevated from criminal to hero.

A scholar who does not share this view is sociologist Nathan Glazer. In an article in the Winter 1992 issue of *The Public Interest* entitled "The Real World of Urban Education," Glazer contends that research shows that expenditure of money does not seem to correlate well with educational success. He suggests that we had better find out where our money is now going before we demand equalization of its distribution.

Other views on the equalization issue include these: "*Brown v. Board of Education:* Time for a Reassessment," by Donald C. Orlich, *Phi Delta Kappan* (April 1991); "Race and Equality of Opportunity: A School Finance Perspective," by C. Phillip Kearney and Li-Ju Chen, *Journal of Education Finance* (Winter 1990); "Toward Educational Change and Economic Justice: An Interview With Herbert Kohl," by Joe Nathan, *Phi Delta Kappan* (May 1991); and "Ghetto Schools Are Getting Worse: Why Not Give Choice a Chance?" by Bill Bradley, *The Philadelphia Inquirer* (March 12, 1992).

Further information can be obtained in other issues of the *Journal of Education Finance*; in the *Journal of Negro Education* special issue on "Urban Future" (Summer 1989); in the *Phi Delta Kappan* special report on "Children of Poverty" (October 1990); in the National School Boards Association report *A Survey of Public Education in the Nation's Urban School Districts* (1989); in the Committee for Economic Development's *Children in Need: Investment Strategies for the Educationally Disadvantaged* (1987); and in the book *Outside In: Minorities and the Transformation of American Education* (1989) by Paula S. Fass.

The issue of funding equalization is, of course, related to Issue 12 in this volume, "Can Schools Prevent Urban Dropouts?" Since the federal political climate has direct bearing on the interpretation of justice and equity, linkage may also be made with Issue 8, "Should National Goals Guide School Performance?" and Issue 9, "Can 'Choice' Lead the Way to Educational Reform?"

ISSUE 8

Should National Goals Guide School Performance?

YES: Denis P. Doyle, from "America 2000," *Phi Delta Kappan* (November 1991)

NO: Evans Clinchy, from "America 2000: Reform, Revolution, or Just More Smoke and Mirrors?" *Phi Delta Kappan* (November 1991)

ISSUE SUMMARY

YES: Hudson Institute scholar Denis P. Doyle lauds "America 2000" as a history-making initiative in federal policy.
NO: Evans Clinchy, a scholar at the Institute for Responsive Education, finds a major internal contradiction in the document and calls for serious rethinking.

Social, political, and economic aims for education would certainly seem to be natural and acceptable both historically and on the contemporary scene. Government-supported schools are expected to serve the predominant goals of society, including those of economic development.

In recent years, a large number of national reports appear to have placed economic reconstruction and growth firmly in the driver's seat when it comes to reconsidering educational objectives and making curricular decisions. These reports include the National Commission on Excellence in Education's *A Nation at Risk,* the Education Commission of States' *Action for Excellence,* the Twentieth Century Fund's *Making the Grade,* and the National Science Foundation's *Educating Americans for the 21st Century.*

In 1990 the nation's governors and the Bush administration adopted six national goals designed to build "schools of the 21st century." The plan envisions all children starting school ready to learn, at least 90 percent of students graduating from high school, all students being able to cope with challenging subject matter (particularly math and science), all adults being literate and responsible citizens, and all graduates of the nation's schools being able to compete in a global economy. These goals guide the "America 2000" legislative initiative put forth by the Bush administration and its education secretary Lamar Alexander. This initiative called for a "New American Schools Program" (funding at least one "break-the-mold" school in each congressional district), a "Merit Schools Program" (rewarding schools for academic improvement), changes in teacher training and certification, expansion of parental choice, and a national testing program.

Now that the Republican administration has been retired by the electorate, the issue of national goals in general and the "America 2000" plan in particular is open to further consideration. Of particular interest for debate are the proposals to move toward national examinations, to establish a national curriculum, and to expand the concept of "choice" to include private and parochial schools. The shape of the Clinton administration's education policy has yet to emerge as of this writing, but Clinton made educational reforms a priority in Arkansas during his years as governor, and during the presidential campaign, he promised to make education a top domestic priority.

Behind the arguments over such proposals lies the basic question of the balance among federal, state, and local power in shaping school policy. Does "top-down" planning produce results? The reforms initiated at the federal and state levels in the 1980s have produced, at best, mixed results. Perhaps Deborah W. Meier in "Myths, Lies, and Public Schools," *The Nation* (September 21, 1992) is correct in asserting that "the debate over education reform belongs in local communities. Only such a community-centered debate will restore the public's sense that it has a stake in public schools." Another critical aspect is pointed to by Keith Geiger, president of the National Education Association, in "Schools, Society and the Economy," *Vital Speeches of the Day* (July 1, 1991): "Our national leaders *say* education is a priority. But the investment that would make that priority a reality has not been forthcoming."

The Washington Post (October 19, 1992) has stated editorially that "America 2000" is "a crusade worth sticking with," although in the 1992 election campaign there was too much emphasis on "choice" and "vouchers" as an appeasement to the religious right and too little emphasis on "inventing new American schools" with more rigorous classroom standards and national achievement tests. The *Post* indicated that 44 states and more than 2,000 communities have already joined the crusade.

In the articles that follow, Denis P. Doyle argues for acceptance of the national goals embodied in the "America 2000" plan and counters the criticism leveled at it. Evans Clinchy attacks the plan as an authoritarian, top-down scenario that will lead more to manipulation than to school improvement.

YES

Denis P. Doyle

AMERICA 2000

No doubt future historians will view the 1980s as the education decade—not a decade in which specific education problems were solved, but a decade in which problems of education as a whole achieved national significance. It is a difference with a meaning. Since the end of World War II, bits and pieces of education have gained national significance: aid to GIs, aid to the poor, aid to the disadvantaged, aid to the handicapped.

The Servicemen's Readjustment Act (the GI Bill), arguably the most important piece of education legislation ever enacted, is a quintessential example of the federal role as we have come to understand it. A narrowly defined subset of the population is identified; a program is designed around its members' educational needs—typically a "deficit" that only the federal government can alleviate; congressional authorization and appropriations follow. From time to time the appropriation is increased, but nothing else of note changes. Such has been the history of student financial aid, Title I (now Chapter 1), the Education for All Handicapped Children Act (now the Individuals with Disabilities Act), and a host of other programs large and small.

It was only a matter of time, I suppose, before incremental and targeted programs such as these were incorporated into a more broadly based set of programs for all Americans. The logic and political momentum behind such a transformation has a sense of historical inevitability about it. But not even the most detached and apolitical observer could fail to note the extraordinary role reversal that this development has brought about. Who is calling for an assertive national role in education in the 1990s? Who is calling for national standards? Who is putting local control, if not at risk, at least on notice? Conservatives you say? Wonder of wonders, it is none other than conservatives.

And who is now opposed? Liberals. How can this be? Until recently, wasn't it an article of liberal faith that there be a vigorous federal role in education and an equally central article of the conservative faith that there be no federal role at all? Indeed, the notion of a major federal role is so closely identified with the left end of the political spectrum that it is startling to see a proposal for just such a role emanate from the Bush Administration. And all the more interesting for that.

This development is particularly striking when contrasted with the persistent pattern of the postwar era; it was not just that liberals proposed more of the same and conservatives, less. Until the Johnson Administration, there was powerful resistance on both sides of the aisle to the creation of a significant national role. To this day, every piece of federal education legislation, whether it bears the stamp of Johnson or Nixon, Ford or Carter, Reagan or Bush, opens with an obligatory disclaimer, disavowing any federal intention (noble or otherwise) to meddle in what has historically been a state and local matter.

To be sure, there is a reason for this practice. From time immemorial, Americans and their elected officials in the Congress and in the White House have viewed a vigorous federal role in education with emotions ranging from skepticism to derision to fear. To oversimplify only slightly, American attitudes toward a federal role in education were shaped by the three R's of politics: race, religion, and region.

First, race. Northerners were afraid that a federal role would institutionalize the separation of the races across the country, not just in the South; Southerners, at least a large number of them, were afraid that the races would be integrated by federal intervention. Second, religion. Catholics were afraid that federal action would inextricably shut Catholic schools out of public funding, as the various Blaine Amendments had done at the state level in the 19th century; anti-Catholics were afraid that federal activity would legitimize public support of Catholic education (as is the practice in most

other democracies). Third, region. Americans everywhere—in all four corners of the nation and from all walks of life—had developed an almost mythic attachment to local control. Thus did an uncanny collocation of interests combine to stop in its tracks any move to strengthen the federal role.

It fell to the federal courts to put an end to the issue of race. The implementation of the *Brown* decision—to be undertaken with "all deliberate speed"—marked a conceptual break with the past. Out with *Plessy*, in with a future of racial integration.

And President Johnson did in the specter of religion—at least for 25 years. To secure the votes of big-city Democrats on behalf of the Elementary and Secondary Education Act (ESEA), Johnson had to include Catholic (and Lutheran and other denominational) schools in Title I. Not until *Aguilar v. Felton*, two decades later, did religious schools lose their federal funds. (And whereas advocates of parochial schools had lent their support to the ESEA, making it possible to enact Title I, when Catholic schools were finally denied participation in the program, there were no public school allies at their side.)

But if the conceptual logjam over federal aid to education was finally broken, the practical matter of providing federal funds for all students was not resolved. Indeed, the old plan put forth by the National Education Association and embodied in the slogan "one-third, one-third, one-third" sounds positively quaint today. Is there anyone anywhere who would seriously expect the distribution of school funding ever to become one-third federal, one-third state, and one-third local?

But if that plan is not to be, the central question of the federal role in education remains: Is it to be enlarged, and, if so, in what manner and serving which children?

WHAT SETS AMERICA 2000 APART IS THAT it is the first serious policy initiative in the nation's history to address that issue. And it does so by breaking the mold— decisively and in a new way. This education reform plan, unveiled by [former] President George Bush and [former] Secretary of Education Lamar Alexander in April 1991, is not more of the same; it is altogether different. It is not a conventional spending program, nor is it anti-government. It embraces the private sector, but it does not reject a public role. It uses Washington for what it is best at— mobilizing public opinion and focusing national energy—without creating bureaucratic structures.

America 2000 is vigorous, optimistic, and upbeat. It is a program that either Roosevelt, Theodore or Franklin, would have been at ease with. It is a program that Ike or JFK, LBJ or Ford would have found congenial. No doubt Nixon or Carter, not to mention Reagan, would be at home with it, because it calls for hard work, private initiative, self-reliance, and freedom from bureaucratic intrusion. It represents a return to an era that was less cynical and disingenuous. It contains echoes of Sputnik (response to outside forces), of the energy and idealism of the Peace Corps, and of the vision and moral fervor of Jimmy Carter.

Interestingly, if America 2000 plays poorly inside the "beltway," it plays powerfully in the rest of the nation. The recent Gallup/Phi Delta Kappa poll of public attitudes toward education reveals how Americans of all backgrounds and regions respond to the plan. Even without asking specific questions about America 2000, the poll makes it clear that Americans overwhelmingly support the underlying concepts: choice, higher standards, radical reform, and national testing.

Indeed, the enthusiastic reception that America 2000 has received beyond the beltway is matched only by the disdain heaped on it by what may best be thought of as "the education policy analysts in exile," the educators who have not had a home in the executive branch since Carter. Nowhere are they represented more fully than in the William T. Grant Foundation's quick compilation of responses to America 2000, *Voices from the Field*. That short report presented an unsurprising chorus of disapproval, ranging from the arch to the merely skeptical. Of the 30 pieces collected therein, only two (one of which was my own) could be said to support America 2000; the remaining 28 criticize it—or even harshly attack it.

The real significance of *Voices from the Field* is that public education is becoming politicized in a manner and to a degree without precedent. And the politicization is most intense and most obvious at the national level, where the effort is most modest. Uncle Sam pays for less than 8% of elementary and secondary education, sets few education policies of note, and does less of consequence. Yet nowhere is education more obviously "political" than in Washington. It reminds me of the old chestnut about the bitterness of academic politics: perhaps the fights are so unpleasant because the stakes are so low. At least they always have been. How else can we explain the intensity and unpleasantness of the response to America 2000?

When the plan was announced, it was met with warmth, even enthusiasm; on the day America 2000 was released, no less a critic of the Bush Administration than Albert Shanker, president of the American Federation of Teachers, observed on CBS's "Nightwatch" that it was a historic event: "America 2000 is the first time the federal government has announced its commitment to all elementary and secondary schoolchildren."

Shanker's observation was on target. But the honeymoon was short-lived. Within weeks Shanker was attacking Bush and Alexander, as were others in the education establishment. "If they want to pick a fight, they've picked one," said Shanker. From statesman to pugilist in a few short weeks is a remarkable transition even by Washington standards.

As it turns out, Shanker's ire can be explained in a word: choice. Keith Geiger, president of the rival National Education Association, has attacked America 2000 for the same reason. Choice is a dread word to educators, conjuring up nightmare visions of market discipline, consumer sovereignty, and accountability. Choice means an environment in which individual consumers—clients—would actually be free to abandon schools that are failing, an environment in which teachers and principals could escape from the tender mercies of senior administrators and school boards. The one thing a monopolist fears above all other things is choice; it is the enemy of apparatchiks everywhere, the enemy of central planners.

Yet it is precisely what the American public says it wants. In poll after poll, support for "choice" has been high and consistent; indeed, only among "leaders" is support for choice nonexistent or even lukewarm. Among the rank and file, support for choice is wide and deep. . . .

How has it happened that choice, the darling of the left on such matters as abortion or human rights, has become the central excuse for attacking America 2000? Is fear of choice simple paternalism, the conviction that a remote bureaucracy knows better than you what is good for you? Is the fear of choice more than the monopolists' understandable desire to hang on to power? Is it more than simple and unvarnished anti-Catholicism (a sentiment that has been aptly described as the "anti-Semitism of intellectuals")? Is fear of choice some kind of code for "more money," the rallying cry of educators everywhere and always?

The answer, of course, is all of the above. And that answer reflects the barrenness, the sterility of the debate about education at the federal level, as well as the atavistic fear of what might happen were a serious federal role to emerge. Choice is at best a stalking-horse, at worst a symbol. It cannot be forced on an unwilling people, though opponents of choice act as thought it might be.

To compound the irony, the Administration did not make choice the centerpiece of its plan; opponents did. As a practical matter, there is little the federal government can do about choice except talk—admittedly an important activity in a democracy, but hardly a dangerous one. The President proposes; the Congress disposes. The "choice" about choice will be made in state houses and at the local level. Uncle Sam may be for it, but he cannot impose it. However, to discuss it at all raised interesting issues, as does the debate about national standards.

Consider, for a moment, the consequences of a federal role in education in which federal policy, if not dominant, were at least the equal of state and local policies. Today—with the notable and important exception of civil rights, which are not limited to education—the federal role is modest at the elementary and secondary level. Indeed, in substantive terms, there can be no role for the federal government in *education*, except that role which states are willing to accept voluntarily. Thanks to the 10th Amendment (the reserve powers clause), those powers not specifically enumerated for the federal government are "reserved" for the states. Education is such a power—and such a responsibility. If Uncle Sam wants to spend money on education he may, but federal education programs are conditional—the offer of federal funds is conditioned on the acceptance of federal rules and regulations. No compliance, no money. But the state or locality that refuses to comply loses only the money. Fiats, edicts, and pronunciamentos are not part of the federal role.

To be sure, the central role of federal government in protecting the civil rights of all Americans in all settings has produced a particularly vigorous federal presence in the nation's schools. But protecting civil rights is not the same as making education policies or specifying practices. It does not deal directly with such matters as textbook selection, curriculum decisions, testing and measurement, conditions of work, hiring, promotion, compensation, retirement benefits, building design and construction, transportation, nutrition, the length of the school day and year, grading, conditions for graduation, disciplinary standards, extracurriculars, and financing. In short, every one of the important things that schools do, or fail to do, falls outside the ambit of the federal government.

Indeed, as study after study has revealed, it is not even clear that "federal" programs—Chapter 1, for example—are subject to much meaningful federal control. It is not simply that Uncle Sam exercises little oversight—there are few program auditors, and most are former state and local employees who work hand-in-glove with their former colleagues. But even if there were a great deal of oversight, the capacity of states and localities to confuse, dissemble, dissimulate, hide, prevaricate, and generally run circles around all but the most ardent Washington gumshoes is legendary. Who has not been impressed with the ease and skill of a Chapter 1 director effortlessly deflecting potentially embarrassing questions? Indeed, that capacity is undoubtedly one of the unwritten qualifications for the job. No superintendent worth his or her salt would permit Washington to do more than *appear* to play an important role.

From the beginning of the federal role in education, with the creation of an education office to "collect statistics" and of Justin Morrill's land grant colleges, there has been a light federal hand on the reins. Even the GI Bill (which Robert Maynard Hutchins, president of the University of Chicago, predicted "would turn American colleges and universities into intellectual hobo jungles") did little to disturb the tempo of life in higher education. Although the GI Bill transformed American life, as a government education program it was simply "much more" of the same. . . .

[O]NE ROLE THAT THE FEDERAL GOVERNment has played successfully for well over a century in a variety of endeavors is that of catalyst for redesign and restructuring: in the 19th century with harbors, bridges, canals, railroads, and land grant colleges (with their heavy emphasis on applied research and development); in the 20th century with airports, the interstate highway system, and heavy-duty research and development, basic and applied, in fields as diverse as medicine, agriculture, space, and particle physics.

The fact that Uncle Sam is only indirectly a stakeholder in education should be an asset rather than a liability. Uncle Sam does not (as a rule) own and operate schools, and the federal contribution to the states, localities, institutions, and individuals that do, while important, is a paltry sum as measured against overall expenditures for education. The lesson for education should be abundantly clear. Uncle Sam is ideally suited to act as a stimulus to change, as funder of "venture capital," and as the one party in the system with a truly national, even global, perspective.

WHAT DOES UNCLE SAM NEED TO DO? Provide the intellectual and political "space," as well as access to resources, to design the "school of the future" from the ground up. The New American Schools Development Corporation, funded by the private sector, has the flexibility and agility to move rapidly and decisively. It can act as "venture capitalist" in ways the public sector could not. (A little-noted provision in the enabling legislation for the—late and unlamented?—National Institute of Education permitted it to receive gifts, grants, and bequests of private funds.)

And a federally funded "new American schools" program will permit the vision of research and development in education to become a reality, as states, districts, and communities of parents, teachers, and children see the success of the new schools. Here is a bold, even daring vision—one that recognizes the national interest but does not compromise local initiative.

Albert Shanker, in a prescient moment, once observed that the trouble with educational research is that "all education experiments are doomed to succeed." Prescient, to be sure, but Secretary Alexander's proposal does not fit the mold that inspired Shanker's comment. For the first time the federal government can address the needs and interests of all students—not just the legitimate but limited needs of the disadvantaged and dispossessed—without imposing its views, values, or standards on the nation. America 2000 reconciles the national interest with the role the federal government has historically played.

President Bush and Secretary Alexander announced America 2000 with the genuine hope that the nation's educators would rally to the cause—it is, after all, the right and proper thing to do. There is no more important domestic business than education and no more pressing responsibility than improving the education of our children. In this judgment the President and the secretary were surely right; moreover, they recognized the fact that the American people shared their concern. The only question that remained was whether or not those who speak for the education establishment did as well. As I write this in late September, the jury is still out. But the direction in which they are leaning is not hard to discern, and it offers scant comfort to those who had hoped that there might be a demonstration of statesmanship on the part of at least some of education's leaders.

Unfortunately, most have chosen to denounce choice, as if choice alone were the President's plan, and to continue rattling their tin cups, as if money were the only thing that mattered. It is a peculiar and ill-tempered view for educators to hold. Has not the time finally come for all of us to agree that money, while a part of the answer, is not the whole answer?

At one level, of course, concern with money—or lack thereof—is a perfectly appropriate reaction to the crises in education, because there is not (nor will there ever be) as much money as we might like for education. Limited resources are a reality. The same is true for health, leisure, retirement, defense—you name it; the list is nearly endless. Consequently, thinking about the implications of limited resources is precisely what reformers must do. To approach education as though the only solution to the problem of limited resources is to raise the limit is counterproductive.

There are other solutions. The one that comes immediately to mind is the application of technology to education. Others include such obvious steps as reinvesting the high school diploma with meaning, making it a degree worth earning. One way to begin might be for schools to raise expectations for students, letting them know that they can participate only so long as they work and work hard. A radical idea, to be sure, but an idea that should at least receive equal consideration with increased funding.

It is in this sense, of course, that the worst fears of the education interest groups are well-founded: budgets for education will be limited, at least for as long as the human mind can foresee. The 1990s provide simply one more example of a perennial problem. What can be changed, however, is the way in which we respond to the problem of limited resources. By way of contrast, imagine conducting a serious conversation about medicine and health care without considering cost containment. It simply isn't possible. Why should education be any different? Indeed, the challenge facing the new American schools is how to do the job better with the same resources.

In the larger economy, the growth of productivity has been the engine of prosperity for the West. Thus, for the first time in history, it is possible to imagine large numbers of people living above a subsistence level. The analogy is clear: it should be possible to imagine educating everyone at levels of expenditure that are realistic and that will enjoy broad public support.

Modern economists have developed an arcane but perfectly plausible explanation of most of the productivity gains of the past 50 years: an increase in human capital. What is human capital? It is what people know and are able to do. Human capital is knowledge, ability, skills, insights, dreams. It is the intellectual—and, yes, moral—vision that transforms dumb matter into goods and services. It is the true source of wealth in the modern era. Not gold, not oil, not diamonds, but people. People who work not just harder, but smarter.

And the social institution that creates human capital—at least the one institution amenable to the influence of policy makers—is the school. It is time, finally, to apply some of the insights about the role of human intelligence in the modern world to that most archaic of our institutions. Schooling cries out for change. Schools must enter the modern world, and the only way they can do so is by trial and error. New schools must be "rolled out" and "tested," precisely as new cars, new computers, new software, or new airplanes are. That's what the New American Schools Development Corporation is all about.

The issue raised by America 2000, then, is not whether to continue treating schools as a production process, but how to transform a moribund institution into a high-performance organization, an organization that works. Schooling can become an enterprise that satisfies its staff; one that satisfies the "workers" (that is, students, for in the modern era students must be workers—not passive vessels, but eager and enterprising seekers of education); and one that satisfies the public, parents, taxpayers, and policy makers.

NO

Evans Clinchy

AMERICA 2000: REFORM, REVOLUTION, OR JUST MORE SMOKE AND MIRRORS?

America 2000 . . . is aimed at implementing the six national goals for education set forth in Charlottesville, Virginia, in 1989 by President Bush and the 50 state governors. It contains a series of federal initiatives that Bush has called "not reform, but revolution."

At first glance, this new federal strategy can easily appear to be the revolutionary set of proposals that Bush and Alexander claim it to be. [Lamar Alexander was secretary of education in the Bush administration.] It presents a number of ideas and programs that could radically change the way our present system of public education is organized and operated. More leisurely study, however, reveals the strategy to be flawed by one major educational/ political blunder and by one massive internal contradiction that, taken together, could render the entire plan not only meaningless but positively dangerous.

FIRST, THE POSITIVE

To be perfectly fair, the proposals contained in America 2000 add up to quite a smorgasbord of ideas and programs. Very much to its credit, America 2000 is in fact the most significant assertion of a federal responsibility for and role in the conduct of public education since the Elementary and Secondary Education Act of 1965. Indeed, it is nothing less than a declaration that the federal government can no longer absolve itself of the responsibility to help create a genuine and truly national policy for education. At least, it cannot shirk the responsibility if this country is to survive into the next century as a continuing model to the world of what a democratic society might be—or even if it is to survive as a first-class economic power.

True, America 2000 pays precious little attention to the crucial question of how the billions of dollars needed to turn all these ideas and proposals into

From Evans Clinchy, "America 2000: Reform, Revolution, or Just More Smoke and Mirrors?" *Phi Delta Kappan* (November 1991). Copyright © 1991 by Phi Delta Kappa, Inc. Reprinted by permission.

reality will be provided. While it is certainly possible for school districts to implement many structural reforms without spending large amounts of money, America 2000 offers little to support the initiatives it endorses beyond the $120 million to $150 million to be raised from the private sector. Although it is encouraging to see private businesses getting involved in the support of the schools, public education is and should be the *public's* business and responsibility. So this maneuver ends up looking like just one more Bush Administration attempt to promote change—and get credit for it—without dipping into the federal treasury or seriously reducing the military budget.

Meanwhile, the nation is in the midst of a recession verging on a true depression. Districts across the country are being decimated by vicious budget slashing. Many schools are being reduced to staffing and budgetary levels that barely allow them to keep the doors open, much less enable harassed and overworked people to plan and put into effect all the marvelous innovations America 2000 envisages.

It is not just ridiculous but downright irresponsible for the federal government to ask states and local communities to meet some fancy set of "new world standards" in the academic core subjects without providing enough money for them to do so. This is like telling General Motors to invent new and wonderful cars that get 50 miles to the gallon, while at the same time ordering them to cut prices and their work force in half—thus making sure that they have neither money nor people to turn loose on the task of thinking up new and wonderful ways to meet the new mileage standards.

The rhetoric of America 2000 clearly requires an annual tripling or quadrupling of the federal investment in public education. But it is not explained to us how we can spend billions to preserve our sources of cheap oil in the Persian Gulf and yet cannot find equal billions to support a "revolution" in our education system. In short, we get little more than the usual fiscal smoke and mirrors out of the Washington establishment. But the lack of a specified source of federal funds is a minor problem compared to the program's educational/political blunder and its massive internal contradiction.

THE BIG BLUNDER

To deal first with the blunder, there appears to be little doubt that parental choice of *public* schools is one of the foundations on which any reform or revolution in public education must be built. As many people have pointed out over the years, public school choice is a necessary but not totally sufficient remedy for what ails us. Parental choice must be combined with a true diversity of approaches to education, with the ability of teachers and principals also to choose the kind of schooling they wish to practice, and with the school-level autonomy necessary to make diversity possible. Given these large restructurings of the way our public systems operate, choice can be, as Deborah Meier of the Central Park East schools has put it, "the necessary catalyst for the kind of dramatic restructuring that most agree is needed to produce a far better educated citizenry."[1]

But Bush and Alexander have revived the hoary notion of education vouchers that would allow parents to choose nonpublic schools for their children and to pay at least part of the tuition with public money. If the present public/nonpublic school arrangements are maintained, this proposal would effectively destroy public education.

What we would almost inevitably end up with are two quite separate, thoroughly unequal, and de facto racially and economically segregated school systems. One of these would be a well-funded public, private, and parochial system, serving a primarily white (though with some minorities), middle-class, and largely suburban student body. The other would be a minimally funded public system, serving largely our urban poor and minority students. Such a dual system of schooling is unlikely to pass either constitutional muster or, thank goodness, the political scrutiny of a civil-rights-minded Congress.

Nor does Alexander's argument hold water that this proposal is no more than an extension of the ideas contained in the GI Bill. The GI Bill allowed veterans of the armed forces to use public money to attend a public or nonpublic college of their choice. Although it is not exactly clear why it has been constitutionally permissible for public money to go to private and religiously affiliated colleges and universities, the GI Bill applied only to presumably consenting adults who voluntarily chose to take advantage of the opportunity and were—also presumably—capable of resisting the blandishments of sectarian institutions. It did not apply to children and young people who are compelled by law to go to school. In the face of such state coercion, it behooves the courts—and the rest of us—to make sure that all constitutional and civil rights guarantees and safeguards are strictly enforced.

On the other hand, if Alexander is serious in saying that nonpublic schools would have to meet "some" of the criteria of public schools, those of us who strongly support public school choice might temper our opposition. If all schools receiving public money could not discriminate and had to admit all students who apply regardless of their background or achievement levels, if such schools could not expel students for unseemly behavior or low academic achievement, if they had to adhere to affirmative action hiring policies, if they could teach no religion, if they had to meet all the educational and financial accountability requirements that apply to the public schools, and so on, then many of us might be able to go along with this proposal. But then all nonpublic schools would essentially become public schools, and that is a proposition unlikely to appeal to private and parochial school educators or to those parents who wish to use the nonpublic schools precisely *because* those schools do not have to face all the problems that public schools must meet and somehow overcome.

RETHINKING THE GOALS

While the blunder on parental choice is a major flaw in the Bush/Alexander proposals, it is dwarfed by the glaring and destructive internal contradiction that runs through all of America 2000. In order to understand this contradiction and why it exists, we need to remind ourselves of those six national goals that the new strategy is designed to transform from rhetoric into reality.[2]

When the governors and the President convened their "education summit" in Charlottesville and subsequently set forth their national goals, that exercise seemed at first glance not only well-intentioned but relatively harmless. After all, the six goals suggest nothing particularly new or radical. They have been the ostensible—if not always clearly articulated—goals of public education for at least the past 50 years. However, they are goals that our present system of public schooling has not been able to achieve and, in its present form, is unlikely ever to achieve.

Thus, at first blush, the governors and the President seemed simply to be joining the general chorus of responsible voices in this society that are calling for radical restructuring of the public education system. Indeed, most of our leading educational researchers and experts, most captains of business and industry, our teacher unions, our major professional organizations, and thousands of just plain folks strongly believe that our existing system must somehow be thoroughly reorganized—even reinvented—if it is adequately to serve our children and young people and the nation itself in the years ahead.

Moreover, the America 2000 proposals seem clearly aimed not only at translating the goals into practice but also at achieving the much-desired redesign of this country's public school system. Why else the great emphasis on "research and development" and the creation of high-powered research and development teams to make possible "the generation of new ideas and approaches"? Why else the variety of efforts aimed at making it possible for individual schools all across the country to "break the mold" and create their own "one-of-a-kind high-performance schools"? And why else the involvement of the private sector to the tune of $150 million to $200 million a year to make all of this possible?

How could all of this possibly be wrong-headed? Well, to begin with, the very act of establishing this particular set of national goals and the America 2000 strategy serves to perpetuate the idea, advanced nearly a decade ago in *A Nation at Risk*, that we can solve our present educational problems from the top down. Our public schools will be improved, this approach says, only if those in power in this society—in this case, the federal government and the state governors—establish a set of lofty national goals and a set of "high" national academic standards.

With America 2000 as its implementation strategy, this authoritarian, top-down scenario could well run something like this. Now that the six national goals have been promulgated and the national strategy outlined, the leading authorities and experts in each of the six core academic subjects will be asked (indeed, they are already being asked) to set "new American standards" in their respective fields. Congress and the President will incorporate the new goals and standards into a legislated national education policy. (This is now being done with the filing of S. 2 in the Senate.) All existing and future federal programs will be shaped to flesh out the goals and standards and to tell us how the goals are to be put into practice.

In order to receive federal financial assistance, the 50 states and all local districts will be expected (perhaps required) to subscribe to the goals and to adopt the new national standards. State legislatures will then be encouraged (perhaps required) to codify the goals and standards into state mandates that will then have to be adopted by local districts and schools as a condition of receiving both federal and state funding. State rules and regulations will then be written and imposed on local districts to ensure that the goals and standards are met.

If the governors and the President had stopped after Charlottesville and left the national goals simply as lofty hopes, the danger might not be too serious and could perhaps be overcome—or the whole business could safely be ignored. But, of course, matters did not stop there. The act of goal- and standard-setting has simultaneously unleashed the further authoritarian urge to make everyone *accountable*, to find out whether the national goals are being met by providing the authorities with simple-minded, easily understood—and therefore *quantified*—assessments of whether we as a nation are succeeding in meeting them.

The setting of national goals and the establishment of a national education policy not only reinforce but also expand our system of endless and arbitrary standardized achievement testing that already begins even before kindergarten. They lead directly to an even greater reliance on our existing system of standardized tests and to renewed calls for an even stronger and more elaborate national and international system of measurement and testing. America 2000 not only proposes a new set of "American achievement tests," to be based on those "new world standards," but also urges all colleges and universities to use the tests for admissions and all employers to use them for hiring purposes. . . .

What this entire process of goal-setting, top-down mandating, and lusting for quantifiable assessment data adds up to—whether anyone likes it or not—is the establishment of a *uniform, standardized national curriculum* that all schools will feel compelled to implement. Indeed, the President's Advisory Committee on Educational Policy, a group of leading educa-

tors and businessmen called together to advise the Administration, has recently told the President that such a national curriculum—and the national testing that must inevitably accompany it—should be developed and imposed on all schools.[3]

THE MASSIVE INTERNAL CONTRADICTION

Let us assume for a moment that the President and the secretary of education are perfectly serious about implementing this organizational straitjacket of an established, highly traditional, and perhaps actually mandated national curriculum with its new "high academic standards" and its accompanying batteries of national and international standardized tests. The massive central contradiction in the Bush/Alexander plan can best be illustrated by a series of only slightly rhetorical questions.

If the new strategy is adopted, what happens to all the America 2000 rhetoric about "revolutionary reform," about the research and development of "bold new ideas," about cutting the red tape of federal and state rules and regulations, about the "new generation of American schools," and about giving the people in individual schools the authority to create and put into practice their own vision of what the school will be and how it will operate? What about all those teachers and principals who wish to practice in, those educational experts who recommend, and those parents who want their children to attend schools that are not tied to the antiquated subject-matter compartments or to the traditional, orderly, administratively convenient, and educationally disastrous sequence of age-graded classes that have led to "retention in grade" and other equally barbaric practices? I mean such schools as Montessori schools, "open" schools, or perhaps even microsociety schools, in which the entire curriculum is built around real-life professions and occupations.[4]

And what happens to the many teachers, principals, educational experts, and parents who believe that children and young people should not be subjected to traditional standardized testing? What happens to all those people who believe strongly that the traditional ways in which students are tested and the traditional ways in which the curriculum is constructed, organized, and taught are precisely what is wrong with public education today?

What "revolutionary reforms," what "bold new ideas" are the people in this "new generation of American schools" going to be allowed to pursue as they exercise their new "freedom from federal and state rules and regulations"? Will they be allowed to throw out the traditional curriculum, with its "new world" academic standards and its mandated subject compartments? Can they refuse to subject their students to the "new American achievement tests"? Will they really be allowed to construct schools and school systems that follow none of the established rules and conventional wisdoms?

If schools cannot genuinely and honestly depart from the tried and less than true, what does it mean that high-powered research and development teams and the schools associated with them will now be empowered to "break the mold" and explore "new ways of teaching and learning"?

Now, of course, all the national goalsetters, the advocates of a national curriculum, and those who devise national tests will make haste to counter these

unpleasant questions by saying that the research and development teams, our local school districts, and the individual schools in those districts will be "free" to meet the newly established goals and testing standards and to deliver that national curriculum in their own unique and highly innovative ways. Indeed, the people in our schools will actually be encouraged to do so and financially rewarded for it.

Don't you believe it. Whatever rhetoric may be handed down about radical change and the "freedom" to create bold new ideas, anyone with any experience in the public schools—or in any form of education—knows full well that the existence of an established, mandated curriculum and of established, mandated tests will determine not only *what* will be taught, but in nearly every case *how* it will be taught.

To begin with, the new "high" national standards, the curriculum guides, the learning materials, and the standardized tests created for the new national curriculum will, of course, be based on those arbitrary, unrealistic subject-matter compartments described in the national goals (English, mathematics, science, history, and geography). We know that the world is not organized along these scholarly lines but rather according to those broad, interdisciplinary occupational and professional categories used in microsociety schools—categories such as law, government and politics, business, industry and economics, publishing of all varieties, the communications industry, and so on. Indeed, we are beginning to see the scholarly academic compartments as increasingly confining, irrelevant, and, at the very least, obsolescent.

Yet the chances are very strong that, because of the structure of the national curriculum and the nature of the national tests, we will be forced to continue to rely on the traditional teaching methodology we call "instruction." Under this venerable approach, the creators of curriculum guides and materials almost always begin their task by identifying the "scope and sequence" of each of the subject compartments, specifying both the "skills" that are supposed to be acquired at each grade level and the precise "content" that teachers must "cover" and that students must "know" by the end of each year in school. The skills to be acquired and the contents to be "learned" are then broken down into small, manageable, linear, and logical steps. Students are exposed to and are required to "learn" each piece before moving on to the next one. These "grade-level skills" and this "grade-level content" are what will be tested by the standardized tests given as the culminating activity of the school year.

For instance, if the established eighth-grade curriculum and the national eighth-grade achievement test in American history both call for extensive "coverage" of, say, the Civil War, then the teacher must "teach" and the students must "learn" (i.e., read and remember) the specified material in the specified American history texts. Thus every eighth-grade history teacher is under enormous pressure to start at Fort Sumter and race pell-mell to Appomattox. After all, that eighth-grade teacher is going to be judged a success or failure according to how well his or her students perform on that standardized (and, quite possibly, national) achievement test.

Of course, this means that any teacher's choices about *how* to conduct history classes that deal with the Civil War are severely limited. The traditional, time-tested ways to achieve the ends prescribed by the "coverage" and "learning" of any historical matter are lecturing, having students read textbook assignments, and giving daily or weekly quizzes on the material that needs to be memorized in order to score well on the final test.

In short, "instruction" is what schools do *to* children and young people, the decisions we adults make *for* them, the tasks we impose *upon* them. Instruction has little to do with what children and young people may want to learn or with what they may be interested in and capable of learning well. It has little to do with all those things that might be important and meaningful in *children's* lives rather than the things that we adults think should be important and meaningful.

In his 1982 textbook, *Developmental Psychology*, Howard Gardner, the Harvard developmental psychologist, describes learning in the preschool and nonschool world of children and young people as a process of education that occurs almost exclusively *in the context* in which what is learned will be used. "First, they watch adults weave or hunt; later they participate as helpers; and eventually they assume a key role themselves. There is little talk, little formal teaching; learning comes from doing. No wonder these youngsters perform best when they become actively involved in a task."[5]

The world of formal schooling, according to Gardner, is entirely different:

> For better or worse, the standard classroom is entirely different. There is scarce opportunity for active participation. The teacher talks, often presenting material in abstract, symbolic forms or relying on inanimate sources such as books and diagrams to convey information. . . .

All cognitive abilities exist in all human beings, needing only the proper circumstances or motivation to be elicited. . . . And yet, inflamed in part by the superior rewards given to those who have been to school, a pervasive antagonism often develops between the schools' logical, out-of-context knowledge system and that practical participation in daily activities fostered informally by the culture. If this antagonism is to be lessened, schools . . . must be viewed as comfortable and significant environments, rather than hostile providers of useless knowledge. This means that schools must contain everyday life within their walls, while also revealing the relation between the skills they teach and the problems children find significant.[6]

Yet here we have the President, the nation's governors, and an apparently growing host of educators and businesspeople intent on locking all of us into those traditional compartments of knowledge and forcing teachers to use anachronistic teaching methods. These leaders and experts apparently have no inkling that, for the 98% of our children and young people who will not themselves become academic scholars, these practices may be not only intellectually obsolete but educationally damaging.

There seems to be no awareness that, if these antiquated subject compartments continue to be "taught" in the conventional "instructional" mode of traditional schooling, they may actually inhibit the development of children's intellects and undermine the usefulness in later life—both to students and to society—of what students are "learning" in school. Given the "instructional" habits and practices common in our schools, it is small wonder that our students find school boring and irrelevant and either drop out completely or drop out while remaining in school (by becoming passive automatons). . . .

CARPING IS NOT ENOUGH

It is all well and good for those of us who resist the imposition of mandated goals, or a mandated national curriculum, and of a mandated national testing system to cry havoc and let slip the dogs of opposition. But mere carping on our part is not enough.

Do we have adequate replacements for the six national goals? For the national curriculum, the national tests, and the old authoritarian structure they appear to preserve? Do we have, in short, a way in which our public schools can transform themselves from Gardner's "hostile providers of useless knowledge" into a system that could genuinely serve and dramatically improve public schooling for its clients and so for the nation as a whole?

Well, yes, I think we do. Over the past several decades, largely as a result of the alternative schools movement of the 1960s and the mandated school desegregation of the 1970s and 1980s (which did a great deal to popularize magnet schools), we have gradually begun to create and put into place a new organizational structure for public education. This new structure is based on the deliberate and conscious creation of a broad range of diverse educational and curricular approaches to schooling designed to match the enormous diversity of our students. It includes parental and professional choice among those diverse schools, the individual school autonomy necessary to make that educational diversity possible, and the guaranteed provision of genuine educational equity for our poor and minority students.[7]

But does this new structure provide an adequate replacement for a national (and international) testing system? Does it offer some mechanism that can assure us that we are educating our children and young people as they need to be educated?

Again, I think we are starting to see what such a system might look like, beginning with the fact that parental choice provides us with an automatic means of determining whether a school is providing the high-quality education that parents want. However, a more formal assessment scheme, based on the precepts laid down by John Dewey and others, would not evaluate students according to their scores on tests in those academic compartments. Instead, such a new assessment system would evaluate each student's grasp of how a democratic society (that "real world" out there) works or should work, would evaluate each student's developed ability to operate in the world, and might even evaluate a student's ability to devise ways of making that world behave more equitably and in a more nurturing fashion.

Such a system would assess every student's understanding of what a democratic, constitutional system of laws and government is; of how a free-market economy can be regulated and controlled to serve the larger public interest; of the role that science and technology do play and should play in such a society; of the power and influence of the media; of the crucial role of the arts, the humanities, and philosophy in the conduct of human affairs; and so on. It would also assess every student's ability to put his or her particular vision of life and the world into practice; that is, it would attempt to judge a student's ability to construct a life that is both personally satisfying and socially responsible. Much of the "test-ing" would consist of assessing how well a student could perform "real world" tasks, rather than of counting the number of correct multiple-choice answers.

WHAT ABOUT THE NATIONAL GOALS?

If, as Deborah Meier and many others among us believe, we cannot reform our schools by fiat, with mandates delivered from on high or with accountability schemes tied to a dictated list of measurable outcomes, can we still have a set of national goals that might help us dramatically improve public schooling and enable us to compete better in the world economy? Of course, these would have to be goals that would in no sense be forced on anyone but would simply serve as generally agreed-upon guidelines to help us forge that restructured education system we so desperately need.

Again, yes, I think that this approach is possible—or at least worth a try. An amended set of six national goals could even include most of those put forth by the President and the governors, if in considerably altered form.

Goal 1: By the year 2000, no American child will be born into poverty and therefore be unprepared to take full advantage of a restructured American system of public education. This goal means that all children in this country (from conception through grade 12) will be supplied with all the health and social services they need to ensure their full physical, intellectual, moral, and emotional development. It also means that all American families will receive such services along with whatever economic assistance is necessary to eliminate both the causes of poverty and poverty itself.

Goals 2 and 3: By the year 2000, every American public school system will be restructured so that the following two goals of education, as described by Jean Piaget, can be achieved:

The principal goal of education is to create men [and women] who are capable of doing new things, not simply of repeating what other generations have done—[people] who are creative, inventive, discoverers.

The second goal of education is to form minds which can be critical, can verify and not accept everything they are offered. The great danger today is of slogans, collective opinions, ready-made trends of thought. We have to be able to resist individually, to criticize, to distinguish between what is proven and what is not. So we need pupils who are active, who learn early to find out by themselves, partly by their own spontaneous activity and partly through materials we set up for them: who learn early to tell what is verifiable and what is simply the first idea to come to them.[8]

These two goals mean that the entire existing curricular structure of American public schooling must be rethought and recast to make sure that, from preschool through high school, the emphasis is not simply on the rote accumulation of facts and the mere acquisition of basic skills but on the continuous *development* of each child's intellectual, social, and moral capacities. Only then will students be able to construct a powerful vision of the world and of their place in it and to develop the ability to use their minds well so that they can become responsible citizens who are able to create the innovations and new ideas that can improve this society—and perhaps even make us "first in the world in science and math."

Goal 4: By the year 2000, there will be a school to fit the needs, talents, and interests of every student, be that student a preschool child, a student of conventional school age, or an adult in need of further education. This goal means that there will be a true diversity of schools and a wide range of differing approaches to public education, so that no student or returning adult will feel the need to drop out or abandon his or her education because the schooling offered is boring or irrelevant. Schooling will be closely connected to the realities of the larger society. Only then is there a chance that the high school graduation rate will reach 90% (or more), and only then will all students be equipped to become competent citizens with the necessary skills to enable the country to compete in the world economy.

Goal 5: By the year 2000, every American public school will be an integrated school of student, parent, and professional choice. This goal means that the American public school system will be restructured so that every school or educational program is open to and can be chosen by those students, parents, teachers, and administrators who share a vision of what that school should be and can do. To ensure that our public schools will be genuinely and equitably integrated, access to all schools will be guaranteed to all students, regardless of race, ethnic group, sex, or economic status.

Goal 6: By the year 2000, our public school system will be restructured so that every American public school of choice (and thus every school) will have the autonomy to develop its distinctive approach to public schooling. This final goal means that each individual public school will be empowered to control—and will be responsible to the public for—its own destiny, its own success or failure. Schools will have control of their own lump-sum budgets, will be able to select their own staffs, and will be able to develop their own distinctive programs.

ARE THESE GOALS ATTAINABLE?

By the year 2000? Not bloody likely! But that is hardly the important point. What *is* important is that by that millennial year we should be well on our way to reinventing our system of public education along the lines laid out for us by these new goals. If we achieve no more than that over the next decade, we will at the very least have put ourselves on the path to constructing a system of public education that will finally be doing most of what our public schools were always meant to do.

NOTES

1. Deborah Meier, "Choice Can Save Public Education," *The Nation*, 4 March 1991, pp. 253, 266–71.

2. See the special section on the national goals in the December 1990 issue of the *Phi Delta Kappan*, pp. 264–315.

3. See "Advisory Panel Presents National Test Plan to Bush," *Education Week*, 23 January 1990, p. 25.

4. For a description of how a microsociety school operates, see George Richmond, "The Future School: Is Lowell Pointing Us Toward a Revolution in Education?," *Phi Delta Kappan*, November 1989, pp. 232–36. See also Evans Clinchy, *A Consumer's Guide to Schools of Choice* (Boston: Institute for Responsive Education, January 1987).

5. Howard Gardner, *Developmental Psychology* (Boston: Little, Brown, 1982), p. 448.

6. Ibid., pp. 448, 451–52.

7. See Evans Clinchy, "Public School Choice: Absolutely Necessary but Not Wholly Sufficient," *Phi Delta Kappan*, December 1989, pp. 289–94; and Mary Anne Raywid, "Public Choice, Yes; Vouchers, No!," *Phi Delta Kappan*, June 1987, pp. 762–69.

8. Jean Piaget, quoted in David Elkind and Eleanor Duckworth, "The Educational Implications of Piaget's Work," in Charles E. Silberman, ed., *The Open Classroom Reader* (New York: Random House, 1973), p. 196.

POSTSCRIPT

Should National Goals Guide School Performance?

Ernest Boyer, president of the Carnegie Foundation for the Advancement of Teaching, in "Educational Goals: An Action Plan," *Vital Speeches of the Day* (June 1, 1990), states that "We are moving in this country from a local to a national view of education and we need better arrangements to guide the way. . . . The challenge is to develop a *national* agenda for school renewal, while retaining leadership at the state and local levels." A central criticism of the Bush administration's "America 2000" approach is that it went well beyond agenda setting and charted a politically inspired policy path leading to a redefinition of the concept of "public education." A focal point of this redefinition is the expansion of "choice" as a reform mechanism; this is addressed more thoroughly in Issue 9 that follows.

For further discussion of national goals and the politics of education, the following sources are recommended: Daniel Patrick Moynihan's "Educational Goals and Political Plans," *The Public Interest* (Winter 1991) and Linda Darling-Hammond's "National Goals and America 2000: Of Carrots, Sticks, and False Assumptions," *The Education Digest* (December 1991), in which she contends that making schools "compete" without investing more to improve them means greater segregation and inequality for many, with improved education for few. She goes on to say, "If . . . standard-setting is the solution, we will lose perhaps our last chance to create a new model for schools in the twenty-first century, one that delivers more than rhetoric about educational excellence and equality."

Joel Spring's critique of political and economic purposes in education has been a central theme of his earlier books *The Sorting Machine* and *Educating the Worker-Citizen* and his more recent work *Conflict of Interest: The Politics of American Education* (1988). Other books on the topic include *Making Schools Better* (1992) by Larry Martz (see especially Chapter 1, "Revolution in Small Bites"); *Educational Renaissance: Our Schools at the Turn of the Twenty-first Century* (1991) by Marvin Cetron and Margaret Gayle; *We Must Take Charge: Our Schools and Our Future* (1991) by Chester E. Finn, Jr.; *Smart Schools, Smart Kids: Why Do Some Schools Work?* (1991) by Edward B. Fiske; Thomas Toch's *In the Name of Excellence* (1991); George H. Wood's *Schools That Work: America's Most Innovative Public Educational Programs* (1992); and Theodore Sizer's *Horace's School: Redesigning the American High School* (1992).

PART 2

Specific Issues

In this section, the issues debated probe concerns that currently face educators and policymakers. How these debates are resolved will affect the future direction of education in our society.

Can "Choice" Lead the Way to
  Educational Reform?

Will the "Edison Project" Prompt
  Major Reforms?

Is Home Schooling a Viable Alternative?

Can Schools Prevent Urban Dropouts?

Should Literacy Be Based on
  Traditional Culture?

Do Black Students Need an Afrocentric
  Curriculum?

Should Bilingual Education Programs
  Be Abandoned?

Does Tracking Create Educational
  Inequality?

Is Mainstreaming Beneficial to All?

Do "Discipline Programs" Promote
  Ethical Behavior?

Are Current Sex Education Programs
  Lacking in Moral Guidance?

Should Schools of Education Be
  Abolished?

ISSUE 9

Can "Choice" Lead the Way to Educational Reform?

YES: John E. Chubb and Terry M. Moe, from "America's Public Schools: Choice *Is* a Panacea," *The Brookings Review* (Summer 1990)

NO: Frances C. Fowler, from "The Shocking Ideological Integrity of Chubb and Moe," *Journal of Education* (Summer 1991)

ISSUE SUMMARY

YES: Political science researchers John E. Chubb and Terry M. Moe, authors of the much-discussed *Politics, Markets, and America's Schools,* make the case for choice as a means of true reform.
NO: Frances C. Fowler of Miami University in Oxford, Ohio, analyzes the premises underlying the proposals of Chubb and Moe and finds an anti-democratic tone.

One of the more heated educational debates in recent years has been the one concerned with finding ways to provide parents and learners with a greater range of choices in schooling. Some people see the public school system as a monolithic structure that runs roughshod over individual inclinations and imposes a rigid social philosophy on its constituents. Others feel that the reduced quality of public education, particularly in large urban areas, demands that parents be given support in their quest for better learning environments. Still others agree with sociologist James S. Coleman's contention that "the greater the constraints imposed on school attendance—short of dictating place of residence and prohibiting attendance at private schools—the greater the educational gap between those who have the money to escape the constraints and those who do not."

Measures that emphasize freedom of choice abound and are often connected with desegregation and school reform goals. Some jurisdictions have developed a system of magnet schools to serve the dual purposes of equality and quality; some districts now allow parents to send their children to any public school under their control; and a few urban districts (notably Milwaukee and Kansas City) are experimenting with funding plans to allow private school alternatives.

Two of the much-discussed ideas of dealing with this last possibility are tuition tax credits and voucher plans. The first, provided by the federal, state, or local government, would expand the number of families able to send their children to the school of their choice and would, according to advocates, improve the quality of public schooling by encouraging competition. Voucher plans, first suggested in 1955 by conservative economist Milton Friedman, are designed to return tax monies to parents of school-aged children for use in a variety of authorized public and private educational settings. Opponents of either approach take the position that such moves will turn the public schools into an enclave of the poor and will lead to further racial, socioeconomic class, and religious isolation. The question of church-state separation looms large in the minds of those who oppose these measures. (See Issue 5 for further discussion of this aspect.)

The "America 2000" initiative promulgated by the Bush administration included "choice" as one of its cornerstones. A key influence in the development of that policy position was the Brookings Institution study *Politics, Markets, and America's Schools* by John E. Chubb and Terry M. Moe. In a recent article ("Hobson's Choice," *The New Republic*, July 15 & 22, 1991), Abigail Thernstrom attacks Chubb and Moe's contention that market-driven choice will lead to school improvement. She argues that choice and its implementation device, vouchers, "threaten to further Balkanize American education and thus American culture."

In the selections that follow, Chubb and Moe present the basic assumptions that undergird their analysis of the ills of the public schools and offer a set of recommendations to rejuvenate the process of education in the United States. Frances C. Fowler offers a point-by-point critique of the suggestions made by Chubb and Moe and an incisive interpretation of their ideological bias.

YES

John E. Chubb and
Terry M. Moe

AMERICA'S PUBLIC SCHOOLS:
CHOICE *IS* A PANACEA

For America's public schools, the last decade has been the worst of times and the best of times. Never before have the public schools been subjected to such savage criticism for failing to meet the nation's educational needs—yet never before have governments been so aggressively dedicated to studying the schools' problems and finding the resources for solving them.

The signs of poor performance were there for all to see during the 1970s. Test scores headed downward year after year. Large numbers of teenagers continued to drop out of school. Drugs and violence poisoned the learning environment. In math and science, two areas crucial to the nation's success in the world economy, American students fell far behind their counterparts in virtually every other industrialized country. Something was clearly wrong.

During the 1980s a growing sense of crisis fueled a powerful movement for educational change, and the nation's political institutions responded with aggressive reforms. State after state increased spending on schools, imposed tougher requirements, introduced more rigorous testing, and strengthened teacher certification and training. And, as the decade came to an end, creative experiments of various forms—from school-based management to magnet schools—were being launched around the nation.

We think these reforms are destined to fail. They simply do not get to the root of the problem. The fundamental causes of poor academic performance are not to be found in the schools, but rather in the institutions by which the schools have traditionally been governed. Reformers fail by automatically relying on these institutions to solve the problem—when the institutions are the problem.

The key to better schools, therefore, is institutional reform. What we propose is a new system of public education that eliminates most political and bureaucratic control over the schools and relies instead on indirect control through markets and parental choice. These new institutions natu-

From John E. Chubb and Terry M. Moe, "America's Public Schools: Choice *Is* a Panacea," *The Brookings Review* (Summer 1990). Copyright © 1990 by The Brookings Institution. Reprinted by permission.

rally function to promote and nurture the kinds of effective schools that reformers have wanted all along.

SCHOOLS AND INSTITUTIONS

Three basic questions lie at the heart of our analysis. What is the relationship between school organization and student achievement? What are the conditions that promote or inhibit desirable forms of organization? And how are these conditions affected by their institutional settings?

Our perspective on school organization and student achievement is in agreement with the most basic claims and findings of the "effective schools" literature, which served as the analytical base of the education reform movement throughout the 1980s. We believe, as most others do, that how much students learn is not determined simply by their aptitude or family background—although, as we show, these are certainly influential—but also by how effectively schools are organized. By our estimates, the typical high school student tends to learn considerably more, comparable to at least an extra year's worth of study, when he or she attends a high school that is effectively organized rather than one that is not.

Generally speaking, effective schools— be they public or private—have the kinds of organizational characteristics that the mainstream literature would lead one to expect: strong leadership, clear and ambitious goals, strong academic programs, teacher professionalism, shared influence, and staff harmony, among other things. These are best understood as integral parts of a coherent syndrome of organization. When this syndrome is viewed as a functioning whole, moreover, it seems to capture the essential features of what people normally mean

by a team—principals and teachers working together, cooperatively and informally, in pursuit of a common mission.

How do these kinds of schools develop and take root? Here again, our own perspective dovetails with a central theme of educational analysis and criticism: the dysfunctions of bureaucracy, the value of autonomy, and the inherent tension between the two in American public education. Bureaucracy vitiates the most basic requirements of effective organization. It imposes goals, structures, and requirements that tell principals and teachers what to do and how to do it—denying them not only the discretion they need to exercise their expertise and professional judgment but also the flexibility they need to develop and operate as teams. The key to effective education rests with unleashing the productive potential already present in the schools and their personnel. It rests with granting them the autonomy to do what they do best. As our study of American high schools documents, the freer schools are from external control the more likely they are to have effective organizations.

Only at this late stage of the game do we begin to part company with the mainstream. While most observers can agree that the public schools have become too bureaucratic and would benefit from substantial grants of autonomy, it is also the standard view that this transformation can be achieved within the prevailing framework of democratic control. The implicit assumption is that, although political institutions have acted in the past to bureaucratize, they can now be counted upon to reverse course, grant the schools autonomy, and support and nurture this new population of autonomous schools. Such an assumption, however, is not based on a systematic understanding of how these institutions operate and what their consequences are for schools.

POLITICAL INSTITUTIONS

Democratic governance of the schools is built around the imposition of higher-order values through public authority. As long as that authority exists and is available for use, public officials will come under intense pressure from social groups of all political stripes to use it. And when they do use it, they cannot blithely assume that their favored policies will be faithfully implemented by the heterogeneous population of principals and teachers below—whose own values and professional views may be quite different from those being imposed. Public officials have little choice but to rely on formal rules and regulations that tell these people what to do and hold them accountable for doing it.

These pressures for bureaucracy are so substantial in themselves that real school autonomy has little chance to take root throughout the system. But they are not the only pressures for bureaucracy. They are compounded by the political uncertainty inherent in all democratic politics: those who exercise public authority know that other actors with different interests may gain authority in the future and subvert the policies they worked so hard to put in place. This knowledge gives them additional incentive to embed their policies in protective bureaucratic arrangements—arrangements that reduce the discretion of schools and formally insulate them from the dangers of politics.

These pressures, arising from the basic properties of democratic control, are compounded yet again by another special feature of the public sector. Its insti-

tutions provide a regulated, politically sensitive setting conducive to the power of unions, and unions protect the interests of their members through formal constraints on the governance and operation of schools—constraints that strike directly at the schools' capacity to build well-functioning teams based on informal cooperation.

The major participants in democratic governance—including the unions—complain that the schools are too bureaucratic. And they mean what they say. But they are the ones who bureaucratized the schools in the past, and they will continue to do so, even as they tout the great advantages of autonomy and professionalism. The incentives to bureaucratize the schools are built into the system.

MARKET INSTITUTIONS

This kind of behavior is not something that Americans simply have to accept, like death and taxes. People who make decisions about education would behave differently if their institutions were different. The most relevant and telling comparison is to markets, since it is through democratic control and markets that American society makes most of its choices on matters of public importance, including education. Public schools are subject to direct control through politics. But not all schools are controlled in this way. Private schools—representing about a fourth of all schools—are subject to indirect control through markets.

What difference does it make? Our analysis suggests that the difference is considerable and that it arises from the most fundamental properties that distinguish the two systems. A market system is not built to enable the imposition of higher-order values on the schools, nor is it driven by a democratic struggle to exercise public authority. Instead, the authority to make educational choices is radically decentralized to those most immediately involved. Schools compete for the support of parents and students, and parents and students are free to choose among schools. The system is built on decentralization, competition, and choice.

Although schools operating under a market system are free to organize any way they want, bureaucratization tends to be an unattractive way to go. Part of the reason is that virtually everything about good education—from the knowledge and talents necessary to produce it, to what it looks like when it is produced—defies formal measurement through the standardized categories of bureaucracy.

The more basic point, however, is that bureaucratic control and its clumsy efforts to measure the unmeasurable are simply *unnecessary* for schools whose primary concern is to please their clients. To do this, they need to perform as effectively as possible, which leads them, given the bottom-heavy technology of education, to favor decentralized forms of organization that take full advantage of strong leadership, teacher professionalism, discretionary judgment, informal cooperation, and teams. They also need to ensure that they provide the kinds of services parents and students want and that they have the capacity to cater and adjust to their clients' specialized needs and interests, which this same syndrome of effective organization allows them to do exceedingly well.

Schools that operate in an environment of competition and choice thus have strong incentives to move toward the kinds of "effective-school" organizations that academics and reformers would

like to impose on the public schools. Of course, not all schools in the market will respond equally well to these incentives. But those that falter will find it more difficult to attract support, and they will tend to be weeded out in favor of schools that are better organized. This process of natural selection complements the incentives of the marketplace in propelling and supporting a population of autonomous, effectively organized schools. . . .

INSTITUTIONAL CONSEQUENCES

No institutional system can be expected to work perfectly under real-world conditions. Just as democratic institutions cannot offer perfect representation or perfect implementation of public policy, so markets cannot offer perfect competition or perfect choice. But these imperfections, which are invariably the favorite targets of each system's critics, tend to divert attention from what is most crucial to an understanding of schools: as institutional systems, democratic control and market control are strikingly different in their fundamental properties. As a result, each system structures individual and social choices about education very differently, and each has very different consequences for the organization and performance of schools. Each system puts its own indelible stamp on the schools that emerge and operate within it.

What the analysis in our book suggests, in the most practical terms, is that American society offers two basic paths to the emergence of effective schools. The first is through markets, which scarcely operate in the public sector, but which act on private schools to discourage bureaucracy and promote desirable forms of organization through the natural dynamics of competition and choice.

The second path is through "special circumstances,"—homogeneous environments free of problems—which, in minimizing the three types of political pressures just discussed, prompt democratic governing institutions to impose less bureaucracy than they otherwise would. Private schools therefore tend to be effectively organized because of the way their system naturally works. When public schools happen to be effectively organized, it is in spite of their system—they are the lucky ones with peculiarly nice environments.

As we show in our book, the power of these institutional forces is graphically reflected in our sample of American high schools. Having cast our net widely to allow for a full range of noninstitutional factors that might reasonably be suspected of influencing school autonomy, we found that virtually all of them fall by the wayside. The extent to which a school is granted the autonomy it needs to develop a more effective organization is overwhelmingly determined by its sectoral location and the niceness of its institutional environment.

Viewed as a whole, then, our effort to take institutions into account builds systematically on mainstream ideas and findings but, in the end, puts a very different slant on things. We agree that effective organization is a major determinant of student achievement. We also agree that schools perform better the more autonomous they are and the less encumbered they are by bureaucracy. But we do not agree that this knowledge about the proximate causes of effective performance can be used to engineer better schools through democratic control. Reformers are right about where they want to go, but their institutions cannot get them there.

The way to get schools with effective organizations is not to insist that democratic institutions should do what they are incapable of doing. Nor is it to assume that the better public schools, the lucky ones with the nice environments, can serve as organizational models for the rest. Their luck is not transferable. The way to get effective schools is to recognize that the problem of ineffective performance is really a deep-seated institutional problem that arises from the most fundamental properties of democratic control.

The most sensible approach to genuine education reform is therefore to move toward a true institutional solution—a different set of institutional arrangements that actively promotes and nurtures the kinds of schools people want. The market alternative then becomes particularly attractive, for it provides a setting in which these organizations take root and flourish. That is where "choice" comes in.

EDUCATIONAL CHOICE

It is fashionable these days to say that choice is "not a panacea." Taken literally, that is obviously true. There are no panaceas in social policy. But the message this aphorism really means to get across is that choice is just one of many reforms with something to contribute. School-based management is another. So are teacher empowerment and professionalism, better training programs, stricter accountability, and bigger budgets. These and other types of reforms all bolster school effectiveness in their own distinctive ways—so the reasoning goes—and the best, most aggressive, most comprehensive approach to transforming the public school system is therefore one that wisely combines them into a multifaceted reformist package.

Without being too literal about it, we think reformers would do well to entertain the notion that choice *is* a panacea. Of all the sundry education reforms that attract attention, only choice has the capacity to address the basic institutional problem plaguing America's schools. The other reforms are all system-preserving. The schools remain subordinates in the structure of public authority—and they remain bureaucratic.

In principle, choice offers a clear, sharp break from the institutional past. In practice, however, it has been forced into the same mold with all the other reforms. It has been embraced half-heartedly and in bits and pieces—for example, through magnet schools and limited open enrollment plans. It has served as a means of granting parents and students a few additional options or of giving schools modest incentives to compete. These are popular moves that can be accomplished without changing the existing system in any fundamental way. But by treating choice like other system-preserving reforms that presumably make democratic control work better, reformers completely miss what choice is all about.

Choice is not like the other reforms and should not be combined with them. Choice is a self-contained reform with its own rationale and justification. It has the capacity *all by itself* to bring about the kind of transformation that reformers have been seeking to engineer for years in myriad other ways. Indeed, if choice is to work to greatest advantage, it must be adopted *without* these other reforms, since they are predicated on democratic control and are implemented by bureaucratic means. The whole point of a thoroughgoing system of choice is to free the schools from these disabling constraints by sweeping away the old institutions and replacing them with new ones. Taken seriously, choice is not a system-preserving reform. It is a revolutionary reform that introduces a new system of public education.

A PROPOSAL FOR REAL REFORM

The following outline describes a choice system that we think is equipped to do the job. Offering our own proposal allows us to illustrate in some detail what a full-blown choice system might look like, as well as to note some of the policy decisions that must be made in building one. More important, it allows us to suggest what our institutional theory of schools actually entails for educational reform.

Our guiding principle in the design of a choice system is this: public authority must be put to use in creating a system that is almost entirely beyond the reach of public authority. Because states have primary responsibility for American public education, we think the best way to achieve significant, enduring reform is for states to take the initiative in withdrawing authority from existing institutions and vesting it directly in the schools, parents, and students. This restructuring cannot be construed as an exercise in delegation. As long as authority remains "available" at higher levels within state government, it will eventually be used to control the schools. As far as possible, all higher-level authority must be eliminated.

What we propose, more specifically, is that state leaders create a new system of public education with the following properties.

The Supply of Schools

The state will be responsible for setting criteria that define what constitutes a "public school" under the new system. These criteria should be minimal, roughly corresponding to the criteria many states now use in accrediting private schools—graduation requirements, health and safety requirements, and teacher certification requirements. Any educational group or organization that applies to the state and meets these minimal criteria must then be chartered as a public school and granted the right to accept students and receive public money.

Existing private schools will be among those eligible to participate. Their participation should be encouraged, because they constitute a supply of already effective schools. Our own preference would be to include religious schools too, as long as their sectarian functions can be kept clearly separate from their educational functions. Private schools that do participate will thereby become public schools, as such schools are defined under the new choice system.

School districts can continue running their present schools, assuming those schools meet state criteria. But districts will have authority over only their own schools and not over any of the others that may be chartered by the state.

Funding

The state will set up a Choice Office in each district, which, among other things, will maintain a record of all school-age children and the level of funding—the "scholarship" amounts—associated with each child. This office will directly compensate schools based on the specific children they enroll. Public money will flow from funding sources (federal, state, and district governments) to the Choice Office and then to schools. At no point will it go to parents or students.

The state must pay to support its own Choice Office in each district. Districts may retain as much of their current governing apparatus as they wish—superintendents, school boards, central offices, and all their staff. But they have to pay for them entirely out of the revenue they derive from the scholarships of those children who voluntarily choose to attend district-run schools. Aside from the governance of these schools, which no one need attend, districts will be little more than taxing jurisdictions that allow citizens to make a collective determination about how large their children's scholarships will be.

As it does now, the state will have the right to specify how much, or by what formula, each district must contribute for each child. Our preference is for an equalization approach that requires wealthier districts to contribute more per child than poor districts do and that guarantees an adequate financial foundation to students in all districts. The state's contribution can then be calibrated to bring total spending per child up to whatever dollar amount seems desirable; under an equalization scheme, that would mean a larger state contribution in poor districts than in wealthy ones.

While parents and students should be given as much flexibility as possible, we think it is unwise to allow them to supplement their scholarship amounts with personal funds. Such "add-ons" threaten to produce too many disparities and inequalities within the public system, and many citizens would regard them as unfair and burdensome.

Complete equalization, on the other hand, strikes us as too stifling and restrictive. A reasonable trade-off is to allow collective add-ons, much as the current system does. The citizens of each district can be given the freedom to decide whether they want to spend more per child than the state requires them to spend. They can then determine how important education is to them and how much they are willing to tax themselves for it. As a result, children from different districts may have different-sized scholarships.

Scholarships may also vary within any given district, and we strongly think that they should. Some students have very special educational needs—arising from economic deprivation, physical handicaps, language difficulties, emotional problems, and other disadvantages—that can be met effectively only through costly specialized programs. State and federal programs already appropriate public money to address these problems. Our suggestion is that these funds should take the form of add-ons to student scholarships. At-risk students would then be empowered with bigger scholarships than the others, making them attractive clients to all schools—and stimulating the emergence of new specialty schools.

Choice Among Schools

Each student will be free to attend any public school in the state, regardless of district, with the student's scholarship—consisting of federal, state, and local contributions—flowing to the school of choice. In practice most students will probably choose schools in reasonable proximity to their homes. But districts will have no claim on their own residents.

To the extent that tax revenues allow, every effort will be made to provide transportation for students who need it. This provision is important to help open up as many alternatives as possible to all students, especially the poor and those in rural areas.

To assist parents and students in choosing among schools, the state will provide a Parent Information Center within its local Choice Office. This center will collect comprehensive information on each school in the district, and its parent liaisons will meet personally with parents in helping them judge which schools best meet their children's needs. The emphasis here will be on personal contact and involvement. Parents will be required to visit the center at least once, and encouraged to do so often. Meetings will be arranged at all schools so that parents can see firsthand what their choices are.

The Parent Information Center will handle the applications process in a simple fashion. Once parents and students decide which schools they prefer, they will fill out applications to each, with parent liaisons available to give advice and assistance and to fill out the applications themselves (if necessary). All applications will be submitted to the Center, which in turn will send them out to the schools.

Schools will make their own admissions decisions, subject only to nondiscrimination requirements. This step is absolutely crucial. Schools must be able to define their own missions and build their own programs in their own ways, and they cannot do that if their student population is thrust on them by outsiders.

Schools must be free to admit as many or as few students as they want, based on whatever criteria they think relevant—intelligence, interest, motivation, special needs—and they must be free to exercise their own, informal judgments about individual applicants. Schools will set their own "tuitions." They may choose to do so explicitly, say, by publicly announcing the minimum scholarship they are willing to accept. They may also do it implicitly by allowing anyone to apply for admission and simply making selections, knowing in advance what each applicant's scholarship amount is. In either case, schools are free to admit students with different-sized scholarships, and they are free to keep the entire scholarship that accompanies each student they have admitted. That gives all schools incentives to attract students with special needs, since these children will have the largest scholarships. It also gives schools incentives to attract students from districts with high base-level scholarships. But no school need restrict itself to students with special needs, nor to students from a single district.

The application process must take place within a framework that guarantees each student a school, as well as a fair shot at getting into the school he or she most wants. That framework, however, should impose only the most minimal restrictions on the schools.

We suggest something like the following. The Parent Information Center will be responsible for seeing that parents and students are informed, that they have visited the schools that interest them, and that all applications are submitted by a given date. Schools will then be required to make their admissions decisions within a set time, and students who are accepted into more than one school will be required to select one as their final choice. Students who are not accepted anywhere, as well as schools that have yet to attract as many students as they want, will participate in a second round of applications, which will work the same way.

After this second round, some students may remain without schools. At this point, parent liaisons will take informal action to try to match up these students with appropriate schools. If any students still remain unassigned, a special safety-net procedure—a lottery, for example—will be invoked to ensure that each is assigned to a specific school.

As long as they are not "arbitrary and capricious," schools must also be free to expel students or deny them readmission when, based on their own experience and standards, they believe the situation warrants it. This authority is essential if schools are to define and control their own organizations, and it gives students a strong incentive to live up to their side of the educational "contract."

Governance and Organization

Each school must be granted sole authority to determine its own governing structure. A school may be run entirely by teachers or even a union. It may vest all power in a principal. It may be built around committees that guarantee representation to the principal, teachers, parents, students, and members of the community. Or it may do something completely different.

The state must refrain from imposing *any* structures or requirements that specify how authority is to be exercised within individual schools. This includes the district-run schools: the state must not impose any governing apparatus on them either. These schools, however, are subordinate units within district government—they are already embedded in a larger organization—and it is the district authorities, not the schools, that have the legal right to determine how they will be governed.

More generally, the state will do nothing to tell the schools how they must be internally organized to do their work. The state will not set requirements for career ladders, advisory committees, textbook selection, in-service training, preparation time, homework, or anything else. Each school will be organized and operated as it sees fit.

Statewide tenure laws will be eliminated, allowing each school to decide for itself whether or not to adopt a tenure policy and what the specifics of that policy will be. This change is essential if schools are to have the flexibility they need to build well-functioning teams. Some schools may not offer tenure at all, relying on pay and working conditions to attract the kinds of teachers they want, while others may offer tenure as a supplementary means of compensating and retaining their best teachers.

Teachers, meantime, may demand tenure in their negotiations (individual or collective) with schools. And, as in private colleges and universities, the best teachers are well positioned to get it, since their services will be valued by any number of other schools. School districts may continue to offer districtwide tenure, along with transfer rights, seniority preference, and whatever other personnel policies they have offered in the past. But these policies apply only to district-run schools and the teachers who work in them.

Teachers will continue to have a right to join unions and engage in collective bargaining, but the legally prescribed bargaining unit will be the individual school or, as in the case of the district government, the larger organization that runs the school. If teachers in a given school want to join a union or, having done so, want to exact financial or struc-

tural concessions, that is up to them. But they cannot commit teachers in other schools, unless they are in other district-run schools, to the same things, and they must suffer the consequences if their victories put them at a competitive disadvantage in supplying quality education.

The state will continue to certify teachers, but requirements will be minimal, corresponding to those that many states have historically applied to private schools. In our view, individuals should be certified to teach if they have a bachelor's degree and if their personal history reveals no obvious problems. Whether they are truly good teachers will be determined in practice, as schools decide whom to hire, observe their own teachers in action over an extended period of time, and make decisions regarding merit, promotion, and dismissal.

The schools may, as a matter of strategy, choose to pay attention to certain formal indicators of past or future performance, among them: a master's degree, completion of a voluntary teacher certification program at an education school, or voluntary certification by a national board. Some schools may choose to require one or more of these, or perhaps to reward them in various ways. But that is up to the schools, which will be able to look anywhere for good teachers in a now much larger and more dynamic market.

The state will hold the schools accountable for meeting certain procedural requirements. It will ensure that schools continue to meet the criteria set out in their charters, that they adhere to nondiscrimination laws in admissions and other matters, and that they collect and make available to the public, through the Parent Information Center, information on their mission, their staff and course offerings, standardized test scores (which we would make optional), parent and student satisfaction, staff opinions, and anything else that would promote informed choice among parents and students.

The state will not hold the schools accountable for student achievement or other dimensions that call for assessments of the quality of school performance. When it comes to performance, schools will be held accountable from below, by parents and students who directly experience their services and are free to choose. The state will play a crucial supporting role here in monitoring the full and honest disclosure of information by the schools—but it will be only a supporting role.

CHOICE AS A PUBLIC SYSTEM

This proposal calls for fundamental changes in the structure of American public education. Stereotypes aside, however, these changes have nothing to do with "privatizing" the nation's schools. The choice system we outline would be a truly public system—and a democratic one.

We are proposing that the state put its democratic authority to use in creating a new institutional framework. The design and legitimation of this framework would be a democratic act of the most basic sort. It would be a social decision, made through the usual processes of democratic governance, by which the people and their representatives specify the structure of a new system of public education.

This framework, as we set it out, is quite flexible and admits of substantial variation on important issues, all of them matters of public policy to be decided by representative government. Public officials and their constituents would be free to take their own approaches to taxation, equalization, treatment of religious schools, additional funding for disadvantaged students, parent add-ons, and other controversial issues of public concern, thus designing choice systems to reflect the unique conditions, preferences, and political forces of their own states.

Once this structural framework is democratically determined, moreover, governments would continue to play important roles within it. State officials and agencies would remain pivotal to the success of public education and to its ongoing operation. They would provide funding, approve applications for new schools, orchestrate and oversee the choice process, elicit full information about schools, provide transportation to students, monitor schools for adherence to the law, and (if they want) design and administer tests of student performance. School districts, meantime, would continue as local taxing jurisdictions, and they would have the option of continuing to operate their own system of schools.

The crucial difference is that direct democratic control of the schools—the very *capacity* for control, not simply its exercise—would essentially be eliminated. Most of those who previously held authority over the schools would have their authority permanently withdrawn, and that authority would be vested in schools, parents, and students. Schools would be legally autonomous: free to govern themselves as they want, specify their own goals and programs and methods, design their own organizations, select their own student bodies, and make their own personnel decisions. Parents and students would be legally empowered to choose among alternative schools, aided by institutions designed to promote active involvement, well-informed decisions, and fair treatment.

DEMOCRACY AND EDUCATIONAL PROGRESS

We do not expect everyone to accept the argument we have made here. In fact, we expect most of those who speak with authority on educational matters, leaders and academics within the educational community, to reject it. But we will regard our effort as a success if it directs attention to America's institutions of democratic control and provokes serious debate about their consequences for the nation's public schools. Whether or not our own conclusions are right, the fact is that these issues are truly basic to an understanding of schools, and they have so far played no part in the national debate. If educational reform is to have any chance at all of succeeding, that has to change.

In the meantime, we can only believe that the current "revolution" in public education will prove a disappointment. It might have succeeded had it actually been a revolution, but it was not and was never intended to be, despite the lofty rhetoric. Revolutions replace old institutions with new ones. The 1980s reform movement never seriously thought about the old institutions and certainly never considered them part of the problem. They were, as they had always been, part of the solution—and, for that matter, part of the definition of what democracy and public education are all about.

This identification has never been valid. Nothing in the concept of democracy requires that schools be subject to direct control by school boards, superintendents, central offices, departments of education, and other arms of government

Nor does anything in the concept of public education require that schools be governed in this way. There are many paths to democracy and public education. The path America has been trodding for the past half-century is exacting a heavy price—one the nation and its children can ill afford to bear, and need not. It is time, we think, to get to the root of the problem.

NO

THE SHOCKING IDEOLOGICAL
INTEGRITY OF CHUBB AND MOE

In the fall of 1990, John Chubb and Terry Moe's book—still called by what was apparently its pre-publication title of *What Price Democracy? Politics, Markets, and America's Schools*—was debated at a national education conference. The debate itself was tame. A carefully neutral moderator introduced the speakers and provided smooth transitions between them. The first speaker, an education professor at a prestigious private university, praised the book and announced his agreement with its policy proposals. The second, an education professor at a less prestigious private university, called it the most important book on education in a decade. He regretted only that the authors "bashed democracy over the head." The third was less positive: he criticized Chubb and Moe's statistics and found them wanting. Only the fourth suggested that both Chubb and Moe's premises and their conclusions were questionable.

After the debate, the floor was opened to audience participation. The room became hot, both physically and emotionally. One man blurted that he considered the book "a conclusion in search of an analysis." Several others raised questions about desegregation, education of the handicapped, and the selectivity of private schools. Yet the anger in the room remained largely inchoate and inarticulate. Afterward, muttered arguing could be heard in the halls and elevators.

At the end of this review I will seek to explain the reactions of both the panel and the audience. But first I will have to explain what is really going on in Chubb and Moe's book. In doing so, I will not analyze their statistics; others have done that. Nor will I discuss how the implementation of their proposal would affect equity in American education although that is important. Rather, I will focus on their ideology. I will describe how it shapes and misshapes their book I will also discuss its meaning for American education First, however, I will summarize their major argument.

From Frances C. Fowler, "The Shocking Ideological Integrity of Chubb and Moe," *Journal of Education*, vol. 173, no. 3 (Spring 1991). Copyright © 1991 by the Trustees of Boston University. Reprinted by permission.

THE ARGUMENT OF THE BOOK

Chubb and Moe begin *Politics, Markets, and America's Schools* with a discussion of the current education reform movement. Uncritically accepting the premise that it is the poor quality of public education which has caused the United States to become uncompetitive in the international economy, they announce that all reforms proposed to date will fail because they do not attack the root problem. The *real* problem, as they see it, is the institutions which govern public education. In their words:

> Our analysis shows that the system's familiar arrangements for direct democratic control do indeed impose a distinctive structure on the educational choices of all the various participants—and that this structure tends to promote organizational characteristics that are ill-suited to the effective performance of American public schools. (p. 21)

In Chapter 2 Chubb and Moe elaborate on their theory. As public institutions, public schools are naturally political, bureaucratic, coercive, hierarchical, and filled with conflict. Pulled in many directions by interest groups and labor unions, they cannot possibly educate children well. In contrast, private schools are subject to market forces which encourage responsiveness to their "clientele." Their decentralized autonomy, "social homogeneity," and strong principals permit them to organize effectively. Thus, they successfully educate their students.

The next three chapters describe Chubb and Moe's research. Using data from the High School and Beyond survey of the early 1980s and their own Administrator and Teacher Survey, they ran a series of regression analyses and other statistical tests. Their findings are displayed in 49 tables. On the strength of this analysis, they conclude that private schools perform better than public ones and that their superiority is related to their organizational characteristics.

The last chapter contains Chubb and Moe's policy proposal. They advocate abolishing the democratic governance of public schools. In its place a choice program should be established. Although the authors do not use the word "voucher," in essence they propose an unregulated voucher plan. All schools—public and private—which met "minimal criteria" would participate. Parents would receive "scholarships" for their children. These could be used at any school willing to accept their children as students. Schools would be free to develop their own admissions criteria (subject to nondiscrimination rules), establish their own tuition fees, and expel students. Meanwhile, tenure laws would be repealed, and each school would be free to devise its own system of internal governance. Teacher certification requirements would be minimal, and the state would not hold schools accountable for student achievement or any other performance measures. Chubb and Moe are not optimistic that their proposal will be adopted, but they believe that their book will be successful if it "directs attention to America's institutions of democratic control" (p. 228).

THE IDEOLOGICAL CHARACTER OF THE BOOK

In form, *Politics, Markets, and America's Schools* appears to be a scholarly work which has been popularized to appeal to a general, but educated, audience. In the foreword, the president of the Brookings

Institution writes that it "is the culmination of a large study" (p. x) and lists five funding agencies. The book contains 49 statistical tables, and its four appendices provide detailed information about technical aspects of the study's methodology. The 254 footnotes cite most of the major relevant works in the areas of politics of education, effective schools, and political science.

Like most scholarly works this book includes a theoretical framework. The authors never identify their theory by name. Among political scientists, however, Moe is considered a "peripheral member of the rational choice school" (Almond, 1990, p. 127). Rational choice theorists, assuming that political institutions function like markets and that individuals seek to maximize their material interests, use economic models to analyze politics. They distrust political processes and consider markets more efficient (Almond, 1990).

These beliefs are evident in Chubb and Moe's development of their theory. They argue that democratic control of education leads to bureaucracy, hierarchy, and inefficiency. In contrast, markets encourage autonomy, discretion, diversity, and responsiveness. They are therefore more efficient than politically controlled systems. Chubb and Moe elaborate upon their theory by adding to it some elements of Social Darwinism. Market systems perform a type of "natural selection," so that only the best organizations "survive," (p. 33). They also "promote desirable forms of organization through the natural dynamics of competition and choice" (p. 190). Of course, this theory closely resembles what Bruce Cooper (1988) labels neoconservative ideology.

Genuine scholars use theoretical frameworks to give coherence and meaning to their inquiry, but they do not allow their theories to become intellectual blinders. Rather, they test them by bringing them into contact with real phenomena. When the evidence disconfirms their theories, they modify or abandon them. In *Politics, Markets, and America's Schools*, however, Chubb and Moe repeatedly evade evidence which might raise doubts about the validity of their theory. Numerous examples could be cited, but this discussion will be limited to three: their handling of the nature of private education, their handling of international comparisons, and their handling of the social context of schools.

The authors never define "public" or "private" (the lack of careful definitions is a pervasive problem in the book), but their theory leads them to assume that public and private schools are very different. Because public institutions seek to "impose" "higher-order values" (p. 62) upon society, they inevitably become bureaucratic and hierarchical. In contrast, private institutions are free "to find their niche—a specialized segment of the market to which they can appeal" (p. 55). Since much of the book extols private schools and their organizational strengths, one would expect to find some details about private education in it. At the very least, one would expect some discussion of its demographic characteristics. Such information is lacking. The most detailed descriptions are provided in two brief passages:

> About half of all private schools are Catholic, and the rest are a diverse lot of religious schools, college preparatory schools, military academies, schools for children with special problems or talents, and many other types of schools as well. (p. 27)

The authority to control each private school is vested in the school's owner—which may be an individual, a partnership, a church, a corporation, a nonprofit agency, or some other form of organization. (p. 32)

These descriptions suggest considerable diversity among American private schools, an idea consistent with the demands of the authors' theory. These descriptions are, however, inaccurate. When Chubb and Moe's data were collected in the early 1980s, American private education was dominated by religious organizations. Fully 70% of private school students attended Catholic schools; another 22.2% attended Lutheran, Jewish, and Evangelical schools. Other types of schools enrolled a mere 7.8% of the private school population (Erickson, 1985).

American private education is almost exclusively a religious enterprise. One question which Chubb and Moe should therefore have addressed is this one: In what sense are churches "private" institutions? Like "public" institutions, churches hold "higher-order values" which they often seek to impose upon others. Like "public" institutions, their organization is often bureaucratic and hierarchical. Is it possible that the terms "public" and "private" are not as sharply dichotomous as Chubb and Moe believe, but rather points on a continuum? If so, where do churches fall on that continuum? It is arguable that, in comparing public and private schools, the authors actually compared similar organizations. It is also arguable that the slightly higher achievement scores of private school students result, not from the natural dynamics of market forces, but from the strong religious commitment of private school teachers, administrators, parents, and students. Chubb and Moe do not

address these issues. Their theory blinds them to such possibilities—and also to the real nature of American private education.

In their handling of international comparisons, Chubb and Moe also avoid dealing with facts which might disconfirm their theory. Like many who are concerned about the quality of American public education, they refer to the superior educational performance of such countries as Japan, Germany, and France. They also mention the current inability of the United States to compete effectively in international markets. Such comments seem strangely out of place in this book, for Japan, Germany, and France operate large public school systems which are democratically controlled. Not until page 66 do the authors hint that this fact might pose a problem for their argument. There a number discreetly refers readers to a long footnote, printed on page 289, which reads in part:

In principle, one should be able to learn . . . by taking advantage of institutional variation across nations—by comparing, for instance, the American system of public education with the educational systems of Japan or France. This is not our purpose here . . . an enormous amount of new research would have to be carried out. . . . American public bureaucracies tend to be far more constraining and formally complex than bureaucracies in parliamentary systems. . . . Nations are different—and appearances can be deceiving.

Of course, Chubb and Moe cannot have it both ways. If nations are too different to permit comparisons, then they should have refrained from making cross-national comparisons of student achievement and economic performance, in the first place. Once again, they have evaded evidence which would disconfirm their theory that democratically controlled institutions are inherently inefficient. I cannot speak to the Japanese situation, but I have spent considerable time in both French and German schools. A close examination of public education in those countries would reveal organizational structures which combine centralized bureaucracy with participatory democracy at the building level. It would also reveal powerful teachers unions which "co-manage" the school system with administrators. Finally, it would reveal a general belief that public education is more prestigious than private education.

These findings would not fit well within Chubb and Moe's theoretical framework. Instead, they would raise questions such as these: Is the problem in American schools too little democracy rather than too much? Do French and German teachers work better than their American colleagues because their strong unions make them feel empowered and secure? Does the American tendency to denigrate everything public make it difficult for our public schools to command the respect which they need in order to accomplish their mission? Such questions move far beyond the narrow constraints of Chubb and Moe's theory. It is not surprising that they chose not to look at education in other countries.

The real nature of their theory becomes clearest at the end of their discussion of the social context of American public schools. In a 14-page analysis of the causes of student achievement, Chubb and Moe make some important admissions. They acknowledge the importance of family background and of family economic resources. They also admit that causality can be reciprocal—that although

school organization can affect student achievement, student characteristics may also cause certain types of school organizations to develop. Possibly they realized that they would lose credibility if they completely ignored these issues. Then, having made these concessions, they write in a revealing paragraph:

> We do believe we have a workable method of analysis. . . . Despite all we have said about the problem of reciprocal causality, we believe that the key influences on student achievement tend to run in one direction. We believe that school control affects school organization more than the other way around. . . . We also believe that this causal chain is firmly anchored at the front end by institutions. (p. 114; my italics)

No evidence is provided for these "beliefs." Nor is a logical argument offered in their support. Nothing could be clearer: Chubb and Moe's "theory" is actually a matter of belief. It functions in their book, not as a theory subject to confirmation or disconfirmation by evidence, but as an ideology. In short, their book is not a scholarly work. It is a sophisticated piece of propaganda written to support a policy proposal.

THE ANTIDEMOCRATIC CHARACTER OF THE BOOK

The most disturbing fact about *Politics, Markets, and America's Schools* is neither that it is ideological nor that it is propaganda. The most disturbing fact about it is that it is openly antidemocratic. In all fairness to Chubb and Moe, it must be said that they do not directly attack democracy itself. Rather, they carefully qualify their arguments in order to limit their attack to the democratic control of public education. However, anyone who accepts the premises underlying their attack on the democratic control of public schools can easily extend their argument to all public institutions.

Chubb and Moe's first premise is that the "direct democratic control" of American education causes it to be inefficient. Of course, a major inaccuracy lies at the heart of this premise—American public education is *not* governed by a system of "direct democratic control." Its governance system employs indirect, or representative, democratic structures such as school boards, superintendents, and state legislatures. Chubb and Moe never mention the possibility that more elements of truly *direct* democratic control might solve some of the problems of American schools. Presumably they believe that both direct and representative democratic control share the same weakness: because they impose "higher-order values" on schools they are inefficient.

Unfortunately, Chubb and Moe never identify these "higher-order values." However, a close reading of the book and a careful analysis of what is and is not said suggests that these "higher-order values" include the core democratic values of freedom, equality, and fraternity. For example, the authors advocate the repeal of teacher tenure. Historically, one reason for the passage of tenure laws was to ease political pressures on teachers to teach and live only in those ways which suited their school boards. Since Chubb and Moe never explain how the intellectual and personal freedom of teachers will be protected under their system, it is fair to conclude that such freedoms are probably included among their "higher-order values."

They seem somewhat more concerned about student equality than about teacher freedom; they express some concern about equal educational opportunity. Yet they qualify it with statements like: "Complete equalization . . . strikes us as too stifling and restrictive" (p. 220). They also fail to address the problem of unequal resources and how it might affect the ability of parents to choose schools for their children. Because of such qualifications and omissions, one wonders if such policies as desegregation and education of the handicapped fall within the scope of their "higher-order values." Certainly, they say very little about those issues.

The suspicion that their commitment to equality is weak is reinforced by their rejection of the idea that democratic fraternity means learning to live with people different from oneself. Instead, they argue that "social homogeneity" is important to schools' performance because it reduces conflict about goals (pp. 62–63). Again, "social homogeneity" is never clearly defined. Nonetheless, in the total context of the book, one is justified in thinking that it almost certainly includes homogeneity of social class and religious affiliation. It may also include homogeneity of race, ethnicity, and language. In any event, Chubb and Moe seem to understand fraternity as living among one's own kind rather than led to value cultural differences by encountering them during one's formative years.

Although Chubb and Moe never clearly define the "higher-order values" which public education "imposes," they are sure that those values have a negative impact upon the schools. To be precise, the imposition of these values causes undesirable organizational characteristics to develop. These include bureaucracy, unresponsiveness, and goal displacement. The result is inefficiency. They directly link these negative qualities to "democratic control." Nothing can convey the flavor of their critique as well as their own words:

> In this sense, democracy is essentially coercive. The winners get to use public authority to impose their policies on the losers. (p. 28)

> Democracy cannot remedy the mismatch between what parents and students want and what the public schools provide. Conflict and disharmony are built into the system. (p. 34)

> In sum, the politics of democratic control promotes the piece-by-piece construction of a peculiar set of organizational arrangements that are highly bureaucratic. (p. 44)

> The key to understanding why America's public schools are failing is to be found in a deeper understanding of how its traditional institutions of democratic control actually work. The nation is experiencing a crisis in public education not because these democratic institutions have functioned perversely or improperly or unwisely, but because they have functioned quite normally. Democratic control normally produces ineffective schools. This is how it works. (p. 227)

Chubb and Moe could hardly be clearer. The problem is not the way that Americans have understood democracy or the particular set of democratic institutions which Americans have developed. The problem is democracy itself. Democracy is political; it is difficult; it is also inefficient. Clearly, if democratic control "normally produces ineffective schools" (p. 227), one is justified in concluding that Chubb and Moe probably believe that it also produces ineffective cities, states, and nations. In short, democracy is just ineffective.

The second basic premise of the book is that market control systems can remedy most of the flaws in democratic institutions. Although the authors concede that market systems have imperfections, they do not discuss these flaws in depth. Instead, they propose changing the governance of American schools from a political control system to a market control system. The "guiding principle" of this reform would be that "public authority must be put to use in creating a system that is almost entirely beyond the reach of public authority" (p. 218). They recommend doing this by amending state constitutions, because "the legal foundation of the new system would then be very difficult to change or violate once put in place" (p. 309). Under their proposal, the authority to govern schools would devolve to the building level and autonomous schools would compete for students. This competition would supposedly promote effective school organizations and higher academic performance.

A key element in their proposal is the role of the school principal. Since a market system depends on the responsiveness of those who operate enterprises to their "clients," principals would have to be empowered to lead. Chubb and Moe believe that principals should be given "concentrated authority" (p. 52) so that they can shape their schools. In particular, the principal should be completely in control of personnel decisions in his (the feminine pronoun is never used) school. He should have the authority "to build a hand-picked team of 'right-thinking' teachers" (p. 52). Such a team could work smoothly together to attract "a specialized clientele" (p. 60). Teachers who ceased to be effective team players would be "eliminated" (p. 50).

In their last paragraph, Chubb and Moe write that "there are many paths to democracy" (p. 229). Given their casual attitude toward definitions, they might argue that their proposal is, in fact, democratic. It is simply another "path to democracy." But the broad outlines of their proposal suggest a different conclusion. Authority over education is to be removed from the public; the new system is to be made very difficult to change; managers exercising "concentrated authority" are to play a major role in it. Such systems are not unheard of in the history of governance structures. They are not, however, usually called "democratic." They have other names.

THE REACTIONS OF THE DEBATERS AND THEIR AUDIENCE

Returning to the debate of Chubb and Moe's book at the 1990 education conference, it is easy to understand why the members of the audience became angry. Almost all were university professors; almost all were Americans. They had come to the conference consciously expecting to hear reports of research which conformed to their conception of the nature of scholarship. Unconsciously, they had come expecting that all policy proposals would be expressed in traditional American political discourse. Neither expectation was fulfilled.

It is not quite so easy to understand why only one person—the last panelist—challenged Chubb and Moe's ideas. The others took easier ways out. They maintained neutrality; or they criticized the methodology of the study; or, at most, they raised obvious equity issues. Yet the inchoate anger in the room suggested that these responses were felt as inadequate even as they were offered. Why? I

would like to suggest that by revealing the real implications of Chubb and Moe's ideology the debate also revealed the contradiction that lies at the heart of traditional American political discourse. It was that revelation which left the audience emotional.

Robert Dahl, one of the grand old men of American political science, has argued that in the late 19th century an "ideological transfer" occurred in the United States (Dahl, 1977, p. 7). At that time the "agrarian order that . . . was extraordinarily congenial to democracy was . . . displaced by a new socioeconomic order of corporate capitalism that was much less compatible" (p. 7). Yet supporters of the new order continued to speak in the ideological terms of the order which had been displaced. The old democratic terminology of the early nineteenth century was simply applied to the new economic institutions. For example, arguments against government regulation of individuals were "transferred" to corporations. As a result, American political thinking and discourse contain inner contradictions.

Of course, the same inner contradictions occur in the politics of American education. Public schools are an inheritance from the early 19th century. Later education movements, such as the cult of efficiency, contained ideological elements which conflicted with the basic premises of public education (Callahan, 1962). Yet, for generations the sacred aura around public schools prevented people from thinking such ideological concepts through to their logical conclusions. The democratic ideas of Thomas Jefferson and others were simply juxtaposed with ideas drawn from Social Darwinism and Scientific Management. They sounded good together, and few people noticed that they contradicted each other. This contradictory political discourse was the discourse which those attending the education conference expected to hear.

But Chubb and Moe have ideological integrity. They elevate efficiency above all other values; they idealize market control systems; they believe that "nature" causes the dynamics of competition and selection in human societies. Moreover, they are willing to let "nature" have its way, unchallenged by "higher-order values" such as human concepts of social justice or political freedom. Of course, these ideas have nothing whatever to do with democracy—*but, unlike most Americans of the last century, Chubb and Moe follow them through to their logical conclusion.* They attack democracy. Given their ideological premises, this attack makes perfect sense.

Only one person in the audience that day was able to answer Chubb and Moe adequately—that is to say, at the level of theory. He was a critical theorist. Had Dahl been in the audience, he too could have responded adequately. So could anyone else who was well grounded in social or political theory. But most of the panel and the audience were unable to respond. Accustomed to the old, contradictory discourse, they were caught short. As Dahl says, it "distorts our understanding of ourselves and of our possibilities" (p. 1).

The panelist who called *Politics, Markets, and America's Schools* one of the most important books of the decade was, however, correct. This is an important book for three reasons. First, it clearly reveals the conflict between the historic democratic ideals of the United States and neo-conservative ideology. Second, it clearly reveals the central educational issue of the 1990s. That issue is not school choice,

or restructuring, or accountability, or even international competitiveness. It is whether the United States will continue to have a school system which is, in any meaningful sense, public. Finally, it reveals the level at which the debate over the future of American education must be enjoined. Chubb and Moe's ideology is consistent with their conclusions and policy recommendations. In *Politics, Markets, and America's Schools* they move beyond the contradiction identified by Dahl. It is time for other Americans to move beyond that contradiction as well. Chubb and Moe should be answered in clear, consistent, and theoretical terms by those American scholars who are not willing to discard democracy. It is time for more ideological integrity.

REFERENCES

Almond, G. A. (1990). *A discipline divided: Schools and sects in political science.* Newbury Park, CA: SAGE Publications.

Callahan, R. E. (1962). *Education and the cult of efficiency.* Chicago: University of Chicago Press.

Cooper, B. S. (1988). School reform in the 1980s: The New Right's legacy. *Educational Administration Quarterly, 24,* 282–298.

Dahl, R. A. (1977). On removing certain impediments to democracy in the United States. *Political Science Quarterly, 92,* 1–20.

Erickson, D. A. (1985). Choice and private schools: Dynamics of supply and demand. In D. C. Levy (Ed.), *Private education: Studies in choice and public policy* (pp. 82–109). New York: Oxford University Press.

POSTSCRIPT

Can "Choice" Lead the Way to Educational Reform?

Legislation designed to increase parental choice was debated a number of times in the past two years in the U.S. Congress. A typical Republican position was that the country desperately needs choices in education but that the powerful special interest groups (such as teachers' unions) are not interested in the feelings of the majority of the American people but are interested only in more money for pet projects. A typical Democratic stance was that vouchers provide encouragement and a publicly funded mechanism to abandon neighborhood public schools and leave them with less support.

Two factors weighed heavily in the legislative consideration of choice: the effect on equalization of opportunity and the implications for separation of religion and education. The first of these is treated by Stanley C. Trent in "School Choice for African-American Children Who Live in Poverty: A Commitment to Equity or More of the Same?" *Urban Education* (October 1992) and by Charles V. Willie in "Controlled Choice: An Alternative Desegregation Plan for Minorities Who Feel Betrayed," *Education and Urban Society* (February 1991). The second is discussed by Americans for Religious Liberty in "School Choice: Panacea or Scam?" *Voice of Reason* (Winter 1991); by David Bernstein in "Religion in School: A Role for Vouchers," *Current* (May 1992); by John E. Coons in " 'Choice' Plans Should Include Private Option," *Education Week* (January 17, 1990); and by Dennis L. Evans in "The Risks of Inclusive 'Choice' Plans," *Education Week* (February 14, 1990).

Some pungent editorial commentary on choice is provided by Virginia I. Postrel, "Bad Choice," *Reason* (July 1991); Alan Reynolds, "Al in Wonderland," *Reason* (June 1992); and Chris Pipho, "The Vouchers Are Coming!" *Phi Delta Kappan* (October 1991). Also see "Class Action," *Saturday Night* (September 1992), in which Barry Cooper discusses the problems that exist in the Canadian school system and argues for the implementation of a voucher system similar to the one currently being tested in parts of the United States.

Two works that cover the topic rather comprehensively are *Choice in Public Education* (1990) edited by Boyd H. Walberg and *School Choice: Issues and Answers* (1991) by Ruth Randall and Keith Geiger. Other journal articles include these: William Bainbridge and Steven Sundre, "School Choice: The Education Issue of the 1990s," *Children Today* (January/February 1991); John G. Boswell, "Improving Our Schools: Parental Choice Is Not Enough," *The World & I* (February 1990); Deborah Meier, "Choice Can *Save* Public Education," *The Nation* (March 4, 1991); and Lois D. Whealey, "Choice or Elitism?" *The American School Board Journal* (April 1991).

ISSUE 10

Will the "Edison Project" Prompt Major Reforms?

YES: Geoffrey Morris, from "Whittling at the Wall," *National Review* (September 14, 1992)

NO: Jonathan Kozol, from "Whittle and the Privateers," *The Nation* (September 21, 1992)

ISSUE SUMMARY

YES: Geoffrey Morris, executive editor of *National Review*, describes and lauds Chris Whittle's new plan for a nationwide network of private, for-profit, secondary schools.
NO: Social activist Jonathan Kozol sees the plan, called the Edison Project, as corporate exploitation and a threat to public schooling.

Using the call of "America 2000" to "reinvent" the schools of this country and public acceptance of the idea that "choice" may be extended to the private sector, entrepreneur Christopher Whittle has initiated plans for a coast-to-coast system of new private schools. Whittle, who has been dubbed "the Ross Perot of American Education," calls this effort the Edison Project (after the inventive genius of Thomas Alva Edison) and has hired former Yale University president Benno Schmidt as its central administrator.

Whittle's Channel One commercial-supported newscasts are being broadcast to some 9,000 schools serving an estimated 6.6 million students. It is his hope that the new Edison Project will have opened 200 profit-making private schools by the year 1996.

It is Whittle's opinion that most existing schools are stuck in the sixteenth century, out of touch with today's technology and life-styles. In an article by Mary Ellin Barrett (*USA Weekend,* August 23–25, 1991) he is quoted as saying, "All we take for granted about schools should be questioned, from class size to the fact that a teacher is required at all."

According to Whittle and Schmidt, the Edison Project is starting with questions, on the assumption that "a good institution never has The Answer." The curricular emphasis will be on "less" rather than "more," and communication technology will play a central role. Innovation will be the key feature: students serving as "pilots" rather than "passengers," teachers staying with the same students for longer periods of time, curricular focus on one subject for a whole day—or week—or month, and an emphasis on the forest (meaning) rather than the trees (subject matter facts). The successful innovations, Whittle says, will become models for the improvement of the public schools.

Detractors, however, do not share his optimism about eventual positive effects on public education and fear that his profit-oriented schools will not be accountable and will not have open admissions. They feel also that students may be mentally manipulated by materials produced by Whittle's communications company and its partner Time Warner.

An editorial in *The Nation* (June 15, 1992) entitled "Next—McSchool" claims that the Edison Project will be impossible without the federal government's funneling of money (through a tuition tax credit or voucher system) to parents who want their children to attend a Whittle school. Bush administration secretary of education Lamar Alexander was a strong supporter; Robert Riley, the new head of the Education Department under President Clinton, may be less enthusiastic. But the editorial predicts that the Clinton administration will "undoubtedly be technology-friendly, middle-class-based, and entrepreneurophilic." Arnold Fege of the national Parent Teachers Association is concerned about the growing corporate influence on the public schools, stating that "Business wants the curriculum to include a strong business agenda" (as quoted in John S. Friedman, "Big Business Goes to School," *The Nation*, February 17, 1992).

In the articles selected to illustrate thinking on this issue, Geoffrey Morris outlines the Whittle project in more detail and offers a positive appraisal of its potential impact. Jonathan Kozol, author of *Savage Inequalities*, puts forth a decidedly negative portrayal of the social and political ramifications of Whittle's enterprise and privatization in general.

YES

Geoffrey Morris

WHITTLING AT THE WALL

At first glance, Chris Whittle seems an unlikely entrant to the education business. He's a yuppie, an entrepreneurial overachiever. He doesn't blush at the prospect of making a lot of money. Education, on the other hand, is usually thought of as a labor of love.

But Whittle, like most Americans, realizes the nation's public schools aren't doing the job. Additional money that goes into them is inversely proportional to the success of their students. For Whittle, today's public schools are the equivalent of East Berlin: "If you want institutions to change, you've got to have a West Berlin that gives them a place to go." Whittle's plan: to open a nationwide franchise of 200 schools by 1996.

All that currently exists of Whittle's venture is a general philosophy, incorporated into its name, the Edison Project: "You can't make a light bulb out of a candle," says the 44-year-old Whittle. "The power sources are different." And, he likes to add, "light bulbs are cheaper." His venture is not about reform, he explains. It's a whole new way of educating America.

He is now spending some $60 million to get his idea into the blueprint stage. He has hired seven core thinkers: John Chubb of the Brookings Institution; Lee Eisenberg, former editor-in-chief of *Esquire* (which Whittle used to own); Chester Finn, who served under William Bennett at the Education Department; Nancy Hechinger, an imaginative video producer; Sylvia Peters, an inner-city Chicago principal who transformed a bureaucratic nightmare into a working school; Daniel Biederman, president of the Grand Central and 34th Street Partnerships in New York, which cleans public lands with private money; and Dominique Browning, former assistant managing editor at *Newsweek*. Clearly an assemblage that is far outside the education establishment.

Then there's Benno Schmidt, CEO and president of the venture, who resigned as president of Yale this spring, frustrated at an opposition faculty and student body, and discouraged at the growing bands of multiculturalists.

This brain trust meets fairly regularly, tossing around ideas, hoping a plan will eventually materialize. There's disagreement, but happy disagreement, says Chester Finn. The group is currently in free thought—no constraints, no limitations on their ideas. Finn hypothesizes that "we may throw the whole education process out the window." Teaching "may not be broken down into subjects, and the schools may not be split up into classrooms. . . . But we just don't know."

The schools may open for 12-hour days, with pupils and teachers coming in shifts. Summer is not necessarily vacation time. The schools may include children as young as a year old. *Time* and *Newsweek*, Whittle says, may be required reading. And it's almost certain that computers and video will play a major role. For instance, when challenged with the prospect that he'll have to have 100 to 1 student-to-teacher ratios in order to cut costs, Whittle says more like 10,000 to 1— or 100,000 to 1—by using electronically the "country's best lecturers." Another possibility is to have students clean toilets and hallways—you know, it builds discipline, instills pride . . . saves money. Not your standard Thomas Jefferson High School.

Benno Schmidt's main task is to raise $2 to $3 billion to get the schools built and running. Schmidt's strong suit as Yale president was his fund-raising ability: the endowment grew from $1.7 billion when he started in 1986 to $3 billion today. But it's one thing to raise $1 billion for one of the nation's most prestigious universities and quite another to do it for something that is just an idea of a man who has made his money not in education but in publishing magazines.

Whittle has already entered the education business, however—with Channel One, a 12-minute news program shown to students in participating schools. Much like MTV's news, Channel One deals with the day's burning issues—

such as how to stop environmental destruction of the world—and does so with slick charts and graphics. News stories are broken up with ads. That's where Whittle makes the money—about $100 million in ad revenue a year.

But parents complain they have a hard enough time keeping kids away from the TV and in front of the books *after* school. Now what will happen, when kids are in front of the tube *during* school? In certain school districts, protests are forcing administrators to pull the show. On top of that, a study of students who watched Channel One revealed recently that it had had little success in informing kids about current events. Whittle Communications doesn't dispute the study.

The Edison Project, however, is much more ambitious—and the people Whittle has brought in to run it are motivated to create an enduring system of education and not simply a money-making enterprise. The project is getting rave reviews. Hamilton Jordan has nothing but praise for the brain child, which is why he signed on to help with public relations (with a brief leave of absence to run the ill-fated Perot campaign).

"I'm in his corner," says Peter Flanigan, who spearheaded a project in New York to get individuals to sponsor poor inner-city youths at Catholic schools.

But Edison's most promising reviews are from the American Federation of Teachers and the National Education Association, both of which are severely critical. Their main complaint is that the idea of a school is not to make a profit. In addition, they say, Chris Whittle doesn't understand the problems of educating a diverse and multilingual student body. But of course their main worry is that Whittle will succeed in building a West Berlin.

One obvious question is: Why should a parent enroll his kids at Whittle Elementary and not (depending on his circumstances) Cardinal Hayes in Harlem or some posh prep school in New England? Inner-city parents who want to get their children out of the God-forsaken public schools and into a private school with a proven track record have a hard enough time scraping together the $2,500 tuition at Catholic schools, much less the $5,000 for Whittle. And those who can afford to pay Whittle's tuition can find the extra two grand for the prestigious private schools.

What Whittle likes to say is that "we are constantly thinking about how other people can replicate what we're doing. . . . We're not trying to create an elitist $7,000-a-student system that will draw away the more affluent students from public schools. Current public-school spending per student averages about $5,000. We want to come in at $4,995." Some 20 per cent of the students will be on scholarship, he hopes. "We want to provide a better education at a lower cost. We want to be copied."

Let's hope the brain trust at Whittle headquarters in Knoxville, Tennessee, has plans to copy other models in making its own. The group's own Sylvia Peters did wonders with a Chicago school, mostly through motivation and discipline. There are dozens of examples nationwide like hers. New York's Catholic high schools report a 95 per cent on-time graduation rate. And some 80 per cent go on to college. Meanwhile, the public schools send about 50 per cent on to college. And there's really no question as to what differentiates the two systems. New York's Catholic schools have about 35 administrators; resources go to books and teachers, not studies and chauffeurs.

The city public-school system, on the other hand, has some 20,000 administrators. The other difference is high standards and high expectations. There's discipline and a willingness to talk about virtues and steer away from vices. Successful religious and secular schools encourage honesty and civility and family commitment. Whether Modern Man Whittle can, or is willing to, deal with such old-fashioned notions is not clear.

Many of his brain trust know the value of basics: reading, discipline, homework, and a moral framework. The educators in the project, particularly Chester Finn and John Chubb, were attracted to Edison because they have been researching and hypothesizing their entire careers. Now they can put their thoughts into practice.

Some have said that Whittle is relying on his friend [former] Education Secretary Lamar Alexander to push through a voucher program, which would allow parents to take federal dollars and put them into whichever school they want their children to attend—public, Catholic, Whittle. Whittle claims "the voucher system is not at all critical" to his project. "I would never build a business plan on vouchers—though sometime around 2005, vouchers will be a reality."

It's not certain whether the Edison Project will ever become a reality. It has tremendous obstacles to mount both educationally and financially. It has good people on its side and an ambitious and competent leader in Benno Schmidt. Everything Whittle has touched in the past has turned to gold—but he has never tried to build a West Berlin before.

NO

Jonathan Kozol

WHITTLE AND THE PRIVATEERS

A "growing bunch of entrepreneurs," *The New York Times* reported in a 1991 education supplement, "are suggesting that unabashed capitalism can succeed" in the delivery of education "where bureaucracy and altruism have failed." If private corporations can achieve what government cannot, the *Times* went on, "why should they not make money in the process?"

A number of corporations are now setting out to do exactly that. Burger King has opened "Burger King Academies," fully accredited quasi-private high schools, in fourteen cities. I.B.M. and Apple are contemplating the idea of starting schools-for-profit too. Educational Alternatives, a profit-making firm in Minneapolis, now runs a public school for profit in Miami, under contract to Dade County, and recently won contracts to run public schools in Baltimore and Duluth. "It's open season on marketing," says the corporation's president.

But the most ambitious plan to date for profit-making schools are those announced in May 1991 by Chris Whittle, founder and chairman of Whittle Communications, a publisher of upscale consumer-oriented magazines. Whittle has pioneered already in the sale of television news-and-advertising packages to public schools. Now, "the impresario of captive-audience marketing," as *The New York Times* describes him, plans to open 200 profit-making schools by 1996 and foresees as many as 1,000 schools serving 2 million children within another decade. Although Whittle is the front man, the media conglomerate Time Warner holds 38 percent of the stock in the Edison Project, as the venture is called, and has an option to obtain another 30 percent. Another one-quarter of the stock is held by a British tabloid publisher, Associated Newspapers.

Whittle's commercials for Snickers, Burger King and other products on Channel One, shown in 10,000 schools, are required viewing for almost 8 million students daily—more than a third of all teenagers in the nation's schools. *U.S. News & World Report* notes that Whittle is tapping "the potential for widespread commercial penetration" of a student market in which more than $80 billion worth of products are sold yearly. At $157,000 for a thirty-second ad—double the advertising rate of prime-time network news—Whittle grosses $630,000 from the four ads run each day, bringing him gross annual revenues of more than $100 million.

It is easy to see why advertisers are prepared to pay these rates. Under the contract that school districts sign, 90 percent of the children in a school must watch the program 90 percent of the time, each of the programs must be watched in its entirety, a show cannot be interrupted and the teacher does not have the right to turn it off. In return for twelve minutes of students' time each day, schools get the loan of a satellite dish and TV sets for each classroom.

Because the students are obliged by law to be in school, and because the schools that have accepted Whittle's contract are obliged to show the ads, Whittle offers advertisers something that no ordinary television network can provide: an audience that is forced to watch these advertisements almost every day. By any standard, the deal he offers advertisers is terrific.

Whittle's Edison Project—which, according to *The Wall Street Journal*, he intends to use as "an expanded outlet" for advertisements—carries all of this a great deal further. The schools will charge tuition of $5,500—roughly the same as the national average spent per pupil in public schools. In order to cut costs, Whittle proposes saving on teacher salaries by using volunteers, classroom aides and computerized instruction, and he proposes using the students themselves to do some of the work of school custodians. Twenty percent of students will be granted scholarships, although the kids on scholarships will, for the most part, be in separate schools from those who pay. In an inner-city school, he says, 95 percent of the

kids will be on scholarship, while in suburban settings only 1 percent may be on scholarship. Whittle appears untroubled by the certainty that he is thereby guaranteeing segregated schooling.

Although Whittle promises he will not be selective in admissions, he does not address the likelihood that those who seek and win admission to his schools will be self-selecting. His promise, furthermore, is one he may well circumvent by simple strategies like opting not to offer services for kids with special needs.

Whittle's agenda meshes nicely with the voucher program advocated by the Bush Administration in its education plan, "America 2000." Whittle's ties to Lamar Alexander, [former president] Bush's Education Secretary, have already been explored by journalists [see John S. Friedman, "Big Business Goes to School," February 17]. Alexander, a friend of Whittle's for some twenty years, initially served on Whittle's board and also worked as a consultant to, and held stock in, his corporation—a relationship from which he profited financially. (Having bought four Whittle Communications shares in 1988 for $10,000, Alexander and his wife then sold them back to Whittle for $330,000 five months later—a transaction that attracted only brief attention from the Senate during Alexander's confirmation hearings.)

Whittle's White House connections were rendered even more explicit when he hired longtime Bush and Reagan operative Chester Finn Jr. to serve as his adviser. Finn, according to *The Boston Globe*, is being paid $1 million on a three-year Whittle contract. Finn, of course, is also close to Alexander and is generally acknowledged to be the author of "America 2000." Whittle's announcement of the Edison Project, moreover, followed the release of "America 2000" by a mere five weeks. While Bush, with the help of Finn, was arguing the virtues of the voucher system, which would open up the schooling market to the private sector, Whittle—also helped by Finn—was staking out his first claim on that market.

Benno Schmidt, the former president of Yale whom Whittle recruited to head the Edison Project, denies that he and Whittle are adversaries of the public schools. Schmidt insists that his purpose is to offer a challenge and a model that can only help public schools. But Whittle himself, in a careless moment, made his real intentions all too clear. "You have to have a West Berlin for East Berlin to fall," he told *The New York Times*, "and what we're really doing here is building West Berlin." This fascinating metaphor, in which he likens the American common school to the collapsing Stalinist monstrosity of East Berlin, is consistent with the language used by many voucher advocates. John Chubb, a proponent of vouchers who like Finn has now been added to the Whittle payroll, stated a few years ago that what he is proposing "is as different from our present system as capitalism is from socialism." Chubb, who now appears with regularity on network television, makes explicit his distaste for public schools, which he describes as "captives" of democracy.

Once a handful of Whittle's schools exist—and, with the corporate funds he has available, the first schools he opens are likely to be dazzling creations—they may well be exploited as a further selling point for vouchers. Parents, he says, who already "pay tax dollars" for the public schools, "are going to have to make a decision about whether they want to pay twice." Whittle undoubtedly hopes that the parents of the children he enrolls—

and the favorable press he orchestrates— will generate a national demand for the diversion of tax money into private education.

He has, moreover, shown already that he is prepared to pour enormous sums of money into lobbying campaigns. In California, where there has been strong resistance to his television package, Whittle has spent some $640,000 to recruit high-powered legislative lobbyists. How much might he someday spend to lobby Congress for a voucher system? The question, in a sense, is academic; Finn and Chubb and Schmidt are, in effect, his lobbyists already.

Under the entrepreneurial model Whittle represents, public schools will of course be obliged to advertise in order to compete with Whittle's marketing, causing a diversion of scarce funds from teaching into selling. This is, moreover, a competition that public educators, having neither marketing experience nor capital, are unlikely to win. With public education starved for funds after a decade of Reaganite attrition and with many public schools in disrepair, Whittle's initial boutique offerings are likely to appear spectacular.

IF THE GOALS OF CHUBB AND FINN AND Whittle should be realized, what might education someday look like in America? A vivid answer is given by Chubb, who is now one of the seven members of the Edison design team. Public schools, he has written, "must take whoever walks in the door." As a result, "they do not have the luxury of being able to select" the students who may be "best suited" to their goals. A private school, by contrast, has the right to keep out students who may need "more slowly paced instruction." Under a voucher system, he says, instead of public schools that try to serve a large diversity of students in one setting, we would see "a constellation" of "different schools serving different kinds of students differently." Such schools, he suggests, "might target their appeals" to "chosen segments" of the population.

Excellence in public schools, says Chubb, is undermined because so "many of their students come from families that put little or no emphasis on education." The virtue of the voucher-funded schools that he proposes, Chubb asserts, is that, like private schools today, they would be attractive to the kinds of kids whose parents are "informed," "supportive" and "encourage education." Children of the other kind of parents—"parents who may cause problems"—are, he says, "the ones most likely to drop out." What would happen to these children? "Larger numbers of . . . specialized schools," he claims, would soon emerge and would presumably address the needs of children from such families. Strip away the fancy language here and we are looking at a social Darwinist scenario, a triage operation that will filter off the fortunate and leave the rest in schools where children of the "better" parents do not need to see them.

Unlike his new employer, Chubb is honest to a fault. If his goals should someday be achieved, what we have known as public education will be granted a new definition and a different role in our society. What is now regarded as a right will come to be seen as just one more commercial product—or, more properly, a line of differentiated products. Whatever common bonds still hold together cities and communities are likely to be weakened or dissolved. As parents scramble to get children into one of Whittle's schools—or, for that matter, any other "voucher school"—they will by necessity view almost every other parent

as a rival. They will feel no obligation to raise tax-support for public schools attended by their neighbors' children. Instead of fighting for systematic excellence and equity for all, we will have taught them to advance their own kids at whatever cost to other people's children.

To the extent that liberal education writers have demurred at Whittle's plans, they have focused chiefly on the dangers of commercialism in the classroom. But the commercial products Whittle sells may be far less pernicious than his non-commercial products: an attitude, a set of values, a body of political beliefs as well. Whittle disclaims any wish to sell his ideologies to children. He speaks of education as a strictly neutral and mechanical experience. As every teacher knows, however, schools are never neutral. Consciously or not, they shape the soul and style of the future adult population.

When business enters education, therefore, it sells something more important than the brand names of its products. It sells a way of looking at the world and at oneself. It sells predictability instead of critical capacities. It sells a circumscribed, job-specific utility. "I'm in the business," says Elaine Mosley, the principal of a corporate-sponsored high school in Chicago, "of developing minds to meet a market demand."

The literature on school reform now being churned out by the private sector is unsentimental and straightforward on these matters. Students are described, and valued, not as children but as "workers." They are seen as future "assets" or "productive units"—or else, failing that, as pint-sized human deficits who threaten our productive capacities—but not as human beings who have value in themselves. The package of skills the child learns, or doesn't learn, is called the "product" of the school. Sometimes the child is referred to as "the product." A heightened emphasis on testing is one logical result of this utilitarian approach and promises a future in which "product testing" of commodities called "students" will be more and more pronounced.

When wedded to the reach and power of a firm such as Time Warner, a school's potential for reshaping the entire world view of a youthful population is almost unlimited. One hesitates to contemplate the possibilities when schools, movies, books, magazines and cable-system offerings are governed, produced and orchestrated by a single corporate directorate. Words attributed to religious leaders of the past—"give me a child at the age of 5"—should give us pause. Do we want to give this power to Chris Whittle—or to the corporate inheritors of Henry Luce?

Ironically, the road that leads to Whittle's enterprise may have been paved to a degree by liberals who have supported the idea of market choice and competition in the public schools while reassuring us that we can ward off any threat of private-school vouchers. In effect, they have been saying: "It will go thus far—and no farther."

I see no reason why. Once we accept the ideology of competition as the engine of reform, we will be hard-pressed to say why only certain people ought to be allowed to be competitors. If "parental option" is to be the pedagogic gospel, who is to say which options are to be permitted and which will be disallowed? Already ideologues at places like the Heritage Foundation are making just this argument: If choice is good, who are you to draw the line at choices only you approve of? Right-wing intellectuals who make this point are better debaters than

most educators on the left; they are also infinitely more successful at encapsulating their ideas and selling them to politicians and the public. They shrewdly see the drive for public schools of choice as an initial thrust—inadequate but tolerable for now—in a campaign that will eventuate in an unfettered market system.

Old friends of mine in the "alternative schools" tell me with some confidence: "We're not afraid of people such as Whittle. We have something special here that he can't duplicate." I don't think they understand the forces they are facing. No matter what the "special" thing they do, they cannot do it with the flair and promotional momentum that a massive private company can generate; nor can they profit from the same economies of scale. Business can and will construct dramatic new school buildings, set up space-age science and computer centers, target specific clienteles. Anything, moreover, that progressives have that is unique can be appropriated (even if adulterated) and repackaged to look better in commercial form. Their pedagogy, where it seems of interest to the public, can be copied and reprocessed to provide a Whittle school with a soupçon of liberal inventiveness and charm. Their teachers can be weaned away by better salaries. Their administrators can be bought away as well. Business can also mouth the words of people like Paul Goodman, Paulo Freire and John Holt as frequently as we do. Deborah Meier, no doubt to her dismay, is cited constantly at conservative symposiums sponsored by business corporations. . . .

The last thing I want is to create divisiveness among progressive educators, who are already embattled in their efforts at reform; many of the innovations they have tried to introduce in public education—local school autonomy, empowerment of parents—are enormously important. I do, however, feel uneasy at the risks involved when people I admire end up, even quite unwillingly, helping to propel the juggernaut that Whittle, Finn and Bush are riding. I don't know exactly how we can avoid this, but I think we should be far more circumspect about these possibilities.

Whittle's enterprise, moreover, may be only the beginning. With the end of the cold war and the scaling back of military spending, military-industrial companies like Honeywell and Raytheon may well shift their horizons soon and start to look at education as an even better realm than war for future "penetration." An education-industrial complex cannot fail to represent a tempting prospect.

Those who dismiss this danger ought to listen to the statements made by business strategists and by their friends in power. "It is time," says Deputy Educa-tion Secretary David Kearns, the former C.E.O. of Xerox, for business "to take ownership of the schools." We would do well to take him at his word. [Having President] Clinton in [the White House] may postpone the arrival of this train but will not derail it. Whittle has shown his business friends how easily resistance on the part of local citizens can be defeated by a mix of doublespeak and savvy. Any man who, in a mere three years, has won the power to indoctrinate 8 million kids with advertising every day is likely to do very well at breaking open the next market.

"A radical reprivatizing of the public realm is now well under way," notes Pennsylvania State University Professor Henry Giroux. Strategists at corporate think tanks are already mobilizing their resources for the next encounter. If we are serious, we should be mobilizing too.

POSTSCRIPT

Will the "Edison Project" Prompt Major Reforms?

"Reinventing," "restructuring," "new American schools," and "privatization" are the buzzwords of the current dialogue on change in education.
Ernest Boyer of the Carnegie Foundation has said that real reform needs to
occur in the minds of educators and citizens alike; both need to rethink what
a school should be. Theodore Sizer of the Coalition for Essential Schools (a
more modest-sized network of innovative schools) states that we have been
forced to rethink the ideas and practices that shape schooling.

In considering the possible effects on school reform of Whittle's project,
subquestions must also be addressed: Are private schools clearly superior to
public schools? If so, why? Should the government provide supplementary
aid to parents who choose a private school alternative? In regard to the first,
the most-discussed comparisons are *Public and Private Schools* (1981) by James
Coleman and *Public and Private Schools: The Impact of Communities* (1987) by
James Coleman and Thomas Hoffer. These studies showed that private
schools were superior in discipline, academic standards, and parental support and public schools were ahead in breadth of curriculum, affective
development, and pluralistic enrollment. Some contrary evidence is presented in a study by the National Assessment of Educational Progress (see
"NAEP: No Difference Between Public and Private High Schools," *Education
Today*, April 20, 1981) and by American Federation of Teachers president
Albert Shanker in "Do Private Schools Outperform Public Schools?" *American Educator* (Fall 1991). Another useful article is "The New Private Schools
and Their Historical Purpose," by Patricia Lines, *Phi Delta Kappan* (January
1986).

The question of public aid for private schools has been debated for
decades, dating back to the beginnings of the Catholic school system in the
United States. The over-20,000 private schools in the United States enroll
some 5 million students. Since about 75 percent of these schools are
religiously affiliated, separation of church and state concerns have blocked
all but token public aid. Here are some sources that address this question:
Frances C. Fowler's "The French Experience With Public Aid to Private
Schools," *Phi Delta Kappan* (January 1987); Mary Anne Raywid's "Public
Choice, Yes; Vouchers, No!" *Phi Delta Kappan* (June 1987); and David W.
Kirkpatrick's book *Choice in Schooling: A Case for Tuition Vouchers* (1990).

The Edison Project itself, being newly launched, has not been widely
discussed in print. Besides sources cited in the issue introduction, see
Marilee Rist's "Whittling Away at Public Education," *The Executive Educator*
(September 1991).

ISSUE 11

Is Home Schooling a Viable Alternative?

YES: David Guterson, from "When Schools Fail Children: An English Teacher Educates His Kids at Home," *Harper's Magazine* (November 1990)

NO: Jennie F. Rakestraw and Donald A. Rakestraw, from "Home Schooling: A Question of Quality, an Issue of Rights," *The Educational Forum* (Fall 1990)

ISSUE SUMMARY

YES: David Guterson, a public school teacher, explains why he and his wife educate their own children at home.

NO: Jennie F. Rakestraw and Donald A. Rakestraw, assistant professors at Georgia Southern College, examine the history and legal status of home schooling and raise questions about the balance of power between parents' interests and society's.

Historically, compulsory school attendance laws have been justified in a variety of ways—parental inability or unwillingness to educate their offspring, a social need to elevate the level of moral behavior, the need to maintain the social and economic machinery, the desire to widen opportunities for social mobility, the need to acculturate an immigrant population, and the need to pass on the cultural heritage and "civilize" the young. Compulsory attendance laws in the United States date back to 1852, and only in recent decades have they come under serious attack.

The first barrage came primarily from the radical reformers of the 1960s and 1970s. Paul Goodman's *Compulsory Mis-education and the Community of Scholars* (1964), Ivan Illich's *Deschooling Society* (1970), and many books written by John Holt demanded that government monopolization of the paths of learning be demolished. According to Illich, compulsory, government-controlled schooling treats knowledge as a commodity, deadens the individual's will to learn, and establishes an artificial structure for "success" that socially damages those who are unable to take advantage of the system. He further contends that "the whole enterprise of formal education is based on the false assumption that learning will be assured, maximized, and made more efficient if it is administered by specially prepared professionals in a special place at a prescribed time according to a preconceived plan to a group of children of a certain age."

The second assault came primarily from the Christian fundamentalists in the 1980s who saw the secularism of the public schools as a threat to the values being taught at home. Using the U.S. Supreme Court decision in *Wisconsin v. Yoder* (1972), which exempted the Amish sect from compliance with compulsory attendance laws, increasing numbers of parents engaged in home schooling on religious grounds. Support groups, such as the Christian Liberty Academy, provided parents with materials for conducting school at home. By the mid-1980s almost every state had given permission for some form of home schooling. Some jurisdictions mandated strict controls, some liberalized existing attendance laws, some clarified "home schooling" as a fulfillment of the law while upholding the right of the state to enforce regulations, while still others virtually abandoned their compulsory attendance laws.

What this leaves us with in the 1990s, according to Patricia M. Lines in "An Overview of Home Instruction," *Phi Delta Kappan* (March 1987), is a "small but vigorous and diverse" movement. Although estimates vary widely, the home-schooling movement serves about 1 percent of the total school-age population. Lines reports that the current reasons parents give for educating their children at home include concern about the methods and materials used in the schools, the child's inability to adapt to formal schooling, concerns about a lack of moral climate in the schools, and the inability of the schools to provide individualized attention to their children's needs.

This specific issue is related to the somewhat broader issue of parental choice (see Issue 9) and the fundamental problems involved in the relationship between church and state (see Issue 5). In the selections that follow, public school teacher David Guterson provides an in-depth analysis of his reasons for keeping his own children away from formal schooling. Although not arguing directly against the rights of parents to select such an option, educators Jennie F. Rakestraw and Donald A. Rakestraw examine some of the difficulties involved in choosing that course of action.

YES

David Guterson

WHEN SCHOOLS FAIL CHILDREN

Although it remains unarticulated among us, we Americans share an allegiance to schools, an assumption that schools are the foundation of our meritocracy and the prime prerequisite to a satisfying existence. In fact, to the oft-cited triumvirate of what is ineluctable in life—birth, death, and taxes—we are prone to add an unspoken fourth: education in classrooms.

In my classroom at a public high school in an upper-middle-class milieu where education is taken relatively seriously, we read with great purpose precisely those stories that tacitly reaffirm this loyalty to schools: In *Lord of the Flies* a pack of schoolboys degenerate into killers because no teachers are around to preserve the constraints of civilization. In *To Kill a Mockingbird* the venerable Atticus Finch insists that, for all of its shortcomings—and despite the fact that his daughter, Scout, is best educated by his own good example and by life in the larger web of Maycomb County—Maycomb Elementary is *mandatory. The Catcher in the Rye* is in large part the story of its protagonist's maladjustment to schools, and J. D. Salinger is highly critical of the hypocrisy behind a good education; still he ultimately offers up Mr. Antolini—an English teacher—as Holden Caulfield's last best hope.

The doctrine that school is necessary, which we early imbibe while within the very belly of the beast, is inevitably reinforced after we are disgorged. The daily implacability with which the media report the decline of schools, the constant knell of ominous statistics on the sorry state of American education, the curious popularity of such books as E. D. Hirsch's *Cultural Literacy* and Allan Bloom's *Closing of the American Mind,* are signs and portents, yes—but they also serve to bolster our shared assumption that school is required not merely because we attended it but also because our common life is in such a precarious state. Our national discussion about education is a desperate one, taking place, as it does, in an atmosphere of crisis, but it does not include in any serious way a challenge to the notion that *every child should attend school.* Why? Because, quite simply, there is no context for such a challenge: We live in a country where a challenge to the universal necessity of schools is not merely eccentric, not merely radical, but fundamentally un-American.

Yet there *are* those who have challenged not exactly the schools' raison d'être but the reason for their children's being *in* them. The children of such people have come to be called by a powerful misnomer, by a Newspeak conjoining: "homeschoolers." These children are not really *home*schoolers at all but rather young persons who do not go to school and are educated outside of institutions, persons best defined by what they don't do as opposed to what they do. There are currently about 300,000 homeschoolers in the United States—truants from one perspective, but, from another, following in the footsteps of Thomas Jefferson, Thomas Edison, Woodrow Wilson, Margaret Mead, and Andrew Wyeth.

A substantial majority of homeschooling parents in America are fervently religious and view schools as at odds with Christian doctrine. Overall, however, they are a diverse lot—the orthodox and the progressive, the Fundamentalist Christian and the libertarian, the urban, the rural, the social skeptic, the idealist, the self-sufficient, and the paranoid. And studies show little or no correlation between the degree of religious content in a homeschooling program or the level of its formal structure—ranging from orthodox "structuralists," with homes set up as miniature schools, to informal programs guided only by a child's ability to learn—or the education or affluence of homeschooling parents (or lack of affluence; the median annual income of homeschooling families is somewhere between $20,000 and $30,000) and the surprising academic success of homeschooled children, who tend to score well above average on standardized achievement tests.

But despite this—and despite the fact that teaching one's own was the norm in the United States until the 1850s—homeschooling today is little more than a fringe movement, an uprising perceived by many as a sort of insult and by others as a severe admonishment: *Take more interest in your children, like us!* (A Gallup poll revealed that 70 percent of the American population disapproved of homeschooling.) The movement inspires guilt in the hearts of too many parents—a lot of them baby boomers energetically seeking money and success yet worried that their children are growing up estranged from them—guilt and the sort of rage normally reserved for heretics and cultists.

Few people realize that the homeschooling movement is populated by a large number of educators or ex-educators—parents who teach or who have taught in the schools but keep their children out of them. Their paradoxical behavior makes them at first a curiosity and finally an affront to the schools that hired them; their students are confounded by their apparent hypocrisy; their colleagues are apt to tread delicately around the subject. So saying, I'll add my own confession: I am one of these walking contradictions. I teach my neighbors' children in my high school classroom, but my wife and I teach ours at home.

WE CAME TO THIS DECISION, I SHOULD admit from the outset, viscerally, with our understanding incomplete, pondering no more than a year's trial run. We were like most parents in the turmoil we felt far in advance of our oldest son's first step onto the school bus but unlike most in our response to it: We became existentially worried.

At first it seemed this anxiety signified that something was fundamentally wrong with us. Were we overzealous, overprotective, paranoid? It was our duty, we tried to tell ourselves, to override our parental instincts; school, after all, was ineluctable. And so my wife attempted to visit the local kindergarten (to no avail—its principal's policy forbade such visits) in order to assure herself that nothing dreadful might occur within its walls. Meanwhile I sought to convince myself that my own experience of student life as nightmarishly dreary and an incomparable waste of time was my own experience, only that, and that nothing legitimate could be deduced from it. And this was true: I could deduce nothing.

I wish I could write that my wife and I had excellent reasons for deciding to homeschool. We didn't. It was in the gut, and the gut, we knew, could be wrong either way. In May of 1986 we read books, in June we talked, July we wrung hands, August felt deep and hot and still, September came, and then one morning the big yellow bus arrived, waited a minute with its doors open, and our child did not get on it.

That fall we took to answering our inquisitors—friends, acquaintances, siblings, grandparents—with the all-purpose and ultimately evasive assertion that to hold a child out of kindergarten was not really so unusual, that many people do it.

Not schoolteachers, they replied.

But since then, each of our three sons has missed the bus, so to speak, and we find ourselves flung headlong into a life neither of us would have predicted.

AS IT TURNS OUT, IT IS A LIFE OUR FAMILY likes, and this is our chief reason for continuing to homeschool. Our days and our children's days are various. They pass with no sense that learning is separate from life, an activity that begins at a specific point in the morning and arbi-

trarily ends at another in the afternoon. Instead, learning proceeds *from* our children, spurred by their interests and questions. A winter day on which snow falls is the natural starting point for discussion and reading about meteorology, weather fronts, road salts, sloped roofs, Alaska, polar bears, the invention of touring skis. A spring evening spent on a blanket in the yard as the stars begin to show themselves is a proper time for talk of constellations, for bringing out a star chart, for setting up a telescope, for questions about satellites, eclipses, comets, meteors, navigation, Columbus, the Apollo space program. When the weather is poor for roaming out of doors, our boys— five, seven, and nine—might spend hours playing Scrabble or chess, or read to one another, or draw pictures, or comb through atlases and encyclopedias because the maps and pictures interest them. At dinner, if it is impending war in the Middle East that is in the news, the atlases and encyclopedias might end up on the table, and we might be there for two hours or more, eating, asking questions, looking up precise answers, discovering how oil is formed in the ground, why people fight over it, how Islam differs from other religions, why a person has to drink more water when it's hot, and why camels have humps.

There are hours in the morning—two at most—when my wife sits down with our nine-year-old and is systematic about writing and mathematics; later, they will practice violin together. Evenings are my time for nurturing our children's interest in geography, for discussing the day's news, and for reading poems to them before they go to bed. We try to be consistent about these matters, and yet no two days are ever much alike, and the curriculum is devised by us according to our children's needs and implemented by us according to our strengths and weaknesses as parents and teachers. Thus:

AUGUST 30: Reading: *The Wooden Horse;* violin: *Witches' Dance;* writing: letter to Adam, final draft; science: gas cannon, carbon dioxide.
SEPTEMBER 26: Visit to the chicken-butchering plant and Point Defiance Zoo; violin practice; journal and writing.
OCTOBER 16: Neighborhood recycling; banking; violin practice; Chess Club; finished letter to Aunt Mary.
NOVEMBER 7: *Mouse and the Motorcycle,* Chapters 3 and 4; math drill, multiplying by 4 and 5; violin practice; cursive writing; swimming with Nathan.

What else? An ant farm, a bug jar, a pair of field glasses, a rabbit cage, old appliances to take apart. An aquarium, a terrarium, a metronome, a collection of petrified wood, another of shells, a globe, a magnifying glass, a calculator, a microscope. Felt pens, watercolors, dry cell batteries, paper-airplane kits. Swimming teachers, lithographers, bakers, canoe builders, attorneys, inventors, flutists, fishermen. And time to ponder all of them. To read the information on the backs of baseball cards, dig butter clams, dye rice paper, weave on a homemade frame loom. To plant potatoes, tell tall tales, watch birds feed. To fashion a self in silence.

And people too, many of them, a large and shifting variety. Friends from Little League and music lessons, acquaintances made on the basketball court and in art classes. The group of homeschoolers with whom our boys put on plays, beachcomb at low tide, play chess.

And salmon. Perhaps it began, one night, with merely eating one. Or with reading *Red Tag Comes Back.* Or with the man at the side of the road with the purse seine laid out in his yard. At any rate, the salmon life-cycle exhibit at the Seattle Aquarium and walking among the gill-netters at Fisherman's Terminal. And cleaning debris from a salmon stream, standing in it, one Saturday. Visiting the hatchery on the Elwha River, the fish ladders at the Rocky Reach Dam, the Pacific Science Center display on the Nootka people. Then seeing their grandfather's catch from the Hakai Peninsula, the bones and organs, the digestive tracts of fish—the blood and murder—and mulling over eating what was once living and the relative ethics of sportfishing. And then one day, abruptly—perhaps a plane has flown overhead or they have seen from the yard a crow fly—it is *flight* that interests them, the Wright Brothers, Charles Lindbergh, Amelia Earhart, draft and lift and thrust and wingspan, the Museum of Flight, the Boeing plant, pitch, yaw, and roll. . . .

Their education is various, alive, participatory, whole—and, most of all, *theirs.* Quite frankly, no school can hope to match it. It is an education tuned to their harmonies, local and intimate as opposed to generic and imposed. They have not learned to be fearful of learning, to associate it with pain and dreariness, with competition, anxiety, dread. My wife and I hope that they will continue in this, that adolescence will find them earnestly seeking, that they will see enough of schools—by visiting them—to know what they are missing. We hope that colleges, if college is what they want, will recognize their strengths without school transcripts. (Admissions boards, incidentally, increasingly recognize homeschooled children as legitimate candidates.) And that their social lives will continue to be vigorous and sane, will continue to include people of all sorts and all ages. And finally that the life we have developed as a family will sustain itself on through *their* children, that our intimacy will not end when *they* are parents.

It is not always, of course, so idyllic, so wonderful, so easy to wax romantic over. Much of the time, though, it is satisfying and full, a fruitful existence for us all. We recognize that in the long run it may have drawbacks, but in the long run no life is perfect. We can't know, finally, if this is what is best for our children and, like all parents, we are playing it by ear to some extent, hoping to guess correctly what it is we should *do*. We do know that homeschooling has given us a life we wouldn't otherwise have, and we are thankful for that.

AT THE SAME TIME, I GO ON TEACHING English in a public high school. There my students might bemoan the dreary meaninglessness of classroom life and rail against its absurdities but also profess skepticism at the very mention of homeschooling. How are your kids going to make friends? they ask. Who's going to teach them algebra? How do you expect them to get into college? When do you find time to teach them anyway? What if you weren't a teacher—could you do it? Why are you *here*, Mr. Guterson?

Excellent questions, I say, sooner or later, in the approving voice of a high school English teacher. But answering them I feel the orbit of my reasoning widen—what high school students call "digression"—because in the end you can't discuss homeschooling as if it were divorced from other raging social issues. In fact, bring it up with your students' parents and you're soon fending off a touchy debate about such sacred matters as work, children, money, leisure time, and, above all, the self. Before long you are listening to hysterical pronouncements about democracy, capitalism, enculturation, the Japanese, and nearly everything else.

Let's take, for example, the assertion that children who don't go to school won't be "socialized." Most people believe school is the primary training ground for the social life we experience when we emerge from school: In its halls and classrooms, these skeptics recollect with mixed emotions, one sorts out the broad panoply of human types and then adjusts oneself to them, finds ways to modulate one's persona in the face of the great shifting tide of humanity. In this vision of things, the homeschooled child figures as an eternal outsider who, because he or she never attended school, will remain forever uninitiated in the tricky nuances of adult society. He will miss his cues at cocktail parties, he will not understand the subtleties of behaviors that come his way at the office or on the bus.

Furthermore, say homeschooling's detractors, homeschooling is *undemocratic*. They take at face value the portrait of schools as the irreplaceable agents of enculturation and, as E. D. Hirsch would have it, of cultural literacy. Jefferson's vision, after all, was that school would be democracy's proving ground, a place where all comers would take their best shot at the American Dream and where that dream would ultimately find its most basic and most enduring sustenance. Not to show up at all—at all!—is thus to give in to the forces of cultural decline, to withdraw at the moment of national crisis, and to suggest openly that if Rome is really burning, the best response is not to douse the flames or even to fiddle away beside the baths but to go home and lock the door.

Critics of homeschooling are likely to add that for America to work we must act in concert to repair our schools; that few parents are, in fact, well qualified to teach children the broad range of things they need to know; that homeschooling allows the bigoted and narrow-minded to perpetuate their types; that despite all the drawbacks to a peer-dominated world, such a world is required if children are to grapple with relationships more egalitarian than family ones. And more: Send your child to the school of hard knocks, they say, where some bigger boy will shove him from his place in line or steal his blocks or vandalize his fingerpaintings, where he will learn forbearance and self-reliance and meet in the form of his teacher an adult who is less than perfect and less than fully attentive to his every need—where, in short, life in all of its troubling glory will present itself daily to him. A dark inversion, perversely true, of Robert Fulghum's *All I Really Need to Know I Learned in Kindergarten.*

LET ME ADDRESS THESE CRITICISMS IN ORDER. Evidence in support of homeschooling's academic virtues is both overwhelming and precisely what we would expect if we gave the matter some reflection. Public educators have complained, into a steady, implacable wind, that with much smaller classes and more one-to-one contact they might make better academic headway. Small wonder, then, that homeschoolers score consistently well above the norm on standardized achievement tests: They're learning under the ideal conditions—alone or in groups small enough to make real learning possible—that schoolteachers persistently cry out for.

Recently, a strong case has been made that achievement tests don't tell us any-thing that matters, because they are culturally biased and because they are *tests*—and tests are attended by various levels of anxiety and a wide range of test-taking habits. Here some facts about homeschoolers are in order: They come predominantly from the very middle-class backgrounds that standardized achievement tests reportedly favor, and their parents are, for the most part, deeply interested in their education as well as themselves better educated than the average American adult. Thus, homeschoolers' test scores might best be compared with those of schoolchildren who come from similar test-favoring backgrounds and whose parents also are well educated and involved. Furthermore, it's true that some homeschooling parents teach "to" standardized tests—some classroom teachers do also—because states require that their children take them or because college entry is largely contingent on test scores in the absence of a school grade-point average. (Harvard, for example, admits homeschooled children and takes their SAT scores very seriously.)

Researchers have probed as well the more slippery question of whether homeschooled children are properly socialized. John Wesley Taylor V, using the Piers-Harris Self-Concept Scale—a measure of the "central core of personality"—concluded that "few homeschooling children are socially deprived." Mona Maarse Delahooke placed them in the "well-adjusted" range on a personality measure known as the Roberts Apperception Test for Children; Jon Wartes, in surveys of 219 Washington State homeschoolers, found that at least half spent more than twenty hours a month in organized community activities and that more than two thirds spent twenty to thirty plus hours a month with other children of varying ages. Linda Montgomery, after studying the leadership skills of homeschooled children, concluded that "homeschooling is not generally repressive of a student's potential leadership, and may in fact nurture leadership at least as well as does the conventional system." In my experience, homeschoolers are less peer-dependent than schoolchildren and less susceptible to peer pressure. In this regard, the research merely corroborates what seems to most observers obvious.

But although homeschooling may work, it is by no means easy. Most American adults are fully competent, of course, to learn whatever they have to learn—facts, skills, methods, strategies—in order to teach their children. But should they want to do it, they should strive to be good at it, and they should face the endeavor seriously. It should bring them satisfaction; it should feel like important work. *No one* should undertake to home-school without coming to terms with this fundamental truth: It is the fabric of your own life you are deciding about, not just your child's education.

THIS MATTER — THE FABRIC OF A HOME-schooling life—is the concern of some critics who assert that in practice home-schooling is patently sexist, that its most obvious result is the isolation of women in the home, away from the fulfillments of the workplace. (That there may be fulfillments in the home, for both sexes, as educators of children, is another issue entirely.) Yet the question of who does what in a relationship is no more or less important with regard to homeschooling than with regard to anything else: who works outside the home, who works inside, who does the dishes, changes oil in the car, shops for food, flies to Miami on a business trip. The question of *who does what* remains: who takes responsibility for the child's introduction to long division, drives her to swimming lessons, teaches him to throw a baseball, shows her how to use a calculator. Homeschooling is, in fact, no more inherently sexist than anything else in a marriage (and is less so than schools), and if in many homeschooling families the mother is the prime mover and first cause of education and the father an addendum and auxiliary, this is a reflection on the culture at large and not on the phenomenon of homeschooling.

There are others who assert that although homeschooling might serve well for the American middle class, other groups—the poor, the disenfranchised, the immigrant—need schools to flourish. After all, the public schools have historically been a crucial conduit of upward mobility, they say, and point out the Vietnamese immigrants of the last twenty years, whose kids get full scholarships from places like the University of Texas and Columbia. Yet the mobility they describe is next to nonexistent; a permanent underclass is the reality in this country, and schools do as much as any other institution to reinforce this state of affairs. By systematizing unfairness, inequality, and privilege, schools prepare the children of the underclass to accept as inevitable the coming drudgery of their adult lives. At my school, for example, "basic" students are more likely to serve meals in Foods I while "honors" students join an organization called Future Business Leaders of America and enroll in courses like Leadership and Humanities. In both its social and academic structure, my school best instructs the disenfranchised in the cruel truth that disenfranchisement is permanent.

To say that homeschoolers, for the sake of American democracy, *must* be institutionalized is an undemocratic proposition. Both the courts and state governments recognize this, for homeschooling is legal in one form or another everywhere in the United States. The Supreme Court thus far has not ruled in any explicit way on homeschooling. The closest it came, in 1972, was to declare that Wisconsin's compulsory-education law could not, in fact, compel three Amish families to send their children to high school. Yet legal tension about homeschooling persists—mostly as First, Ninth, and Fourteenth Amendment issues: freedom of religion and the right to privacy—for the states have an interest in seeing children educated and are, rightly, concerned that in at least some cases "homeschool" ends up meaning no school. (When homeschooling parents in question are deemed incompetent, the courts have consistently—and properly—ruled against them.) Moreover, and more importantly, does anyone really believe that schools make students better democrats? Do they serve the individual and democratic society? I give them an A only for prompting peer-group relations of a sort conducive to the workings of our *economy:* Schools are in their social fabric nasty, competitive, mean-spirited, and status-conscious in the manner of the adult institutions they mimic.

Could there be something in the very nature of the school as an institution that prevents it from fully realizing its mandate to inform, educate, and develop both the individual and his or her society? Or, to put it another way, could there be something in its *manner* of being that prevents it from realizing its *reason* for being? At the high school where I teach, as at most, students come and go in sets of thirty or so at approximately one-hour intervals, an arrangement convenient to the daunting task of administering a crowd of more than 800 young people but not necessarily conducive to their education or in the best interests of society. The arrangement is instead both relatively expedient and indicative of the schools' custodial function—in essence, their primary one, since we have structured schools in such a manner as to allow this function to precede all others. Schools *keep* students first, and any education that happens along the way is incidental and achieved against the odds. It may be, finally, that schools temporarily *prevent* us from getting the education we persist in getting outside and beyond schools, where the conditions of life provide more natural motivations and learning is less abstract. *Never let your schooling get in the way of your education,* advised Mark Twain, who never attended school.

THE SCHOOL I TEACH IN IS FORTUNATE TO employ some excellent teachers, honorable and earnest men and women who are quietly heroic for the sake of their students and whose presence does much to salvage some good from an otherwise untenable institution. They bring humanity to an inhumane setting and pit it against the *design* of schools, which were envisioned as factories dedicated to the efficient production of predictable, formulaic human beings.

But I find myself, like many teachers, beating my head against the classroom wall on a daily, even hourly, basis. My students are compelled to herd themselves from room to room, to sit in daily confinement with other people of precisely their age and approximately their social class, to hear me out on "Sailing to

Byzantium" whether or not they are ready. They are scrutinized, sorted, graded, disciplined, and their waking hours are consumed by this prison life: thirty hours a week, thirty-six weeks a year, seven to ten hours a week of "homework" twelve years running—the heart of their young lives consumed by it. What can we expect of them as adults, other than that they become, as New York City Teacher of the Year John Taylor Gatto says, "dependent human beings, unable to initiate lines of meaning to give substance and pleasure to their existence"? Penned up and locked away, shaped by television and school instead of by their community, they must struggle as adults for a satisfying life they can neither grasp nor envision.

CONFINING CHILDREN TO SCHOOL IS EM-blematic of the industrialized twentieth century, but it is also convenient for our current generation of young parents, which might best be characterized in general terms as terrifyingly selfish, persistently immature, and unable to efface its collective ego for the sake of the generation that will follow it and is *already* following it. While these people go about the business of saving the world—or of extracting everything they can from it—their children (they can hardly believe they have children, can hardly grasp the privilege of nurturing them when they are so thoroughly occupied by their attentions to themselves) need *someplace* to go. The truth is that for too many contemporary parents the school system is little more than convenient day care—day care they can feel good about as long as they don't reflect on it too deeply.

Many parents I know put more hours into their golf games or their wardrobes or into accumulating enough capital for the purchase of unnecessary luxuries than into their child's education. Because they are still children themselves, it simply doesn't occur to them to take an active role in their child's learning—in part because they expect the schools to do it all, in part because there isn't room in their souls for anybody to loom as large as themselves. For many the solution is simply to buy an education as one buys a BMW—your child's school as yet another commodity to show off. So when I talk about homeschooling I am talking about choosing less affluence in the name of more education. I am talking about giving matters intense and vital thought before one ships one's child off to school.

And while it's easy—and understandable—for parents to protest that one hasn't the time or energy for homeschooling, there is much, short of pulling children out of school, that parents can undertake today. Homeschooling is only the extreme form of a life in which all of us can and should take part. The notion of parents as educators of their children is, in the broad sense, neither extreme nor outlandish, and we should consider how instinctively parents engage in the instruction of their children—at the dinner table, for example—and how vital a role an expanded homeschooling movement might play in repairing families. We should think clearly about the problems of schools, ask ourselves why every attempt to correct them seems doomed to fail, replace in our hearts the bankrupt notion of "quality time" with a reassessment of our role as parents. We should recognize that schools will never solve the bedrock problems of education because the problems are problems of *families*, of cultural pressures that the schools reflect and thus cannot really remedy.

Today it is considered natural for parents to leave their children's education entirely in the hands of institutions. In a better world we would see *ourselves* as responsible and our schools primarily as resources. Schools would cease to be *places* in the sense that prisons and hospitals are places; instead, education would be embedded in the life of the community, part of the mechanics of our democracy, and all would feel a devotion to its processes. Parents would measure their inclinations and abilities and immerse themselves, to varying degrees and in varying ways, in a larger educational system designed to *assist* them. Schools—educational resource centers—would provide materials, technology, and expertise instead of classrooms, babysitters, and bureaucrats.

Admittedly, I am a professional educator, part of this vast bureaucracy. Yet I see no contradiction in what I am doing: coming each day to where young people are, attempting within the constraints of the institution to see to their education. Each year I come to admire many of my students, to like them so well that I am sad to see them go; each year there are moments in which I am gratified, even moved, by a sentence a student has written in an essay, by a question somebody asks. Yet for all this, for all the quiet joys of the classroom, I am forever aware of some amorphous dissatisfaction, some inkling that things might be better. It seems to me that many of my students should simply be elsewhere, that they would be better served by a different sort of education, that their society would be better served by it, too. I believe this education is one their parents can best provide and that they should expect schools to assist them. These parents love their children with a depth that, finally, I can't match—and finally, teaching is an act of love before it is anything else.

NO

Jennie F. Rakestraw and
Donald A. Rakestraw

HOME SCHOOLING: A QUESTION OF QUALITY, AN ISSUE OF RIGHTS

Home schooling is an educational practice that is spreading throughout grassroots America. Fifteen years ago it was rare to find parents teaching their children at home rather than sending them to traditional schools. But in recent years, there has been a surprising increase of interest in, and commitment to, home schooling. In 1986, Lines, a policy analyst for the U.S. Department of Education, estimated that there were between 120,000 and 260,000 home-schooled children in the United States. Public school officials, state legislators, and professional educators have had to take notice of the presence of these home-schooling families and, at times, take action about them. When parents educate their children at home, they depart from the mass-schooling ethic that has been perceived as a cornerstone of the 20th-century American way of life. This departure has raised questions concerning who holds responsibility for providing education and who is accountable for insuring quality education. Not surprisingly, such questions have been fundamental issues of home schooling and keynotes of continuing debate.

Although states have had reasonable and obvious interest in education, advocates of home schooling have regarded their parental freedom to educate as a Constitutional right, a moral duty and, for some, a Biblical command. With their opinions concerning educational philosophy, curriculum, socialization, institutionalization of children, and teacher qualifications usually at variance with public school practices, home educators have felt their decisions to home-school a matter of conscience. Home schooling, meanwhile, has a foundation in American history and has developed a legal foundation in most states. Even so, home schools face skepticism. They have reappeared out of the past with a new face, one that looks unfamiliar and maybe even unsafe. Are parents able to meet *all* the needs of their children in the home setting? Can we concede that parents are ultimately responsible and accountable for the education of their children?

From Jennie F. Rakestraw and Donald A. Rakestraw, "Home Schooling: A Question of Quality, an Issue of Rights," *The Educational Forum*, vol. 55, no. 1 (Fall 1990). Copyright © 1990 by Kappa Delta Pi, an international honor society in education. Reprinted by permission. References omitted.

THE HISTORICAL BACKGROUND

We believe that the historical perspective must be taken when deciding on the advisability of home schooling. And we would be wise to examine how the contemporary movement toward home schooling evolved, as well as how effective these schools are in meeting children's academic and social needs.

During America's colonial and early national periods, home schooling was commonplace and, as a matter of fact, a predominant form of education. The primary responsibility for education clearly rested with parents. Although the Constitution of the United States addressed a wide range of powers, limitations, and duties, it did not expressly mention education. It was only after the passing in 1791 of the Tenth Amendment in the Bill of Rights that education became a function of the states. At that point, the states were empowered to provide education, but schooling still was not universal, compulsory, or tax supported. Although state-sponsored "charity schools" were established to provide formal schooling locally to those in need, American education remained a private and religious effort until the late 1800s. Private schools, many of which were church supported, assumed a large role in providing academic as well as religious instruction. There was no division between religious and secular authority and the Bible was considered the moral guide for the nation and, consequently, for the developing educational system.

During the 19th century, the state's interest in education grew. Universal public education was the means by which individual liberty and a democratic state would be guaranteed. The interests and goals of the state, in contrast with those of the church, were considered to be representative of the people. The purposes of the state, namely, to promote cultural, economic, and social equality, gradually superseded the purposes of the church in American education. After the Civil War, the majority of states passed legislation providing for free public education. Even though the concept of public education had been slow to gain acceptance, every state established public schools by the early 1900s. Nevertheless, the presumption of family responsibility and control remained, and parents could use the "right of excusal" to have their children excused from any objectionable course or programs of study. Parents believed schools should conform to their values and reinforce their authority, while preparing their children for success in American society. Public education was regarded as a service to families, "an opportunity to which children were entitled, not as a requirement to be imposed."

The free educational opportunities offered by public schools were not always accepted. Indifferent parents, inadequate school facilities, rejection of a regimented school setting by children, opportunities for child labor, and the generally low standard of living—all worked against the efforts of public education. In due time, the problems of child neglect and exploitation prompted the passage of compulsory school attendance laws and child labor laws. By 1918 every state had a compulsory attendance law in effect, and the relationship between families and schools changed. The locus of responsibility had shifted from the family to the institutionalized school operated by the state. Since schools were responsive to group, rather than individual, demands, various social groups began to battle over whose values, pedagogy, and world view should be adopted by public schools. This created a problem for parents who, while accepting the idea of public education itself, perhaps did not realize that public education, when mandated by compulsory attendance laws, would usurp their rights over their children's education. By yielding to state compulsory attendance laws, parents found themselves increasingly removed from the responsibility for their children's education.

The goals of public education, generally condoned, reflected a national concern over (a) advancing the ideals of, and preserving, a democracy, (b) economically strengthening the country, and (c) equalizing opportunity among races and classes of people. In addition, the socialization of children in the school was a major emphasis of compulsory education, as it provided a powerful means of political control. Indeed, some have claimed that the essence of the common school movement was "its rhetorical commitment to the deliberate use of education as a tool for social manipulation and social progress."

Naturally, many Americans questioned the appropriateness and effectiveness of school socialization and, from the beginning, public education has been challenged and pressured to reform. In the more recent past, when Sputnik was launched by the Soviet Union in 1957, the event shocked the American public and its educational system. The satellite undermined the American people's confidence in their educational and technological superiority, as well as their sense of national security. Fear and survival became the motive for change. The attitudes and emotions thus provoked during the late 1950s greatly affected American educational policies and cre-

ated an era of self-inspection, criticism, and disequilibrium. Many of the educational innovations and practices of the present can be traced to this period. Not only were alternative public schools established to counteract the growth of private schools, but some parents withdrew their children from traditional schools and initiated the contemporary home education movement. Since the 1960s, skepticism has continued to increase over how acceptable and even necessary public education is to the education and socialization of children and to the maintenance of American democracy. The renewed interest in home schooling has been an outgrowth of this sentiment.

Present-day home schools have thus evolved from a dissatisfaction with organized public schooling, a dissatisfaction based on philosophical differences in educational thought. For instance, during the 1960s and early 1970s, educators and noneducators alike called for reforms. Many recognized the need for changes but felt they should be implemented within the framework of the existing educational system. For example, Silberman described the schools as "grim, joyless places" but argued that they need not be: "Public schools *can* be organized to facilitate joy in learning and esthetic expression and to develop character. . . . This is no utopian hope." Yet, for some, this unrealized hope is indeed utopian and has not been fulfilled.

Others believed in a radicalization of the school, while still others contended that reform was impossible and that schools should simply be abolished. Holt, as an example, once felt that school reform was possible, but has since reconsidered his position. He now believes that the conditions for true education "do not exist and cannot be made to exist within compulsory, coercive, competitive schools." According to him:

> While the question "Can the schools be reformed?" kept turning up "No" for an answer, I found myself asking a much deeper question. Were schools, however organized, however run, necessary at all? Were they the best place for learning? Were they even a good place? Except for people learning a few specialized skills, I began to doubt that they were.

Holt has therefore encouraged concerned parents to withdraw their children from institutionalized schools and to teach them at home. Moore has also advocated home schooling on the basis of his research, through the Hewitt Research Foundation, on the effects of institutionalizing young children. He suggested that children should not be enrolled in formal school programs before ages 8 to 10 unless they are severely disadvantaged or handicapped. Instead, parents should be assured their rights by the state to teach their children "systematically" at home.

While the home schooling movement, under the leadership of Holt and Moore, has expanded and stabilized in every state, the fundamental issue still remains: Who holds responsibility for the education of American children? With this question unanswered, many local school officials faced difficult, multi-faceted decisions involving home-schooling families. These decisions sometimes led to the charging, prosecution, and imprisonment of parents for child neglect and/or violation of state compulsory school attendance laws. Nevertheless, every state has been allowing home schooling in some form or another, even while impos-

ing some regulations to protect the right of the state to an educated citizenry.

The legal foundation of home schooling has involved numerous court rulings and individual state's compulsory education statutes. The acceptance of home schooling implies that, although states have assumed a prominent role in providing education over the years, ultimate responsibility stays with parents. Many public educators cringe at the notion, but President Reagan was voicing a widely-held opinion when he in 1984 stated that, "The primary right, duty and responsibility of educating children belongs to parents. Their wishes should be heeded."

THE QUESTION OF QUALITY

In heeding the parental wishes, however, we must be careful that the quality of education is preserved. Public educators have often contended that some parents do not have the ability or the patience to teach their children well. Observations have been made that home-schooled children tend to be students with better-than-average potential but that their achievement is uneven due to a "spottiness" in the parents' preparation. Some school officials have been concerned about the lack of documentation and objective evaluation of home-schooled children. Some state legislators and school officials have addressed these concerns, and, since 1980, 28 states have adopted home school statutes or regulations. Compulsory attendance laws in 31 states now explicitly recognize an exception for home schooling. In legally providing for home schooling, most of these statutes established varying sets of requirements for home schools, including such criteria as teacher qualifications, achievement testing, and record keeping. . . .

In addition to academic concerns, the socialization of home-schooled children has been a primary consideration. Many educators insist that peer interaction in the school environment is necessary for normal development and speculate that home schooling will produce social isolates. Home schooling has also been criticized as elitist, appealing mainly to educated, middle-class families. Critics also fear that the domination of parents over their children would deny the protection of society to the neglected or indoctrinated child. Some have even questioned the motives of parents who home-school their children, suspecting that some mothers use home schooling as a rationalization to stay home while others home-school for status or ego reasons. These criticisms and concerns have mounted in parallel with the growth of home schooling. . . .

THE EFFECTIVENESS OF HOME SCHOOLING

In spite of concerns over academic progress, several studies have found that home-schooled children achieve higher than national averages on standardized measures. For example, the Tennessee Education Department reported that home-schooled students in Grades 2, 3, 6, and 8 in that state scored higher in every major area of the Stanford Achievement Test than the statewide public school averages for the 1985–1986 school year. Similar results were reported in studies by the New York and Washington State Departments of Education. In Alabama, home-schooled children in Grades 2, 3, 5, and 6 scored in 1986 at or above the national norms in all areas of the Stanford Achievement Test. In Illinois, a study concluded that home-schooled children are not disadvantaged academicallyby their home-school setting.

A few studies have examined the achievement of home-schooled children working with differing home-school curricula. Two such studies were conducted by home-school curriculum publishers: the Hewitt Research Foundation found that the average standardized test score of children, who use the Hewitt-Moore Child Development Center home-school curriculum, was approximately at the 80th percentile, while researchers at the Christian Liberty Academy found that home-schooled children who use their curriculum performed two to three grade levels above the national norms. In addition, studies done since 1981 by the Alaska Department of Education have found that the home-schooled children in the first through eighth grades outperformed their classroom counterparts on the California Achievement Test and the Alaska Statewide Assessment Tests.

Now, the effects of home schooling on the socialization of children have been more difficult to examine, since there is apparently no convenient instrument available to measure the equivocal elements of socialization. However, Taylor, himself a proponent of home schooling, used a self-concept inventory with a sampling of home-schooled children and found that these children scored higher than conventionally-schooled children in all areas on the scale. His conclusion was that few home-schooled children are socially deprived. Other studies that have surveyed parents' reasons for home-schooling commonly report that parents see socialization as a negative aspect of school. They wish to help their children develop social skills without negative peer influences, learning socialization skills from parent models in the home rather than from peer models in the school. While those wary of home schooling worry about the children's socialization, the parents worry about the quality of socialization that takes place in traditional schools.

THE "THREAT" OF THE HOME SCHOOLING MOVEMENT

Home schooling has been regarded as a major educational movement in America even though the actual number of home-schooled children is still negligible, being less than 1 percent of the school-age children. Nevertheless, there is apprehension over possible negative effects that this movement could have on public schooling. Even as the function and effectiveness of public education in today's society have been questioned, schools seem to have maintained a certain level of general support. Thus, Jackson, for one, advanced an argument that previous challenges to public education simply reaffirmed how deep-rooted our society's allegiance to public education had become.

On their part, advocates of home schooling have maintained that granting the right to educate their children would not significantly deplete public school attendance or damage the system. For any family not to opt for the convenience of public schooling would be not only impractical but also inconsistent with the typical American lifestyle. Rather than rocking the foundations of American schooling, the definition and concept of education would merely be revised and broadened. Toffler, for instance, visu-

alized an increased role of families in the education of children and maintained that home schoolers should be aided by the schools and not regarded as "freaks or lawbreakers."

Of course, the prevalence of home schooling in the future of American education cannot be clearly foreseen now. Nevertheless, [it] is ironic to note that several current trends have encouraged the growth of home schooling. The increased emphasis on parent education, parental choice and participation in the educational process, and alternative educational options worked indirectly to promote the home-schooling movement. Widely-publicized issues concerning secular humanism in public education and the reassessment of teacher certification requirements have provided added incentives for home schoolers. In addition, recent national reports such as A *Nation at Risk*, offering many sweeping indictments and reform recommendations, have been seen as evidence that public education is moving farther away from the educational ideals of home-schooling parents. Any future dissatisfactions with public education will increase the possibility of more families turning to home schooling.

COMPULSORY PUBLIC SCHOOLING IN THE United States originated from genuine societal needs and has grown strong as an American institution. However, future needs might create a more distinctive place for home schooling. Parental freedom to home school has been promoted as a right which a democratic society should allow. Before it can become a viable educational alternative, nevertheless, underlying issues regarding the balance of power between parents and society over the education of children must be settled. Only mutual interest in the welfare of the child, a cooperative spirit, and a genuine objectivity in discussing the sensitive issues surrounding home schooling will provide satisfactory solutions.

POSTSCRIPT

Is Home Schooling a Viable Alternative?

A recent Gallup poll shows that the majority of respondents is opposed to home schooling. Yet many of the reasons that home-schooling parents give are shared by many others who are unable to join the movement. A new wave of court actions related to home schooling is anticipated in the 1990s, which will call into question the legality of strict state or district regulations imposed on home schoolers (the state of Missouri, for example, stipulates 1,000 hours of instruction per year, 600 of which must be devoted to reading, language arts, mathematics, social studies, and science, and 400 of which must be accommodated at the home-school site).

Some questions that must be considered as the controversy over home schooling gets ironed out in the coming years are these: Do home-schooling parents exert too much mind control over their children? Is the "peer independence" of home-schooled children a gain or a loss for them? What effects do the lack of facilities and extracurricular activities have? Should home-schooling parents receive financial aid or tax benefits?

These and other questions are addressed in a wide variety of books and articles on the subject. Two classic works are *School Can Wait* (1979) by Raymond and Dorothy Moore and *Teach Your Own* (1981) by John Holt. Holt's newsletter *Growing Without Schooling* is also an interesting source.

Also recommended are: "The New Pioneers of the Home-Schooling Movement," Diane Divoky, *Phi Delta Kappan* (February 1983); "Compulsory Education and Home Schooling: Truancy or Prophecy?" Mary Anne Pitman, *Education and Urban Society* (May 1987); "Home Schooling and Compulsory School Attendance," Josef Wendel et al., *School Law Bulletin* (Summer 1986); and "Home Schooling Litigation Tests State Compulsory Education Laws," Sally Banks Zakariya, *The American School Board Journal* (May 1988).

Collections of articles addressing the topic are presented in the Winter 1988 issue of *Religion and Public Education*, the November 1988 issue of *Education and Urban Society*, and the February 1989 issue of *Educational Review*. The January 1988 issue of *Education and Urban Society* also offers two excellent overviews: "The Context of Home Schooling in the United States," by J. Gary Knowles, and "Home Schools: A Synthesis of Research on Characteristics and Learner Outcomes," by B. D. Ray.

Recent books of note include Cheryl Gorder's new edition of *Home Schools: An Alternative* (1990) and *Home Schooling: Political, Historical, and Pedagogical Perspectives* (1991) by Jane van Galen and Mary Anne Pitman.

ISSUE 12

Can Schools Prevent Urban Dropouts?

YES: Larry Cuban, from "At-Risk Students: What Teachers and Principals Can Do," *Educational Leadership* (February 1989)

NO: Paul Woodring, from "A New Approach to the Dropout Problem," *Phi Delta Kappan* (February 1989)

ISSUE SUMMARY

YES: Professor of education and former school superintendent Larry Cuban offers some basic assumptions and specific guidelines for dealing with the urban dropout problem.
NO: Paul Woodring, an emeritus professor of educational psychology, attacks the conventional wisdom and turns his attention outside the schools.

The present nationwide dropout rate in American schools is somewhere in the vicinity of 25 percent by most calculations. In large urban districts and among certain minority groups the figures are closer to 50 percent. There are those who believe that a dramatic turnaround in dropout rates is possible; but even among those who support the goal of a 90 percent high school completion rate by the year 2000, there is a great deal of disagreement regarding the best way to accomplish such a goal. There are also those who believe that not only is the goal unrealistic but that the completion of the type of schooling that now prevails is not a desirable aim for many young people. Rutgers University professor Jackson Toby, for one, contends that "stay-ins" damage the quest for excellence in public education and often pose a threat to students who really want to learn. "Isn't it better for everybody," he states, "if some students drop out?"

The reasons why students drop out are many: personal or family problems, excessive absence or truancy, lack of interest or motivation, desire for or need of a job, failing grades, difficulty communicating with school professionals, and low levels of identification with school goals and activities. To deal with the situation, school systems have developed early detection programs and prevention and recovery programs. The former place an emphasis on working with the family to provide support and encouragement, building self-esteem through positive social interaction with peers and teachers, and providing alternative courses that may trigger a more enthusiastic response. The latter focus on better health and counseling centers, better teacher training, a more personalized school atmosphere, and full-time evening schools.

Approximately 80 percent of the nation's larger school districts provide opportunities to attend alternative schools for those students who are not responding well to the standard offerings. Harlem Prep in New York City, which originated in 1967; Philadelphia's Parkway Program, begun in 1968; and numerous "school-without-walls" programs have established long records of success. More recently, magnet schools, challenge programs, and special schools for those who have already dropped out have been initiated.

More research was done on the dropout phenomenon between 1987 and 1989 than in the previous 20, according to Robert DeBlois in "Keep At-Risk Students in School: Toward a Curriculum for Potential Dropouts," *NASSP Bulletin* (April 1989). Drawing on the ideas of philosopher John Dewey and the practices of dropout prevention approaches that are currently successful, DeBlois lists these essential components of good alternative schools: a meaningful vocational orientation, a focus on interdisciplinary team projects, and an emphasis on mastery learning in a continuous process curriculum that is individualized and flexible. Although these components are directed at potential dropouts, a case could be made for their applicability to programs for all students.

In the articles that follow, Larry Cuban contends that, even though much of the educational reform movement of the 1980s missed urban schools, there is still hope for improvement of their programs and a reduction in dropout rates. The key to this is the creation of a true sense of attachment between students and the schools. Paul Woodring does not share this optimism and, in fact, contends that prolonging the schooling of some children has already contributed greatly to disorder in the schools and has made the high school diploma almost meaningless.

YES

Larry Cuban

AT-RISK STUDENTS: WHAT TEACHERS AND PRINCIPALS CAN DO

You want to know what is happening in big city classrooms? Ask a teacher, talk to an assistant principal, visit a school and listen to students. Whatever you do, don't be fooled by the buzzwords from today's policymakers: *school-site management, high academic standards, core curriculum, restructured schools, teacher-run schools,* and the like. The buzzwords give a skewed picture of what occurs daily in classrooms; real school improvement has yet to penetrate most urban schools.

The truth is that recent state reforms have largely bypassed millions of students in urban schools across the nation (Carnegie Foundation for the Advancement of Teaching 1988, Committee for Economic Development 1987, and Ford Foundation, 1987). I said "largely." There are, of course, numerous efforts under way. The above reports note instances of gifted teachers' and principals' producing results that are outstanding in any situation but mind-boggling in the face of daily conditions in at-risk schools (Corcoran, Walker, and White, 1988). Turnaround schools, where staffs have converted educational disasters into schools where parents clamor for entry, do exist. Teachers like Garfield High's Jaime Escalante and Rabun Gap's Eliot Wigginton inspire and educate their students year after year. Administrators like Harlem's Deborah Meier and Los Angeles' George McKenna help teachers put forth their best again and again. Such successes are reported, then amplified like an echo in a cavern. But in numbers, they are a faint sound in the Grand Canyon of hundreds of thousands of classrooms and millions of students' lives.

I say this not to disparage these successes or the intentions of the reformers; I say this only to point out that recent reforms aimed at school and classroom improvement sailed over urban schools. Furthermore, I distinguish between slogans and the gritty realities facing teachers daily. Policymakers and headline writers frequently assume that changes in school governance, district boundaries, curriculum, or decision-making authority automatically lead to classroom changes in urban schools. Not so. The historical record unforgivingly documents such flawed assumptions in the stale buzz-words of earlier decades: *decentralization, teacher-proof curriculum, merit pay, individualized instruction,* and so on. We must tell policymakers that we know they cannot mandate or direct what matters in schools and classrooms.

After spending a quarter-century in classrooms and schools, I have reached a few conclusions, my operating assumptions.

• The future of urban schools is the primary issue facing the nation's educational system. If the system is left as it is, the social and individual costs of inadequate schooling will severely corrode the social fabric of the nation.

• The students in these schools, like students everywhere, bring strengths to their classrooms and dream dreams of academic success.

• There are teachers and principals who not only want to improve what occurs in their schools but have done so in the face of massive obstacles.

• As grim as some of the working conditions are, as complicated and tough as the children's lives are, there is a slim but significant margin of constructive change available to teachers and principals who are determined to stretch the minds and fashion the character of low-income, ethnic, and language-minority children.

To practitioners who share these assumptions, I ask two questions: (1) Is there sufficient knowledge available to make fundamental changes in a classroom and school? (2) What can principals and teachers do that will improve what children experience in urban schools?

IS SUFFICIENT KNOWLEDGE AVAILABLE?

Yes, it is. Drawing on practitioner wisdom accumulated through experience and on research findings, we have sufficient knowledge to make changes in schools and classrooms. Some of our practitioner wisdom is captured in the work of gifted principals and teachers who simply know what has to be done and do it. Some of our knowledge appears in syntheses of research such as the U.S. Department of Education's booklet *Schools That Work: Educating Disadvantaged Children.*

We know about the necessary conditions that have to be in place for improvement to occur. We know about the importance of a school culture where both children and adults share common values about respect, intellectual achievement, and caring for one another. We know that key decisions in curriculum, instruction, and school organization need to occur at the school site with the substantial participation of the entire staff.

But no pat formulas to grow effective schools yet exist. Knowing how to put together the right combination of people, things, and ideas to create a productive setting that supports at-risk students and the adults that work with them remains just out of our reach so far. It is the difference between having all the parts of a car lying around and knowing exactly how to put them together to make the car run. We know the necessary parts of an effective school, but we lack the know-how to put them together in just the right order. Still, knowing what the right pieces are is a solid advance (Purkey and Smith 1983).

HOW, THEN, CAN PRINCIPALS AND TEACHERS IMPROVE URBAN SCHOOLS?

By *improve,* I mean *create* schools and classrooms that build attachment in students toward completing school, increase the students' desire to learn, build self-esteem, and enhance academic performance. Let me take up the features of programs that have appeared in the literature and that coincide with practitioner wisdom about what works with at-risk students in urban schools (Comer 1980, Leinhardt and Bickel 1987).

1. *Size.* Successful schools and programs enroll as few as 50 students but seldom more than a few hundred. This smallness helps to foster enduring relationships among adults and students; in these programs, everyone knows everyone else, at least to some extent. Also, the potential for students to participate in activities is greater in small programs. Further, a class size of 15–20 students per teacher permits a level of personalizing instruction unavailable in more crowded settings. In secondary schools these programs can be housed as schools-within-a-school or separated from the main building. For example, Bret Harte Intermediate School in Los Angeles, Orr High School in Chicago, and Theodore Roosevelt High School in the Bronx adopted "houses" and similar arrangements to combat largeness and anonymity (Carnegie 1988).

2. *Staff.* Teachers often *choose* to work in these programs and classes, thus making a commitment to at-risk students in their decisions to volunteer. When this kind of commitment is wedded to personal and cultural knowledge about these pupils and a willingness to experiment with methods and techniques, these like-minded teachers develop into a spirited professional cadre who enjoy working together. Principals of these programs endorse classroom changes and provide tangible and emotional support. Further, district officials, the superintendent, and the school board actively nourish such endeavors and provide resources to help the program accomplish its purposes. Chambers Academy, a small public school in New York City, has 11 teachers who spend at least three hours a week with small groups of students in advisory sessions in addition to teaching two or more courses to the very same students (Carnegie 1988).

3. *Flexibility.* Because the program is small and purpose is to rescue kids from what appears to be a grim future, teachers and principals usually employ varied nontraditional approaches. There is seldom any ability grouping. Few, if any, distinctions are made between students other than, perhaps, age. Tests are used to figure out what kind of match is needed between the student and the difficulty level of materials and between the student and teacher methods. In effect, these successful programs reflect the concept of continuous progress or non-gradedness. Passing and failing are not public displays where some students move ahead and others stay behind; mastery and achievement become personal benchmarks along a trail toward larger goals.

Time is restructured into schedules quite different from regular school: secondary teachers frequently spend unusual amounts of time each day with students; team teaching is common for larger chunks of the school day. One teacher may work with a group of students not for a semester or even a year, but for two or even three years; the same high school teacher may teach three subjects. In-school learning is frequently mixed with out-of-school work or other tasks. Finally, these programs often coordinate an array of social services that the students need. The teacher, adviser, or special staff make linkages with social services, and the pressing needs of each student are dealt with by people who know the child (Lotto 1982, Wehlage 1983).

4. *School As Community.* These programs avoid the conventional model of school, where the teachers' primary concern is academic achievement, where students remain anonymous or emotionally distant from the teacher, and where rewards and penalties dominate the relationship between teacher and students. Rather, these small, flexible programs have in common a model of a community, an extended family where achievement is important and so is caring for one another. Building a sense of belonging to a group—in effect, a supportive environment—is consciously sought as a means of increasing self-esteem and achievement. Of course, the community model exists in regular schools, especially in small elementary schools or on high school athletic teams, clubs, bands, and drill teams; programs for at-risk students work hard to cultivate this community spirit and group cohesion so crucial to their success (Comer 1980).

OPTIONS FOR INSTRUCTION

When we move from matters of organization and climate to instruction, there are at least three directions teachers can consider. First, the literature on teacher effectiveness links certain teaching practices to test score gains. The pedagogy called *direct instruction* or *active teaching*, for example, claims that if teachers of

at-risk students use these practices in teaching reading and math at certain elementary grades, achievement test scores will increase. This model of teaching has frequently been folded into efforts aimed at building effective schools (Brophy and Good 1986).

Direct instruction has a fairly large body of research evidence to support its use of very specific teaching tactics for certain skills in elementary classrooms; it seems to fit at-risk students, and it particularly fits the inclinations of teachers familiar with the characteristics of such children.

However, critics of direct instruction have pointed out its deficits in content, its emphasis on routine work that proves tedious, its emphasis on test scores as the only measure of learning, its low expectations for teaching reasoning and critical thinking at the elementary level, and its inapplicability to secondary school subjects. Yet this approach, harnessed to the folk wisdom of veteran teachers, suggests that familiar techniques of managing a class, introducing and explaining material, will have some payoff in higher test scores—if that is the goal.

Second, there are instructional approaches that build on the strengths that children bring to school, instructional strategies that make linkages with life experiences of students and exploit a growing knowledge about active learning and the importance of student involvement in developing higher-order thinking skills. Such ways of teaching at-risk children (for example, whole language programs) further develop children's store of language, connect abstract ideas with children's background, and move back and forth between student experiences and school concepts (Au 1980, Heath 1983, Banks 1987).

Third, there is a growing body of evidence that mixed ability and multi-age groupings within and across classrooms have positive effects on student motivation and learning. Cooperative learning approaches that target culturally different children have demonstrated an array of positive outcomes including test score gains. By contrast, pullout programs or within-class grouping by ethnicity or aptitude often have unintended negative effects on students' learning (Leinhardt and Bickel 1987, Slavin 1983, Cohen 1986, Kennedy et al. 1986).

What these three alternatives mean for classroom teachers is that they can choose among them or blend them into their own individual repertoires. Teachers making these choices also need to know the cultural backgrounds of their students, show skill in connecting subject matter to student experiences, and construct classroom activities in which students participate actively in acquiring what is to be learned.

KEEN SATISFACTIONS

Are the resulting schools or programs very different from the familiar ones where silence, mixed with reprimands, worksheets and order, dominates the school day? Indeed, they are. Does this mean more work for principals and teachers? Indeed, it does. Will this produce keen satisfactions from seeing growth in students? Indeed, it will. The rewards are intensely personal and sharply felt; they last a lifetime.

There is, then, a window of opportunity open to teachers and principals who can still gather their courage, wits, and energy to improve the lives of at-risk children. But the work must be accomplished by teachers and administrators.

We cannot look to policies, regulations, and slogans to do the job.

REFERENCES

Au, K. (1980). "Participation Structures in a Reading Lesson with Hawaiian Children: Analysis of a Culturally Appropriate Instructional Event." *Anthropology and Education Quarterly* 11: 91–115.

Banks, J. (1987). "Ethnicity, Class, and Cognitive Styles: Research and Teaching Implications." Paper presented at American Educational Research Association, Washington, D.C.

Brophy, J., and T. Good. (1986). "Teacher Behavior and Student Achievement." In *Handbook of Research on Teaching*, edited by Merlin Wittrock. New York: Macmillan.

Carnegie Foundation for the Advancement of Teaching. (1988). *The Imperiled Generation.* New York: Carnegie Foundation for the Advancement of Teaching.

Cohen, E. (1986). *Designing Groupwork.* New York: Teachers College Press.

Comer, J. (1980). *School Power.* New York: Free Press.

Committee For Economic Development. (1987). *Children in Need: Investment Strategies for the Educationally Disadvantaged.* New York: Committee for Economic Development.

Corcoran, T., L. Walker, and L. White. (1988). *Working in Urban Schools.* Washington, D.C.: Institute for Educational Leadership.

Ford Foundation. (1987). *The Forgotten Half: Non-College Youth in America.* New York: Ford Foundation.

Heath, S. B. (1983). *Ways With Words.* New York: Cambridge University Press.

Kennedy, M., R. Jung, and M. Orland. (1986). *Poverty, Achievement and the Distribution of Compensatory Education Services.* Washington, D.C.: U.S. Department of Education.

Leinhardt, G., and W. Bickel. (1987). "Instruction's the Thing Wherein to Catch the Mind That Falls Behind." *Educational Psychologist* 22: 177–207.

Lotto, L. S. (1982). "The Holding Power of Vocational Curricula: Characteristics of Effective Dropout Prevention Programs." *Journal of Vocational Education Research* 7, 4: 39–49.

Purkey, S., and M. S. Smith. (1983). "Effective Schools: A Review." *Elementary School Journal* 40: 427–452.

Slavin, R. (1983). *Cooperative Learning.* New York: Longman.

Wehlage, G. (1983). *Effective Programs for the Marginal High School Student.* Bloomington, Ind.: Phi Delta Kappa Educational Foundation.

NO

Paul Woodring

A NEW APPROACH TO THE DROPOUT PROBLEM

The nationwide drive to keep all adolescents in high school until they graduate—to "cut the dropout rate to zero by the year 2000"—undoubtedly has the support of millions of Americans who have not thought deeply about the consequences. Unfortunately, the results of such an effort are certain to be disappointing, even in the unlikely event that the goal is achieved.

In 1951 Robert Ulich of the Harvard Graduate School of Education warned us that "prolongation of school age is not in itself a blessing, but may even be a curse to civilization, unless there goes together with the prolongation a revolutionary rethinking and restructuring of the total program from the secondary school upward" [Robert Ulich, *Crisis and Hope in American Education* (Boston: Beacon Press, 1951), p. 28]. This warning has not been heeded. No such rethinking or restructuring has occurred. Instead, we have persisted in thinking that just keeping all boys and girls in school longer will solve the problems of illiteracy, crime, and unemployment. In reality, while it has solved none of these problems, the prolongation of schooling has already contributed greatly to disorder in the schools and has made the high school diploma almost meaningless.

More years in school will not cure illiteracy. Anyone who has survived 10 years of schooling without learning to read is not likely to become literate as a result of sitting in classes for two more years. If high school teachers are required to spend their time trying to teach adolescents to read, they will have no time for the more advanced education that the rest of their students need, want, and are ready for. The achievement of literacy is the task of the elementary school or of a remedial program for adults.

Keeping juvenile delinquents in school does not prevent crime. It brings crime into the schools. The cliché "school keeps them off the streets" is nonsense. At best, school keeps adolescents off the streets for only five or six hours a day for half the days of the year. This leaves ample time for those who are so disposed to engage in gang warfare and other illegal and antisocial activities. It seems safe to say that potential dropouts do not spend much time on homework.

While it is true that dropouts have trouble finding jobs, there is no persuasive evidence that the same individuals would be any more employable after more years in school. In the past, vocational education programs kept many students in school while preparing them for employment. But such programs do not solve the problems of today's urban dropouts. Courses that prepare students for the skilled trades, for secretarial work, or for scientific agriculture require intelligence and high levels of motivation; they are not designed for slow or reluctant learners.

Moreover, the conviction that high school diplomas are essential for everyone is of recent origin. Edison, Carnegie, Rockefeller, and Ford became high achievers in an industrial society without high school diplomas. Throughout the 19th century, many senators, governors, merchants, and even Presidents of the United States had only a few years of schooling. The fact that Abraham Lincoln was able to compose the Gettysburg Address without the aid of speechwriters is evidence that it is possible to become highly literate without much formal education.

In most parts of the U.S., free public high schools did not come into existence until the last quarter of the 19th century. In 1900 only 6% of the appropriate age group graduated from high school. Somewhere along the way, the other 94% dropped out. In the 1920s only half of our young people even entered high school, and half of those who did enter did not stay for four years. In other words, 75% were dropouts. In 1950, 41% dropped out.

Estimates of the percentage of young people who drop out today range from 14% to 27%, depending on whose figures you choose to accept. (William James once observed that the chief use of statistics is to refute the figures of other statisticians.) The 14% figure comes from the U.S. Census Bureau, which counts as a dropout anyone past the age of 18 who has not graduated from high school and who is no longer enrolled. This is probably the best national figure we can obtain because different school districts count dropouts in different ways, while some do not count them at all.

In any case, it seems clear that the present percentage of dropouts is the lowest in history. The much higher figures often bruited about in the media are for selected cities, not for the entire nation. It is notable that the highest rates are now in the major metropolitan areas, whereas, a generation or two ago, they were in the rural areas. This may explain why dropouts are getting more attention today: most editors and writers live in cities.

THE EFFORT TO KEEP ALL ADOLESCENTS IN high school until they graduate is now on a collision course with the equally insistent demand for higher standards for promotion and graduation. Some of today's school reformers see no conflict. They persist in believing that all adolescents could master the traditional academic disciplines if only they were sufficiently "challenged." They demand a single high school curriculum for all that would include foreign languages, mathematics through calculus, three years of science, three years of social studies, and four years of literature that would include translations of the greatest literature of the western world.

Such a curriculum would be splendid for the academically talented, but it shows no evidence of the kind of rethinking and restructuring advocated by Ulich. The only teachers who think this curriculum could be made effective for all students are those who teach in highly selective private schools that avoid the problem of educating slow learners by not admitting them in the first place. Public school teachers, who face the full range of intellectual capacity in their classrooms, laugh at the idea of teaching Dostoevski and differential calculus to *all* their students. They doubt the wisdom of teaching foreign languages to students who are still having trouble with English. They know that requiring such a program of everyone would cause the number of dropouts to rise.

While some students drop out because they are unable to comprehend what is being taught, many leave for other reasons. Those who are emotionally disturbed might be helped by the services of a good school psychologist, but the prospects are less bright for those who have become addicted to drugs at an early age. Some students drop out in the hope of finding jobs to support their families, only to discover that no jobs are available. Nearly a million teenage girls become pregnant each year, and half of them never finish high school.

But this still leaves a substantial number who, when asked their reasons for leaving, are prone to say that they are bored and that they "can't stand being cooped up in a classroom all day." Such adolescent restlessness is not at all unusual, even among those of good intelligence. In an earlier era, these young people could have gone West, though many were content to return to the farm where they could take pride in doing the work of adults. Because such opportunities are no longer available, today's dropouts pose a growing social problem.

If all reluctant learners were *required* to remain in school—and if we could recruit enough truant officers to enforce the requirement—the schools would become custodial rather than educational institutions. Indeed, some high schools in our major cities have already moved a long way in that direction, as is indicated by falling standards, growing disorder, and despair among teachers. Because the schools cannot solve this problem without endangering the education of those students who are ready and eager to learn, we must look beyond the schools for a solution.

WHAT URBAN DROPOUTS MOST NEED IS A complete change of environment. They need an environment that takes them out of the city slums with their pervasive crime and readily available drugs. One possible way of doing this might be the establishment of a revised version of the Civilian Conservation Corps (CCC) of the 1930s. In the CCC young men were organized into companies of about 200, under the direction of reserve army officers, and sent to national parks and national forests to build roads, trails, and bridges; to construct campgrounds for tourists; and to fight forest fires. They were provided good food and medical services.

Each CCC company had an education officer who offered evening courses, and many boys who had been restless in school found it much more interesting to study geology, biology, surveying, and astronomy while living in a tent in a mountain valley. Men who are now of retirement age recall the CCC experience as a turning point in their lives. Many later returned to school and prospered there. I have known several as colleagues on university faculties. (The new CCC might have two or three education officers in each company, instead of one.)

Today, there should also be a similar program for women. Many girls who find high schools too confining would love the experience of building mountain trails or engaging in other activities that were once considered "men's work." The success of the Women's Army Corps (WACs) in World War II gave clear evidence that women could thrive under wilderness conditions. Those WACs whom I knew in New Guinea and other South Sea islands had higher morale than the men, and many of them were only a little older than today's dropouts.

The CCC program of the 1930s provided work and valuable learning experience for about three million men. At its peak it enrolled about half a million a year—approximately equal to the yearly number of dropouts today. If we could afford such a program during the years of the Great Depression, surely we can afford it in today's more affluent society. It would relieve high schools of the responsibility for the boys and girls who are profiting least from what high schools now provide and who are most likely to cause problems for teachers and for other students. At the same time, it would provide the dropouts with experience that would make them more employable when they return to their homes.

I am not proposing a new version of the CCC as a panacea for all the ills of schooling; there are no panaceas for problems so complex. I offer it as an example of the kind of rethinking that becomes possible once we reject the conventional wisdom that simply keeping everyone in school longer will solve our problems.

POSTSCRIPT

Can Schools Prevent Urban Dropouts?

"Withered Hopes, Stillborn Dreams: The Dismal Panorama of Urban Schools" is the title of a 1988 article by Gene Maeroff. It represents the feelings of many—experts and laypeople alike—that we are nearing the time when many of our big city public school systems will become inoperable.

Nevertheless, a stream of opinion and research and experimentation keeps hopes glimmering. A 1988 study by the Grant Foundation, *The Forgotten Half*, charts a path that includes greater flexibility in allowing people to return to school, expansion of work-study programs, development of community service projects, better career information and counseling, and the provision of tutors and mentors. Other proposals for action flow from books, such as *Illiterate America* (1985) by Jonathan Kozol; *Before It's Too Late* (1988) by Anne Wheelock and Gayle Dorman; and *School Dropouts: Patterns and Policies* (1986) by Gary Natriello. The most recent attempt to shed light on the problem is a book featuring interviews of teenagers by teenagers, *When I Was Young I Loved School: Dropping Out and Hanging In* (1989) edited by Anne Sheffield and Bruce Frankel.

Recent journal articles such as the following take a variety of stances on the issue: "The Dropout Controversy: Dropouts and Grownups—Coercion or Choice?" Chester Finn and Jackson Toby, *Public Interest* (Summer 1989); "Dropout Prevention: Trinkets and Gimmicks or Deweyan Reconstruction," Joseph Gerics and Miriam Westheimer, *Teachers College Record* (Fall 1988); "Rich Schools, Poor Schools: The Persistence of Unequal Education," Arthur Wise, *College Board Review* (Spring 1989); "The Student Incentive Plan: Mitigating the Legacy of Poverty," George Richmond, *Phi Delta Kappan* (November 1990); and "Educating Poor Minority Children," James P. Comer, *Scientific American* (November 1988).

A number of journals have devoted issues to the dropout theme: the May 1987 issue of *Education and Urban Society*, which contains specific studies of black and Hispanic students and a fine article by Margaret D. LeCompte on the cultural context; the May/June 1988 issue of *Black Scholar*; the February 1989 issue of *Educational Leadership*; and the June 1990 issue of *Phi Delta Kappan*. Finally, the October 1989 issue of *Phi Delta Kappan* includes a summary of the Phi Delta Kappa study of students at risk by Jack Frymier and Bruce Gansneder. Relevant books include *Dropouts in America: Enough Is Known for Action* (Institute for Educational Leadership, 1987) by Andrew Hahn, Jacqueline Danzberger, and Bernard Lefkowitz; *Improving the Urban High School* (1990) by Karen S. Louis and Matthew B. Miles; *Liberating Schools: Education in the Inner City* (1991) edited by David Boaz; *Dealing With the Dropout Problem* (1990) by N. L. Gage; and *Making Schools Work for Under-achieving Minority Students* (1990) edited by Josie G. Bain and Joan L. Herman.

ISSUE 13

Should Literacy Be Based on Traditional Culture?

YES: E. D. Hirsch, Jr., from "Restoring Cultural Literacy in the Early Grades," *Educational Leadership* (December 1987/January 1988)

NO: James A. Banks, from "Multicultural Literacy and Curriculum Reform," *Educational Horizons* (Spring 1991)

ISSUE SUMMARY

YES: Professor of English E. D. Hirsch, Jr., insists that higher levels of literacy must be achieved through a renewed emphasis on traditional information and a common culture.
NO: Professor of education James A. Banks argues that the nation's demographic makeup necessitates a curriculum reshaped along multicultural lines.

Focus on the lack of cultural literacy in the United States, as defined by E. D. Hirsch, Jr., in his book *Cultural Literacy* and by Allan Bloom in his popular book *The Closing of the American Mind* (1987), has renewed the blaze of controversy over the role a student's social experiences should play in shaping schools. Can there be a specific designation of the knowledge essential to the attainment of cultural understanding in a given society? When that society is multicultural, should so-called literacy be drawn exclusively from the dominant cultural source within that society? Although John Dewey (see Issue 1) advocated a flexible curriculum geared to personal interests and social problems, Robert M. Hutchins identified the Great Books (of the Western world) as the key to cultural understanding and social functioning.

The subtitle of Allan Bloom's 1987 book is *How Higher Education Has Failed Democracy and Impoverished the Souls of Today's Students,* and it stirred fears in a manner similar to the earlier "Nation at Risk" document. Mortimer J. Adler's *Paideia Proposal,* William J. Bennett's *To Reclaim a Legacy,* Lynne Cheney's *American Memory,* Diane Ravitch and Chester Finn, Jr.'s *What Do Our 17-Year-Olds Know?* and Bennett's "James Madison" curricula are all 1980s documents that sounded alarms about the state of education in the United States and offered fairly consistent methods for redirecting educational efforts.

The pattern enunciated in these works centers on the internalization of cultural knowledge and on the study of original works drawn primarily from the United States' European heritage. Early and consistent exposure to the chronological development of that heritage through the public schools as well as the larger community are seen as vital elements in the "recovery" process.

A number of critics, however, are concerned about the almost total emphasis on a Eurocentric perspective. Molefi Kete Asante, for example, has written forcefully on his advocacy of "multicultural literacy," and Ira Shor's book *Culture Wars: School and Society in the Conservative Restoration, 1969–1984* (1987) claims that the underlying motivation of the movement is "to restore conservative themes and 'right words' that establish raw authority at the top while discrediting the [liberal] 1960s."

In the articles presented here, E. D. Hirsch, Jr., observes that the teaching of traditional knowledge through good literature has been severely undermined. He contends that the uniformity of literature textbooks that prevailed in decades past has evaporated under the influence of erroneous doctrines and slogans, which have come to dominate educational decisions. Everyone, he contends, must be able to participate in the national culture—the disadvantaged as well as the advantaged—and this requires uniform exposure to a common body of materials. In rebuttal James A. Banks contends that the "national culture" that Hirsch espouses is dominated by a traditional Eurocentric canon, which ignores the social construction of knowledge and current cultural realities.

YES   E. D. Hirsch, Jr.

RESTORING CULTURAL LITERACY
IN THE EARLY GRADES

In recent decades we have assumed that the early curriculum should be "child-centered" and "skill-centered." Yet there is a growing consensus among reading researchers that adequate literacy depends upon the specific information called "cultural literacy," and we should therefore begin to impart traditional literate culture to children at the earliest possible age.

The need to begin such instruction early is based on technical as well as social considerations. From a purely technical standpoint, our children need traditional background information early to make sense of significant reading materials, and thus gain further information that enables them to make further progress in reading and learning. From a social standpoint, the need to start as early as possible is even more urgent. Young children from the middle class sometimes receive necessary literate information outside the school, but disadvantaged children rarely have access to literate background information outside the school. Therefore, to change the cycle of illiteracy that debars disadvantaged children from high literacy, we need to impart enough literate information from preschool through third grade to ensure continued progress in literacy on the part of all our children.

EXAMINING THE EDUCATIONAL SLOGANS

Now that these basic truths are becoming widely known, it is time to question and qualify some educational slogans inconsistent with those truths that have actively hindered the teaching of literate information to young children. I do not suggest that the three slogans I shall examine constitute all the intellectual barriers to curriculum reform in the early grades (sheer inertia must never be underestimated). But the harmful slogans are powerful and widely spread. Calling them into doubt might help foster the urgently needed reform of giving young children early instruction in our traditional literate culture.

1. *The home is more decisive for literacy than the school.* No one with common sense would doubt that a child whose parents actively encourage conscientious performance in school will do better, all things equal, than a child whose parents discourage academic performance. We know that many children are all too heavily influenced by the anti-academic values (usually defensive reactions) of their parents and peers. Every conscientious teacher, principal, and supervisor tries to counteract the anti-school ethic that is especially powerful and self-defeating among just those disadvantaged children who are most in need of a pro-school ethic. Although few of us in education have the time or opportunity to abolish the anti-school ethic in all its defensive manifestations, one good sign of the times is that we are getting help. Parents and the public at large have identified the problem, and are trying to help the schools combat it.

But quite apart from lamenting the negative influences of anti-academic attitudes, some educators have held a rather defeatist view about the possibility of breaking the illiteracy cycle. They accept as axiomatic the slogan that the educational and economic level of the home is more decisive for high literacy than the school can ever be, no matter how supportive the attitudes of the home. This defeatist attitude dates, of course, from the first Coleman report of 1966. Since that time, the slogan that the socioeconomic status of the home is inherently decisive for academic achievement has been part of the received wisdom of many specialists in education.

The slogan is, of course, true as a description of educational outcomes under our current educational arrangements. Children from middle-class homes perform better on the whole than children from poor homes, no matter what schools they attend or what moral support they receive in the home. Viewed in broad, statistical terms, a child's socioeconomic status is at present the decisive factor in academic performance. But two inferences from the first Coleman report are open to serious criticism: first, the inference that the state of affairs described by the report is inherent and inevitable, and, second (a corollary of the first), that any attempt to reverse the sociological finding by specific school policies would be futile. These doleful inferences are used to support the claim that we can at best try to change the attitudes and actions of parents, but that nothing of consequence regarding the cycle of illiteracy will be accomplished by changing the policies of our already-beleaguered schools.

We must, of course, acknowledge that all attempts to reinforce children's education within the home are welcome. Parental help is useful not only for motivating students, but also for increasing their time-on-task and attitude to learning. My aim in criticizing the slogan of the decisiveness of the home is not to discourage vigorous appeals to parents to help, supervise and encourage their children's learning. My purpose, rather, is to insist that, despite the importance of the home, our schools can do a much better job of teaching literacy to all students, even without effective reinforcement from the home.

There is positive evidence, not considered by the first Coleman report, that under a different curriculum our schools can make children acceptably literate even when they come from illiterate homes. The positive evidence is just as compelling as the negative evidence cited

212 / 13. SHOULD LITERACY BE BASED ON TRADITIONAL CULTURE?

in the report. In fact, the positive evidence is more compelling, because it takes into account a larger number of instances and a greater amount of experimental data. I mean by this the historical record.

In the later nineteenth and early twentieth century, American schools succeeded in creating a literate middle class by teaching children of illiterate parents. One factor in their success, lacking in our schools today, was the use of a traditional literate curriculum. Ruth Elson has demonstrated the uniformity of American textbooks in the 19th century, and to her study may now be added Kathryn Neeley's examination of school readers between the 1840s and the 1940s. Both studies find a consistent tendency in earlier schoolbooks to teach common, traditional materials. The commonalty of our elementary curriculum in the early twentieth century gave students from literate and illiterate families alike a common foundation in the literate culture, which, as I show in *Cultural Literacy*, is a prerequisite to mature literacy.

Looking outside the United States and taking a still broader historical view of home influence produces evidence that is even more decisive. In the eighteenth century, the established of wide-scale national literacy in Britain, France, and Germany (and every other literate country) was first accomplished through the school, not through the home. In Perpignan, for example, literacy in the French language was achieved by schools that taught children who heard and spoke no French in their homes. Indeed, their Catalan-speaking parents were not literate in any language, and were in fact *opposed* to their children's learning French in school.

The only way national literacy could have been achieved in such large multilinguistic nations as France and Great Britain was through the deliberate agency of a national school system that conveyed a common core of literate culture. Parents in Wales, for example, did not always approve of or cooperate with schools that taught English to their children. Nonetheless, Welsh schools graduated pupils who were literate in English language and culture. The cooperation of parents was certainly not available in the schools of Brittany, where Breton-speaking parents opposed the teaching of French. But that did not prevent the schools of Brittany from producing pupils who were literate in French language and culture. In short, the schools can impart high literacy even under severe handicaps, if they do so by teaching not only the mechanical skills of decoding but also the literate national culture. Ernest Gellner has pointed out that all literate national cultures in the modern world have been school-transmitted cultures rather than home-transmitted cultures, and has explained in detail why the pattern has necessarily been followed in every modern nation.

Why, then, did we accept the slogan that the socioeconomic status of the home is more decisive than the policies of the school in achieving mature literacy? What lies behind the well-documented findings of the first Coleman report?

The best explanation I can devise is this: Up to about 1945 in many schools (give or take a decade to allow for the slowness of curricular change), literacy *had* been effectively taught to disadvantaged students under a largely traditional curriculum. It was not until the 1940s that older generations of teachers and administrators had retired in large numbers and were replaced by disciples of Dewey and Kilpatrick, who imposed the latest child- and skill-centered textbooks. Up to the 1940s or so, many of our schools were still able to graduate highly literate students who had come from illiterate homes. They effected this transformation through a traditional curriculum both for native black children as well as for children from immigrant European families.

But by the 1940s, with the newer theories ever more dominant in teachers, administrators, and textbooks, our public schools were turning slowly and overwhelmingly to less traditional, more up-to-date, child-centered materials that gradually ceased to transmit our traditional literate culture. This curricular change constituted a particularly catastrophic turn for the early grades. The effects of the change were not immediately noticed, because the earlier curriculum had already created a large number of literate homes that continued to supply their children with the traditional literate information that had disappeared from the schools.

Thus the new curriculum was not at first disabling for those children who were lucky enough to come from highly literate homes, where they received traditional (originally school-transmitted) literate culture. But the new curriculum did cease to supply literate background information to children from illiterate homes, and consequently those unfortunates did not receive the needed information from any source. This hypothesis probably explains why the Coleman report of 1966 turned out to be inconsistent with the larger historical record. Unhappily, this hypothesis about the effects of the new curriculum may also explain why our schools in the past four decades have done little to improve the educational and economic status of children from illiterate homes.

The practical implication of these historical observations, when coupled with the data from reading research, is to suggest that we should once again teach all of our children the elements of our traditional literate culture, starting at an early age. That means, for instance, teaching Mother Goose at school, instead of assuming that Mother Goose rhymes might bore children who have already heard them. The argument about boredom has an easy answer; if parents don't want their children to be bored, and if they know that our schools are going to teach Mother Goose, they can read their kids *Pat the Bunny* or *The Cat in the Hat* or whatever else they choose, with full confidence that "Jack and Jill" are on the way.

In sum, we cannot validly generalize the findings of the Coleman report of 1966. We cannot justifiably continue to repeat the easy slogan that the home is the fundamental determinant of literacy. Our children are not trapped in a cycle of sociological determinism. As late as the 1930s and 1940s our schools were our chief, and at times our only conveyors of our literate traditions. History and common sense suggest that our schools can successfully resume that primary responsibility with better results than ever before. The home should, of course, foster a pro-school ethic, and should, where possible, enhance, enlarge, and encourage the teaching of our literate traditions. But it is our schools which must make sure that our literate traditions are successfully conveyed to every child from every sort of home.

2. *Schools should stress general skills and broad understanding, not mere facts.* Along with the new child- and skill-centered curriculum went an antipathy to "mere facts." The phrases "rote-learning" and "piling up of facts" are still used today as scapegoat terms against a traditional education that has not in fact existed in our public schools for several decades. In the 1920s such terms of abuse radiated from lectures at Teachers College, Columbia, and slowly spread to schools of education throughout the nation. You will immediately recognize that these scapegoat terms still function as banner slogans, even though the education they attack has long since vanished from the scene. On the other hand, the typical terms of approval in educational writing since the '20s continue to be such phrases as "relevant materials" that are "meaningful to the child," and that inculcate "higher-order skills."

Since we now know that, in order to become literate, young children must gain a store of traditional information at an early age, it is time to reconsider the pejorative use of phrases like "memorization," (better to say "learning by heart") and "piling up facts" as though they were insult terms. Many "higher-order skills" of literacy are gained *only* by piling up information. No study of language acquisition, for instance, has challenged the commonsense observation that children learn the names of objects by repeatedly being told those names until they remember them. Thus, at the very roots of language acquisition we find memorization and the piling up of facts. Later on, in earliest training, children must learn the alphabet by heart. I cannot conceive how a child could acquire the alphabet other than by memorization and the piling up of facts. The

same applies to the multiplication table, the days of the week, and the months of the year. There's no other way of acquiring those skills.

Of course everybody knows these things. I do not wish to make the shibboleths of modern educational theory seem totally without merit. My point is subtler and gentler. Only recently have we come to understand that "Jack and Jill" and "George Washington" belong to an alphabet that must be learned by heart, and which is no less essential to higher-order literacy skills than the alphabet itself. Certain linguistically based concepts (researchers call them "schemata") belong to the very ABCs of literacy. The methods by which children learn these higher-order ABCs can be exciting and fun, or they can be deadening and painful. Good teachers always try to choose the pleasant over the painful, if only because the pleasant is more effective. But learning the higher-order ABCs, like learning the alphabet itself, does require learning by heart and piling up information.

The negative connotations of terms like "mere facts" and "memorization" arise from the theory that acquiring facts is inferior to "meaningful" learning experiences that cause children to take interest in and understand the significance of what they are being taught. It is assumed that the piling up of information cannot be meaningful, or interesting, or motivational to children. Given such alternatives, who would choose to be meaningless and dull? To reinforce this anti-fact, anti-memorization view, psychology since the time of Herbart has instructed us that the only materials that are meaningful to children are those that resonate with their own imaginations and experiences. Hence, the humane principle of meaningful, nonrote instruction has been reinforced by the scientific principle that curricular materials should connect directly with the experiences of young children.

But expert teaching and well-conceived texts, not modernity of content, are the bridges of relevance that connect reading materials with a child's experience. The life experiences of children who enter American classrooms are much too varied to form a definite content basis for child-centered materials. Moreover, most of the literate culture that children will need for later life consists of traditional, intergenerational materials. Consequently, their literacy is more effectively enhanced when they are successfully taught durable, traditional subjects like Ulysses and the Cyclops than when they are taught ephemera like Dick and Jane at the Supermarket.

It's quite doubtful that "mere facts" are really meaningless to young children, any more than they are to adults. We should unblinkingly face the truth that many of the facts we adults know are not perfectly interconnected in our minds. Meaningfulness does not require complete clarity and coherence, or even powerful emotion. E. B. White once said that he learned how to write just as he learned how to drive, without understanding what went on under the hood. How many adults can explain coherently what happens when they switch on a TV set? Most of us just know the less-than-coherent facts about TV: the picture comes on when we punch the power switch, it changes when we change the channel switch, and it goes off when we punch the power switch again. In the technological era, many of us still live in the "magic years"; things happen for us as they happen for children in ways that

we do not fully understand and cannot accurately explain.

Take another example. The names that we give to objects and concepts rarely have any coherent logic to them. It is the nature of language to be arbitrary. *Dog* has no more inherent rightness or logical aptness than *chien* or *Hund*. We have just gotten used to the words. This is as true for adults as for children. In short, the world of adults, like that of children, is at least partly incoherent and arbitrary. The child's world is less coherent and certainly less accurate than our own, but the differences are of degree, not kind. Perhaps many differences between children and adults have been, as Mark Twain said of reports of his death, greatly exaggerated.

Much of the essential information that we adults need can be gained only by being "piled up" as schemata in our memories. If parents and teachers waited until children could adequately understand the alphabet, they would wait until the first year of a doctoral program in linguistics. If they waited until children could adequately understand the first line of "My country, 'tis of thee," they would wait until tenth grade before divulging the words of the song. (Does anyone know an elementary school child who can explain the linguistic meaning of the words "My country, 'tis of thee"? For that matter, does anyone believe that a first-grader can understand "The Star-Spangled Banner," whose readability score probably ranks at the eleventh- or twelfth-grade level? Shall we therefore defer teaching "The Star-Spangled Banner" until twelfth grade?)

Even the most ardent proponents of "meaningful" instruction and "higher-order skills acquisition" must accept such inconsistencies when slogans about developmental learning readiness are applied to the early grades. I don't know anyone who is so opposed to learning by heart as to deplore the teaching of the alphabet, or "The Star-Spangled Banner," or "America." But if we acquiesce in accepting *those* incompletely understood elements into the curriculum, why should we exclude other "mere facts" that are equally useful to literacy? Answer: We should *not* exclude those traditional facts, but recognize that young children need many, many items of traditional information that are no less necessary to literacy than the alphabet and "The Star-Spangled Banner."

Another grave weakness in the theory that children are interested only in immediately meaningful, child-centered materials is that young children take great joy in learning vaguely understood information that will only later be fully meaningful to them. Although many of the facts that children need to learn are meaningless to them in a linguistic sense, they are nonetheless highly meaningful to them in a social sense. Children give their own context to such items, and correctly believe them to belong to the fabric of the adult community they wish to join. Children thrive only as members of a community. From the cradle, they take to language and culture like ducks to water. They come into the world with an appetite for acculturation. It is impractical, indeed absurd, to thwart that *natural* appetite for culture on the basis of an abstract theory about learning readiness. Nothing better expresses the absurdity than Dewey's deploring the "facility" with which young children absorb the cultural facts we pile upon them, or his approval of Rousseau's fatuous remark that "the apparent ease with which children learn is their ruin."

3. *The optimal contents of a language arts curriculum can be determined on scientific principles.* This doctrine about the early curriculum is less a slogan than an unexamined assumption. Science is a neutral servant of our educational purposes. Science represents the reality principle in education. It does not set our goals; it serves them. It helps define their inherent limits, and indicates the best avenues for us to follow in order to achieve them. Any more substantial claim for the role of science in education is a misleading claim.

Suppose, for example, that our primary goal is to achieve high literacy for all children. How can science guide us in choosing the *specific* materials to reach that goal? One currently used, so-called "scientific" approach is to use a quantitatively determined first-grade vocabulary for first grade, a second-grade vocabulary for second grade, and so on. And how does science yield up these graded vocabularies? By word frequency studies. The most frequent words should be taught first, the next frequent next, and so on.

There are serious difficulties hidden under this apparently neutral, apparently scientific approach. Assuming that makers of children's texts use common sense, as McGuffey did long before there were any word frequency studies, they wouldn't have to take special measures to supply young children with the most frequent words of English. They could assume that children would encounter those primary words with approximately the standard frequency in *any* reasonably chosen reading materials. They could rely on the fact that any diverse sampling of texts in a language will produce a similar list of its most frequent words. For instance, the Francis-Kucera frequency list, taken from the huge Brown University corpus consisting of several million words, puts the word *from* in position 26. The Carroll-Davies-Richman (CDR) frequency list, taken from a corpus of elementary and secondary school materials, puts the word *from* in position 23. It is safe to assume that *any* intelligently chosen materials for the early grades will provide automatic reinforcement of the most frequent words of the English language.

An even stronger reason for not depending on word frequencies to determine suitable elementary reading materials is that after a certain point—somewhere after the top few thousand words—word frequencies depend entirely on the particular corpus of texts chosen to determine them. But what is the right corpus for the early grades? No one can answer that question on neutral scientific grounds. There is no purely objective, scientific way of choosing the right corpus for determining the correct grade-level of words. Consider, for example, some implications for choosing proper names in texts for early grades by means of the Carroll-Davies-Richman frequency list. On the basis of the most frequent words from 1 to 10,000, the corpus tells us that early texts should contain:

- The Alamo *but not* The Iliad
- Jack and Jill *but not* Cinderella
- Blake *but not* Milton
- Helen Keller *but not* Joan of Arc
- Moses *but not* Jesus
- Galileo *but not* Copernicus
- John Glenn *but not* Charles Lindbergh
- Louis Pasteur *but not* Marie Curie
- Scrooge *but not* Dickens
- Edison *but not* Locke
- Einstein *but not* Socrates
- Hitler *but not* Churchill

This list on its face suggests the inappropriateness of using word frequency as a "scientific" basis for the content of the language arts curriculum. In fact, such a use of word frequency is quite *unscientific* when we simply take the existing word frequencies that are found in current school materials as "objective" guides for determining the proper frequencies for new school materials.

Understanding this, suppose we did agree upon an appropriate corpus for determining grade-by-grade vocabulary according to word frequency. One characteristic of such a corpus would be that it must be constantly revised to reflect changes in the literate culture. Otherwise, the frequency analysis might become quite misleading. Consider this example. The biggest analyzed corpus of English that we have is the one at Brown University, compiled by Francis and Kucera. This corpus not only takes materials from a deliberately indiscriminate sampling of genres, it also remains stuck in the year 1961. Thus, according to the frequencies of the Brown corpus, the first surname that our children should learn after Washington is Khrushchev.

What inference should we draw from this interesting fact? Not, of course, that first-graders should be taught about Nikita Khrushchev before they are taught about Abraham Lincoln. Rather, we should draw the inference that it is all too easy to misapply scientific data. Consider, by contrast, the *scientific* virtues of simply asking a group of literate adults to choose the words and concepts that are most important for children to know to become literate adults. These people will do a much better job than either the Brown or the CDR frequency lists, in part because the corpus of texts they have read will be many, many times bigger than even the huge Brown corpus, and in part because their sense of the most appropriate words will be constantly adjusting itself to significant cultural change. Consequently, their judgments will be far less likely to exhibit the Khrushchev effect. This advantage alone will make their judgments more, not less, scientific than the current word frequency approach. Of course, these observations imply no criticism of the valuable work of Carroll, Davies, and Richman, Francis, and Kucera, but are directed toward the unsound, uncritical use of quantitative research.

Other examples of pseudoscience in education could teach us the same moral: there can be no substitute for informed judgments by educated adults regarding the most important contents to be taught to children. If we as a nation decide that we want our children to possess mature literacy, there is no substitute for asking literate persons collectively to decide upon the contents required for mature literacy. After we make that determination, we need to develop an effective sequence of those core contents and effectively present them during the 13 years of schooling. Science can surely help us accomplish those jobs, but science alone is not in a position to tell us which words, concepts, and facts we need to teach.

CHANGING A LOSING GAME

In criticizing certain slogans and assumptions that are current among some educators, my purpose has, of course, been a constructive one. I take no pleasure in showing prized educational doctrines to be half-truths. Rather, I have tried to focus on just those doctrines, slogans, and assumptions that have actively impeded the teaching of traditional literate information to young children. Only by imparting that information early can we achieve higher literacy and greater social justice. Any half-truth or slogan, no matter how dearly held, that stands in the way of that aim should be ruthlessly cast aside. Our children are more important than our theories.

We have given our theories a reasonable chance during the past four decades, and in light of the current ignorance explosion among young people, our results do not tend to confirm our theories. Even those educators who do not agree with my specific proposals for higher national literacy may nonetheless readily agree with the great tennis player Bill Tilden, whose immortal strategic advice holds for educational policy just as well as for tennis matches: "Always change a losing game."

NO

James A. Banks

MULTICULTURAL LITERACY AND CURRICULUM REFORM

Most reports urging educational reform in the 1980s paid scant attention to helping citizens develop the knowledge, attitudes, and skills necessary to function effectively in a nation and world increasingly diverse ethnically, racially, and culturally. Two of the most influential works published late in the decade not only failed to describe the need for multicultural literacy and understanding, but also ran counter to the U.S. multicultural movement.

E. D. Hirsch's and Allan Bloom's widely reviewed and discussed books, both published in 1987, were regarded by many as having cogently made the case for emphasizing the traditional western-centric canon dominating school and university curricula, a canon threatened, according to Bloom and other western traditionalists, by movements to incorporate more ethnic and women's content into curricula. Hirsch's works appear more sympathetic to ethnic and women's concern's than Bloom's. However, Hirsch's formulation of a list of memorizable facts is inconsistent with multicultural teaching, since it ignores the notion of knowledge as a social construction with normative and political assumptions. Regarding knowledge as a social construction and viewing it from diverse cultural perspectives are key components of multicultural literacy.

There is growing recognition among educators and the general public that tomorrow's citizens should acquire the knowledge, skills, and attitudes critical to functioning in a diverse, complex world. Several factors contribute to this growing recognition, including the *demographic imperative*, significant population growth among people of color, and increasing enrollments of students of color in the nation's schools. Because of higher birthrates among people of color compared to whites and the large influx each year of immigrants from Asia and Latin America, one in three Americans is forecast to be a person of color by the turn of the century. Between 1981 and 1986, about 89 percent of legal immigrants to the United States came from non-European nations. Most came from Asia (47 percent) and Latin America (38 percent). This significant population growth will have tremendous impact

From James A. Banks, "Multicultural Literacy and Curriculum Reform," *Educational Horizons* (Spring 1991). Copyright © 1991 by Pi Lambda Theta, an international honor and professional association in education, 4101 E. Third St., Bloomington, IN 47407-6626. Reprinted by permission. Notes omitted.

on the nation's social institutions, including the work force, the courts, the economic system, and the schools. The ethnic texture of the nation's schools will become increasingly diverse as well as low income as we enter the twenty-first century. About 46 percent of school-age youths will be of color by the year 2000. This will contrast sharply with the ethnic and racial makeup of teacher populations; teachers of color are expected to decline from about 12.5 percent of the nation's teaching force in 1980 to about 5 percent by the year 2000.

Growing recognition of the changing nature of the nation's work force and the predicted gap between needs and skills are other factors motivating educators and the general public to focus on multicultural concerns. When the twenty-first century arrives, there will be a large number of retirees and too few new workers. People of color will constitute a disproportionate share of the work force in the next century. Between 1980 and 2000, about 83 percent of new entrants to the labor force will be women, people of color, or immigrants; native white males will make up only 15 percent. However, if the current educational levels of students of color are not increased significantly, most students will not have the knowledge and skills to meet the requirements of a global, primarily service-oriented job market. Consequently, corporations will export work to foreign nations that have more skilled workers—a trend that already has begun. While work opportunities are exported, low-income inner-city residents become increasingly disempowered in the process.

THE RASH OF RECENT RACIAL INCIDENTS on the nation's campuses is yet another factor stimulating discussion and concrete action regarding multicultural education and curriculum reform. More than two hundred such incidents were reported in the press between 1986 and 1988; an unknown number has not been publicized. Racial incidents have occurred on all types of campuses, including liberal ones like the University of California, Berkeley; Stanford University; and the University of Wisconsin, Madison. African Americans and Jews have been frequent victims in such incidents, which have stunned and perplexed administrators and motivated many students of color and their white allies to demand ethnic studies requirements and reform of required ethnic content.

Despite rough beginnings and a tenuous status, ethnic studies courses are becoming institutionalized at most major universities, including Berkeley, the University of Minnesota, and Bowling Green State University. The ethnic studies program at Berkeley, for example, grants a doctoral degree; the University of Washington has established an interdisciplinary Department of American Ethnic Studies. Amid a bitter campus controversy and national debate, Stanford replaced a required freshman western culture course with one called "Culture, Ideas, and Values," which includes the study of at least one non-western culture and works by women, minorities, and people of color.

Ethnic studies courses in high schools have not fared as well as those at universities. Most school districts have tried to incorporate such content into the existing curriculum rather than establishing separate courses. The rationale for this approach is intellectually defensible and laudable, but the approach has had mixed results. In most schools, the *textbook* is the curriculum. In the early 1970s, when the civil rights movement was at its apex and publishers were being pressured to integrate textbooks, large bits and pieces of ethnic content were introduced.

But when the civil rights movement lost much of its momentum and influence during the Reagan years, the impetus for textbook publishers to include this content waned, and publishers consequently slowed their pace. However, the momentum has now resumed as a result of changing demographics and pressure exerted by people of color, especially those in large urban school districts and in populous states with state textbook adoption policies, such as California and Texas.

THE CURRICULUM CANON BATTLE

Parents and students of color are now pushing for reforms that go beyond separate ethnic studies courses and programs. They are urging public school educators and university faculties to integrate ethnic content into mainstream curricula and to transform the canons and paradigms on which school and university curricula are based. Acrid and divisive controversies have arisen on several campuses over attempts to incorporate ethnic content into the mainstream curriculum or to require all students to take ethnic studies courses. A heated and bitter debate also has arisen over attempts to incorporate ethnic content into public school curricula. Much of this controversy focuses on attempts to infuse curricula with content about African Americans and African contributions to western civilization—efforts often called *Afrocentric*. Today's curriculum controversies are in some ways more wrenching than those of the 1960s and 1970s, when attempts were made to establish separate ethnic studies courses and programs.

At universities throughout the United States, a vigorous debate is raging between those who defend the established Eurocentric, male-dominated curriculum and those who argue that the curriculum and its canon must be transformed to more accurately reflect race, ethnic, and cultural diversity.

A canon is a "norm, criterion, model or standard used for evaluating or criticizing." It is also "a basic general principle or rule commonly accepted as true, valid and fundamental." A specific and identifiable canon is used to define, select, and evaluate knowledge in school and university curricula in the United States and other western nations. Rarely is this canon explicitly defined or discussed, and it is often taken for granted, unquestioned, and internalized by writers, researchers, teachers, professors, and students. Consequently, it often marginalizes the experiences of people of color, Third World nations and cultures, and the perspectives and histories of women.

African-American scholars such as George Washington Williams, Carter G. Woodson, and W. E. B. DuBois challenged the established canon in social science and history in the nineteenth and twentieth centuries. Their scholarship was influential in the African-American academic community but largely ignored by the white world. The ethnic studies movement, growing out of the civil rights movement of the 1960s and 1970s, seriously challenged the Eurocentric canon. Later, this canon also was challenged by the women's studies movement. These movements are forcing an examination of the canon used to select and judge knowledge imparted in school and university curricula.

Feeling that their voices often have been silenced and their experiences minimized, women and people of color are struggling to be recognized in the curriculum and to have their important historical and cultural works canonized. This struggle can best be understood as a battle over who will participate in or control the formulation of the canon or standard used to determine what constitutes a liberal education. The guardians and defenders of the traditional, established canon apparently believe it best serves their interests and, consequently, the interests of society and the nation.

A struggle for voice has emerged because of a powerful resistance movement to multicultural studies. Two organizations were founded to resist multicultural curriculum reform: the Madison Center, organized by William Bennett when he was secretary of education, and the National Association of Scholars. Resistance also has been articulated in a series of popular and education articles and editorials severely critical of the multicultural education movement.

SPECIAL INTERESTS AND THE PUBLIC INTEREST

Ethnic and women's studies often are called *special interests* by individuals and groups now determining and formulating curricula. *Special interest* is defined as a "person or group seeking to influence policy often narrowly defined." The term implies an interest that is particularlistic and inconsistent with the paramount goals and needs of the nation. To be in the public good, interests must extend beyond the needs of a unique or particular group.

An important question is, Who formulates the criteria for determining what is a *special interest*? Powerful, traditional groups already have shaped curricula, institutions, and structures in their image and interests. The dominant culture tends to view a special interest as any one that challenges its power, ideologies, and paradigms, particularly if interest groups demand that institutional canons, assumptions, and values be transformed. History is replete with examples of dominant groups defining their own interests as being in the public interest.

One way those in power marginalize and disempower those who are structurally excluded from the mainstream is by labeling such individuals visions, histories, goals, and struggles as "special interests." This serves to deny excluded groups the legitimacy and validity of full participation in society and its institutions.

Only a curriculum that reflects the collective experiences and interests of a wide range of groups is truly in the national interest and consistent with the public good. Any other curriculum reflects only special interests and, thus, does not meet the needs of a nation that must survive in a pluralistic, highly interdependent global world. Special interest curricula, such as history and literature emphasizing the primacy of the West and the history of European-American males, are detrimental to the public good, since they do not help students acquire life skills and perspectives essential for surviving in the twenty-first century.

The ethnic and women's studies movements do not constitute efforts to promote special interests. Their major aims are to transform the curriculum so that it is more truthful and inclusive and reflects the histories and experiences of the diverse groups making up American society. Such movements serve to democratize school and university curricula, rather than strengthen special interests.

For a variety of complex reasons, including the need to enhance our nation's survival in a period of serious economic and social problems, it behooves educators to rethink such concepts as special interests, the national interest, and the public good. Groups using such terms should be identified, along with their purposes for using them, and the use of these terms in the context of a rapidly changing world should be evaluated.

Our concept of cultural literacy should be broader than Hirsch's, which is neutral and static. Knowledge is dynamic, changing, and constructed within a social context. Rather than transmitting knowledge in a largely uncritical way, as Hirsch suggests, educators should help students recognize that knowledge reflects the social context in which it is created and that it has normative and value assumptions.

A MULTICULTURAL CURRICULUM

It is imperative that curricula be transformed to help students view concepts, issues, and problems from diverse cultural perspectives. Merely inserting ethnic and gender content into existing curricular structures, paradigms, and assumptions is not enough. Totally transformed, multicultural curricula motivate students to view and interpret facts, events, concepts, and theories from varying perspectives.

Students and teachers also bring their own biases and points of view to the knowledge they encounter. What students learn reflects not only what they encounter in the curriculum, but also the perceptions of the medium (the teacher). The multicultural classroom is a place where multiple voices are both heard and legitimized, including the vanquished and victims, students and teachers, the textbook writer, and those whose culture is transmitted by oral traditions.

Hirsch's contention that all U.S. citizens should master a common core of knowledge is logical and defensible. But who will participate in formulating this knowledge? And whose interests will it serve? There must be broad participation in identifying, constructing, and formulating the knowledge we expect all our citizens to master. Such knowledge should reflect cultural democracy and serve the needs of all citizens.

Knowledge that satisfies these criteria can best be described as multicultural, and when mastered by students, multicultural literacy is acquired. Multicultural literacy is far preferable to cultural literacy, which connotes knowledge and understanding selected, defined, and constructed by elite groups within society. Multicultural literacy, on the other hand, connotes knowledge and understanding that reflect the broad spectrum of interests, experiences, hopes, struggles, and voices of society.

KNOWLEDGE AS SOCIAL CONSTRUCTION

The knowledge construction process is an important dimension of multicultural education. It describes ways teachers help students understand, investigate, and determine how implicit cultural assumptions, frames of references, perspectives, and biases within a discipline influence how knowledge is created. This process teaches students that knowledge reflects the social, political, and economic context in which it is created. Knowledge created by elite and powerless groups within the same society also tends to differ in significant ways.

Students can analyze the knowledge construction process in science, for example, by studying how racism has been perpetuated by genetic theories of intelligence, Darwinism, and eugenics. In his important book, *The Mismeasurement of Man*, Stephen Jay Gould describes how scientific racism developed and was influential in the nineteenth and twentieth centuries. Scientific racism also has influenced significantly the interpretations of mental ability tests in the United States. When students are examining how science has supported racist practices and ideologies, they also should examine how science has contributed to human justice and equality. Biological theories about the traits and characteristics that human groups share, as well as anthropological theories that challenged racist beliefs during the post–World War II period, especially the writings of Franz Boas and Ruth Benedict, are good examples of how science and scientists have helped eradicate racist beliefs, ideologies, and practices. Students should learn how science, like other disciplines, has been both a supporter and eradicator of racist beliefs and practices.

Students can examine the knowledge construction process in the social sciences and humanities when they study such units and topics as the European discovery of America and America's westward movement. Students can discuss the latent political messages contained in these concepts and how they are used to justify the domination and destruction of Native American cultures.

Students can be asked why the Americas are called the *New World* and why people from England are often called *settlers* and *pioneers* in textbooks, while people from other lands are usually called *immigrants*. Students can be asked to think of words that might have been used by the Lakota Sioux to describe the same people that a textbook might label *settlers* and *pioneers*. Such terms as *invaders, conquerors,* and *foreigners* may come to their minds. The goal of this exercise is not to teach students that Anglo immigrants who went West were invaders, but to help them view settlers from the perspectives of both Anglos and Lakota Sioux.

Other important goals are to help students develop empathy for both groups and to give voice to all the participants in U.S. history and culture. Students will gain a thorough understanding of the settlement of the West as well as other events only when they are able to view these from diverse ethnic and cultural perspectives and construct their own versions of the past and present.

When studying the westward movement, a teacher might ask, Whose point of view does the westward movement reflect, European Americans' or the Lakota Sioux's? Who was moving West? How might a Lakota Sioux historian describe this period in U.S. history? What are other ways of thinking and describing the westward movement?

The West, thus, was not the West for the Sioux; it was the center of the universe. For people living in Japan, it was the East. Teachers also can help students look at the westward movement from the viewpoint of those living in Mexico and Alaska: The West was the North for Mexicans and the South for Alaskans. By helping students view the westward movement from varying perspectives, teachers can help them understand why knowledge is a social construction that reflects people's cultural, economic, and power positions within a society.

TEACHING STUDENTS TO KNOW, TO CARE, AND TO ACT

The major goals of a curriculum that fosters multicultural literacy should be to help students to know, to care, and to act in ways that will develop and foster a democratic and just society where all groups experience cultural democracy and empowerment. Knowledge is an essential part of multicultural literacy, but it is not the only component. Knowledge alone will not help students develop empathy, caring, and a commitment to humane and democratic change. To help our nation and world become more culturally democratic, students also must develop commitment to personal, social, and civic action as well as knowledge and skills to participate in effective civic action.

ALTHOUGH KNOWLEDGE, CARING, AND action are conceptually distinct, in the classroom they are highly interrelated. In my multicultural classes for teacher education students, I use historical and sociological knowledge about the experiences of different ethnic and racial groups to inform as well as enable students to examine and clarify their personal attitudes about ethnic diversity. These knowledge experiences are also vehicles that enable students to think of actions they can take to actualize their feelings and moral commitments.

Knowledge experiences that I use to help students examine their value commitments and think of ways to act include reading *Balm in Gilead: Journey of a Healer*, Sara Lawrence Lightfoot's powerful biography of her mother, one of the nation's first African-American child psychiatrists; the historical overviews of various U.S. ethnic groups in my book, *Teaching Strategies for Ethnic Studies*, and several video and film presentations, including selections from "Eyes on the Prize II," the award-winning history of the civil rights movement produced by Henry Hampton. To enable students to focus their values regarding these experiences, I ask them such questions as, How did the book or film make you feel? and Why do you think you feel that way? To enable them to think about ways to act on their feelings, I ask such questions as, How interracial are your own personal experiences? Would you like to live a more interracial life? What are some books you can read or popular films you can see that will enable you to act on your commitment to live a more racially and ethnically integrated life? The power of these kinds of experiences is often revealed in student papers, as illustrated by this excerpt from a paper by a student after he had viewed several segments of "Eyes on the Prize II":

> I feel that my teaching will now necessarily be a little bit different forever simply because I myself have changed . . . I am no longer quite the same person I was before I viewed the presentations—my horizons are a little wider, perspectives a little broader, insights a little deeper. That is what I gained from "Eyes on the Prize II."

The most meaningful and effective way to prepare teachers to involve students in multicultural experiences that will enable them to know, care, and participate in democratic action is to involve teachers themselves in multicultural experiences that focus on these goals. When teachers have gained knowledge about cultural and ethnic diversity, looked at that knowledge from different ethnic and cultural perspectives, and taken action to make their own lives and communities more culturally sensitive and diverse, they will have the knowledge and skills needed to help transform the curricular canon as well the hearts and minds of their students. Only then will students in our schools and colleges be able to attain the knowledge, skills, and perspectives needed to participate effectively in next century's global society.

POSTSCRIPT

Should Literacy Be Based on Traditional Culture?

During the past 20 years or so the public schools have been encouraged to embrace multiculturalism as a curricular focus. The "No One Model American" statement (issued by the American Association of Colleges of Teacher Education in 1972) set the tone by calling for an educational effort to support cultural diversity and global understanding. During the 1980s conservatives attempted to rekindle an emphasis on cultural commonalities shaped by Western tradition.

The issue is complex and difficult to resolve. For further exploration, you may want to consult the following sources: the December 1987 issue of *Language Arts*; Margaret Bedrosian's "Multi-ethnic Literature: Mining the Diversity," *Journal of Ethnic Studies* (Fall 1987); and Hirsch's more detailed examination of concrete proposals for change in "Cultural Literacy: Let's Get Specific," *NEA Today* (January 1988).

A 1988 yearbook of the National Society for the Study of Education (NSSE), edited by Ian Westbury and Alan C. Purves, is entitled *Cultural Literacy and the Idea of General Education*. It is related to an earlier NSSE effort edited by Benjamin Ladner, *The Humanities in Precollegiate Education* (1984), which contains excellent articles by John J. McDermott ("Cultural Literacy: Time for a New Curriculum") and Benjamin DeMott ("The Humanities and the Summoning Reader"). Although both volumes contain constructive thinking on the possibilities of improvement, the 1988 collection ends on a pessimistic note. In "The Fortress Monastery: The Future of the Common Core," Mark Holmes concludes that "a universal, common core much beyond the ABCs seems unlikely."

In 1989 Lynne Cheney, head of the National Endowment for the Humanities, kept the controversy alive in *50 Hours: A Core Curriculum for College Students*. Also, the March 1989 issue of *The Clearing House* was devoted to the topic of cultural literacy.

Recent books on the topic include William J. Bennett's *Our Children and Our Country: Improving America's Schools and Affirming the Common Culture* (1988); *Multicultural Literacy: Opening the American Mind* (1988) by Simonson and Walker; *Battle of the Books: The Curriculum Debate in America* (1990) by James Atlas; and Sonia Nieto's *Affirming Diversity: The Socio-Political Context of Multicultural Education* (1992).

The question remains: how to foster social unity while preserving cultural diversity? The schools must increase their efforts to better prepare members of minority groups to function effectively in the mainstream of society. At the same time, the schools must honestly portray the varying values and lifestyles that are found throughout the nation and all areas of the globe.

ISSUE 14

Do Black Students Need an Afrocentric Curriculum?

YES: Molefi Kete Asante, from "The Afrocentric Idea in Education," *Journal of Negro Education* (Spring 1991)

NO: Arthur M. Schlesinger, Jr., from "The Disuniting of America," *American Educator* (Winter 1991)

ISSUE SUMMARY

YES: Black studies professor Molefi Kete Asante puts forth his argument for providing black students with an Afrocentric frame of reference, which will enhance their self-esteem and learning.
NO: Noted historian Arthur M. Schlesinger, Jr., documents his concerns about the recent spread of Afrocentric programs, the multiculturalization of the curriculum, and the use of history as therapy.

A more specific manifestation of the argument over multicultural emphases in the curriculum of the public schools can be seen in the recent experimentation with Afrocentric frameworks in predominantly black neighborhood schools and in the attempts to create all-black male classes and schools. Although many school districts are revising the curriculum to embrace a more multicultural perspective, some (such as Atlanta, Georgia) are developing and using an African-centered curricular base. Movement in this direction has been inspired, at least in part, by the work of Temple University scholar Molefi Kete Asante, framer of the Afrocentric idea in his 1980 book *Afrocentricity.*

The Afrocentrists feel that the traditional emphasis on white European history and culture, and the disregard of African history and culture, alienates black schoolchildren who are unable to feel an attachment to the content being offered. Many who support the Afrocentrists would agree with Asa G. Hilliard III, a professor of educational psychology, who has stated that there is a vast amount of important information about African people that *everyone*, not only black schoolchildren, should be aware of.

In his much-discussed book, *The Disuniting of America: Reflections on a Multicultural Society* (1991), historian Arthur M. Schlesinger, Jr., denounces this movement as an extreme example of a "cult of ethnicity." Agreeing with

228

Schlesinger, David Nicholson (in " 'Afrocentrism' and the Tribalization of America: The Misguided Logic of Ethnic Education Schemes," *The Washington Post*, September 23, 1990) argues that "the sweeping call for 'curricula of inclusion' is based on untested, unproven premises. Worse, because it intentionally exaggerates differences, it seems likely to exacerbate racial and ethnic tensions."

To which Kariamu Welsh, a proponent of Asante's position, would reply:

> The eyes of the African-American must be on his own center, one that reflects and resembles him and speaks to him in his own language. . . . If one understands properly African history, an assumption can never be made that Afrocentricity is a back to 'anything' movement. It is an uncovering of one's true self, it is the pinpointing of one's center, and it is the clarity and focus through which black people must see the world in order to escalate. [From the foreward to Asante's book.—Ed.]

Lending support to his position, a study by a North Carolina University researcher showed that studying Africa and African American history and culture leads to improved overall academic performance by black students.

A different slant emerges from the insights of Richard Cohen, a *Washington Post* columnist writing in an October 7, 1990, column: "Changing the curriculum in school districts where blacks predominate would tend only to put these students further outside the mainstream. They would know what others do not, which is all right. But they would not know what most others do—and that's been the problem in the first place."

A subissue of the basic controversy involves providing not only an Afrocentric curriculum for black students but all-male classes or even all-male schools. Some commentators claim that the federal inattention to poor urban families in the 1980s provided the impetus for proposing such classes and schools. As Larry Cuban states in "Desperate Remedies for Desperate Times," *Education Week*, November 20, 1991, "To advocate a single-sex school, an Afrocentric curriculum taught by black male teachers who enforce strict rules is, indeed, a strong response to a desperate situation." The effort attempts to combat the present epidemic of academic failure and male-on-male violence.

In the articles that follow, Molefi Kete Asante establishes the necessity of Afrocentric programs, examines theoretical and philosophical underpinnings of his view, and charts a path for implementation at all levels of education. Arthur M. Schlesinger, Jr., questions the basic assumptions from which Asante's argument flows and expresses fears about divisive strategies and historical manipulation.

YES

Molefi Kete Asante

THE AFROCENTRIC IDEA IN EDUCATION

INTRODUCTION

Many of the principles that govern the development of the Afrocentric idea in education were first established by Carter G. Woodson in *The Mis-education of the Negro* (1933). Indeed, Woodson's classic reveals the fundamental problems pertaining to the education of the African person in America. As Woodson contends, African Americans have been educated away from their own culture and traditions and attached to the fringes of European culture; thus dislocated from themselves, Woodson asserts that African Americans often valorize European culture to the detriment of their own heritage (p. 7). Although Woodson does not advocate rejection of American citizenship or nationality, he believed that assuming African Americans hold the same position as European Americans vis-à-vis the realities of America would lead to the psychological and cultural death of the African American population. Furthermore, if education is ever to be substantive and meaningful within the context of American society, Woodson argues, it must first address the African's historical experiences, both in Africa and America (p. 7). That is why he places on education, and particularly on the traditionally African American colleges, the burden of teaching the African American to be responsive to the long traditions and history of Africa as well as America. Woodson's alert recognition, more than 50 years ago, that something is severely wrong with the way African Americans are educated provides the principal impetus for the Afrocentric approach to American education.

In this article I will examine the nature and scope of this approach, establish its necessity, and suggest ways to develop and disseminate it throughout all levels of education. Two propositions stand in the background of the theoretical and philosophical issues I will present. These ideas represent the core presuppositions on which I have based most of my work in the field of education, and they suggest the direction of my own thinking about what education is capable of doing to and for an already politically and economically marginalized people—African Americans:

1. Education is fundamentally a social phenomenon whose ultimate purpose is to socialize the learner; to send a child to school is to prepare that child to become part of a social group.

2. Schools are reflective of the societies that develop them (i.e., a White supremacist-dominated society will develop a White supremacist educational system).

DEFINITIONS

An alternative framework suggests that other definitional assumptions can provide a new paradigm for the examination of education within the American society. For example, in education, *centricity* refers to a perspective that involves locating students within the context of their own cultural references so that they can relate socially and psychologically to other cultural perspectives. Centricity is a concept that can be applied to any culture. The centrist paradigm is supported by research showing that the most productive method of teaching any student is to place his or her group within the center of the context of knowledge (Asante, 1990). For White students in America this is easy because almost all the experiences discussed in American classrooms are approached from the standpoint of White perspectives and history. American education, however, is not centric; it is Eurocentric. Consequently, non-White students are also made to see themselves and their groups as the "acted upon." Only rarely do they read or hear of non-White people as active participants in history. This is as true for a discussion of the American Revolution as it is for a discussion of Dante's *Inferno*; for instance, most class-

room discussions of the European slave trade concentrate on the activities of Whites rather than on the resistance efforts of Africans. A person educated in a truly centric fashion comes to view all groups' contributions as significant and useful. Even a White person educated in such a system does not assume superiority based upon racist notions. Thus, a truly centric education is different from a Eurocentric, racist (that is, White supremacist) education.

Afrocentricity is a frame of reference wherein phenomena are viewed from the perspective of the African person. The Afrocentric approach seeks in every situation the appropriate centrality of the African person (Asante, 1987). In education this means that teachers provide students the opportunity to study the world and its people, concepts, and history from an African world view. In most classrooms, whatever the subject, Whites are located in the center perspective position. How alien the African American child must feel, how like an outsider! The little African American child who sits in a classroom and is taught to accept as heroes and heroines individuals who defamed African people is being actively de-centered, dislocated, and made into a nonperson, one whose aim in life might be to one day shed that "badge of inferiority": his or her Blackness. In Afrocentric educational settings, however, teachers do not marginalize African American children by causing them to question their own self-worth because their people's story is seldom told. By seeing themselves as the subjects rather than the objects of education—be the discipline biology, medicine, literature, or social studies—African American students come to see themselves not merely as seekers of knowledge but as integral participants in it. Because all content areas are adaptable to an Afrocentric approach, African American students can be made to see themselves as centered in the reality of any discipline.

It must be emphasized that Afrocentricity is *not* a Black version of Eurocentricity (Asante, 1987). Eurocentricity is based on White supremacist notions whose purposes are to protect White privilege and advantage in education, economics, politics, and so forth. Unlike Eurocentricity, Afrocentricity does not condone ethnocentric valorization at the expense of degrading other groups' perspectives. Moreover, Eurocentricity presents the particular historical reality of Europeans as the sum total of the human experience (Asante, 1987). It imposes Eurocentric realities as "universal"; i.e., that which is White is presented as applying to the human condition in general, while that which is non-White is viewed as group-specific and therefore not "human." This explains why some scholars and artists of African descent rush to deny their Blackness; they believe that to exist as a Black person is not to exist as a universal human being. They are the individuals Woodson identified as preferring European art, language, and culture over African art, language, and culture; they believe that anything of European origin is inherently better than anything produced by or issuing from their own people. Naturally, the person of African descent should be centered in his or her historical experiences as an African, but Eurocentric curricula produce such aberrations of perspective among persons of color.

Multiculturalism in education is a non-hierarchical approach that respects and celebrates a variety of cultural perspectives on world phenomena (Asante, 1991).

The multicultural approach holds that although European culture is the majority culture in the United States, that is not sufficient reason for it to be imposed on diverse student populations as "universal." Multiculturalists assert that education, to have integrity, must begin with the proposition that all humans have contributed to world development and the flow of knowledge and information, and that most human achievements are the result of mutually interactive, international effort. Without a multicultural education, students remain essentially ignorant of the contributions of a major portion of the world's people. A multicultural education is thus a fundamental necessity for anyone who wishes to achieve competency in almost any subject.

The Afrocentric idea must be the stepping-stone from which the multicultural idea is launched. A truly authentic multicultural education, therefore, must be based upon the Afrocentric initiative. If this step is skipped, multicultural curricula, as they are increasingly being defined by White "resisters" (to be discussed below) will evolve without any substantive infusion of African American content, and the African American child will continue to be lost in the Eurocentric framework of education. In other words, the African American child will neither be confirmed nor affirmed in his or her own cultural information. For the mutual benefit of all Americans, this tragedy, which leads to the psychological and cultural dislocation of African American children, can and should be avoided.

THE REVOLUTIONARY CHALLENGE

Because it centers African American students inside history, culture, science, and so forth rather than outside these subjects, the Afrocentric idea presents the most revolutionary challenge to the ideology of White supremacy in education during the past decade. No other theoretical position stated by African Americans has ever captured the imagination of such a wide range of scholars and students of history, sociology, communications, anthropology, and psychology. The Afrocentric challenge has been posed in three critical ways:

1. It questions the imposition of the White supremacist view as universal and/or classical (Asante, 1990).

2. It demonstrates the indefensibility of racist theories that assault multiculturalism and pluralism.

3. It projects a humanistic and pluralistic viewpoint by articulating Afrocentricity as a valid, nonhegemonic perspective.

SUPPRESSION AND DISTORTION: SYMBOLS OF RESISTANCE

The forces of resistance to the Afrocentric, multicultural transformation of the curriculum and teaching practices began to assemble their wagons almost as quickly as word got out about the need for equality in education (Ravitch, 1990). Recently, the renowned historian Arthur Schlesinger and others formed a group called the Committee for the Defense of History. This is a paradoxical development because only lies, untruths, and inaccurate information need defending. In their arguments against the Afrocentric perspective, these proponents of Eurocentrism often clothe their arguments in false categories and fake terms (i.e., "pluralistic" and "particularistic" multiculturalism) (Keto, 1990; Asante, 1991). Besides, as the late African scholar Cheikh Anta Diop (1980) maintained: "African history and Africa need no defense." Afro-

centric education is not against history. It is *for* history—correct, accurate history— and if it is against anything, it is against the marginalization of African American, Hispanic American, Asian American, Native American, and other non-White children. The Committee for the Defense of History is nothing more than a futile attempt to buttress the crumbling pillars of a White supremacist system that conceals its true motives behind the cloak of American liberalism. It was created in the same spirit that generated Bloom's *The Closing of the American Mind* (1987) and Hirsch's *Cultural Literacy: What Every American Needs to Know* (1987), both of which were placed at the service of the White hegemony in education, particularly its curricular hegemony. This committee and other evidences of White backlash are a predictable challenge to the contemporary thrust for an Afrocentric, multicultural approach to education.

Naturally, different adherents to a theory will have different views on its meaning. While two discourses presently are circulating about multiculturalism, only one is relevant to the liberation of the minds of African and White people in the United States. That discourse is Afrocentricity: the acceptance of Africa as central to African people. Yet, rather than getting on board with Afrocentrists to fight against White hegemonic education, some Whites (and some Blacks as well) have opted to plead for a return to the educational plantation. Unfortunately for them, however, those days are gone, and such misinformation can never be packaged as accurate, correct education again.

Ravitch (1990), who argues that there are two kinds of multiculturalism— *pluralist multiculturalism* and *particularist multiculturalism*—is the leader of those professors whom I call "resisters" or opponents to Afrocentricity and multiculturalism. Indeed, Ravitch advances the imaginary divisions in multicultural perspectives to conceal her true identity as a defender of White supremacy. Her tactics are the tactics of those who prefer Africans and other non-Whites to remain-on the mental and psychological plantation of Western civilization. In their arrogance the resisters accuse Afrocentrists and multiculturalists of creating "fantasy history" and "bizarre theories" of non-White people's contributions to civilization. What they prove, however, is their own ignorance. Additionally, Ravitch and others (Nicholson, 1990) assert that multiculturalism will bring about the "tribalization" of America, but in reality America has always been a nation of ethnic diversity. When one reads their works on multiculturalism, one realizes that they are really advocating the imposition of a White perspective on everybody else's culture. Believing that the Eurocentric position is indisputable, they attempt to resist and impede the progressive transformation of the monoethnic curriculum. Indeed, the closets of bigotry have opened to reveal various attempts by White scholars (joined by some Blacks) to defend White privilege in the curriculum in much the same way as it has been so staunchly defended in the larger society. It was perhaps inevitable that the introduction of the Afrocentric idea would open up the discussion of the American school curriculum in a profound way.

Why has Afrocentricity created so much of a controversy in educational circles? The idea that an African American child is placed in a stronger position to learn if he or she is centered—that is, if the child sees himself or herself within the content of the curriculum rather than at its margins—is not novel (Asante,

1980). What is revolutionary is the movement from the idea (conceptual stage) to its implementation in practice, when we begin to teach teachers how to put African American youth at the center of instruction. In effect, students are shown how to see with new eyes and hear with new ears. African American children learn to interpret and center phenomena in the context of African heritage, while White students are taught to see that their own centers are not threatened by the presence or contributions of African Americans and others.

THE CONDITION OF EUROCENTRIC EDUCATION

Institutions such as schools are conditioned by the character of the nation in which they are developed. Just as crime and politics are different in different nations, so, too, is education. In the United States a "Whites-only" orientation has predominated in education. This has had a profound impact on the quality of education for children of all races and ethnic groups. The African American child has suffered disproportionately, but White children are also the victims of monoculturally diseased curricula.

The Tragedy of Ignorance

During the past five years many White students and parents have approached me after presentations with tears in their eyes or expressing their anger about the absence of information about African Americans in the schools. A recent comment from a young White man at a major university in the Northeast was especially striking. As he said to me: "My teacher told us that Martin Luther King was a commie and went on with the class." Because this student's teacher made no effort to discuss King's ideas, the student maliciously had been kept ignorant. The vast majority of White Americans are likewise ignorant about the bountiful reservoirs of African and African American history, culture, and contributions. For example, few Americans of any color have heard the names of Cheikh Anta Diop, Anna Julia Cooper, C. L. R. James, or J. A. Rogers. All were historians who contributed greatly to our understanding of the African world. Indeed, very few teachers have ever taken a course in African American Studies; therefore, most are unable to provide systematic information about African Americans.

Afrocentricity and History
Most of America's teaching force are victims of the same system that victimizes today's young. Thus, American children are not taught the names of the African ethnic groups from which the majority of the African American population are derived; few are taught the names of any of the sacred sites in Africa. Few teachers can discuss with their students the significance of the Middle Passage or describe what it meant or means to Africans. Little mention is made in American classrooms of either the brutality of slavery or the ex-slaves' celebration of freedom. American children have little or no understanding of the nature of the capture, transport, and enslavement of Africans. Few have been taught the true horrors of being taken, shipped naked across 25 days of ocean, broken by abuse and indignities of all kinds, and dehumanized into a beast of burden, a thing without a name. If our students only knew the truth, if they were taught the Afrocentric perspective on the Great Enslavement, and if they knew the full story about the

events since slavery that have served to constantly dislocate African Americans, their behavior would perhaps be different. Among these events are: the infamous constitutional compromise of 1787, which decreed that African Americans were, by law, the equivalent of but three-fifths of a person (see Franklin, 1974); the 1857 Dred Scott decision in which the Supreme Court avowed that African Americans had no rights Whites were obliged to respect (Howard, 1857); the complete dismissal and nonenforcement of Section 2 of the Fourteenth Amendment to the Constitution (this amendment, passed in 1868, stipulated as one of its provisions a penalty against any state that denied African Americans the right to vote, and called for the reduction of a state's delegates to the House of Representatives in proportion to the number of disenfranchised African American males therein); and the much-mentioned, as-yet-unreceived 40 acres and a mule, reparation for enslavement, promised to each African American family after the Civil War by Union General William T. Sherman and Secretary of War Edwin Stanton (Oubre, 1978, pp. 18–19, 182–183; see also Smith, 1987, pp. 106–107). If the curriculum were enhanced to include readings from the slave narratives; the diaries of slave ship captains; the journals of slaveowners; the abolitionist newspapers; the writings of the freedmen and freedwomen; the accounts of African American civil rights, civic, and social organizations; and numerous others, African American children would be different, White children would be different—indeed, America would be a different nation today.

America's classrooms should resound with the story of the barbaric treatment of the Africans, of how their dignity was stolen and their cultures destroyed. The recorded experiences of escaped slaves provide the substance for such learning units. For example, the narrative of Jacob and Ruth Weldon presents a detailed account of the Middle Passage (Feldstein, 1971). The Weldons noted that Africans, having been captured and brought onto the slave ships, were chained to the deck, made to bend over, and "branded with a red hot iron in the form of letters or signs dipped in an oily preparation and pressed against the naked flesh till it burnt a deep and ineffaceable scar, to show who was the owner" (pp. 33–37). They also recalled that those who screamed were lashed on the face, breast, thighs, and backs with a "cat-o'-nine tails" wielded by White sailors: "Every blow brought the returning lash pieces of grieving flesh" (p. 44). They saw mothers with babies at their breasts basely branded and lashed, hewed and scarred, till it would seem as if the very heavens must smite the infernal tormentors with the doom they so richly merited" (p. 44). Children and infants were not spared from this terror. The Weldons tell of a nine-month-old baby on board a slave ship being flogged because it would not eat. The ship's captain ordered the child's feet placed in boiling water, which dissolved the skin and nails, then ordered the child whipped again; still the child refused to eat. Eventually the captain killed the baby with his own hands and commanded the child's mother to throw the dead baby overboard. When the mother refused, she, too, was beaten, then forced to the ship's side, where "with her head averted so she might not see it, she dropped the body into the sea" (p. 44). In a similar vein a captain of a ship with 440 Africans on board noted that 132 had to be thrown overboard to save water (Feldstein, 1971,

p. 47). As another wrote, the "groans and soffocating [*sic*] cries for air and water coming from below the deck sickened the soul of humanity" (Feldstein, 1971, p. 44).

Upon landing in America the situation was often worse. The brutality of the slavocracy is unequalled for the psychological and spiritual destruction it wrought upon African Americans. Slave mothers were often forced to leave their children unattended while they worked in the fields. Unable to nurse their children or to properly care for them, they often returned from work at night to find their children dead (Feldstein, 1971 p. 49). The testimony of Henry Bibb also sheds light on the bleakness of the slave experience:

> I was born May 1815, of a slave mother . . . and was claimed as the property of David White, Esq. . . . I was flogged up; for where I should have received moral, mental, and religious instructions, I received stripes without number, the object of which was to degrade and keep me in subordination. I can truly say that I drank deeply of the bitter cup of suffering and woe. I have been dragged down to the lowest depths of human degradation and wretchedness, by slaveholders. (Feldstein, 1971, p. 60)

Enslavement was truly a living death. While the ontological onslaught caused some Africans to opt for suicide, the most widespread results were dislocation, disorientation, and misorientation— all of which are the consequences of the African person being actively de-centered. The "Jim Crow" period of second-class citizenship, from 1877 to 1954, saw only slight improvement in the lot of African Americans. This era was characterized by the sharecropper system, disenfranchisement, enforced segregation, internal migration, lynchings, unemployment, poor housing conditions, and separate and unequal educational facilities. Inequitable policies and practices veritably plagued the race.

No wonder many persons of African descent attempt to shed their race and become "raceless." One's basic identity is one's self-identity, which is ultimately one's cultural identity; without a strong cultural identity, one is lost. Black children do not know their people's story and White children do not know the story, but remembrance is a vital requisite for understanding and humility. This is why the Jews have campaigned (and rightly so) to have the story of the European Holocaust taught in schools and colleges. Teaching about such a monstrous human brutality should forever remind the world of the ways in which humans have often violated each other. Teaching about the African Holocaust is just as important for many of the same reasons. Additionally, it underscores the enormity of the effects of physical, psychological, and economic dislocation on the African population in America and throughout the African diaspora. Without an understanding of the historical experiences of African people, American children cannot make any real headway in addressing the problems of the present.

Certainly, if African American children were taught to be fully aware of the struggles of our African forebears they would find a renewed sense of purpose and vision in their own lives. They would cease acting as if they have no past and no future. For instance, if they were taught about the historical relationship of Africans to the cotton industry—how African American men, women, and children were forced to pick cotton from "can't see in the morning 'til can't see at night," until the blood ran from the tips of their fingers where they were pricked by the hard boll; or if they were made to visualize their ancestors in the burning sun, bent double with constant stooping, and dragging rough, heavy croaker sacks behind them—or picture them bringing those sacks trembling to the scale, fearful of a sure flogging if they did not pick enough, perhaps our African American youth would develop a stronger entrepreneurial spirit. If White children were taught the same information rather than that normally fed them about American slavery, they would probably view our society differently and work to transform it into a better place.

CORRECTING DISTORTED INFORMATION

Hegemonic education can exist only so long as true and accurate information is withheld. Hegemonic Eurocentric education can exist only so long as Whites maintain that Africans and other non-Whites have never contributed to world civilization. It is largely upon such false ideas that invidious distinctions are made. The truth, however, gives one insight into the real reasons behind human actions, whether one chooses to follow the paths of others or not. For example, one cannot remain comfortable teaching that art and philosophy originated in Greece if one learns that the Greeks themselves taught that the study of these subjects originated in Africa, specifically ancient Kemet (Herodotus, 1987). The first philosophers were the Egyptians Kagemni, Khun-anup, Ptahhotep, Kete, and Seti; but Eurocentric education is so disjointed that students have no way of discovering this and other knowledge of the organic relationship of Africa to the rest of human history. Not only did Africa contribute to human history, African civilizations predate all other civilizations. Indeed, the human species originated on the continent of Africa—this is true whether one looks at either archaeological or biological evidence.

Two other notions must be refuted. There are those who say that African American history should begin with the arrival of Africans as slaves in 1619, but it has been shown that Africans visited and inhabited North and South America long before European settlers "discovered" the "New World" (Van Sertima, 1976). Secondly, although America became something of a home for those Africans who survived the horrors of the Middle Passage, their experiences on the slave ships and during slavery resulted in their having an entirely different (and often tainted) perspective about America from that of the Europeans and others who came, for the most part, of their own free will seeking opportunities not available to them in their native lands. Afrocentricity therefore seeks to recognize this divergence in perspective and create centeredness for African American students.

CONCLUSION

The reigning initiative for total curricular change is the movement that is being proposed and led by Africans, namely, the Afrocentric idea. When I wrote the first book on Afrocentricity (Asante, 1980), now in its fifth printing, I had no idea that in 10 years the idea would both shake up and shape discussions in education, art, fashion, and politics. Since the publication of my subsequent works, *The Afrocentric Idea* (Asante, 1987) and *Kemet, Afrocentricity, and Knowledge* (Asante, 1990), the debate has been joined in

earnest. Still, for many White Americans (and some African Americans) the most unsettling aspect of the discussion about Afrocentricity is that its intellectual source lies in the research and writings of African American scholars. Whites are accustomed to being in charge of the major ideas circulating in the American academy. Deconstructionism, Gestalt psychology, Marxism, structuralism, Piagetian theory, and so forth have all been developed, articulated, and elaborated upon at length, generally by White scholars. On the other hand, Afrocentricity is the product of scholars such as Nobles (1986), Hilliard (1978), Karenga (1986), Keto (1990), Richards (1991), and Myers (1989). There are also increasing numbers of young, impressively credentialled African American scholars who have begun to write in the Afrocentric vein (Jean, 1991). They, and even some young White scholars, have emerged with ideas about how to change the curriculum Afrocentrically.

Afrocentricity provides all Americans an opportunity to examine the perspective of the African person in this society and the world. The resisters claim that Afrocentricity is anti-White; yet, if Afrocentricity as a theory is against anything it is against racism, ignorance, and monoethnic hegemony in the curriculum. Afrocentricity is not anti-White; it is, however, pro-human. Further, the aim of the Afrocentric curriculum is not to divide America, it is to make America flourish as it ought to flourish. This nation has long been divided with regard to the educational opportunities afforded to children. By virtue of the protection provided by society and reinforced by the Eurocentric curriculum, the White child is already ahead of the African American child by first grade. Our efforts thus must concentrate on giving the African

American child greater opportunities for learning at the kindergarten level. However, the kind of assistance the African American child needs is as much cultural as it is academic. If the proper cultural information is provided, the academic performance will surely follow suit.

When it comes to educating African American children, the American educational system does not need a tune-up, it needs an overhaul. Black children have been maligned by this system. Black teachers have been maligned. Black history has been maligned. Africa has been maligned. Nonetheless, two truisms can be stated about education in America. First, some teachers *can and do* effectively teach African American children; secondly, if some teachers can do it, others can, too. We must learn all we can about what makes these teachers' attitudes and approaches successful, and then work diligently to see that their successes are replicated on a broad scale. By raising the same questions that Woodson posed more than 50 years ago, Afrocentric education, along with a significant reorientation of the American educational enterprise, seeks to respond to the African person's psychological and cultural dislocation. By providing philosophical and theoretical guidelines and criteria that are centered in an African perception of reality and by placing the African American child in his or her proper historical context and setting, Afrocentricity may be just the "escape hatch" African Americans so desperately need to facilitate academic success and "steal away" from the cycle of miseducation and dislocation.

REFERENCES

Asante, M. K. (1980). *Afrocentricity: The theory of social change.* Buffalo, NY: Amulefi.

Asante, M. K. (1987). *The Afrocentric idea.* Philadelphia: Temple University Press.

Asante, M. K. (1990). *Kemet, Afrocentricity, and knowledge.* Trenton, NJ: Africa World Press.

Bloom, A. (1987). *The closing of the American mind.* New York: Simon & Schuster.

Feldstein, S. (1971). *Once a slave: The slave's view of slavery.* New York: William Morrow.

Franklin, J. H. (1974). *From slavery to freedom.* New York: Knopf.

Herodotus. (1987). *The history.* Chicago: University of Illinois Press.

Hilliard, A. G., III. (1978, June 20). *Anatomy and dynamics of oppression.* Speech delivered at the National Conference on Human Relations in Education, Minneapolis, MN.

Hirsch, E. D. (1987). *Cultural literacy: What every American needs to know.* New York: Houghton Mifflin.

Howard, B. C. (1857). *Report of the decision of the Supreme Court of the United States and the opinions of the justices thereof in the case of Dred Scott versus John F. A. Sandford, December term, 1856.* New York: D. Appleton & Co.

Jean, C. (1991). *Beyond the Eurocentric veils.* Amherst, MA: University of Massachusetts Press.

Karenga, M. R. (1986). *Introduction to Black studies.* Los Angeles: University of Sankore Press.

Keto, C. T. (1990). *Africa-centered perspective of history.* Blackwood, NJ: C. A. Associates.

Nicholson, D. (1990, September 23). Afrocentrism and the tribalization of America. *The Washington Post,* p. B-1.

Nobles, W. (1986). *African psychology.* Oakland, CA: Black Family Institute.

Oubre, C. F. (1978). *Forty acres and a mule: The Freedman's Bureau and Black land ownership.* Baton Rouge, LA: Louisiana State University Press.

Ravitch, D. (1990, Summer). Multiculturalism: E pluribus plures. *The American Scholar,* pp. 337–354.

Richards, D. (1991). *Let the circle be unbroken.* Trenton, NJ: Africa World Press.

Smith, J. O. (1987). *The politics of racial inequality: A systematic comparative macro-analysis from the colonial period to 1970.* New York: Greenwood Press.

Van Sertima, I. (1976). *They came before Columbus.* New York: Random House.

Woodson, C. G. (1915). *The education of the Negro prior to 1861: A history of the education of the colored people of the U.S. from the beginning of slavery.* New York: G. P. Putnam's Sons.

Woodson, C. G. (1933). *The Mis-education of the Negro.* Washington, DC: Associated Publishers.

Woodson, C. G. (1936). *African background outlined.* Washington, DC: Association for the Study of Afro-American Life and History.

NO

Arthur M. Schlesinger, Jr.

THE DISUNITING OF AMERICA

Most white Americans through most of American history simply considered colored Americans inferior and unassimilable. Not until the 1960s did integration become a widely accepted national objective. Even then, even after legal obstacles to integration fell, social, economic, and psychological obstacles remained. Both black Americans and red Americans have every reason to seek redressing of the historical balance. And indeed the cruelty with which white Americans have dealt with black Americans has been compounded by the callousness with which white historians have dealt with black history.

Even the best historians: Frederick Jackson Turner, dismissing the slavery question as a mere "incident" when American history is "rightly viewed"; Charles and Mary Beard in their famous *The Rise of American Civilization*, describing blacks as passive in slavery and ludicrous in Reconstruction and acknowledging only one black achievement—the invention of ragtime; Samuel Eliot Morison and Henry Steele Commager, writing about childlike and improvident Sambo on the old plantation. One can sympathize with W. E. B. Du Bois's rage after reading white histories of slavery and Reconstruction; he was, he wrote, "literally aghast at what American historians have done to this field . . . one of the most stupendous efforts the world ever saw to discredit human beings. . . ."

The job of redressing the balance has been splendidly undertaken in recent years by both white and black historians. Meticulous and convincing scholarship has reversed conventional judgments on slavery, on Reconstruction, on the role of blacks in American life.

BUT SCHOLARLY RESPONSIBILITY WAS ONLY ONE FACTOR BEHIND THE CAMPAIGN of historical correction. History remains a weapon. "History's potency is mighty," Herbert Aptheker, the polemical chronicler of slave rebellions, has written. "The oppressed need it for identity and inspiration." (Aptheker, a faithful Stalinist, was an old hand at the manipulation of history.)

For blacks the American dream has been pretty much of a nightmare, and, far more than white ethnics, they are driven by a desperate need to vindicate

From Arthur M. Schlesinger, Jr., "The Disuniting of America," *American Educator* (Winter 1991). Adapted from Arthur M. Schlesinger, Jr., *The Disuniting of America: Reflections on a Multicultural Society* (W. W. Norton, 1992). This book was first published by Whittle Books as part of The Larger Agenda Series. Reprinted by permission of Whittle Communications, L.P.

their own identity. "The academic and social rescue and reconstruction of Black history," as Maulana Karenga put it in his influential *Introduction to Black Studies* ("a landmark in the intellectual history of African Americans," according to Molefi Kete Asante of Temple University), "is . . . [an] indispensable part of the rescue and reconstruction of Black humanity. For history is the substance and mirror of a people's humanity in others' eyes as well as in their own eyes . . . not only what they have done, but also a reflection of who they are, what they can do, and equally important what they can become. . . ."

One can hardly be surprised at the emergence of a there's-always-a-black-man-at-the-bottom-of-it-doing-the-real-work approach to American history. "The extent to which the past of a people is regarded as praiseworthy," the white anthropologist Melville J. Herskovits wrote in his study of the African antecedents of American blacks, "their own self-esteem would be high and the opinion of others will be favorable."

White domination of American schools and colleges, some black academics say, results in Eurocentric, racist, elitist, imperialist indoctrination and in systematic denigration of black values and achievements. "In the public school system," writes Felix Boateng of Eastern Washington University, "the orientation is so Eurocentric that white students take their identity for granted, and African-American students are totally deculturalized"—deculturalization being the "process by which the individual is deprived of his or her culture and then conditioned to other cultural values." "In a sense," says Molefi Kete Asante, the Eurocentric curriculum is "killing our children, killing their minds."

In history, Western-civilization courses are seen as cultural imperialism designed to disparage non-Western traditions and to impress the Western stamp on people of all races. In literature, the "canon," the accepted list of essential books, is seen as an instrumentality of the white power structure. Nowhere can blacks discover adequate reflection or representation of the black self.

Some black educators even argue ultimate biological and mental differences, asserting that black students do not learn the way white students do and that the black mind works in a genetically distinctive way. Black children are said, in the jargon of the educationist, to "process information differently." "There are scientific studies that show, at early ages, the difference between Caucasian infants and African infants," says Clare Jacobs, a teacher in Washington, D.C. "Our African children are very expressive. Every thought we have has an emotional dimension to it, and Western education has historically subordinated the feelings." Charles Willie of Harvard finds several distinct "intelligences" of which the "communication and calculation" valued by whites constitute only two. Other kinds of "intelligence" are singing and dancing, in both of which blacks excel.

Salvation thus lies, the argument goes, in breaking the white, Eurocentric, racist grip on the curriculum and providing education that responds to colored races, colored histories, colored ways of learning and behaving. Europe has reigned long enough; it is the source of most of the evil in the world anyway; and the time is overdue to honor the African contributions to civilization so purposefully suppressed in Eurocentric curricula. Children from nonwhite minorities, so long persuaded of their inferiority by the white hegemons, need the support and inspiration that identification with role models of the same color will give them.

The answer, for some at least, is "Afrocentricity," described by Asante in his book of that title as "the centerpiece of human regeneration." There is, Asante contends, a single "African Cultural System." Wherever people of African descent are, we respond to the same rhythms of the universe, the same cosmological sensibilities. . . . Our Africanity is our ultimate reality."

THE BELATED RECOGNITION OF THE PLUralistic character of American society has had a bracing impact on the teaching and writing of history. Scholars now explore such long-neglected fields as the history of women, of immigration, of blacks, Indians, Hispanics, and other minorities. Voices long silent ring out of the darkness of history.

The result has been a reconstruction of American history, partly on the merits and partly in response to ethnic pressures. In 1987, the two states with both the greatest and the most diversified populations—California and New York—adopted new curricula for grades one to twelve. Both state curricula materially increased the time allotted to non-European cultures.

The New York curriculum went further in minimizing Western traditions. A two-year global-studies course divided the world into seven regions—Africa, South Asia, East Asia, Latin America, the Middle East, Western Europe, and Eastern Europe—with each region given equal time. The history of Western Europe was cut back from a full year to one quarter of the second year. American history was reduced to a section on the

Constitution; then a leap across Jefferson, Jackson, the Civil War, and Reconstruction to 1877.

In spite of the multiculturalization of the New York state history curriculum in 1987—a revision approved by such scholars as Eric Foner of Columbia and Christopher Lasch of Rochester—a newly appointed commissioner of education yielded to pressures from minority interests to consider still further revision. In 1989, the Task Force on Minorities: Equity and Excellence (not one historian among its seventeen members) brought in a report that argued: the "systematic bias toward European culture and its derivatives" has "a terribly damaging effect on the psyche of young people of African, Asian, Latino, and Native American descent." The dominance of "the European-American monocultural perspective" explains why "large numbers of children of non-European descent are not doing as well as expected."

Dr. Leonard Jeffries, the task force's consultant on African-American culture and a leading author of the report, discerns "deep-seated pathologies of racial hatred" even in the 1987 curriculum. The consultant on Asian-American culture called for more pictures of Asian-Americans. The consultant on Latino culture found damning evidence of ethnocentric bias in such usages as the "Mexican War" and the "Spanish-American War." The ethnically correct designations should be the "American-Mexican War" and the "Spanish-Cuban-American War." The consultant on Native American culture wanted more space for Indians and for bilingual education in Iroquois.

A new curriculum giving the four other cultures equitable treatment, the report concluded, would provide "children from Native American, Puerto Rican/Latino,

Asian-American, and African-American cultures . . . higher self-esteem and self-respect, while children from European cultures will have a less arrogant perspective."

The report views division into racial groups as the basic analytical framework for an understanding of American history. Its interest in history is not as an intellectual discipline but rather as social and psychological therapy whose primary function is to raise the self-esteem of children from minority groups. Nor does the report regard the Constitution or the American Creed as means of improvement.

Jeffries scorns the Constitution, finding "something vulgar and revolting in glorifying a process that heaped undeserved rewards on a segment of the population while oppressing the majority." The belief in the unifying force of democratic ideals finds no echo in the report. Indeed, the report takes no interest in the problem of holding a diverse republic together. Its impact is rather to sanction and deepen racial tensions.

THE RECENT SPREAD OF AFROCENTRIC PROgrams to public schools represents an extension of the New York task force ideology. These programs are, in most cases, based on a series of "African-American Baseline Essays" conceived by the educational psychologist Asa Hilliard.

Hilliard's narration for the slide show "Free Your Mind, Return to the Source: The African Origin of Civilization" suggests his approach. "Africa," he writes, "is the mother of Western civilization"—an argument turning on the contention that Egypt was a black African country and the real source of the science and philosophy Western historians attribute to Greece. Africans, Hilliard continues,

also invented birth control and carbon steel. They brought science, medicine, and the arts to Europe; indeed, many European artists, such as Browning and Beethoven, were, in fact, "Afro-European." They also discovered America long before Columbus, and the original name of the Atlantic Ocean was the Ethiopian Ocean.

Hilliard's African-American Baseline Essays were introduced into the school system of Portland, Oregon, in 1987. They have subsequently been the inspiration for Afrocentric curricula in Milwaukee, Indianapolis, Pittsburgh, Washington, D.C., Richmond, Atlanta, Philadelphia, Detroit, Baltimore, Camden, and other cities and continue at this writing to be urged on school boards and administrators anxious to do the right thing.

John Henrik Clarke's Baseline Essay on Social Studies begins with the proposition that "African scholars are the final authority on Africa." Egypt, he continues, "gave birth to what later became known as Western civilization, long before the greatness of Greece and Rome." "Great civilizations" existed throughout Africa, where "great kings" ruled "in might and wisdom over vast empires." After Egypt declined, magnificent empires arose in West Africa, in Ghana, Mali, Songhay—all marked by the brilliance and enlightenment of their administrations and the high quality of their libraries and universities.

Other Baseline Essays argue in a similar vein that Africa was the birthplace of science, mathematics, philosophy, medicine, and art and that Europe stole its civilization from Africa and then engaged in "malicious misrepresentation of African society and people . . . to support the enormous profitability of slavery." The coordinator of multicultural/multi-ethnic education in Portland even says that Napoleon deliberately shot off the nose of the Sphinx so that the Sphinx would not be recognized as African.

Like other excluded groups before them, black Americans invoke supposed past glories to compensate for real past and present injustices. Because their exclusion has been more tragic and terrible than that of white immigrants, their quest for self-affirmation is more intense and passionate. In seeking to impose Afrocentric curricula on public schools, for example, they go further than their white predecessors. And belated recognition by white America of the wrongs so viciously inflicted on black Americans has created the phenomenon of white guilt—not a bad thing in many respects, but still a vulnerability that invites cynical exploitation and manipulation.

I AM CONSTRAINED TO FEEL THAT THE CULT of ethnicity in general and the Afrocentric campaign in particular do not bode well either for American education or for the future of the republic. Cultural pluralism is not the issue. Nor is the teaching of Afro-American or African history the issue; of course these are legitimate subjects. The issue is the kind of history that the New York task force, the Portland Baseline essayists, and other Afrocentric ideologues propose for American children. The issue is the teaching of *bad* history under whatever ethnic banner.

One argument for organizing a school curriculum around Africa is that black Africa is the birthplace of science, philosophy, religion, medicine, technology, of the great achievements that have been wrongly ascribed to Western civilization. But is this, in fact, true? Many historians and anthropologists regard Mesopotamia as the cradle of civilization; for a recent

discussion, see Charles Keith Maisels' *The Emergence of Civilization*.

The Afrocentrist case rests largely on the proposition that ancient Egypt was essentially a black African country. I am far from being an expert on Egyptian history, but neither, one must add, are the educators and psychologists who push Afrocentrism. A book they often cite is Martin Bernal's *Black Athena*, a vigorous effort by a Cornell professor to document Egyptian influence on ancient Greece. In fact, Bernal makes no very strong claims about Egyptian pigmentation; but, citing Herodotus, he does argue that several Egyptian dynasties "were made up of pharaohs whom one can usefully call black."

Frank M. Snowden Jr., the distinguished black classicist at Howard University and author of *Blacks in Antiquity*, is most doubtful about painting ancient Egypt black. Bernal's assumption that Herodotus meant black in the 20th-century sense is contradicted, Snowden demonstrates, "by Herodotus himself and the copious evidence of other classical authors."

Frank J. Yurco, an Egyptologist at Chicago's Field Museum of Natural History, after examining the evidence derivable from mummies, paintings, statues, and reliefs, concludes in the *Biblical Archaeological Review* that ancient Egyptians, like their modern descendants, varied in color from the light Mediterranean type to the darker brown of upper Egypt to the still darker shade of the Nubians around Aswan. He adds that ancient Egyptians would have found the question meaningless and wonders at our presumption in assigning "our primitive racial labels" to so impressive a culture.

After Egypt, Afrocentrists teach children about the glorious West African emperors, the vast lands they ruled, the civilization they achieved; not, however, about the tyrannous authority they exercised, the ferocity of their wars, the tribal massacres, the squalid lot of the common people, the captives sold into slavery, the complicity with the Atlantic slave trade, the persistence of slavery in Africa after it was abolished in the West. As for tribalism, the word *tribe* hardly occurs in the Afrocentric lexicon; but who can hope to understand African history without understanding it.

The Baseline Essay on science and technology contains biographies of black American scientists, among them Charles R. Drew, who first developed the process for the preservation of blood plasma. In 1950 Drew, grievously injured in an automobile accident in North Carolina, lost quantities of blood. *"Not one* of several nearby white hospitals," according to the Baseline Essay, "would provide the blood transfusions he so desperately [*sic*] needed, and on the way to a hospital that treated Black people, he died." It is a hell of a story—the inventor of blood-plasma storage dead because racist whites denied him his own invention. Only it is not true. According to the biographical entry for Drew written by the eminent black scholar Rayford Logan of Howard for the *Dictionary of American Negro Biography,* "Conflicting versions to the contrary, Drew received prompt medical attention."

Is it really a good idea to teach minority children myths—at least to teach myths as facts?

THE DEEPER REASON FOR THE AFROCEN-tric campaign lies in the theory that the purpose of history in the schools is essentially therapeutic: to build a sense of self-worth among minority children. Eu-rocentrism, by denying nonwhite children any past in which they can take pride, is held to be the cause of poor academic performance. Race consciousness and group pride are supposed to strengthen a sense of identity and self-respect among nonwhite students.

Why does anyone suppose that pride and inspiration are available only from people of the same ethnicity? Plainly this is not the case. At the age of twelve, Frederick Douglass encountered a book entitled *The Columbian Orator* containing speeches by Burke, Sheridan, Pitt, and Fox. "Every opportunity I got," Douglass later said, "I used to read this book." The orations "gave tongue to interesting thoughts of my own soul, which had frequently flashed through my mind, and died away for want of utterance. . . . What I got from Sheridan was a bold denunciation of slavery and a powerful vindication of human rights. The reading of these documents enabled me to utter my thoughts." Douglass did not find the fact that the orators were white an insuperable obstacle.

Or hear Ralph Ellison: "In Macon County, Alabama, I read Marx, Freud, T. S. Eliot, Pound, Gertrude Stein, and Hemingway. Books that seldom, if ever, mentioned Negroes were to release me from whatever 'segregated' idea I might have had of my human possibilities." He was freed, Ellison continued, not by the example of Richard Wright and other black writers but by artists who offered a broader sense of life and possibility. "It requires real poverty of the imagination to think that this can come to a Negro only through the example of other Negroes."

Martin Luther King, Jr. did pretty well with Thoreau, Gandhi, and Reinhold Niebuhr as models—and remember, after all, whom King (and his father) were named for. Is Lincoln to be a hero only for those of English ancestry? Jackson only for Scotch-Irish? Douglass only for blacks? Great artists, thinkers, leaders are the possession not just of their own racial clan but of all humanity.

As for self-esteem, is this really the product of ethnic role models and fantasies of a glorious past? Or does it not result from the belief in oneself that springs from achievement, from personal rather than from racial pride?

Columnist William Raspberry notes that Afrocentric education will make black children "less competent in the culture in which they have to compete." After all, what good will it do young black Americans to hear that, because their minds work differently, a first-class education is not for them? Will such training help them to understand democracy better? Help them to fit better into American life?

Will it increase their self-esteem when black children grow up and learn that many of the things the Afrocentrists taught them are not true? Black scholars have tried for years to rescue black history from chauvinistic hyperbole. A. A. Schomburg, the noted archivist of black history, expressed his scorn long ago for those who "glibly tried to prove that half of the world's geniuses have been Negroes and to trace the pedigree of nineteenth-century Americans from the Queen of Sheba."

The dean of black historians in America today is John Hope Franklin. "While a black scholar," Franklin writes, "has a clear responsibility to join in improving the society in which he lives, he must understand the difference between hard-hitting advocacy on the one hand and the highest standards of scholarship on the other."

THE USE OF HISTORY AS THERAPY MEANS the corruption of history as history. All major races, cultures, nations have committed crimes, atrocities, horrors at one time or another. Every civilization has skeletons in its closet. Honest history calls for the unexpurgated record. How much would a full account of African despotism, massacre, and slavery increase the self-esteem of black students? Yet what kind of history do you have if you leave out all the bad things?

"Once ethnic pride and self-esteem become the criterion for teaching history," historian Diane Ravitch points out, "certain things cannot be taught." Skeletons must stay in the closet lest outing displease descendants.

No history curriculum in the country is more carefully wrought and better balanced in its cultural pluralism than California's. But hearings before the State Board of Education show what happens when ethnicity is unleashed at the expense of scholarship. At issue were textbooks responsive to the new curriculum. Polish-Americans demanded that any reference to Hitler's Holocaust be accompanied by accounts of equivalent genocide suffered by Polish Christians. Armenian-Americans sought coverage of Turkish massacres; Turkish-Americans objected. Though black historians testified that the treatment of black history was exemplary, Afrocentrists said the schoolbooks would lead to "textbook genocide." Moslems complained that an illustration of an Islamic warrior with a raised scimitar stereotyped Moslems as "terrorists."

"The single theme that persistently ran through the hearings," Ravitch writes, "was that the critics did not want anything taught if it offended members of their group."

In New York the curriculum guide for eleventh-grade American history tells students that there were three "foundations" for the Constitution: the European Enlightenment, the "Haudenosaunee political system," and the antecedent colonial experience. Only the Haudenosaunee political system receives explanatory subheadings: "a. Influence upon colonial leadership and European intellectuals (Locke, Montesquieu, Voltaire, Rousseau); b. Impact on Albany Plan of Union, Articles of Confederation, and U.S. Constitution."

How many experts on the American Constitution would endorse this stirring tribute to the "Haudenosaunee political system"? How many have heard of that system? Whatever influence the Iroquois confederation may have had on the framers of the Constitution was marginal; on European intellectuals it was marginal to the point of invisibility. No other state curriculum offers this analysis of the making of the Constitution. But then no other state has so effective an Iroquois lobby.

President Franklin Jenifer of Howard University, while saying that "historical black institutions" like his own have a responsibility to teach young people about their particular history and culture, adds, "One has to be very careful when one is talking about public schools. . . . There should be no creation of nonexistent history."

Let us by all means teach black history, African history, women's history, Hispanic history, Asian history. But let us teach them as history, not as filiopietistic commemoration. When every ethnic and religious group claims a right to approve or veto anything that is taught in public schools, the fatal line is crossed between cultural pluralism and ethnocentrism. An evident casualty is the old idea that whatever our ethnic base, we are all Americans together.

THE ETHNICITY RAGE IN GENERAL AND Afrocentricity in particular not only divert attention from the real needs but exacerbate the problems. The cult of ethnicity exaggerates differences, intensifies resentments and antagonisms, drives ever deeper the awful wedges between races and nationalities. The end game is self-pity and self-ghettoization. Afrocentricity as expounded by ethnic ideologues implies Europhobia, separatism, emotions of alienation, victimization, paranoia.

If any educational institution should bring people together as individuals in friendly and civil association, it should be the university. But the fragmentation of campuses in recent years into a multitude of ethnic organizations is spectacular—and disconcerting.

Stanford University, writer Dinesh D'Souza reports in his book *Illiberal Education*, has "ethnic theme houses." The University of Pennsylvania gives blacks—6 percent of the enrollment—their own yearbook. Campuses today, according to one University of Pennsylvania professor, have "the cultural diversity of Beirut. There are separate armed camps. The black kids don't mix with the white kids. The Asians are off by themselves. Oppression is the great status symbol."

Oberlin was for a century and a half the model of a racially integrated college. "Increasingly" Jacob Weisberg, an editor at *The New Republic*, reports, "Oberlin students think, act, study, and live apart." Asians live in Asia House, Jews in "J" House, Latinos in Spanish House, blacks in African-Heritage House, foreign students in Third World House. Even the Lesbian, Gay, and Bisexual Union has broken up into racial and gender factions. "The result is separate worlds."

Huddling is an understandable reaction for any minority group faced with new and scary challenges. But institutionalized separatism only crystallizes racial differences and magnifies racial tensions. "Certain activities are labeled white and black," says a black student at Central Michigan University. "If you don't just participate in black activities, you are shunned."

Militants further argue that because only blacks can comprehend the black experience, only blacks should teach black history and literature, as, in the view of some feminists, only women should teach women's history and literature. "True diversity," according to the faculty's Budget Committee at the University of California at Berkeley, requires that courses match the ethnic and gender identities of the professors.

The doctrine that *only* blacks can teach and write black history leads inexorably to the doctrine that blacks can teach and write *only* black history as well as to inescapable corollaries: Chinese must be restricted to Chinese history, women to women's history, and so on. Henry Louis Gates of Duke University criticizes "ghettoized programs where students and members of the faculty sit around and argue about whether a white person can think a black thought?" As for the notion that there is a "mystique" about black studies that requires a person to have black skin in order to pursue them—that, John Hope Franklin observes succinctly, is "voodoo."

The separatist impulse is by no means confined to the black community. Another salient expression is the bilingualism movement. The presumed purpose of bilingualism is transitional: to move non-English-speaking children as quickly as possible from bilingual into all-English classes.

Alas, bilingualism has not worked out as planned: rather the contrary. Testimony is mixed, but indications are that bilingual education retards rather than expedites the movement of Hispanic children into the English-speaking world and that it promotes segregation more than it does integration. Bilingualism "encourages concentrations of Hispanics to stay together and not be integrated," says Alfredo Mathew Jr., a Hispanic civic leader, and it may well foster "a type of apartheid that will generate animosities with others, such as Blacks, in the competition for scarce resources and further alienate the Hispanic from the larger society."

"The era that began with the dream of integration," author Richard Rodriguez has observed, "ended up with scorn for assimilation." The cult of ethnicity has reversed the movement of American history, producing a nation of minorities—or at least of minority spokesmen—less interested in joining with the majority in common endeavor than in declaring their alienation from an oppressive, white, patriarchal, racist, sexist, classist society. The ethnic ideology inculcates the illusion that membership in one or another ethnic group is the basic American experience.

The contemporary sanctification of the group puts the old idea of a coherent society at stake. Multicultural zealots reject as hegemonic the notion of a shared commitment to common ideals. How far the discourse has come from Crevecoeur's "new race," from Tocqueville's civic participation, from Bryce's "amazing solvent" from Myrdal's "American Creed"!

Yet what has held the American people together in the absence of a common ethnic origin has been precisely a common adherence to ideals of democracy and human rights that, too often transgressed in practice, forever goad us to narrow the gap between practice and principle.

America is an experiment in creating a common identity for people of diverse races, religions, languages, cultures. If the republic now turns away from its old goal of "one people," what is its future?—disintegration of the national community, apartheid, Balkanization, tribalization?

POSTSCRIPT

Do Black Students Need an Afrocentric Curriculum?

How can equal educational opportunities be ensured? What are the current realities of the U.S. educational system, and how should inequalities be addressed? Can opportunities for educational success for black schoolchildren be improved by making the changes Asante recommends? Or is there merit to Schlesinger's contention that Afrocentric programs have the potential to teach myths as facts and do not bode well for addressing the problems of race and inequality in the schools or in U.S. society?

Sources for further exploration of this issue are multiple. For additional insight into the thinking of the opponents presented here, see Asante's "Afrocentric Curriculum" in *Educational Leadership* (December 1991) and Schlesinger's "The American Creed: From Dilemma to Decomposition" in *New Perspectives Quarterly* (Summer 1991). An interesting appraisal of the situation may be found in James Comer's "Racism and the Education of Young Children," *Teachers College Record* (Spring 1989).

Special collections of articles on Afrocentrism may be found in the *Journal of Negro Education* (Summer 1992), which features the thoughts of James A. Banks, Asa G. Hilliard III, Maxine Greene, and Lisa Delpit; *Counseling Psychologist* (April 1989); and *Time* magazine (July 8, 1991). Another good source is the *Journal of Black Studies*, whose December 1990 issue contains two especially interesting pieces: "Afrocentric Cultural Consciousness and African-American Male-Female Relationships," by Yvonne R. Bell et al., and Bayo Oyebade's "African Studies and the Afrocentric Paradigm: A Critique." The September 1989 issue features William Oliver's "Black Males and Social Problems: Prevention Through Afrocentric Socialization." Of further interest is Eileen Oliver's "An Afrocentric Approach to Literature: Putting the Pieces Back Together," *English Journal* (September 1988).

See also these probing articles: Midge Decter's "E Pluribus Nihil: Multiculturalism and Black Children," *Commentary* (Fall 1991); Diane Ravitch's "Multiculturalism: E Pluribus Plures," *American Scholar* (Summer 1990); and C. Vann Woodward's "Equal But Separate," *The New Republic* (July 15 & 22, 1991), which reviews Schlesinger's *The Disuniting of America*. On the topic of all-male instruction, see the October 1991 issue of *Emerge*, particularly articles by Bray and Benjamin. Finally, some penetrating insights can be gained from *Going to School: The African-American Experience* (1990) edited by Kofi Lomotey.

ISSUE 15

Should Bilingual Education Programs Be Abandoned?

YES: Diane Ravitch, from "Politicization and the Schools: The Case of Bilingual Education," *Proceedings of the American Philosophical Society* (June 1985)

NO: Donaldo Macedo, from "English Only: The Tongue-Tying of America," *Journal of Education* (Spring 1991)

ISSUE SUMMARY

YES: History of education professor Diane Ravitch finds inadequate evidence of success in bilingual education programs and expresses concern over the effort's politicization.

NO: Donaldo Macedo, an associate professor of linguistics, deplores the incessant attack on bilingual education by Ravitch and other conservatives and explores the pedagogical and political implications of abandoning such programs.

The issue of accommodating non-English-speaking immigrants by means of a bilingual education program has been controversial since the late 1960s. Events of the past decades have brought about one of the largest influxes of immigrants to the United States in the nation's history. And the disadvantages that non-English-speaking children and their parents experience during the childrens' years of formal schooling has received considerable attention from educators, policymakers, and the popular press.

Efforts to modify this type of social and developmental disadvantage have appeared in the form of bilingual education programs initiated at the local level and supported by federal funding. Approaches implemented include direct academic instruction in the primary language and the provision of language tutors under the English for Speakers of Other Languages (ESOL) program. Research evaluation of these efforts has produced varied results and has given rise to controversy over the efficacy of the programs themselves and the social and political intentions served by them.

A political movement at the national and state levels to establish English as the official language of the United States has gained support in recent years. Supporters of this movement feel that the bilingual approach will lead to the kind of linguistic division that has torn Canada apart.

Perhaps sharing some of the concerns of the "official English" advocates, increasing numbers of educators seem to be tilting in the direction of the immersion approach. In a recent book, *Forked Tongue: The Politics of Bilingual Education* (1990), Rosalie Pedalineo Porter, a teacher and researcher in the field of bilingual education for over 15 years, issues an indictment of the policies and programs that have been prevalent. One of her central recommendations is that "limited-English children must be placed with specially trained teachers in a program in which these students will be immersed in the English language, in which they have as much contact as possible with English speakers, and in which school subjects, not just social conversations, are the focus of the English-language lessons from kindergarten through twelfth grade."

Amado M. Padilla of Stanford University has examined the rationale behind "official English" and has also reviewed the effectiveness of bilingual education programs (see "English Only vs. Bilingual Education: Ensuring a Language-Competent Society," *Journal of Education*, Spring 1991). Padilla concludes that "the debate about how to assist linguistic minority children should focus on new educational technologies and *not* just on the effectiveness of bilingual education or whether bilingualism detracts from loyalty to this country."

In the first of the articles that follow, Diane Ravitch finds the effort to continue the policy of bilingual education to be overpoliticized. She contends that the program "exemplifies a campaign on behalf of social and political goals that are only tangentially related to education." She claims that "the aim is to use the public schools to promote the maintenance of distinct ethnic communities, each with its own cultural heritage and language." Donaldo Macedo, arguing from an opposing point of view, claims that the conservative ideology that propels the antibilingual education forces ignores the evidence supporting it and fails to recognize the need for preparing students for the ever-changing, multilingual, and multicultural world of the twenty-first century. An "English only" approach, he states, relegates the immigrant population to the margins of society.

YES

Diane Ravitch

POLITICIZATION AND THE SCHOOLS: THE CASE OF BILINGUAL EDUCATION

There has always been a politics of schools, and no doubt there always will be. Like any other organization populated by human beings, schools have their internal politics; for as long as there have been public schools, there have been political battles over their budget, their personnel policies, their curricula, and their purposes. Anyone who believes that there was once a time in which schools were untouched by political controversy is uninformed about the history of education. The decision-making processes that determine who will be chosen as principal or how the school board will be selected or whether to pass a school bond issue are simply political facts of life that are part and parcel of the administration, financing, and governance of schools. There is also a politics of the curriculum and of the profession, in which contending forces argue about programs and policies. It is hard to imagine a school, a school system, a university, a state board of education, or a national department of education in which these kinds of political conflicts do not exist. They are an intrinsic aspect of complex organizations in which people disagree about how to achieve their goals and about which goals to pursue; to the extent that we operate in a democratic manner, conflict over important and even unimportant issues is inevitable.

There is another kind of politics, however, in which educational institutions become entangled in crusades marked by passionate advocacy, intolerance of criticism, and unyielding dogmatism, and in which the education of children is a secondary rather than a primary consideration. Such crusades go beyond politics-as-usual; they represent the politicization of education. Schools and universities become targets for politicization for several reasons: First, they offer a large captive audience of presumably impressionable minds; second, they are expected to shape the opinions, knowledge, and values of the rising generation, which makes them attractive to those who want to influence the future; and third, since Americans have

From Diane Ravitch, "Politicization and the Schools: The Case of Bilingual Education," *Proceedings of the American Philosophical Society*, vol. 129, no. 2 (June 1985). Copyright © 1985 by The American Philosophical Society. Reprinted by permission.

no strong educational philosophy or educational tradition, almost any claim—properly clothed in rhetorical appeals about the needs of children or of American society—can make its way into the course catalogue or the educational agenda.

Ever since Americans created public schools, financed by tax dollars and controlled by boards of laymen, the schools have been at the center of intermittent struggles over the values that they represent. The founders of the common school, and in particular Horace Mann, believed that the schools could be kept aloof from the religious and political controversies beyond their door, but it has not been easy to keep the crusaders outside the schoolhouse. In the nineteenth century, heated battles were fought over such issues as which Bible would be read in the classroom and whether public dollars might be used to subsidize religious schools. After the onset of World War I, anti-German hostility caused the German language to be routed from American schools, even though nearly a quarter of the high school population studied the language in 1915. Some of this same fervor, strengthened by zeal to hasten the process of assimilation, caused several states to outlaw parochial and private schools and to prohibit the teaching of foreign language in the first eight years of school. Such laws, obviously products of nationalism and xenophobia, were struck down as unconstitutional by the United States Supreme Court in the 1920s. The legislative efforts to abolish nonpublic schools and to bar the teaching of foreign languages were examples of politicization; their purpose was not to improve the education of any child, but to achieve certain social and political goals that the sponsors of these laws believed were of overwhelming importance.

Another example of politicization in education was the crusade to cleanse the schools of teachers and other employees who were suspected of being disloyal, subversive, or controversial. This crusade began in the years after World War I, gathered momentum during the 1930s, and came to full fruition during the loyalty investigations by state and national legislative committees in the 1950s. Fears for national security led to intrusive surveillance of the beliefs, friends, past associations, and political activities of teachers and professors. These inquiries did not improve anyone's education; they used the educational institutions as vehicles toward political goals that were extraneous to education.

A more recent example of politicization occurred on the campuses during the war in Vietnam. Those who had fought political intrusions into educational institutions during the McCarthy era did so on the ground of academic freedom. Academic freedom, they argued, protected the right of students and teachers to express their views, regardless of their content; because of academic freedom, the university served as a sanctuary for dissidents, heretics, and skeptics of all persuasions. During the war in Vietnam, those who tried to maintain the university as a privileged haven for conflicting views, an open marketplace of ideas, found themselves the object of attack by student radicals. Student (and sometimes faculty) radicals believed that opposition to the war was so important that those who did not agree with them should be harassed and even silenced.

Faced with a moral issue, the activist argued, the university could not stand above the battle, nor could it tolerate the expression of "immoral" views. In this spirit, young radicals tried to prevent those with whom they disagreed from speaking and teaching; towards this end, they heckled speakers, disrupted classes, and even planted bombs on campus. These actions were intended to politicize schools and campuses and, in some instances, they succeeded. They were advocated by sincere and zealous individuals who earnestly believed that education could not take place within a context of political neutrality. Their efforts at politicization stemmed not from any desire to improve education as such, but from the pursuit of political goals.

As significant as the student movement and the McCarthy era were as examples of the dangers of politicization, they were short-lived in comparison to the policy of racial segregation. Segregation of public school children by their race and ancestry was established by law in seventeen states and by custom in many communities beyond those states. The practice of assigning public school children and teachers on the basis of their race had no educational justification; it was not intended to improve anyone's education. It was premised on the belief in the innate inferiority of people whose skin was of dark color. Racial segregation as policy and practice politicized the schools; it used them to buttress a racist social and political order. It limited the educational opportunities available to blacks. Racial segregation was socially and politically so effective in isolating blacks from opportunity or economic advancement and educationally so devastating in retarding their learning that our society continues to pay a heavy price to redress the cumulative deficits of generations of poor education.

The United States Supreme Court's 1954 decision, *Brown v. Board of Education*, started the process of ending state-im-

posed racial segregation. In those southern states where segregation was the cornerstone of a way of life, white resistance to desegregation was prolonged and intense. The drive to disestablish racial segregation and to uproot every last vestige of its effects was unquestionably necessary. The practice of assigning children to school by their race and of segregating other public facilities by race was a national disgrace. However, the process through which desegregation came about dramatically altered the politics of schools; courts and regulatory agencies at the federal and state level became accustomed to intervening in the internal affairs of educational institutions, and the potential for politicization of the schools was significantly enlarged.

The slow pace of desegregation in the decade after the *Brown* decision, concurrent with a period of rising expectations, contributed to a dramatic buildup of frustration and rage among blacks, culminating in the protests, civil disorders, and riots of the mid-1960s. In response, Congress enacted major civil rights laws in 1964 and 1965, and the federal courts became aggressive in telling school boards what to do to remedy their constitutional violations. Initially, these orders consisted of commands to produce racially mixed schools. However, some courts went beyond questions of racial mix. In Washington, D.C., a federal district judge in 1967 directed the school administration to abandon ability grouping, which he believed discriminated against black children. This was the first time that a federal court found a common pedagogical practice to be unconstitutional.[1]

In the nearly two decades since that decision, the active intervention of the federal judiciary into school affairs has ceased to be unusual. In Ann Arbor, Michigan, a federal judge ordered the school board to train teachers in "black English," a program subsequently found to be ineffectual in improving the education of black students. In California, a federal judge barred the use of intelligence tests for placement of students in special education classes, even though reputable psychologists defend their validity. In Boston, where the school board was found guilty of intentionally segregating children by race, the federal judge assumed full control over the school system for more than a decade; even reform superintendents who were committed to carrying out the judge's program for desegregation complained of the hundreds of court orders regulating every aspect of schooling, hiring, promotion, curriculum, and financing. In 1982, in a case unrelated to desegregation, a state judge in West Virginia ordered the state education department to do "no less than completely reconstruct the entire system of education in West Virginia," and the judge started the process of reconstruction by setting down his own standards for facilities, administration, and curriculum, including what was to be taught and for how many minutes each week.[2]

Perhaps this is as good a way of bringing about school reform as any other. No doubt school officials are delighted when a judge orders the state legislature to raise taxes on behalf of the schools. But it does seem to be a repudiation of our democratic political structure when judges go beyond issues of constitutional rights, don the mantle of school superintendent, and use their authority to change promotional standards, to reconstruct the curriculum, or to impose their own pedagogical prescriptions.

Now, by the definition of politicization that I earlier offered—that is, when educational institutions become the focus of dogmatic crusaders whose purposes are primarily political and only incidentally related to children's education—these examples may not qualify as politicization, although they do suggest how thin is the line between politics and politicization. After all, the judges were doing what they thought would produce better education. The court decisions in places like Ann Arbor, Boston, California, and West Virginia may be thought of as a shift in the politics of schools, a shift that has brought the judiciary into the decision-making process as a full-fledged partner in shaping educational disputes, even those involving questions of pedagogy and curriculum.

The long struggle to desegregate American schools put them at the center of political battles for more than a generation and virtually destroyed the belief that schools could remain above politics. Having lost their apolitical shield, the schools also lost their capacity to resist efforts to politicize them. In the absence of resistance, demands by interest groups of varying ideologies escalated, each trying to impose its own agenda on the curriculum, the textbooks, the school library, or the teachers. Based on the activities of single-issue groups, any number of contemporary educational policies would serve equally well as examples of politicization. The example that I have chosen as illustrative of politicization is bilingual education. The history of this program exemplifies a campaign on behalf of social and political goals that are only tangentially related to education. I would like to sketch briefly the bilingual controversy, which provides an overview of the new politics of education and demonstrates the tendency within this new politics to use educational programs for noneducational ends.

Demands for bilingual education arose as an outgrowth of the civil rights movement. As it evolved, that movement contained complex, and occasionally contradictory, elements. One facet of the movement appealed for racial integration and assimilation, which led to court orders for busing and racial balance; but the dynamics of the movement also inspired appeals to racial solidarity, which led to demands for black studies, black control of black schools, and other race-conscious policies. Whether the plea was for integration or for separatism, advocates could always point to a body of social science as evidence for their goals.

Race consciousness became a necessary part of the remedies that courts fashioned, but its presence legitimized ethnocentrism as a force in American politics. In the late 1960s, the courts, Congress, and policymakers—having been told for years by spokesmen for the civil rights movement that all children should be treated equally without regard to their race or ancestry—frequently heard compelling testimony by political activists and social scientists about the value of ethnic particularism in the curriculum.

Congress first endorsed funding for bilingual education in 1968, at a time when ethnocentrism had become a powerful political current. In hearings on this legislation, proponents of bilingual education argued that non-English-speaking children did poorly in school because they had low self-esteem, and that this low self-esteem was caused by the absence of their native language from the classroom. They claimed that if the children were taught in their native tongue and about their native culture, they

would have higher self-esteem, better attitudes toward school, and higher educational achievement. Bilingual educators also insisted that children would learn English more readily if they already knew another language.

In the congressional hearings, both advocates and congressmen seemed to agree that the purpose of bilingual education was to help non-English speakers succeed in school and in society. But the differences between them were not then obvious. The congressmen believed that bilingual education would serve as a temporary transition into the regular English language program. But the bilingual educators saw the program as an opportunity to maintain the language and culture of the non-English-speaking student, while he was learning English.[3]

What was extraordinary about the Bilingual Education Act of 1968, which has since been renewed several times, is that it was the first time that the Congress had ever legislated a given pedagogical method. In practice, bilingual education means a program in which children study the major school subjects in a language other than English. Funding of the program, although small within the context of the federal education budget, created strong constituencies for its continuation, both within the federal government and among recipient agencies. No different from other interest groups, these constituencies pressed for expansion and strengthening of their program. Just as lifelong vocational educators are unlikely to ask whether their program works, so career bilingual educators are committed to their method as a philosophy, not as a technique for language instruction. The difference is this: techniques are subject to evaluation, which may cause them to be revised or discarded; philosophies are not.

In 1974, the Supreme Court's *Lau v. Nichols* decision reinforced demands for bilingual education. The Court ruled against the San Francisco public schools for their failure to provide English language instruction for 1,800 non-English-speaking Chinese students. The Court's decision was reasonable and appropriate. The Court said, "There is no equality of treatment merely by providing students with the same facilities, textbooks, teachers, and curriculum; for students who do not understand English are effectively foreclosed from any meaningful education." The decision did not endorse any particular remedy. It said "Teaching English to the students of Chinese ancestry who do not speak the language is one choice. Giving instruction to the group in Chinese is another. There may be others."[4]

Despite the Court's prudent refusal to endorse any particular method of instruction, the bilingual educators interpreted the *Lau* decision as a mandate for bilingual programs. In the year after the decision, the United States Office of Education established a task force to fashion guidelines for the implementation of the *Lau* decision; the task force was composed of bilingual educators and representatives of language minority groups. The task force fashioned regulations that prescribed in exhaustive detail how school districts should prepare and carry out bilingual programs for non-English-speaking students. The districts were directed to identify the student's primary language, not by his proficiency in English, but by determining which language was most often spoken in the student's home, which language he had learned first, and which language he

used most often. Thus a student would be eligible for a bilingual program even if he was entirely fluent in English.[5]

Furthermore, while the Supreme Court refused to endorse any given method, the task force directed that non-English-speaking students should receive bilingual education that emphasized instruction in their native language and culture. Districts were discouraged from using the "English as a Second Language" approach, which consists of intensive, supplemental English-only instruction, or immersion techniques, in which students are instructed in English within an English-only context.

Since the establishment of the bilingual education program, many millions of dollars have been spent to support bilingual programs in more than sixty different languages. Among those receiving funding to administer and staff such programs, bilingual education is obviously popular, but there are critics who think that it is educationally unsound. Proponents of desegregation have complained that bilingual education needlessly segregates non-English speakers from others of their age. At a congressional hearing in 1977, one desegregation specialist complained that bilingual programs had been funded "without any significant proof that they would work. . . . There is nothing in the research to suggest that children can effectively learn English without continuous interaction with other children who are native English speakers."[6]

The research on bilingual education has been contradictory, and studies that favor or criticize the bilingual approach have been attacked as biased. Researchers connected to bilingual institutes claim that their programs resulted in significant gains for non-English-speaking children.

But a four-year study commissioned by the United States Office of Education concluded that students who learned bilingually did not achieve at a higher level than those in regular classes, nor were their attitudes toward school significantly different. What they seemed to learn best, the study found, was the language in which they were instructed.[7]

One of the few evidently unbiased, nonpolitical assessments of bilingual research was published in 1982 in the *Harvard Educational Review*. A survey of international findings, it concluded that "bilingual programs are neither better nor worse than other instructional methods." The author found that in the absence of compelling experimental support for this method, there was "no legal necessity or research basis for the federal government to advocate or require a specific educational approach."[8]

If the research is in fact inconclusive, then there is no justification for mandating the use of bilingual education or any other single pedagogy. The bilingual method may or may not be the best way to learn English. Language instruction programs that are generally regarded as outstanding, such as those provided for Foreign Service officers or by the nationally acclaimed center at Middlebury College, are immersion programs, in which students embark on a systematic program of intensive language learning without depending on their native tongue. Immersion programs may not be appropriate for all children, but then neither is any single pedagogical method. The method to be used should be determined by the school authorities and the professional staff, based on their resources and competence.

Despite the fact that the Supreme Court did not endorse bilingual education, the lower federal courts have tended to treat this pedagogy as a civil right, and more than a dozen states have mandated its use in their public schools. The path by which bilingual education came to be viewed as a civil right, rather than as one method of teaching language, demonstrates the politicization of the language issue in American education. The United States Commission on Civil Rights endorsed bilingual education as a civil right nearly a decade ago. Public interest lawyers and civil rights lawyers have also regarded bilingual education as a basic civil right. An article in 1983 in the *Columbia Journal of Law and Social Problems* contended that bilingual education "may be the most effective method of compensatory language instruction currently used to educate language-minority students."[9] It based this conclusion not on a review of educational research but on statements made by various political agencies.

The article states, for example, as a matter of fact rather than opinion: " . . . by offering subject matter instruction in a language understood by language-minority students, the bilingual-bicultural method maximizes achievement, and thus minimizes feelings of inferiority that might accompany a poor academic performance. By ridding the school environment of those features which may damage a language-minority child's self-image and thereby interfere with the educative process, bilingual-bicultural education creates the atmosphere most conducive to successful learning."[10]

If there were indeed conclusive evidence for these statements, then bilingual-bicultural education *should* be imposed on school districts throughout the country. However, the picture is complicated;

there are good bilingual programs, and there are ineffective bilingual programs. In and of itself, bilingualism is one pedagogical method, as subject to variation and misuse as any other single method. To date, no school district has claimed that the bilingual method succeeded in sharply decreasing the dropout rate of Hispanic children or markedly raising their achievement scores in English and other subjects. The bilingual method is not necessarily inferior to other methods; its use should not be barred. There simply is no conclusive evidence that bilingualism should be preferred to all other ways of instructing non-English-speaking students. This being the case, there are no valid reasons for courts or federal agencies to impose this method on school districts for all non-English speakers, to the exclusion of other methods of language instruction.

Bilingual education exemplifies politicization because its advocates press its adoption regardless of its educational effectiveness, and they insist that it must be made mandatory regardless of the wishes of the parents and children who are its presumed beneficiaries. It is a political program whose goals are implicit in the term "biculturalism." The aim is to use the public schools to promote the maintenance of distinct ethnic communities, each with its own cultural heritage and language. This in itself is a valid goal for a democratic nation as diverse and pluralistic as ours, but it is questionable whether this goal is appropriately pursued by the public schools, rather than by the freely chosen activities of individuals and groups.

Then there is the larger question of whether bilingual education actually promotes equality of educational opportunity. Unless it enables non-English-

speaking children to learn English and to enter into the mainstream of American society, it may hinder equality of educational opportunity. The child who spends most of his instructional time learning in Croatian or Greek or Spanish is likely to learn Croatian, Greek, or Spanish. Fluency in these languages will be of little help to those who want to apply to American colleges, universities, graduate schools, or employers, unless they are also fluent in English.

Of course, our nation needs much more foreign language instruction. But we should not confuse our desire to promote foreign languages in general with the special educational needs of children who do not know how to speak and read English in an English-language society.

Will our educational institutions ever be insulated from the extremes of politicization? It seems highly unlikely, in view of the fact that our schools and colleges are deeply embedded in the social and political mainstream. What is notably different today is the vastly increased power of the federal government and the courts to intervene in educational institutions, because of the expansion of the laws and the dependence of almost all educational institutions on public funding. To avoid unwise and dangerous politicization, government agencies should strive to distinguish between their proper role as protectors of fundamental constitutional rights and inappropriate intrusion into complex issues of curriculum and pedagogy.

This kind of institutional restraint would be strongly abetted if judges and policymakers exercised caution and skepticism in their use of social science testimony. Before making social research the basis for constitutional edicts, judges and policymakers should understand that social science findings are usually divergent, limited, tentative, and partial.

We need the courts as vigilant guardians of our rights; we need federal agencies that respond promptly to any violations of those rights. But we also need educational institutions that are free to exercise their responsibilities without fear of pressure groups and political lobbies. Decisions about which textbooks to use, which theories to teach, which books to place in the school library, how to teach, and what to teach are educational issues. They should be made by appropriate lay and professional authorities on educational grounds. In a democratic society, all of us share the responsibility to protect schools, colleges, and universities against unwarranted political intrusion into educational affairs.

REFERENCES

1. *Hobson v. Hansen*, 269 F. Supp. 401 (D.D.C., 1967); Alexander Bickel, "Skelly Wright's Sweeping Decision," *New Republic*, July 8, 1967, pp. 11–12.

2. Nathan Glazer, "Black English and Reluctant Judges," *Public Interest*, vol. 62, Winter 1980, pp. 40–54; *Larry P. v. Wilson Riles*, 495 F. Supp. 1926 (N.D. Calif., 1979); Nathan Glazer, "IQ on Trial," *Commentary*, June 1981, pp. 51–59; *Morgan v. Hennigan*, 379 F. Supp. 410 (D. Mass., 1974); Robert Wood, "The Disassembling of American Education," *Daedalus*, vol. 109, no. 3, Summer 1980, pp. 99–113; *Education Week*, May 12, 1982, p. 5.

3. U.S. Congress, Senate, Committee on Labor and Public Welfare, Special Subcommittee on Bilingual Education, 90th Cong., 1st sess., 1967.

4. *Lau v. Nichols*, 414 U.S. 563 (1974).

5. U.S. Department of Health, Education, and Welfare, "Task Force Findings Specifying Remedies Available for Eliminating Past Educational Practices Ruled Unlawful under *Lau v. Nichols*" (Washington, D.C., Summer 1975).

6. U.S. Congress, House, Subcommittee on Elementary, Secondary, and Vocational Education of the Committee on Education and Labor, Bilingual Education, 95th Cong., 1st sess., 1977, pp. 335–336. The speaker was Gary Orfield.

7. Malcolm N. Danoff, "Evaluation of the Impact of ESEA Title VII Spanish/English Bilingual Education Programs" (Palo Alto, Calif.: American Institutes for Research, 1978).

8. Iris Rotberg, "Some Legal and Research Considerations in Establishing Federal Policy in Bilingual Education," *Harvard Educational Review*, vol. 52, May 1982, pp. 148–168.

9. Jonathan D. Haft, "Assuring Equal Educational Opportunity for Language-Minority Students: Bilingual Education and the Equal Educational Opportunity Act of 1974." *Columbia Journal of Law and Social Problems*, vol. 18, no. 2, 1983, pp. 209–293.

10. Ibid., p. 253.

NO

Donaldo Macedo

ENGLISH ONLY: THE TONGUE-TYING
OF AMERICA

During the past decade conservative educators such as ex-secretary of education William Bennett and Diane Ravitch have mounted an unrelenting attack on bilingual and multicultural education. These conservative educators tend to recycle old assumptions about the "melting pot theory" and our "common culture," assumptions designed primarily to maintain the status quo. Maintained is a status quo that functions as a cultural reproduction mechanism which systematically does not allow other cultural subjects, who are considered outside of the mainstream, to be present in history. These cultural subjects who are profiled as the "other" are but palely represented in history within our purportedly democratic society in the form of Black History Month, Puerto Rican Day, and so forth. This historical constriction was elegantly captured by an 11th-grade Vietnamese student in California:

> I was so excited when my history teacher talked about the Vietnam War. Now at last, I thought, now we will study about my country. We didn't really study it. Just for one day, though, my country was real again. (Olsen, 1988, p. 68)

The incessant attack on bilingual education which claims that it serves to tongue-tie students in their native language not only negates the multilingual and multicultural nature of U.S. society, but blindly ignores the empirical evidence that has been amply documented in support of bilingual education. . . . [T]he present overdose of monolingualism and Anglocentrism that dominates the current educational debate not only contributes to a type of mind-tied America, but also is incapable of producing educators and leaders who can rethink what it means to prepare students to enter the ever-changing, multilingual, and multicultural world of the 21st century.

It is both academically dishonest and misleading to simply point to some failures of bilingual education without examining the lack of success of linguistic minority students within a larger context of a general failure of public education in major urban centers. Furthermore, the English Only position points to a pedagogy of exclusion that views the learning of English as education itself. English Only advocates fail to question under what conditions English will be taught and by whom. For example, immersing non-English-speaking students in English as a Second Language [ESL] programs taught by untrained music, art and social science teachers (as is the case in Massachusetts with the grandfather clause in ESL Certification) will hardly accomplish the avowed goals of the English Only Movement. The proponents of English Only also fail to raise two other fundamental questions. First, if English is the most effective educational language, how can we explain that over 60 million Americans are illiterate or functionally illiterate (Kozol, 1985, p. 4)? Second, if education solely in English can guarantee linguistic minorities a better future, as educators like William Bennett promise, why do the majority of Black Americans, whose ancestors have been speaking English for over 200 years, find themselves still relegated to ghettos?

I want to argue in this paper that the answer lies not in technical questions of whether English is a more viable language of instruction or the repetitive promise that it offers non-English-speaking students "full participation first in their school and later in American society" (Silber, 1991, p. 7). This position assumes that English is in fact a superior language and that we live in a classless, race-blind society. I want to propose that decisions about how to educate non-English-speaking students cannot be reduced to issues of language, but rest in a full understanding of the ideological ele-

ments that generate and sustain linguistic, racial, and sex discrimination. That is, educators need to develop, as Henry Giroux has suggested, "a politics and pedagogy around a new language capable of acknowledging the multiple, contradictory, and complex subject positions people occupy within different social, cultural, and economic locations" (1992, p. 27). By shifting the linguistic issue to an ideological terrain we will challenge conservative educators to confront the Berlin Wall of racism, classism, and economic deprivation which characterizes the lived experiences of minorities in U.S. public schools. For example, J. Anthony Lukas succinctly captures the ideological elements that promote racism and segregation in schools in his analysis of desegregation in the Boston Public Schools. Lukas cites a trip to Charlestown High School, where a group of Black parents experienced firsthand the stark reality their children were destined to endure. Although the headmaster assured them that "violence, intimidation, or racial slurs would not be tolerated," they could not avoid the racial epithets on the walls: "Welcome Niggers," "Niggers Suck," "White Power," "KKK," "Bus is for Zulu," and "Be illiterate, fight busing." As those parents were boarding the bus, "they were met with jeers and catcalls 'go home niggers. Keep going all the way to Africa!' " This racial intolerance led one parent to reflect, "My god, what kind of hell am I sending my children into?" (Lukas, 1985, p. 282). What could her children learn at a school like that except to hate? Even though forced integration of schools in Boston exacerbated the racial tensions in the Boston Public Schools, one should not overlook the deep-seated racism that permeates all levels of the school structure. . . .

Against this landscape of violent racism perpetrated against racial minorities, and also against linguistic minorities, one can understand the reasons for the high dropout rate in the Boston public schools (approximately 50%). Perhaps racism and other ideological elements are part of a school reality which forces a high percentage of students to leave school, only later to be profiled by the very system as dropouts or "poor and unmotivated students." One could argue that the above incidents occurred during a tumultuous time of racial division in Boston's history, but I do not believe that we have learned a great deal from historically dangerous memories to the degree that our leaders continue to invite racial tensions as evidenced in the Willie Horton presidential campaign issue and the present quota for jobs as an invitation once again to racial divisiveness.

It is very curious that this new-found concern of English Only advocates for limited English proficiency students does not interrogate those very ideological elements that psychologically and emotionally harm these students far more than the mere fact that English may present itself as a temporary barrier to an effective education. It would be more socially constructive and beneficial if the zeal that propels the English Only movement were diverted toward social struggles designed to end violent racism and structures of poverty, homelessness, and family breakdown, among other social ills that characterize the lived experiences of minorities in the United States. If these social issues are not dealt with appropriately, it is naive to think that the acquisition of the English language alone will, somehow, magically eclipse the raw and cruel injustices and oppression perpetrated against the dispossessed class of minorities in the United States. According to Peter McLaren, these dispossessed minority students who

> populate urban settings in places such as Howard Beach, Ozone Park, El Barrio, are more likely to be forced to learn about Eastern Europe in ways set forth by neo-conservative multiculturists than they are to learn about the Harlem Renaissance, Mexico, Africa, the Caribbean, or Aztec or Zulu culture. (McLaren, 1991, p. 7)

While arguing for the use of the students' native language in their educational development, I would like to make it very clear that the bilingual education goal should never be to restrict students to their own vernacular. This linguistic constriction inevitably leads to a linguistic ghetto. Educators must understand fully the broader meaning of the use of students' language as a requisite for their empowerment. That is, empowerment should never be limited to what Stanley Aronowitz describes as "the process of appreciating and loving oneself" (1985). In addition to this process, empowerment should also be a means that enables students "to interrogate and selectively appropriate those aspects of the dominant culture that will provide them with the basis for defining and transforming, rather than merely serving, the wider social order" (Giroux & McLaren, 1986, p. 17). This means that educators should understand the value of mastering the standard English language of the wider society. It is through the full appropriation of the standard English language that linguistic minority students find themselves linguistically empowered to engage in dialogue with various sectors of the wider society. What I must reiterate is that educators should never allow the limited proficient students' native language to be silenced by a distorted legitimation of the standard English language. Linguistic minority students' language should never be sacrificed, since it is the only means through which they make sense of their own experience in the world.

Given the importance of the standard English language in the education of linguistic minority students, I must agree with the members of the Institute for Research in English Acquisition and Development when they quote Antonio Gramsci in their brochure:

Without the mastery of the common standard version of the national language, one is inevitably destined to function only at the periphery of national life and, especially, outside the national and political mainstream. (READ, 1990)

But these English Only advocates fail to tell the other side of Antonio Gramsci's argument, which warns us:

Each time that in one way or another, the question of language comes to the fore, that signifies that a series of other problems is about to emerge, the formation and enlarging of the ruling class, the necessity to establish more "intimate" and sure relations between the ruling groups and the popular masses, that is, the reorganization of cultural hegemony. (Gramsci, 1971, p. 16)

This selective selection of Gramsci's position on language points to the hidden curriculum with which the English Only movement seeks to promote a monolithic ideology. It is also part and parcel of an ongoing attempt at "reorganization of cultural hegemony" as evidenced by the unrelenting attack by conservative educators on multicultural education and curriculum diversity. . . .

In contrast to the zeal for a common culture and English only, these conservative educators have remained ominously silent about forms of racism, inequality, subjugation, and exploitation that daily serve to wage symbolic and real violence against those children who by virtue of their language, race, ethnicity, class, or gender are not treated in schools with the dignity and respect all children warrant in a democracy. Instead of reconstituting education around an urban and cultural studies approach which takes the social, cultural, political, and economic divisions of education and everyday life as the primary categories for understanding contemporary schooling, conservative educators have recoiled in an attempt to salvage the status quo. That is, they try to keep the present unchanged even though, as Renato Constantino points out:

Within the living present there are imperceptible changes which make the status quo a moving reality. . . . Thus a new policy based on the present as past and not on the present as future is backward for it is premised not on evolving conditions but on conditions that are already dying away. (1978, p. 201)

One such not so imperceptible change is the rapid growth of minority representation in the labor force. As such, the conservative leaders and educators are digging this country's economic grave by their continued failure to educate minorities. As Lew Ferlerger and Jay Mandle convincingly argue, "Unless the educational attainment of minority populations in the United States improves, the country's hopes for resuming high rates of growth and an increasing standard of living look increasingly dubious" (1991, p. 12).

In addition to the real threat to the economic fabric of the United States, the persistent call for English language only in education smacks of backwardness in the present conjuncture of our ever-changing multicultural and multilingual society. Furthermore, these conservative educators base their language policy argument on the premise that English education in this country is highly effective. On the contrary. As Patrick Courts clearly argues in his book *Literacy for Empowerment* (1991), English education is failing even middle-class and upper-class students. He argues that English reading and writing classes are mostly based on workbooks and grammar lessons, lessons which force students to "bark at print" or fill in the blanks. Students engage in grudgingly banal exercises such as practicing correct punctuation and writing sample business letters. Books used in their classes are, Courts points out, too often in the service of commercially prepared ditto sheets and workbooks. Courts's account suggests that most school programs do not take advantage of the language experiences that the majority of students have had before they reach school. These teachers become the victims of their own professional ideology when they delegitimize the language experiences that students bring with them into the classroom.

Courts's study is basically concerned with middle-class and upper-middle-class students unburdened by racial discrimination and poverty, students who have done well in elementary and high school settings and are now populating the university lecture halls and seminar rooms. If schools are failing these students, the situation does not bode well for those students less economically, socially, and politically advantaged. It is toward the linguistic minority students that I would like to turn my discussion now.

THE ROLE OF LANGUAGE IN THE EDUCATION OF LINGUISTIC MINORITY STUDENTS

Within the last two decades, the issue of bilingual education has taken on a heated importance among educators. Unfortunately, the debate that has emerged tends to recycle old assumptions and values regarding the meaning and usefulness of the students' native language in education. The notion that education of linguistic minority students is a matter of learning the standard English language still informs the vast majority of bilingual programs and manifests its logic in the renewed emphasis on technical reading and writing skills.

I want to reiterate in this paper that the education of linguistic minority students cannot be viewed as simply the development of skills aimed at acquiring the standard English language. English Only proponents seldom discuss the pedagogical structures that will enable these students to access other bodies of knowledge. Nor do they interrogate the quality of ESL instruction provided to the linguistic minority students and the adverse material conditions under which these students learn English. The view that teaching English constitutes education sustains a notion of ideology that systematically negates rather than makes meaningful the cultural experiences of the subordinate linguistic groups who are, by and large, the objects of its policies. For the education of linguistic minority students to become meaningful it has to be situated within a theory of cultural production and viewed as an integral part of the way in which people produce, transform, and reproduce meaning. Bilingual education, in this sense, must be seen as a medium that constitutes and affirms the historical and existential moments of lived culture. Hence, it is an eminently political phenomenon, and it must be analyzed within the context of a theory of power relations and an understanding of social and cultural reproduction and production. By "cultural reproduction" I refer to collective experiences that function in the interest of the dominant groups rather than in the interest of the oppressed groups that are objects of its policies. Bilingual education programs in the United States have been developed and implemented under the cultural reproduction model leading to a de facto neocolonial educational model. I use "cultural production" to refer to specific groups of people producing, mediating, and confirming the mutual ideological elements that merge from and reaffirm their daily lived experiences. In this case, such experiences are rooted in the interest of individual and collective self-determination. It is only through a cultural production model that we can achieve a truly democratic and liberatory educational experience. I will return to this issue later.

While the various debates in the past two decades may differ in their basic assumptions about the education of linguistic minority students, they all share one common feature: they all ignore the role of language as a major force in the construction of human subjectivities. That is, they ignore the way language may either confirm or deny the life histories and experiences of the people who use it.

The pedagogical and political implications in education programs for linguistic minority students are far-reaching and yet largely ignored. These programs, for example, often contradict a fundamental principle of reading, namely that students learn to read faster and with better comprehension when taught in their native tongue. The immediate recognition of familiar words and experiences enhances the development of a positive self-concept in children who are somewhat insecure about the status of their language and culture. For this reason, and to be consistent with the plan to construct a democratic society free from vestiges of oppression, a minority literacy program must be rooted in the cultural capital of subordinate groups and have as its point of departure their own language.

Educators must develop radical pedagogical structures which provide students with the opportunity to use their own reality as a basis of literacy. This includes, obviously, the language they bring to the classroom. To do otherwise is to deny minority students the rights that lie at the core of a democratic education. The failure to base a literacy program on the minority students' language means that oppositional forces can neutralize the efforts of educators and political leaders to achieve decolonization of schooling. It is of tantamount importance that the incorporation of the minority language as the primary language of instruction in education of linguistic minority students be given top priority. It is through their own language that linguistic minority students will be able to reconstruct their history and their culture.

I want to argue that the minority language has to be understood within the theoretical framework that generates it. Put another way, the ultimate meaning and value of the minority language is not to be found by determining how systematic and rule-governed it is. We know that already. Its real meaning has to be understood through the assumptions that govern it, and it has to be understood via the social, political, and ideological relations to which it points. Generally speaking, this issue of effectiveness and validity often hides the true role of language in the maintenance of the values and interests of the dominant class. In other words, the issue of effectiveness and validity becomes a mask that obfuscates questions about the social, political, and ideological order within which the minority language exists.

If an emancipatory and critical education program is to be developed in the United States for linguistic minority students in which they become "subjects" rather than "objects," educators must understand the productive quality of language. James Donald puts it this way:

> I take language to be productive rather than reflective of social reality. This means calling into question the assumption that we, as speaking subjects, simply use language to organize and express our ideas and experiences. On the contrary, language is one of the most important social practices through which we come to experience ourselves as subjects. . . . My point here is that once we get beyond the idea of language as no more than a medium of communication, as a tool equally and neutrally available to all parties in cultural exchanges, then we can begin to examine language both as a practice of signification and also as a site for culture struggle and as a mechanism which produces antagonistic relations between different social groups. (Donald, 1982, p. 44)

It is to the antagonistic relationship between the minority and dominant speakers that I want to turn now. The antagonistic nature of the minority language has never been fully explored. In order to more clearly discuss this issue of antagonism, I will use Donald's distinction between oppressed language and repressed language. Using Donald's categories, the "negative" way of posing the minority language question is to view it in terms of oppression—that is, seeing the minority language as "lacking" the dominant standard features which usually serve as a point of reference for the minority language. By far the most common questions concerning the minority language in the United States are posed from the oppression perspective. The alternative view of the minority language is that it is repressed in the standard dominant language. In this view, minority language as a repressed language could, if spoken, challenge the privileged standard linguistic dominance. Educators have failed to recognize the "positive" promise and antagonistic nature of the minority language. It is precisely on these dimensions that educators must demystify the standard dominant language and the old assumptions about its inherent superiority. Educators must develop liberatory and critical bilingual programs informed by a radical pedagogy so that the minority language will cease to provide its speakers the experience of subordination and, moreover, may be brandished as a weapon of resistance to the dominance of the dominant standard language of the curriculum.

In this sense, the students' language is the only means by which they can develop their own voice, a prerequisite to the development of a positive sense of self-worth. As Giroux elegantly states, the students' voice "is the discursive means to make themselves 'heard' and to define themselves as active authors of their worlds" (Giroux & McLaren, 1986,

p. 235). The authorship of one's own world also implies the use of one's own language, and relates to what Mikhail Bakhtin describes as "retelling a story in one's own words" (Giroux & McLaren, 1986, p. 235).

A DEMOCRATIC AND LIBERATORY EDUCATION FOR LINGUISTIC MINORITY STUDENTS

In maintaining a certain coherence with the educational plan to reconstruct new and more democratic educational programs for linguistic minority students, educators and political leaders need to create a new school grounded in a new educational praxis, expressing different concepts of education consonant with the principles of a democratic, multicultural, and multilingual society. In order for this to happen, the first step is to identify the objectives of the inherent colonial education that informs the majority of bilingual programs in the United States. Next, it is necessary to analyze how colonialist methods used by the dominant schools function, legitimize the Anglocentric values and meaning, and at the same time negate the history, culture, and language practices of the majority of linguistic minority students. The new school, so it is argued, must also be informed by a radical bilingual pedagogy, which would make concrete such values as solidarity, social responsibility, and creativity. In the democratic development of bilingual programs rooted in a liberatory ideology, linguistic minority students become "subjects" rather than mere "objects" to be assimilated blindly into an often hostile dominant "common" culture. A democratic and liberatory education needs to move away from traditional approaches, which em-phasize the acquisition of mechanical basic skills while divorcing education from its ideological and historical contexts. In attempting to meet this goal, it purposely must reject the conservative principles embedded in the English Only movement I have discussed earlier. Unfortunately, many bilingual programs sometimes unknowingly reproduce one common feature of the traditional approaches to education by ignoring the important relationship between language and the cultural capital of the students at whom bilingual education is aimed. The result is the development of bilingual programs whose basic assumptions are at odds with the democratic spirit that launched them.

Bilingual program development must be largely based on the notion of a democratic and liberatory education, in which education is viewed "as one of the major vehicles by which 'oppressed' people are able to participate in the sociohistorical transformation of their society" (Walmsley, 1981, p. 74). Bilingual education, in this sense, is grounded in a critical reflection of the cultural capital of the oppressed. It becomes a vehicle by which linguistic minority students are equipped with the necessary tools to reappropriate their history, culture, and language practices. It is, thus, a way to enable the linguistic minority students to reclaim "those historical and existential experiences that are devalued in everyday life by the dominant culture in order to be both validated and critically understood" (Giroux, 1983, p. 226). To do otherwise is to deny these students their very democratic rights. In fact, the criticism that bilingual and multicultural education unwisely question the traditions and values of our so-called "common culture" as suggested by Kenneth T. Jackson (1991) is both antidemocratic and academically dishonest. Multicultural education and curriculum diversity did not create the S & L scandal, the Iran-Contra debacle, or the extortion of minority properties by banks, the stewards of the "common culture," who charged minorities exorbitant loan-sharking interest rates. Multicultural education and curriculum diversity did not force Joachim Maitre, dean of the College of Communication at Boston University, to choose the hypocritical moral high ground to excoriate the popular culture's "bleak moral content," all the while plagiarizing 15 paragraphs of a conservative comrade's text.

The learning of English language skills alone will not enable linguistic minority students to acquire the critical tools "to awaken and liberate them from their mystified and distorted views of themselves and their world" (Giroux, 1983, p. 226). For example, speaking English has not enabled African-Americans to change this society's practice of jailing more Blacks than even South Africa, and this society spending over 7 billion dollars to keep African-American men in jail while spending only 1 billion dollars educating Black males (Black, 1991).

Educators must understand the all-encompassing role the dominant ideology has played in this mystification and distortion of our so-called "common culture" and our "common language." They must also recognize the antagonistic relationship between the "common culture" and those who, by virtue of their race, language, ethnicity, and gender, have been relegated to the margins. Finally, educators must develop bilingual programs based on the theory of cultural production. In other words, linguistic minority students must be provided the opportunity to become actors in the re-

construction of a more democratic and just society. In short, education conducted in English only is alienating to linguistic minority students, since it denies them the fundamental tools for reflection, critical thinking, and social interaction. Without the cultivation of their native language, and robbed of the opportunity for reflection and critical thinking, linguistic minority students find themselves unable to re-create their culture and history. Without the reappropriation of their culture, the valorization of their lived experiences, English Only supporters' vacuous promise that the English language will guarantee students "full participation first in their school and later in American society" (Silber, 1991, p. 7) can hardly be a reality.

REFERENCES

Aronowitz, S. (1985, May). "Why should Johnny read." *Village Voice Literary Supplement*, p. 13.

Black, C. (1991, January 13). Paying the high price for being the world's no. 1 jailor. *Boston Sunday Globe*, p. 67.

Constantino, R. (1928). *Neocolonial identity and counter consciousness*. London: Merlin Press.

Courts, P. (1991). *Literacy for empowerment*. South Hadley, MA: Bergin & Garvey.

Donald, J. (1982). Language, literacy, and schooling. In *The state and popular culture*. Milton Keynes: Open University Culture Unit.

Ferlerger, L., & Mandle, J. (1991). *African-Americans and the future of the U.S. economy*. Unpublished manuscript.

Giroux, H. A. (1983). *Theory and resistance: A pedagogy for the opposition*. South Hadley, MA: Bergin & Garvey.

Giroux, H. (1991). *Border crossings: Cultural workers and the politics of education*. New York: Routledge.

Giroux, H. A., & McLaren, P. (1986). Teacher education and the politics of engagement: The case for democratic schooling. *Harvard Educational Review, 56*(3), 213–238.

Gramsci, A. (1971). *Selections from Prison Notebooks*, (Ed. and Trans. Quinten Hoare & Geoffrey Smith). New York: International Publishers.

Jackson, D. (1991, December 8). The end of the second Reconstruction. *Boston Globe*, p. 27.

Jackson, K. T. (1991, July 7). Cited in a *Boston Sunday Globe* editorial.

Kozol, J. (1985). *Illiterate America*. New York: Doubleday Anchor.

Lukas, J. A. (1985). *Common ground*. New York: Alfred A. Knopf.

McLaren, P. (1991). Critical pedagogy: Constructing an arch of social dreaming and a doorway to hope. *Journal of Education, 173*(1), 9–34.

Olsen, L. (1988). *Crossing the schoolhouse border: Immigrant students and the California public schools*. San Francisco: California Tomorrow.

Silber, J. (1991, May). *Boston University Commencement Catalogue*.

Walmsley, S. (1981). On the purpose and content of secondary reading programs: Educational and ideological perspectives. *Curriculum Inquiry, 11*, 73–79.

POSTSCRIPT

Should Bilingual Education Programs Be Abandoned?

Research comparing the effectiveness of the several approaches to helping linguistically disadvantaged students remains inconclusive. At the same time, the effort is clouded by the political agendas of those who champion first-language instruction and those who insist on some version of the immersion strategy. Politics and emotional commitments aside, what must be placed first on the agenda are the needs of the students and the value of native language in a child's progress through school.

Further specification of some of the trends and viewpoints cited in the issue introduction and in the YES/NO selections may be found in the following sources: "Defusing the Issues in Bilingualism and Bilingual Education," Charles R. Foster, *Phi Delta Kappan* (January 1982); "The Bilingual Education Battle," Cynthia Gorney, *The Washington Post National Weekly Edition* (July 29, 1985); "Synthesis of Research on Bilingual Education," Kenji Hakuta and Laurie J. Gould, *Educational Leadership* (March 1987); and "The English Language Amendment: One Nation . . . Indivisible?" by S. I. Hayakawa, *The World & I* (March 1986).

Some books to note are Jane Miller's *Many Voices: Bilingualism, Culture and Education* (1983), which includes a research review; Kenji Hakuta's *Mirror of Language: The Debate on Bilingualism* (1986); *Bilingual Education: A Sourcebook* (1985) by Alba N. Ambert and Sarah E. Melendez; and *Sink or Swim: The Politics of Bilingual Education* (1986) by Colman B. Stein, Jr. Thomas Weyr's book *Hispanic U.S.A.: Breaking the Melting Pot* (1988) presents a detailed plan of action in light of the prediction that "by the year 2000 as many people in the U.S. will be speaking Spanish as they will English." A helpful overview article is David Rosenbaum's "Bilingual Education: A Guide to the Literature," *Education Libraries* (Winter 1987).

A number of articles may be found in the March 1989 issue of *The American School Board Journal*, the March 1988 issue of *The English Journal*, and the Summer 1988 issue of *Equity and Excellence*. Some especially provocative articles are these: "Bilingual Education: A Barrier to Achievement," Nicholas Sanchez, *Bilingual Education* (December 1987); " 'Official English': Fear or Foresight?" Nancy Bane, *America* (December 17, 1988); and "The Language of Power," Yolanda T. DeMola, *America* (April 22, 1989).

Most recent articles include Charles L. Glenn's "Educating the Children of Immigrants," *Phi Delta Kappan* (January 1992); David Corson's "Bilingual Ed Policy and Social Justice," *Journal of Education Policy* (January–March 1992); and Mary McGroarty's "The Societal Context of Bilingual Education," *Educational Researcher* (March 1992).

ISSUE 16

Does Tracking Create Educational Inequality?

YES: Jeannie Oakes, from "Keeping Track, Part 1: The Policy and Practice of Curriculum Inequality," *Phi Delta Kappan* (September 1986)

NO: Charles Nevi, from "In Defense of Tracking," *Educational Leadership* (March 1987)

ISSUE SUMMARY

YES: Social scientist Jeannie Oakes argues that tracking exaggerates initial differences among students and contributes to mediocre schooling for many who are placed in middle or lower tracks.
NO: Charles Nevi, director of Curriculum and Instruction for the Puyallup School District in Washington, feels that tracking accommodates individual differences while making "high-status knowledge" available to all.

One of John Franklin Bobbitt's scientific management principles, designed for application to public schooling early in this century, was this: Work up the raw material into that finished product for which it is best adapted. During the first four decades of the century, public school officials became more and more captivated by the "efficiency" movement, and, according to Edward Stevens and George H. Wood, in *Justice, Ideology, and Education* (1987), "The ideal of a unified curriculum gave way to the ideal of differentiating students for predetermined places in the work force." The application of these principles of management resulted in a tracking system in schools that tended to reproduce the divisions of the social class system.

Books such as Willard Waller's *The Sociology of Teaching* (1967), Paulo Freire's *The Pedagogy of the Oppressed* (1973), and *Schooling in Capitalist America* (1976) by Samuel Bowles and Herbert Gintis, mounted a pungent criticism of this prevailing practice. In more recent times, during which a conscious effort has been made to "equalize" opportunities for all students regardless of their backgrounds, the race is still rigged. According to Stevens and Wood: "The very structure of the school, particularly its tracking and sorting function, is designed to assure the success of some at the expense of others."

Many people now realize the importance of reducing the social and racial homogeneity of the school environment. As presently structured, the schools seem unable to overcome initial differences based on social and cultural disadvantages whether or not tracking and grouping are employed. The National Association for the Advancement of Colored People (NAACP) has officially called for the elimination of tracking and homogeneous grouping, the utilization of multimethod assessments of ability and achievement, and the assurance that high expectations will be held for all students.

In her 1985 book *Keeping Track*, Jeannie Oakes presents the results of her analysis of a wide selection of tracking studies. She found that there is little evidence that grouping improves the achievement levels of *any* group. She also found that students from disadvantaged backgrounds are given a less demanding and less rewarding set of curricular experiences and that children in the lower tracks suffer losses of self-esteem and develop negative self-concepts.

In the following articles, Jeannie Oakes defines tracking, examines its underlying assumptions, and summarizes what she judges to be the disappointing effects of the practice. She contends that even as they voice commitment to equality and excellence, schools organize and deliver educational experiences in ways that advance neither. Charles Nevi counters with the argument that while students are obviously equal under the law they are not equal in ability. Tracking and grouping provide for these individual differences, he contends, whereas treating all students the same is not a formula for equity or excellence.

YES   Jeannie Oakes

KEEPING TRACK

The idea of educational equality has fallen from favor. In the 1980s policy makers, school practitioners, and the public have turned their attention instead to what many consider a competing goal: excellence. Attempts to "equalize" schooling in the Sixties and Seventies have been judged extravagant and naive. Worse, critics imply that those well-meant efforts to correct inequality may have compromised the central mission of the schools: teaching academics well. And current critics warn that, given the precarious position of the United States in the global competition for economic, technological, and military superiority, we can no longer sacrifice the quality of our schools to social goals. This view promotes the judicious spending of limited educational resources in ways that will produce the greatest return on "human capital." Phrased in these economic terms, special provisions for underachieving poor and minority students become a bad investment. In short, equality is out; academic excellence is in.

On the other hand, many people still argue vociferously that the distinction between promoting excellence and providing equality is false, that one cannot be achieved without the other. Unfortunately, whether "tight-fisted" conservatives or "fuzzy-headed" liberals are in the ascendancy, the heat of the rhetoric surrounding the argument largely obscures a more serious problem: the possibility that the unquestioned *assumptions* that drive school practice and the *basic features of schools* may themselves lock schools into patterns that make it difficult to achieve *either* excellence *or* equality.

The practice of tracking in secondary schools illustrates this possibility and provides evidence of how schools, even as they voice commitment to equality and excellence, organize and deliver curriculum in ways that advance neither. Nearly all schools track students. Because tracking enables schools to provide educational treatments matched to particular groups of students, it is believed to promote higher achievement for all students under conditions of equal educational opportunity. However, rather than promoting higher achievement, tracking contributes to mediocre schooling for *most* secondary students. And because it places the greatest obstacles to achieve-

From Jeannie Oakes, "Keeping Track, Part 1: The Policy and Practice of Curriculum Inequality," *Phi Delta Kappan* (September 1986). Copyright © 1986 by Phi Delta Kappa, Inc. Reprinted by permission.

ment in the path of those children least advantaged in American society—poor and minority children—tracking forces schools to play an active role in perpetuating school and economic inequalities as well. Evidence about the influence of tracking on student outcomes and analyses of how tracking affects the day-to-day school experiences of young people support the argument that such basic elements of schooling can *prevent* rather than *promote* educational goals.

WHAT IS TRACKING?

Tracking is the practice of dividing students into separate classes for high-, average-, and low-achievers; it lays out different curriculum paths for students headed for college and for those who are bound directly for the workplace. In most senior high schools, students are assigned to one or another *curriculum track* that lays out sequences of courses for college-preparatory, vocational, or general track students. Junior and senior high schools also make use of *ability grouping*—that is, they divide academic subjects (typically English, mathematics, science, and social studies) into classes geared to different "levels" for students of different abilities. In many high schools these two systems overlap, as schools provide college-preparatory, general, and vocational sequences of courses and also practice ability grouping in academic subjects. More likely than not, the student in the vocational curriculum track will be in one of the lower ability groups. Because similar overlapping exists for college-bound students, the distinction between the two types of tracking is sometimes difficult to assess.

But tracking does not proceed as neatly as the description above implies. Both curriculum tracking and ability grouping vary from school to school in the number of subjects that are tracked, in the number of levels provided, and in the ways in which students are placed. Moreover, tracking is confounded by the inflexibilities and idiosyncrasies of "master schedules," which can create unplanned tracking, generate further variations among tracking systems, and affect the courses taken by individual students as well. Elective subjects, such as art and home economics, sometimes become low-track classes because college-preparatory students rarely have time in their schedules to take them; required classes, such as drivers' training, health, or physical education, though they are intended to be heterogeneous, become tracked when the requirements of other courses that *are* tracked keep students together for large portions of the day.

Despite these variations, tracking has common and predictable characteristics:

• The intellectual performance of students is judged, and these judgments determine placement with particular groups.

• Classes and tracks are labeled according to the performance levels of the students in them (e.g., advanced, average, remedial) or according to students' postsecondary destinations (e.g., college-preparatory, vocational).

• The curriculum and instruction in various tracks are tailored to the perceived needs and abilities of the students assigned to them.

• The groups that are formed are not merely a collection of different but equally-valued instructional groups. They form a hierarchy, with the most advanced tracks (and the students in them) seen as being on top.

• Students in various tracks and ability levels experience school in very different ways.

UNDERLYING ASSUMPTIONS

First, and clearly most important, teachers and administrators generally assume that tracking promotes overall student achievement—that is, that the academic needs of all students will be better met when they learn in groups with similar capabilities or prior levels of achievement. Given the inevitable diversity of student populations, tracking is seen as the best way to address individual needs and to cope with individual differences. This assumption stems from a view of human capabilities that includes the belief that students' capacities to master schoolwork are so disparate that they require different and separate schooling experiences. The extreme position contends that some students cannot learn at all.

A second assumption that underlies tracking is that less-capable students will suffer emotional as well as educational damage from daily classroom contact and competition with their brighter peers. Lowered self-concepts and negative attitudes toward learning are widely considered to be consequences of mixed-ability grouping for slower learners. It is also widely assumed that students can be placed in tracks and groups both accurately and fairly. And finally, most teachers and administrators contend that tracking greatly eases the teaching task and is, perhaps, the *only* way to manage student differences.

THE RECORD OF TRACKING

Students clearly differ when they enter secondary schools, and these differences just as clearly influence learning. But separating students to better accommodate these differences appears to be neither necessary, effective, nor appropriate.

Does tracking work? At the risk of oversimplifying a complex body of research literature, it is safe to conclude that *there is little evidence to support any of the assumptions about tracking.* The effects of tracking on student outcomes have been widely investigated, and the bulk of this work *does not* support commonly-held beliefs that tracking increases student learning. Nor does the evidence support tracking as a way to improve students' attitudes about themselves or about schooling.[1] Although existing tracking systems *appear* to provide advantages for students who are placed in the top tracks, the literature suggests that students at all ability levels can achieve at least as well in heterogeneous classrooms.

Students who are *not* in top tracks—a group that includes about 60% of senior high school students—suffer clear and consistent disadvantages from tracking. Among students identified as average or slow, tracking often appears to retard academic progress. Indeed, one study documented the fact that the lowered I.Q. scores of senior high school students followed their placement in low tracks.[2] Students who are placed in vocational tracks do not even seem to reap any benefits in the job market. Indeed, graduates of vocational programs may be less employable and, when they do find jobs, may earn lower wages than other high school graduates.[3]

Most tracking research does not support the assumption that slow students suffer emotional strains when enrolled in mixed-ability classes. Often the opposite result has been found. Rather than helping students feel more comfortable about themselves, tracking can reduce self-esteem, lower aspirations, and foster negative attitudes toward school. Some studies have also concluded that tracking leads low-track students to misbehave and eventually to drop out altogether.[4]

The net effect of tracking is to exaggerate the initial differences among students rather than to provide the means to better accommodate them. For example, studies show that senior high school students who are initially similar in background and prior achievement become *increasingly* different in achievement and future aspirations when they are placed in different tracks.[5] Moreover, this effect is likely to be cumulative over most of the students' school careers, since track placements tend to remain fixed. Students placed in low-ability groups in elementary school are likely to continue in these groups in middle school or junior high school; in senior high school these students are typically placed in non-college-preparatory tracks. Studies that have documented increased gaps between initially comparable high school students placed in different tracks probably capture only a fraction of this effect.

Is tracking fair? Compounding the lack of empirical evidence to support tracking as a way to enhance student outcomes are compelling arguments that favor exposing all students to a common curriculum, *even if differences among them prevent all students from benefiting equally.* These arguments counter both the assumption that tracking can be carried out "fairly" and the view that tracking is a legitimate means to ease the task of teaching.

Central to the issue of fairness is the well-established link between track placements and student background characteristics. Poor and minority youngsters (principally black and Hispanic) are disproportionately placed in tracks for low-ability or non-college-bound students. By the same token, minority students are consistently underrepresented in programs for the gifted and talented. In addition, differentiation by race and class occurs within vocational tracks, with blacks and Hispanics more frequently enrolled in programs that train students for the lowest-level occupations (e.g., building maintenance, commercial sewing, and institutional care). These differences in placement by race and social class appear regardless of whether test scores, counselor and teacher recommendations, or student and parent choices are used as the basis for placement.[6]

Even if these track placements are ostensibly based on merit—that is, determined by prior school achievement rather than by race, class, or student choice—they usually come to signify judgments about supposedly fixed abilities. We might find appropriate the disproportionate placements of poor and minority students in low-track classes if these youngsters were, in fact, known to be innately less capable of learning than middle- and upper-middle-class whites. But this is not the case. Or we might think of these track placements as appropriate *if* they served to remediate the obvious educational deficiencies that many poor and minority students exhibit. If being in a low track prepared disadvantaged students for success in higher tracks and opened future educational opportunities to them, we would not question the need for tracking. However, this rarely happens.

The assumption that tracking makes teaching easier pales in importance when held up against the abundant evidence of the general ineffectiveness of tracking and the disproportionate harm it works on poor and minority students. But even if this were not the case, the assumption that tracking makes teaching easier would stand up *only if* the tracks were made up of truly homogeneous groups. In fact, they are not. Even within tracks, the variability of students' learning speed, cognitive style, interest, effort, and aptitude for various tasks is often considerable. Tracking simply masks the fact that instruction for any group of 20 to 35 people requires considerable variety in instructional strategies, tasks, materials, feedback, and guidance. It also requires multiple criteria for success and a variety of rewards. Unfortunately, for many schools and teachers, tracking deflects attention from these instructional realities. When instruction fails, the problem is too often attributed to the child or perhaps to a "wrong placement." The fact that tracking *may* make teaching easier for some teachers should not cloud our judgment about whether that teaching is best for any group of students—whatever their abilities.

Finally, a profound ethical concern emerges from all the above. In the words of educational philosopher Gary Fenstermacher, "[U]sing individual differences in aptitude, ability or interest as the basis for curricular variation denies students equal access to the knowledge and understanding available to mankind." He continues, "[I]t is possible that some students may not benefit equally from unrestricted access to knowledge, but this fact does not entitle us to control access in ways that effectively prohibit all students from encountering what Dewey called the 'funded capital of civilization.' "[7] Surely educators do not intend any such unfairness when by tracking they seek to accommodate differences among students.

WHY SUCH DISAPPPOINTING EFFECTS?

As those of us who were working with John Goodlad on A Study of Schooling began to analyze the extensive set of data we had gathered about 38 schools across the U.S., we wanted to find out more about tracking.[8] We wanted to gather specific information about the knowledge and skills that students were taught in tracked classes, about the learning activities they experienced, about the way in which teachers managed instruction, about the classroom relationships, and about how involved students were in their learning. By studying tracked classes directly and asking over and over whether such classes differed, we hoped to begin to understand why the effects of tracking have been so disappointing for so many students. We wanted to be able to raise some reasonable hypotheses about the ways in which good intentions of practitioners seem to go wrong.

We selected a representative group of 300 English and mathematics classes. We chose these subjects because they are most often tracked and because nearly all secondary students take them. Our sample included relatively equal numbers of high-, average-, low-, and mixed-ability groups. We had a great deal of information about these classes because teachers and students had completed extensive questionnaires, teachers had been interviewed, and teachers had put together packages of materials about their classes, including lists of the topics and skills they taught, the textbooks they used, and the ways in which they evaluated student learning. Many teachers also gave us sample lesson plans, worksheets, and tests. Trained observers recorded what students and teachers were doing and documented their interactions.

The data gathered on these classes provided some clear and consistent insights. In the three areas we studied—curriculum content, instruction quality, and classroom climate—we found remarkable and disturbing differences between classes in different tracks. These included important discrepancies in student access to knowledge, in their classroom instructional opportunities, and in their classroom learning environments.

Access to knowledge. In both English and math classes, we found that students had access to considerably different types of knowledge and had opportunities to develop quite different intellectual skills. For example, students in high-track English classes were exposed to content that can be called "high-status knowledge." This included topics and skills that are required for college. High-track students studied both classic and modern fiction. They learned the characteristics of literary genres and analyzed the elements of good narrative writing. These students were expected to write thematic essays and reports of library research, and they learned vocabulary that would boost their scores on college entrance exams. It was the high-track students in our sample who had the most opportunities to think critically or to solve interesting problems.

Low-track English classes, on the other hand, rarely, if ever, encountered similar types of knowledge. Nor were they expected to learn the same skills. Instruction in basic reading skills held a prominent place in low-track classes, and these skills were taught mostly through workbooks, kits, and "young adult" fiction. Students wrote simple paragraphs, com-

pleted worksheets on English usage, and practiced filling out applications for jobs and other kinds of forms. Their learning tasks were largely restricted to memorization or low-level comprehension.

The differences in mathematics content followed much the same pattern. High-track classes focused primarily on mathematical concepts; low-track classes stressed basic computational skills and math facts.

These differences are not merely curricular adaptations to individual needs, though they are certainly thought of as such. Differences in access to knowledge have important long-term social and educational consequences as well. For example, low-track students are probably prevented from *ever* encountering at school the knowledge our society values most. Much of the curriculum of low-track classes was likely to lock students into a continuing series of such bottom-level placements because important concepts and skills were neglected. Thus these students were denied the knowledge that would enable them to move successfully into higher-track classes.

Opportunities to learn. We also looked at two classroom conditions known to influence how much students will learn: instructional time and teaching quality. The marked differences we found in our data consistently showed that students in higher tracks had better classroom opportunities. For example, all our data on classroom time pointed to the same conclusion: students in high tracks get more; students in low tracks get less. Teachers of high-track classes set aside more class time for learning, and our observers found that more actual class time was spent on learning activities. High-track students were also expected to spend more time doing homework, fewer high-track students were observed to be off-task during class activities, and more of them told us that learning took up most of their class time, rather than discipline problems, socializing, or class routines.

Instruction in high-track classes more often included a whole range of teacher behaviors likely to enhance learning. High-track teachers were more enthusiastic, and their instruction was clearer. They used strong criticism or ridicule less frequently than did teachers of low-track classes. Classroom tasks were more various and more highly organized in high-track classes, and grades were more relevant to student learning.

These differences in learning opportunities portray a fundamental irony of schooling: those students who need more time to learn appear to be getting less; those students who have the most difficulty learning are being exposed least to the sort of teaching that best facilitates learning.

Classroom climate. We were interested in studying classroom climates in various tracks because we were convinced that supportive relationships and positive feelings in class are more than just nice accompaniments to learning. When teachers and students trust one another, classroom time and energy are freed for teaching and learning. Without this trust, students spend a great deal of time and energy establishing less productive relationships with others and interfering with the teacher's instructional agenda; teachers spend their time and energy trying to maintain control. In such classes, less learning is more likely to occur.

The data from A Study of Schooling permitted us to investigate three impor-

tant aspects of classroom environments: relationships between teachers and students, relationships among the students, and the intensity of student involvement in learning. Once again, we discovered a distressing pattern of advantages for high-track classes and disadvantages for low-track classes. In high-track classes students thought that their teachers were more concerned about them and less punitive. Teachers in high-track classes spent less time on student behavior, and they more often encouraged their students to become independent, questioning, critical thinkers. In low-track classes teachers were seen as less concerned and more punitive. Teachers in low-track classes emphasized matters of discipline and behavior, and they often listed such things as "following directions," "respecting my position," "punctuality," and "learning to take a direct order" as among the five most important things they wanted their class to learn during the year.

We found similar differences in the relationship that students established with one another in class. Students in low-track classes agreed far more often that "students in this class are unfriendly to me" or that "I often feel left out of class activities." They said that their classes were interrupted by problems and by arguing in class. Generally, they seemed to like each other less. Not surprisingly, given these differences in relationships, students in high-track classes appeared to be much more involved in their classwork. Students in low-track classes were more apathetic and indicated more often that they didn't care about what went on or that failing didn't bother most of their classmates.

In these data, we found once again a pattern of classroom experience that seems to enhance the possibilities of learning for those students already disposed to do well—that is, those in high-track classes. We saw even more clearly a pattern of classroom experience likely to inhibit the learning of those in the bottom tracks. As with access to knowledge and opportunities to learn, we found that those who most needed support from a positive, nurturing environment got the least.

Although these data do show clear instructional advantages for high-achieving students and clear disadvantages for their low-achieving peers, other data from our work suggest that the quality of the experience of *average* students falls somewhere between these two extremes. Average students, too, were deprived of the best circumstances schools have to offer, though their classes were typically more like those of high-track students. Taken together, these findings begin to suggest *why* students who are not in the top tracks are likely to suffer because of their placements: their education is of considerably lower quality.

It would be a serious mistake to interpret these data as the "inevitable" outcome of the differences in the students who populate the various tracks. Many of the mixed-ability classes in our study showed that high-quality experiences are very possible in classes that include all types of students. But neither should we attribute these differences to consciously mean-spirited or blatantly discriminatory actions by schoolpeople. Obviously, the content teachers decide to teach and the ways in which they teach it are greatly influenced by the students with whom they interact. And it is unlikely that students are passive participants in tracking processes. It seems more likely that students' achievements, attitudes, interests, perceptions of themselves, and behaviors (growing increasingly disparate over time) help produce some of the effects of tracking. Thus groups of students who, by conventional wisdom, seem less able and less eager to learn are very likely to affect teacher's ability or even willingness to provide the best possible learning opportunities. The obvious conclusion about the effects of these track-specific differences on the ability of the schools to achieve academic excellence is that students who are exposed to less content and lower-quality teaching are unlikely to get the full benefit out of their schooling. Yet this less-fruitful experience seems to be the norm when average- and low-achieving students are grouped together for instruction.

I believe that these data reveal frightening patterns of curricular inequality. Although these patterns would be disturbing under any circumstances (and though many white, suburban schools consign a good number of their students to mediocre experiences in low-ability and general-track classes), they become particularly distressing in light of the prevailing pattern of placing disproportionate numbers of poor and minority students in the lowest-track classes. A self-fulfilling prophecy can be seen to work at the institutional level to prevent schools from providing equal educational opportunity. Tracking appears to teach and reinforce the notion that those not defined as the best are *expected* to do less well. Few students and teachers can defy those expectations.

TRACKING, EQUALITY, AND EXCELLENCE

Tracking is assumed to promote educational excellence because it enables schools to provide students with the curriculum and instruction they need to maximize their potential and achieve excellence on their own terms. But the evidence about tracking suggests the contrary. Certainly students bring differences with them to school, but, by tracking, schools help to widen rather than narrow these differences. Students who are judged to be different from one another are separated into different classes and then provided knowledge, opportunities to learn, and classroom environments that are vastly different. Many of the students in top tracks (only about 40% of high-schoolers) do benefit from the advantages they receive in their classes. But, in their quest for higher standards and superior academic performance, schools seem to have locked themselves into a structure that may *unnecessarily* buy the achievement of a few at the expense of many. Such a structure provides but a shaky foundation for excellence.

At the same time, the evidence about tracking calls into question the widely held view that schools provide students who have the "right stuff" with a neutral environment in which they can rise to the top (with "special" classes providing an extra boost to those who might need it). Everywhere we turn we find that the differentiated structure of schools throws up barriers to achievement for poor and minority students. Measures of talent clearly seem to work against them, which leads to their disproportionate placement in groups identified as slow. Once there, their achievement seems to be further inhibited by the type of knowledge they are taught and by the quality of the learning opportunities they are afforded. Moreover, the social and psychological dimensions of classes at the bottom of the hierarchy of schooling seem to restrict their chances for school success even further.

Good intentions, including those of advocates of "excellence" and of "equity," characterize the rhetoric of schooling. Tracking, because it is usually taken to be a neutral practice and a part of the mechanics of schooling, has escaped the attention of those who mean well. But by failing to scrutinize the effects of tracking, schools unwittingly subvert their well-meant efforts to promote academic excellence and to provide conditions that will enable all students to achieve it.

NOTES

1. Some recent reviews of studies on the effects of tracking include: Robert C. Calfee and Roger Brown, "Grouping Students for Instruction," in *Classroom Management* (Chicago: 78th Yearbook of the National Society for the Study of Education, University of Chicago Press, 1979); Dominick Esposito, "Homogeneous and Heterogeneous Ability Grouping: Principal Findings and Implications for Evaluating and Designing More Effective Educational Environments," *Review of Educational Research*, vol. 43, 1973, pp. 163-79; Jeannie Oakes, "Tracking: A Contextual Perspective on How Schools Structure Differences," *Educational Psychologist*, in press; Caroline J. Persell, *Education and Inequality: The Roots and Results of Stratification in America's Schools* (New York: Free Press, 1977); and James E. Rosenbaum, "The Social Implications of Educational Grouping," in David C. Berliner, ed., *Review of Research in Education, Vol. 8* (Washington, D.C.: American Educational Research Association, 1980), pp. 361-01.

2. James E. Rosenbaum, *Making Inequality: The Hidden Curriculum of High School Tracking* (New York: Wiley, 1976).

3. See, for example, David Stern et al., *One Million Hours a Day: Vocational Education in California Public Secondary Schools* (Berkeley: Report to the California Policy Seminar, University of California School of Education, 1985).

4. Rosenbaum, "The Social Implications . . ."; and William E. Shafer and Carol Olexa, *Tracking and Opportunity* (Scranton, Pa.: Chandler, 1971).

5. Karl A. Alexander and Edward L. McDill, "Selection and Allocation Within Schools: Some Causes and Consequences of Curriculum Place-

ment." *American Sociological Review,* vol. 41, 1976, pp. 969–80; Karl A. Alexander, Martha Cook, and Edward L. McDill, "Curriculum Tracking and Educational Stratification: Some Further Evidence," *American Sociological Review,* vol. 43, 1978, pp. 47–66; and Donald A. Rock et al., *Study of Excellence in High School Education: Longitudinal Study, 1980–82* (Princeton, N.J.: Educational Testing Service, Final Report, 1985).

6. Persell, *Education and Inequality . . . ;* and Jeannie Oakes, *Keeping Track: How Schools Struc-*

ture Inequality (New Haven, Conn.: Yale University Press, 1985).

7. Gary D. Fenstermacher, "Introduction," in Gary D. Fenstermacher and John I. Goodlad, eds., *Individual Differences and the Common Curriculum* (Chicago: 82nd Yearbook of the National Society for the Study of Education, University of Chicago Press, 1983), p. 3.

8. John I. Goodlad, *A Place Called School* (New York: McGraw-Hill, 1984).

NO
Charles Nevi

IN DEFENSE OF TRACKING

In his book, *A Place Called School,* John Goodlad presents a dire picture of low-level tracked classes. These classes, he says, are characterized by unmotivated teachers teaching uninspired students; the material has little significant content or relevance. The picture he presents is enough to embarrass any educator who has ever been associated with tracking in any way, other than to rail against it.[1]

In *Keeping Track* Jeannie Oakes takes the same data that were available to Goodlad for *A Place Called School* and adds even more dire information. In addition to considerably more verbiage, Oakes adds a historical perspective and develops the possibility that tracking is a conscious, deliberate conspiracy on the part of the capitalistic bourgeois elements in society. Oakes claims these groups seek to protect their privileges and property by providing low-level educational programs for the less advantaged to keep them content with their menial roles in society.[2]

Goodlad and Oakes muster enough data and emotion so that it is difficult to dispute them. But with a little reflection, something seems amiss in the pictures of tracking that they present. Somehow, one is reminded of a poem by Issa that goes something like this:

The world is a drop of dew,
And yet—and yet . . .

They are stating the obvious, and one hesitates to dispute them, and yet there still seems to be more to the issue.

Despite the criticism of tracking, ability-grouping is a common, even universal characteristic of public education. Others who have studied the issue indicate that it was being practiced at least as early as the turn of the century and that today it is established in "thousands of American schools."[3] Some observers even say that the history of education is the history of tracking. Tracking was born the first time an enterprising young teacher in a one-room schoolhouse in the 1800s divided his or her class into those who knew how to read and those who didn't. Certainly it began when teachers started organizing their students into grade- and age-level groups, a clear indication that some students were going to cover different content or the same content at a different rate.

REASONS FOR TRACKING

As education has become more complex, content more broad, and students more heterogeneous, tracking has increased. In recent years guidelines for certain federal funds—special and gifted education, Chapter 1—require that students be grouped for the purpose of different specialized instruction.

Oakes argues that tradition is one of the main reasons for the existence of tracking. And certainly this historical sorting of students into groups was done for one of the reasons that Oakes gives for tracking today: homogeneous groups are easier to teach.

A variety of additional reasons explain why tracking has become a tradition. It is one method of trying to improve the instructional setting for selected students, or what one researcher refers to as a "search for a better match between learner and instructional environment."[4] Tracking becomes a very common way of attempting to provide for individual differences. Unless everyone is going to be taught everything simultaneously, grouping is necessary. It may be as simple and obvious as putting some students in grade four, or some students into a primer and others into a novel.

Tracking is not an attempt to create differences, but to accommodate them. Not all differences are created by the schools; most differences are inherited. In reading Goodlad, and particularly Oakes, one can get the impression that all students come to school with exactly the same kinds of abilities, aptitudes, and interests. The reality, of course, is that students vary widely. Socioeconomic status does account for differences in students. Learning disabilities may make some students less able to learn than others, and even though educators seldom deal publicly with the fact, some students are more able learners than others. Some students, for whatever reasons, are just plain smarter than others. Other students come to school with a broader and deeper range of experiences, with attitudes that foster learning, and with a positive orientation to school, rather than a neutral or a negative one. The schools did not create these differences, but the schools must accommodate them, and one way is through grouping students according to their needs and abilities. Even Oakes seems to recognize this.

> Schools must concentrate on equalizing the day-to-day educational experiences for all students. This implies altering the structures and contents of schools that seem to accord greater benefits to some groups of students than to others.[5]

EQUALIZING EDUCATIONAL OPPORTUNITY

But how are educational experiences made equal? It is easy to argue that putting all students in the same classes is not going to equalize their expectations. In fact, an approach that treats all students the same and ignores the real differences among them can guarantee unequal experiences for all. Treating all students the same is not a formula for equity or excellence.

Indeed, research supports tracking. A meta-analysis of 52 studies of secondary tracking programs found "only trivial effects on the achievement of average and below average students." The researchers added that "this finding . . . does not support the view of other recent reviewers who claim that grouping has unfavorable effects on the achievement of low-aptitude students. The effect is near zero on the achievement of average and below-average students; it is not negative."[6]

Despite the zero effect on achievement of average and below-average students, these studies did show some benefits for tracking.

> The controlled studies that we examined gave a very different picture of the effects of grouping on student attitudes. Students seemed to like their school subjects more when they studied them with peers of similar ability, and some students in grouped classes even developed more positive attitudes about themselves and about school.[7]

Tracking is more than a tradition. In a balanced view of tracking, the issue becomes not whether tracking is good or bad, but whether any particular example of tracking accomplishes the goal of matching the learner to the instructional environment.

APPROPRIATE TRACKING

If there is such a thing as good and bad tracking, how does one tell the difference? Can we establish objective criteria? Obviously no magic formulas exist, but *Keeping Track* provides a basis for distinguishing between good and bad tracking.

Oakes cites the decision in the court case of Hobson v. Hansen, and calls it "the best known and probably still the most important rule on tracking."[8] The court's decision stated that tracking is

inappropriate and unlawful when it limits educational opportunities for certain students "on the assumption that they are capable of no more." The court also provided a definition of appropriate tracking.

> Any system of ability grouping which, through a failure to include and implement the concept of compensatory education for the disadvantaged child or otherwise fails in fact to bring the great majority of children into the mainstream of public education denies the children excluded equal opportunity and thus encounters the constitutional bar.[9]

This decision suggests the characteristics of appropriate tracking. One obvious consideration is content. Oakes uses the term "high-status knowledge" which she defines initially as "a commodity whose distribution is limited" to enhance its value. But it is also defined as the knowledge that "provides access to the university."[10] For the purposes of this discussion, high-status knowledge can be thought of as the combination of skills, experiences, attitudes, and academic content needed to create an informed and productive member of society. At the risk of using a cliche: it is the idea that knowledge is power, and that the primary function of the schools is to empower students.

Goodlad and Oakes express legitimate concern that students in the lower tracks are denied access to high-status knowledge, increasing the gap between lower- and higher-tracked (or nontracked) students. Tracking is not appropriate when the intent is to provide the lower-track student with an alternative curriculum that does not lead to the high-status knowledge. An appropriate program of tracking has the same expectations for all students and uses low-level tracking only to provide remediation and to upgrade selected students.

Another consideration, not directly addressed by the court but implicit in the decision, relates to the quality of instruction. Goodlad and Oakes apparently never observed good instruction in a lower-level tracked class, and they seem to assume that quality instruction in a lower track is not possible.

It is true that the attitudes, behaviors, and abilities of the students make lower-track classes more difficult to teach. But these conditions do not magically improve when the students are scattered among untracked classes. They only become hidden from view and easier to ignore. Appropriate tracking is an attempt to structure situations in which the students' special needs and abilities can be recognized and considered. It enables students in lower-level tracks to move toward the worthwhile goal of achieving high-status knowledge.

Appropriate tracking, then, can provide the best possible match between the learner and the instructional environment. Teachers using it can build a good instructional climate and motivate students toward attaining high-status knowledge.

Inappropriate tracking assumes that low-track students are not capable of acquiring high-status knowledge, and they must be given something less.

Oakes points out that the judge in the Hobson v. Hansen decision felt he was making an educational decision that would have been better left to educators. The court's decision concluded, "It is regrettable, of course, that in deciding this case, the court must act in an area so alien to its expertise."[11] But alien or not, the court's decision against limiting educational opportunities for some provides the essential basis for distinguishing between appropriate and inappropriate tracking.

NOTES

1. John I. Goodlad, *A Place Called School* (New York: McGraw-Hill, 1983), see esp. pp. 155–57.
2. Jeannie Oakes, *Keeping Track, How Schools Structure Inequality* (New Haven: Yale University Press, 1985), see esp. pp. 191–213.
3. Chen-Lin C. Kulik and James A. Kulik, "Effects of Ability Grouping on Secondary School Students. A Meta-Analysis of Evaluation Findings." *American Educational Research Journal* (Fall 1982): 416.
4. Deborah Burnett Strather, "Adopting Instruction to Individual Needs. An Eclectic Approach." *Phi Delta Kappan* (December 1985): 309.
5. Oakes, p. 205.
5. Oakes, p. 205.
6. Kulik, p. 426.
7. Kulik, p. 426.
8. Oakes, p. 184.
9. Oakes, p. 184.
10. Oakes, pp. 199–200.
11. Oakes, p. 190.

POSTSCRIPT

Does Tracking Create Educational Inequality?

In his *Paideia Proposal*, Mortimer J. Adler argues that all students in the public schools, regardless of ability level, must be given access to the same basic curriculum. For some, the pace will be slower than for others, and in some cases the depth and extent of study in a given area of the curriculum will vary, but there will be no separation into vocational or business or "basic" tracks. The goal of the proposal is to move toward a true democratization of education.

Should the schools end the practice of ability grouping and tracking in the name of democracy and equity? The January 1989 issue of *Update*, a publication of the Association for Supervision and Curriculum Development, contains commentary by prominent educators on this basic question. Robert Slavin feels that a decision to assign a child to an ability group or track at one point in that child's school experience will greatly influence later grouping decisions; therefore, the practice should be used only when there is a clear educational justification and an absence of other alternatives. Ralph Scott contends that fair and equal opportunities should consist of *appropriate* schooling experiences for individual students; therefore, ability grouping is an essential means for effective education. Don Hindman claims that research has made it clear that homogeneous grouping has a detrimental effect on achievement and social development for students in the low and intermediate tracks; for students in the higher group, achievement effects are negligible.

Some helpful articles to consider are Ray C. Rist, "Student Social Class and Teacher Expectations: The Self-Fulfilling Prophecy in Ghetto Education," *Harvard Educational Review* (August 1970); Walter C. Parker, "The Urban Curriculum and the Allocating Function of Schools," *The Educational Forum* (Summer 1985); Jean Anyon, "Social Class and the Hidden Curriculum of Work," *Journal of Education* (Winter 1980); Kenneth A. Sirotnik, "What You See Is What You Get: Consistency, Persistency, and Mediocrity in Classrooms," *Harvard Educational Review* (vol. 53, no. 1, 1983); and "We Must Offer Equal Access to Knowledge," by John I. Goodlad and Jeannie Oakes, *Educational Leadership* (February 1988). The specific issue of separate classes for the gifted and talented is addressed by Arthur R. King, Jr., and Mary Anne Raywid in *Educational Perspectives* (vol. 26, 1989).

Jeannie Oakes has coauthored a relevant book with Martin Lipton, *Making the Best of Schools* (1990), and the issue at hand has been thoroughly explored by Anne Wheelock in *Crossing the Tracks: How "Untracking" Can Save America's Schools* (1992). Also, the October 1992 issue of *Educational Leadership* addresses the theme "Untracking for Equity."

ISSUE 17

Is Mainstreaming Beneficial to All?

YES: Dean C. Corrigan, from "Political and Moral Contexts That Produced Public Law 94-142," *Journal of Teacher Education* (November/December 1978)

NO: Susan Ohanian, from "P.L. 94-142: Mainstream or Quicksand?" *Phi Delta Kappan* (November 1990)

ISSUE SUMMARY

YES: Dean of education Dean C. Corrigan traces the political and moral roots of Public Law 94-142 and concludes that mainstreaming children with disabilities can restore a sense of social purpose to the schools.

NO: Susan Ohanian, a free-lance writer and former teacher, provides case study evidence of dysfunctions in the execution of the federal mandate.

The Education for All Handicapped Children Act of 1975 (Public Law 94-142) is an excellent example of federal influence in translating social policy into practical alterations of public school procedures at the local level. The general social policy of equalizing educational opportunity and the specific social policy of assuring that young people with various physical, mental, and emotional disabilities are constructively served by tax dollars have come together in a law designed to bring the handicapped closer to the public norm.

Legislation of such delicate matters does not ensure success, however. While most people applaud the intentions of the act, there are those who find the expense involved ill-proportioned and those who feel the federal mandate is unnecessary and heavy-handed.

A staunch supporter of the law, Senator Edward M. Kennedy (D-Massachusetts), has stated that "P.L. 94-142 is designed and intended to protect the rights of all—the child, the parents, and the school. . . . Children are being educated who were formerly at home or in state institutions. It is not easy, but it is gratifying" (*Journal of Teacher Education*, November/December 1978). One reason it is not easy is that most of the regular classroom teachers receiving mainstreamed students are ill-prepared for the task. In-service and preservice programs to correct this deficiency are slowly being incorporated.

As Ann A. Abbott points out, in "Durkheim's Theory of Education: A Case for Mainstreaming," *Peabody Journal of Education* (July 1981), French sociologist Emile Durkheim felt that attachment and belonging were essential to human development. If this is the case, the integration of young people with disabilities into regular classroom settings and into other areas of social intercourse, when possible, is highly desirable. Public Law 94-142 prompts a closer identification of individuals who are disabled in order to assure proper placement in appropriate learning environments. It further requires individualized planning and consultation with parents and experts to ensure the efficacy of the placement.

But practical consequences of the law sometimes result in questions about its desirability. In a period of economic restrictions, how much money can society afford to spend on the special needs of certain students? The 1982 U.S. Supreme Court decision in the *Rowley* case, which denied continuous sign language interpretation for a deaf student in a public school, seems to have drawn some limits. Justice William H. Rehnquist, in stating the majority position, contended that the schools are not obliged to provide services "sufficient to maximize each child's potential." In many decisions since the *Rowley* case, however, the lower courts have been generally supportive of parents seeking expanded services for their disabled children.

In 1986 amendments to the original law, in the form of P.L. 99-457, extended the right to educational services to disabled children aged three to five and offered financial and technical assistance in the development of preschool programs for disabled children from birth to age three. In the 1990 legislative reauthorization, the bill was renamed as the Individuals with Disabilities Education Act (IDEA).

The value of the legislation is still in question. In the following articles, Dean C. Corrigan, an advocate of the law, details the history of P.L. 94-142 and explains how its full implementation could improve the overall institution of education. Susan Ohanian suggests that we need to provide meaningful alternatives for handicapped students who do not flourish in the mainstream.

YES

Dean C. Corrigan

POLITICAL AND MORAL CONTEXTS THAT PRODUCED PUBLIC LAW 94-142

The Education for All Handicapped Children Act, Public Law 94-142, received a clear mandate in the U.S. Congress. Passed by votes of 404–7 in the House of Representatives and 87–7 in the Senate, this Act is the most important piece of educational legislation in this country's history.

ROOTS OF P.L. 94-142

Basically, this Act is Civil Rights as well as educational legislation, and can be fully understood only from that perspective. Congressional testimony on P.L. 94-142 indicates the basic rationale in support of providing access to equal educational opportunity for persons with handicaps is that they are *human beings* living in America and therefore have a right to *access* to equal educational opportunity, *even if it costs more to provide it.*

As we implement the educational concepts in P.L. 94-142, we must remember that this Act calls for social, political, and economic reforms as well as educational reforms, or our strategies for change will not succeed.

P.L. 94-142 has its roots in the 1960s Civil Rights movement. The same rationale behind the 1954 Supreme Court decision, *Brown v. Board of Education,* influenced advocates for the handicapped. That is, segregation has harmful effects on both the person who is segregated and the person who does the segregating (Friedman, 1969). Blatt and Kaplan's *Christmas in Purgatory* (1966) vividly described the inhumane treatment of the handicapped in isolated settings. This book and Blatt's later books (1970a, 1970b, 1976) pricked America's conscience by revealing the plight of the handicapped for all to see.

Spurred by the struggle for civil rights in the larger context, parents of handicapped children joined with civil rights lawyers to attack segregated settings for the handicapped on many of the same grounds that other

From Dean C. Corrigan, "Political and Moral Contexts That Produced Public Law 94-142," *Journal of Teacher Education* (November/December 1978). Copyright © 1978 by The American Association of Colleges for Teacher Education. Reprinted by permission.

advocates were attacking segration based on race. The stigma placed on their children by a school system patterned on "regular or general" education for the so-called "normal" and another quite separate system for the so-called "abnormal" came under sharp attack by groups from all segments of the population.

Another emerging factor—financing educational programs—disturbed many parents, and not just the parents of handicapped children. As state and federal financial support for special education grew, it became profitable for school systems to set up "special classes," often away from "regular" school settings. Too often these classes became dumping grounds for "behavior problems," and a place to segregate ethnic or racial minorities (Sarason & Doris, 1978). There was a dramatic increase in classes for the mentally retarded after the 1954 Brown decision, but the disproportionate number of children from ethnic or racial minorities placed in special classes did not go unnoticed by civil rights advocates or the parents of the segragated children.

As educational critics examined schools for other concerns—discrimination in testing, due process in suspensions, confidentiality of records, and racial bias—the ways that handicapped children were identified, evaluated, and placed came under scrutiny.

The advocates' hard work for the handicapped paid off in 1972 when the landmark court case in Pennsylvania ordered zero reject education, that is, access to free public schools for retarded children. Of the 15,000 previously out-of-school children admitted to public schools because of that decree, the greater proportion, some 52%, were only mildly retarded (Gilhool, 1976). The Peter Mill case in

Washington, D.C., extended the zero-reject imperative to *all* handicaps. Parents' rights to due process hearings, as well as the integration imperative, were recognized in these and other cases (Weintraub, Abeson, Bullard, & Lavor).

While the court battles continued, state legislatures began to pass legislation in response to pressure from citizens groups representing the handicapped. Vermont passed its education for the handicapped act in 1972 and Massachusetts in 1974. State legislation included most of the concepts and requirements that appeared later in Congressional legislation. Today, all states except New Mexico have enabling legislation that complements P.L. 94-142.

At the national level, provisions to insure that handicapped children would get "appropriate" education in the so-called "regular education environments" was framed in the Mathias Amendment, P.L. 380, U.S. Code Section 1413. This amendment, fashioned after the model statute developed by the Council for Exceptional Children (CEC), enjoined that handicapped children be educated with children who were not handicapped, but that their education be differentiated by special needs and appropriate service.

As the right to equal access to education in "least restrictive environments" moved down the legal constitutional road, CEC became an active advocate. Its 1972 Policy Statement and the CEC model statute in establishing the changed facts before the Court required that special educators loudly and clearly say that they had changed (Gilhool, 1966). Other professional groups have taken somewhat longer to take a position in support of free "appropriate" education for the handicapped in the mainstream of education.

(The American Association of Colleges for Teacher Education recently stated its position in *Beyond the Mandate*, . . .)

With these court cases and events as a foundation for legislative action, a strong coalition of parents, lawyers, and legislators, supported by the Education Commission of the States, brought P.L. 94-142 through the Congress. This powerful mandate to all educators, a law that Maynard Reynolds calls an educational Magna Carta for all handicapped children, was signed into law on Nov. 29, 1975.

P.L. 94-142 became fully effective on Oct. 1, 1977 (Fiscal Year 1978). To insure that the law's requirements are carried out in every school district in a State, "State plans" are submitted to the U.S. Office of Education Bureau of Education for the Handicapped (BEH).

Throughout the struggle to pass P.L. 94-142, BEH responded with skill, knowledge, commitment, and political savvy. The educational philosophy that guided the Bureau's action was expressed by Edwin Martin, BEH chief and Associate Commissioner of Education. To improve education for *all* children, he believes that the dichotomous constructs existing at all levels of the educational system and in society, in general, must be eliminated. To make human rights a reality in America, the notion that handicapped, black, or any children are different and should be set apart must be rejected. All children are more alike than different in their basic human nature (Martin, 1974). Under Martin's leadership, BEH shifted its concern from children's handicaps to their learning needs, and changed the educational setting from segregated classrooms and institutions to "appropriate" education in the "least restrictive environment."

IMPLICATIONS FOR SCHOOLS

The Education for All Handicapped Children Act identifies the regular classroom as the "least restrictive environment," unless another setting is prescribed as more appropriate to meet a child's special needs. If other settings are used, they must be justifed.

The implications of using regular classrooms are enormous, not the least of which is that all educators—teachers, counselors, administrators, and other support personnel—must be educationally prepared to work with handicapped persons. This calls for a change in roles of all education personnel, particularly special educators who will join and share their expertise with instructional teams as well as students.

The beneficiaries of this act are approximately 12% of the human beings in the United States between the ages of 3 and 21 who have a handicap, as defined in P.L. 94-142.[1] By school year 1978, a "child find" should have been completed and services extended to include persons aged 3 through 21. Some states have gone beyond this age group in their enabling legislation, and have started the "child find" of children age 1, and extended services beyond age 21. Because many agencies work with these age groups, school personnel must view themselves as part of a human service delivery system rather than a school system. New means of linking with these agencies and new systems of pre- and inservice training must be developed to bring about better collaboration.

Another goal discussed for years by educators is parent involvement. This act requires the child's parent, guardian, or surrogate to sign-off on the individualized plan and consultation at each step of identification, evaluation, and placement into an appropriate setting.[2] How these child-parent-teacher relationships are developed, starting with the "child find," will be critical in achieving the act's goals.

P.L. 94-142 requires individually designed education.[3] If not provided, due process procedures offer parents legal alternatives to insure an individualized education for their children. It is critical to note that the legislation addresses individualized *programs* and individualized *instruction*. Even though it is not stipulated, this legislation views the total school and classroom setting, as well as individual interaction between teachers and students, as being educative. School milieu affects the attitudes of students and educators, such as developing an understanding and respect for individual differences of persons with handicaps, and accepting responsibility in the community for protecting the human rights of other persons. Therefore, the plan for mainstreaming includes consideration of the total learning environment.

American schools must be based now on the principle of "no rejects"; every human being has a right to an education and the right to be treated as a person—not an object, or a symbol on a chart, or a category in a student grouping stucture. The labeling and classification of children, and the social stigma that this labeling produces, must be eliminated. . . .

New evaluation systems should include criterion or domain-referenced evaluation practices in which the concepts of expectancy and capacity are related more to access to competent teaching in educational settings than inherent individual learner traits. The current over-reliance on normative testing, and the misinterpretation and misuse of intelligence, achievement, and aptitude tests must be corrected. Also, under P.L. 94-142, parents must be notified that the evaluation instruments will not discriminate in any way against a child on the basis of race or culture.

To develop the kind of individualized-personalized relationships between teachers and students called for by P.L. 94-142, we must eliminate overcrowding and the resulting class loads, easy anonymity, and shallow teacher-pupil contacts. The basic classroom configuration must change.

The educational setting must be organized so that students know what they can do to achieve *success*. The methods used to differentiate instruction should be neither exclusively behavioristic nor cognitive, child centered nor discipline centered. They should be purposefully eclectic. Curricular tracking that fosters a caste system, and the grade level lockstep that ignores what we know about the ways unique selves develop, must be eliminated. The school must develop ways to use the individual's rhythm, learning speed and style, and exceptionality.

IMPLICATIONS FOR TEACHER EDUCATION

Until educators get rid of the special education-regular education dualism in teacher education institutions, public schools will continue to mirror the same dualism. *All* teachers must be prepared to implement P.L. 94-142. Hence, we must reform *all* aspects of teacher education, not just special education departments. . . .

A major shakeup is needed in the form and substance of teacher education from the first introduction through the teacher's entire career. Financial and personal resources must be directed toward strategies that link schools seeking to change with teacher education institutions seeking to break out of established patterns.

CONCLUSIONS

The Education for All Handicapped Children Act calls on educators to reaffirm some fundamental premises of American education. It implies that all children have a right to an educational environment that helps them to become all they are capable of becoming.

P.L. 94-142 calls on educators to eliminate isolation of the handicapped, the prejudice and discrimination that isolation breeds, and the mockery that it makes of the fundamental right of access to equal educational opportunity.

If the individualization plan, the zero reject principle, the due process requirement, the parent involvement directive, and the integration imperative of P.L. 94-142 are implemented for handicapped children, in the end they will be extended to all children. Thus special education will become general education and general education, special.

The teaching profession controls, for better or worse, the environment within which handicapped children will live intellectual-personal lives. We can destroy it and them, or we can give them hope and happiness by giving them a framework of educational ideas and values.

The most severe shortcoming of teaching and teacher education is that we have concentrated on means rather than ends. Too often we have maintained the "illusion of neutrality," but there is no such thing as "value-free" education. There is only the choice to be conscious of and positive about our values or to conceal and confuse them.

What is needed most from our profession is a moral stance on the issues raised by P.L. 94-142. How far should the majority go in accommodating the needs of the minority? Are the schools and teacher education responsible for teaching this generation of children and parents how to take responsibility to assure the human rights of others? If educators and education are to become effective instruments for social progress, we must restore a sense of social purpose to all levels of the educational system.

NOTES

1. In the law, the term handicapped includes nine categories of handicapping conditions. Schools must have programs for children who are: (1) deaf; (2) hard of hearing; (3) mentally retarded; (4) orthopedically impaired; (5) other health impaired; (6) seriously emotionally disturbed; (7) specific learning disability; (8) speech impaired; and (9) visually handicapped.

2. Parents have the right to obtain an impartial due process hearing with regards to these various steps (identification, evaluation, placement). They must first be notified of the time and place of the hearing that they request and of all their procedural rights. Parents may be accompanied and advised by counsel and by individuals with special knowledge or training with respect to handicapped children. Parents have the right to present evidence at the hearing and to confront, cross examine, and compel the attendance of witnesses. They must be supplied with a record of the hearing, including the written findings of fact and a clear written statement of what the decision is and the basis for reaching it. Finally, they have the right to appeal the hearing.

3. The Individualized Education Program (IEP) is defined in Section 602 (19) of Public Law 94-142, Education for All Handicapped Children Act of 1975, as "a written statement for each handicapped child developed in any meeting by a representative of the local education agency or an intermediate educational unit who shall be qualified to provide, or supervise the provision of, specially designed instruction to meet the unique needs of handicapped children; the teacher; the parents or guardian of such child; and, whenever appropriate, such child.

The statement shall include: (1) a statement of the present levels of educational performance;

(2) a statement of annual goals, including short-term instructional objectives; (3) a statement of the specific educational services to be provided to such child, and the extent to which such child will be able to participate in regular educational programs; (4) the projected dates for initiation and anticipated duration of services; (5) appropriate objective criteria and evaluation procedures and schedules for determining, on at least an annual basis, whether instructional objectives are being achieved.

REFERENCES

Blatt, B. *Exodus from pandemonium*. Boston: Allyn and Bacon, 1970. (a)

Blatt, B. *The revolt of the idiots*. Glenn Ridge, N.J.: Exeptional Press, 1976.

Blatt, B. *Souls in extremis*. Boston: Allyn and Bacon, 1970. (b)

Blatt, B., & Kaplan, F. *Christmas in purgatory*. Boston: Allyn and Bacon, 1966.

Friedman, L. (Ed.). *Argument: The oral argument before the Supreme Court in Brown vs. Board of Education of Topeka, 1952–55*. New York: Chelsea House, 1969.

Gilhool, T.K. Changing public policies: Roots and forces. In *Mainstreaming: Origins and Implications*. University of Minnesota, Minneapolis. Minnesota Education, Vol. 2, Number 2, Spring, 1976. p. 9.

Howsam, R.B., Corrigan, D.C., Denemark, G.W., & Nash, R.J. *Educating a profession*. Washington, D.C.: American Association of Colleges for Teacher Education, 1976.

Martin, E.W. An end to dichotomous constructs: A reconceptualization of teacher education. *Journal of Teacher Education*, Fall 1974, 25, 219.

Sarason, S., & Doris, J. Mainstreaming: Dilemmas, opposition, opportunities. In M.C. Reynolds (Ed.), *Futures of education for exceptional students: Emerging structures*. University of Minnesota, Minneapolis: National Systems Project, 1978.

Weintraub, F., Abeson, A., Bullard, J., & Lavor, M.L. (Eds.). *Public policy and the education of exceptional children*. Reston, VA.: Council for Exceptional Children, 1976.

NO

Susan Ohanian

P.L. 94-142: MAINSTREAM OR QUICKSAND?

Recently I have traveled the country telling stories about students who have touched my life in the past 20 years. Without fail, audiences shed tears when I share heartwarming anecdotes about Charles, the oddball 11-year-old I welcomed into my third-grade classroom.

Although these upbeat stories about Charles are true, they are far from the whole truth. You just can't tell the whole story in a 45-minute talk in a crowded room. As John Updike has observed, the larger the audience, the simpler is its range of response. A packed room is the place for black-and-white sketches—mostly white. One roughs in a few bureaucratic enemies and lots of victories, and the audience responds warmly. There is no duplicity here. I savor my triumphs and am eager to give teachers the uplift that such shared victories bring. The auditorium is not the place for the gray ambiguity of unanswered questions, not the place for soul-searching, not the place for a heart-on-the-sleeve teacher to confess her fear that maybe a lot of youngsters like Charles are drowning in the mainstream.

It is devastating for someone like me to be forced to acknowledge that my dealings with Charles had a dark side. After all, we teach because we are convinced that we can make a difference, a lasting difference. Our job is to push back the darkness, to light a candle. And for someone like me, who had taught oddball seventh-graders for so many years, "getting one young" was a dream come true. If seventh grade sometimes proved too late to save a child, surely a third-grade teacher could intervene soon enough.

Even on my gloomy days I still believe that, though my colleagues who refused to mainstream Charles turned out to be right, it was for all the wrong reasons. In his own quirky, idiosyncratic fashion, Charles did learn; in a harum-scarum sort of way he even made a few prodigious leaps. He learned an impressive amount of dinosaur lore; he became an avid note writer; to his classmates' amazement and delight, this boy, who could neither add nor subtract, could shout out the answer to 9×7. Initially so highstrung that he vomited when he thought other students were looking at him, Charles became the boy who stood in front of an audience of 90 and narrated our class production of "The Frog Prince." He went from the boy who circled the room making weird chirping noises whenever his classmates squeezed close together around me for story time, to the boy who sat in the middle of the squeeze and begged me to read more.

But even Charles recognized that all of this was not enough. He was reluctant to go on to fourth grade with the rest of the class and asked me if he could return to my third grade for a second year. "I know where things are," he said. "I could be your aide." I was charmed by his suggestion. "Why not?" I asked his resource teacher. "He did so well this year, just think what he could do with one more year.

She liked the idea too—until a phone call forced us to face reality. Charles' mother informed us that Charles needed quite specific information about sex.

Charles' life passed rapidly before my eyes. He wasn't a winsome little 8-year-old. He was a gangly 12-year-old who couldn't add or subtract with any reliability, couldn't tell time, and couldn't pass a spelling test even when all the words were three-letter rhyming words, such as pan, man, fan. This 12-year-old on the brink of puberty simply could not come back to my third grade enough times. No matter how much affection, acceptance, and information I offered him, he wasn't going to "catch up"—not even with third-graders.

A boy like Charles is so difficult and so "delayed" that it is natural for a teacher to cling to the positive moments—the time he actually discussed dinosaurs with another student, the time he marched down to the principal's office and read him a story. Can I be blamed for letting my nurturing instincts hold sway? For avoiding the larger question of whether spending half the day or more in a "regular" third-grade classroom was truly appropriate to the needs of a boy approaching puberty?

Michael Dorris says that children like Charles inspire wishful thinking; we optimists are convinced that, with lots of love and just one more little push, the child will be okay. In *The Broken Cord*, Dorris tells Adam's story. Dorris adopted Adam at age 3, knowing that the boy had serious problems but armed with the conviction that love and a good environment could overcome all obstacles. Over the years Adam's full-scale WISC [Wechsler Intelligence Scale for Children] score remained constant in the 64–76 range, and his performance in other areas fell below even what might be expected of a child in that range. Dorris remained constant in his belief that Adam teetered "so close to the edge of 'okay' that there was no way he would not succeed."

Adam's teachers seemed to agree. Year after year a string of report cards proclaimed Adam's progress in reading, math, and map skills. One report announced that Adam had "demonstrated good ability and understanding with regard to our unit on geometry." But Dorris finally realized that, although they spent long hours on homework every night, Adam just wasn't managing.

In retrospect Dorris sees that Adam "learned" the same low-level skills year after year. Progress reports to the contrary, Adam at 18 cannot tell time or read a map; he has no notion of money and will cheerfully pay $10 for a doughnut. Never mind any principles of geometry.

For those who insist that the primary purposes of mainstreaming are better socialization and the enhancement of self-esteem, Dorris describes a heartbreaking collision with reality. Despite yearly report cards that proclaimed Adam's great progress in making friends, Dorris notes that, in all his school days, Adam "never once received so much as a telephone call or an invitation from a 'friend.' " When I read that, I cried. For all the satisfaction I took in helping my third-graders learn to be tolerant and even kind to Charles, I have to admit that I never saw any evidence of friendship. Those third-graders tolerated Charles because I was there. I would wager a large sum that Charles has never received a phone call from a classmate, either. Yes, he made charming breakthroughs, giving us occasional, tantalizing glimpses of a more normal boy— but even on his best days, Charles was still an uncomfortable, oddball child.

LONG BEFORE I MET CHARLES, I HAD known Lucille. Immediately after the passage of P.L. 94-142, the Education for All Handicapped Children Act, my school district put all "educable" children entering seventh and eighth grades into a regular academic program. So none of Lucille's teachers knew that she had spent her entire elementary career in special classes. I suspected that something was amiss the first week of school and asked to see her record. The guidance counselor told me Lucille was one of six siblings in special education; she had never been in a regular program until she hit seventh grade. He reminded me of the new federal law.

When I asked why we teachers hadn't been alerted to the special difficulties of Lucille and similar students, he told me that such information was confidential— that it might prejudice teachers and prevent them from treating "educable"

children "equally" with other children in the class. So youngsters dumped willy-nilly into the mainstream were left to suffer embarrassment in front of their peers when they couldn't read aloud or solve math problems at the board or locate rivers on a map.

Lucille was kind, cheerful, cooperative, and always anxious to please. She was very proud of her high marks in spelling as she progressed from third-grade to fourth-grade words. She had good decoding skills and liked using the typewriter and listening to poetry tapes. She seemed to comprehend nothing.

When Lucille first told me she was having a terrible time in science, I tried to avoid the issue. The course was rigorous, modeled on the teacher's own college biology course. But Lucille was so anxious to pass a test—any test—that I went to the teacher, got the questions for an upcoming exam, and began to coach her. Lucille and I worked during the lunch break for three weeks. We labored over the structure of the cell. She drew cells on the chalkboard and cut cells out of construction paper; she made flash cards; we drilled; we invented acronyms to help her remember. Lucille would learn the material one day and forget it by the next, and so every day we started over. She never gave up. She desperately wanted to pass that test.

Lucille appeared in my doorway right after the biology test. "I didn't do too good," she confided, adding in a whisper, "I think I'm going to be sick." I tried to rush her to the lavatory, but we didn't quite make it. Evidence of Lucille's "failure" lay visible in the hallway. The poor child told me that she was sorry she had let me down. But in truth, I'd failed her. I vowed then never again to drill children on such inappropriate material.

I read in texts advocating mainstreaming that disabled students need "a chance to shine," that they "will learn from non-disabled students," that students with disabilities must be "seen as peers of non-disabled students." But nobody can make a disabled student equal, and nobody can promise a disabled student a phone call from a friend.

When following the mandates of P.L. 94-142, we need to figure out just what it means to mainstream children "to the maximum extent appropriate to their needs." Many school districts lump all children with learning problems together in a sort of academic twilight zone. The educable mentally retarded, the low normal, the learning disabled (whatever that means this week), and the emotionally disturbed are all sent off to regular English, science, social studies, and mathematics classes—until the situation becomes too traumatic either for the child or for the teacher. I always figured my district had to see blood before it would *de*-mainstream a child.

TOMMY WAS AMAZING PROOF OF A SYSTEM run amok. His name appeared on my official class list the first day of school. I asked why he wasn't there, and the students replied, "Oh, Tommy never comes to school. Not even in first grade." He was a legend in his own time. I checked the records: Tommy had shown up eight times in sixth grade. He was sent on to seventh grade because he had already been held back three times, and teachers don't like to have tough, streetwise 14- and 15-year-olds in the same classroom with naive 10- and 11-year-olds. Hard-liners who insist on the elimination of social promotion don't seem to be stepping forward with much advice on how to make mainstreaming work harmoni-

ously for the little girl who keeps a teddy bear in her school locker and the randy hulk who should keep condoms in his.

I began agitating for the district to take Tommy's mother to court and get him into school. And for some reason, somebody did something. The departments in charge of social services and probation got together and sent a trainee to pick up Tommy at his front door every morning and escort him to the front door of the school. Predictably, Tommy came in the front door, raced through the building, and disappeared out the back door.

I heard about all this after the fact. Had I known about the plan to escort Tommy to school, I would at least have stood at the back door. But, as with most bureaucratic schemes, teachers are the last to know. And then we know only because the students tell us.

So the social service folks changed their strategy. A woman appeared in my doorway with Tommy and announced, "I'm with *him*." When Tommy sat down, so did she. She pulled out a thick textbook—a psychology text, no less—and read all period, carefully underlining selected portions with yellow highlighter. Tommy did a bit of work when I crouched by his chair. As soon as I moved to someone else, he unleashed his repertoire of obnoxious tricks. When the bell sounded the end of the period, Tommy dashed out of the room; his companion grabbed her book and ran after him.

I phoned the main office and asked what was going on. I was informed that Tommy now had a court-appointed aide to keep tabs on him. "Good," I thought. Tommy needed one-on-one tutoring. The two or three times I'd worked with him had convinced me he could learn. He was, in fact, very cooperative when I worked alone with him. He liked that individual attention. But I had a classful of students, and Tommy was no good at waiting, at taking turns, at working by himself. He had never been in school long enough to learn these necessary rituals. If he could not have the teacher's immediate and total attention, he became indifferent at first, then hostile, and finally destructive. But with his own aide—maybe we had a chance. I immediately began to dream about Tommy getting some of the individual attention he craved, getting used to school, maybe even succeeding in school.

Fat chance. Tommy's aide quickly let me know how mistaken I was. She informed me that she was in our school solely to see that Tommy made it to class. She was not there to teach him, to talk to him, or to respond to him in any way once he was inside a classroom. She was taking graduate courses at night and had her own books to worry about; she certainly wasn't going to be bothered with Tommy's books. That was my job.

Tommy began racing out of his classes faster and faster. For a few days he just ran around the locker areas, letting the pursuing aide keep him in sight. Other students stood and watched and cheered him on. I suspect a few teachers were silently cheering too. Certainly none of us intervened. The aide had set the ground rules: our job was to teach; hers, to chase. The game soon lost its charm for Tommy, and he began dashing out of the building, losing his aide in the city streets, and returning to his life of petty crime. The last I heard, he'd been declared incorrigible and "sent away."

ANOTHER CHILD IN THE MAINSTREAM FOR the first time, Joey, was taking a full academic curriculum when he wrote me this note:

Dear Mrs. O.,
For Christmas Santa brought me skates, coloring books, and shaving cream.

Your friend,
Joey

I didn't know whether to laugh or cry. Certainly the gifts were appropriate. Joey was a lovable child-man: 15 years old, 5'8" tall, 150 pounds. Who could believe that Joey's teachers could possibly follow mainstream mandates and present him the academic curriculum at his appropriate level? And how could Joey's classmates provide something called "socialization" for a boy who needed both coloring books and shaving cream?

Joey's social studies teacher gave him a lot of special attention. But giving a student like Joey only a fraction of the study packet doesn't help him. Behaviorists can insist until the chalk turns to cheese that "all students can learn the school tasks expected of them if the tasks are rigorously programmed and the students are given enough time." Michael Dorris knows it ain't so, and Joey's teachers know it ain't so. Sad to say, youngsters like Joey don't know it. They have the faith of the innocent. They think that if they just work hard enough, they'll get it. While I was trying to teach Joey the difference between a city and a state, he begged me to coach him for a social studies test on the U.S. Constitution. While I was trying to teach him to address an envelope, he worried about writing a term paper on James Madison.

Even the most optimistic of us must admit that, given all the time in the world, Joey is not going to catch up. The school need not accept blame for the fact that he is not going to be a chemist or a cashier—or probably even a member of Congress or a vice president. But the school must shoulder heavy blame for failing to help Joey learn the things he *could have* learned, things he needed to know. Maybe his teachers should have spent less time helping him participate in some small way in lessons on Washington's battle plan, the three branches of government, or the causes of World War I; maybe someone should have helped him learn to tie his shoes and make change for a dollar.

When a seventh-grade teacher of social studies confronts her supervisor with some of the academic dilemmas posed by mainstreaming a boy like Joey, the supervisor insists that the child is in regular classes primarily for social reasons—"to learn how to get along with others, to make friends." The teacher is advised, "Be nice to Joey. Don't pressure him. Don't expect too much." So Joey's curriculum consists of the benign smile, the reassuring word, and the encouraging pat on the head. Social skills are the goal; cognitive development is seldom mentioned.

It is easy to be nice to Joey. He is a lovely boy. But just how "socializing" is it for him to sit in class after class not understanding the material—and being ignored by the "regular" students? The sad fact is that proclaiming equality, legislating equality, and even funding equality have never raised anybody's I.Q. And I'd like to see evidence that these actions ever improved a "poor perceptual-motor development of the body schema" either—or inspired a phone call from a friend.

Proponents of mainstreaming claim that all children can work on the same subject but at different levels. In effect, they say: give every child *A Tale of Two Cities* or *Foundations of Democracy* or *Modern Biology*. The Robins can read the whole book; the Blue Jays need read only half; the Pigeons can copy the table of contents five times. The Robins can dissect a frog; the Blue Jays can watch a movie about a frog; the Pigeons can play leapfrog. So the Robins go to the university, the Blue Jays might make it to a community college, and the Pigeons are cheated from learning what they can learn—what they need to know.

THEN THERE WAS ARNOLD. HE HAD AN I.Q. of 68 and a history of abuse and neglect. He hated changing classes. I had to push him out of my room and down the hall to his next class, but he would run around and sneak in the back door. He was terrified of eating in the cafeteria. He said that the other children stared at him and made fun of him. "Why can't I stay with you?" he would plead. "I'll just sit and read a book—I promise."

So I'd weaken and let him in, and then the litany would begin. "I bet you hate me too. Yeah, you really hate me. Everybody hates me. Everybody in this whole school hates me." Arnold would start listing the 1,126 people in our building, all of whom hated him. On and on he'd go, whining and wheedling for attention and approval. I soon realized I couldn't give Arnold enough. He sucked up approval with the power of an industrial vacuum cleaner, and all it did was make him whine for more.

But I wasn't a saint. After two weeks of keeping him with me during lunch, I locked my door. I figured if I didn't break up my day with at least 15 minutes of peace and quiet, I'd soon be making bizarre noises too.

Arnold set his own course. Lots of days he did nothing but pester everybody in the room. The whole school got a blessed respite when he settled in on his spelling agenda. Always a good speller, Arnold spied the official departmental list for the eighth grade on my desk and decided to learn every word. For him, this was the pinnacle of academic achievement: a seventh-grader learning eighth-grade spelling words.

For two months Arnold studied the list all day—in social studies, math, science, and physical education. He was never without the list. He ignored all other subjects, insisting, "I've got to learn my words." Arnold's other academic teachers were grateful. Studying spelling words gave him something to do. When he was huddled in a corner poring over his words, he wasn't running around the room making frog noises or pinching other students.

Every week or so Arnold would let me know that he was ready to be tested on another section of the list. He never scored less than 80, and he proudly showed off his 100s to the principal, the school nurse, and anyone else who would look. He tried to show his classmates, but no student would let Arnold near enough.

When it came time to do research for oral reports in our class, Arnold's social studies teacher—anxious for something to enter in her grade book—agreed that, if he reported on a famous American, she would give him credit too. For about a month Arnold carried around a boyhood biography of George Washington, frequently interrupting the class with anecdotes about George.

"When George was born," Arnold began his oral report, "his father looked at the dollar bill and said, 'I think I'll call him George Washington,' and that's how the baby got his name." I must have looked startled, because Arnold addressed his next remarks directly to me. "You have seen his picture right there on the dollar bill, haven't you?" He reached into his pocket, pulled out a dollar, and held it up. "That's how he got his name. Right off the money." On the departmental final exam, this boy was expected to explain the difference between communism and democracy.

IF STUDENTS AND TEACHERS ARE DISORIented by mainstreaming, it also sends confusing messages to parents. Bobby's foster father wanted him removed from my class because he "keeps bringing home first-grade homework and first-grade spelling words." The man felt that such baby work was an insult to a seventh-grader. He pointed out that Bobby was passing biology and social studies. So why the problem in language arts? Why didn't I give him seventh-grade work?

It is not easy to tell a parent that mainstreamed students *don't* fail, that his child can't read that biology book, or that a lot of teachers—not knowing how to handle the mainstreaming dilemma— give all mainstreamed students passing marks and give higher marks to the docile ones who cause no problems. How do you explain to a parent that this is called socialization?

Mainstreamed students get 90s on essays copied out of the encyclopedia— essays that stop in the middle of a sentence. "The teacher asked for two pages, so I wrote the two pages," Sophie says without a hint of irony. If the encyclopedia passage she's copying on Pocahontas runs out before the requisite two pages are filled, she just carries on with James Polk. It is all the same to her—all equally meaningless. This is the curriculum of keeping them quiet, the curriculum of copying; it is also the curriculum of coping for the teachers trying to follow as best they can the rules of mainstreaming.

Every year Billy's teachers reported that he was "making good progress with decoding skills," but by the time he reached seventh grade he was in a constant rage because he couldn't read. I don't think anybody lied about that "good progress." He did make progress: every September he started from initial consonants, and by every June he had reached the *cr* blend.

As academic pressures mounted in the middle school, Billy's rages grew more frequent, and his mother was often called to school for his disciplinary hearings. She confided to me that she read only with great difficulty and that Billy's father couldn't read at all. She enrolled Billy in the nearby university reading clinic. Billy was thrilled that his professor was interested in him and was convinced that the professor would perform miracles. After every session, I'd get a blow-by-blow account of what the professor had said, what lesson the professor had taught. Billy was making rapid progress on the same decoding skills he'd "mastered" every year in school. And I hoped that maybe his new optimism could work miracles.

When Billy proudly showed me the "new book" he was reading for the professor, chills went down my spine. Like everyone else in Billy's old school, I'd known about him when he was a hyperactive third-grader; I'd seen him race around the corridors. I'd also seen the vice principal sit and read with him every day—out of that very same book. A lot of earnest, caring teachers had tried very hard with Billy, but, like Michael Dorris' son, Adam, Billy seemed to have had one year of elementary school repeated eight times over.

After half a dozen or so trips to the university lab, when Billy realized that there was no miracle in the good professor's bag of tricks, his enthusiasm evaporated. He became surly and, according to the professor's report, "exhibited acting-out behavior of an antisocial nature." Since the university reading lab did not operate under the same constraints as a public school classroom, the professor kicked him out.

Billy found a life outside the mainstream. He dropped out of school as soon as he legally could and became a petty criminal. He has been in and out of jail ever since. I don't think it had to be that way. I wish we teachers could have acknowledged that Billy wasn't a mainstream child and offered him a different curriculum. Why did he get the same decoding skills year after year in elementary school and then an academic curriculum in middle school? What would have happened if, when Billy hit seventh grade, we'd said, "Okay, there are a few children who aren't going to learn to read—particularly if they are obnoxious, refuse to cooperate, and refuse to work at it"—and tried something else? We never gave Billy any chance to show what he *could* do, so he got even by making everyone around him suffer. But the sad part is, nobody suffered as much as Billy.

SO-CALLED LIBERAL DOCTRINE HOLDS THAT "special classes"—a relic of education's dark ages—produce demoralization, low self-esteem, and inferior education. And I have seen plenty of evidence that they do. In the worst cases, the special education room is just a holding tank with a curriculum of movies and M & M's; even in the best cases, the curriculum has never taken a direction very different from mainstream academics. We never offer true alternatives but are lured time and again by the people who claim that everybody should learn the classics. We are very reluctant to admit that some people should be allowed—even encouraged—to be different.

We are good at accumulating labels: minimal brain dysfunction, perceptual-motor aberration, impaired learning efficiency, sensory deficit, delayed interpretation of input, and so on. Maybe we should spend less time on labels and more time providing meaningful alternatives for all students who don't flourish in the mainstream. As moved and challenged as I was by Dorris' book, I think little good will be served if it only inspires bureaucrats to look for children who qualify for the label "fetal alcohol syndrome." Of what use is any label to child or teacher if the school system can't come to grips with how to educate the child who is different?

Michael Dorris points out that in the media it is chic to portray the learning disabled as "invariably conscientious, anxious to please, desirous to make a good impression." But Adam taught Dorris to face hard facts: "Adam was not like that. Though I knew him to be sweet, gentle-hearted, and generous, the face he showed to the world was sullen. He avoided work whenever possible, refused to pay attention to his appearance, was slow to motivate, and only occasionally told the truth. His attitude discouraged even those who began their association with him enthusiastically. . . ."

For years Dorris was blinded by his dreams for Adam and not able to see him whole. Now that he has recognized the boy's shortcomings, it doesn't mean that he loves Adam less. Recognizing the shortcomings of special children doesn't mean that I care about them less. It just means that I am finally ready to move beyond slogans and to admit to some dark disappointments. I won't give up lighting candles, but I'm ready to admit the limits of candlelight. I'm ready to stop letting dreams of a more equitable society blind me to the very real and very different educational needs of special children.

POSTSCRIPT

Is Mainstreaming Beneficial to All?

One wit has claimed that P.L. 94-142 is really a "full employment act for lawyers." Indeed, much litigation regarding the identification, classification, placement, and specialized treatment of children with handicaps has been initiated. The parental involvement aspect of the law invites cooperation but can lead to conflict. Also, some parents of nondisabled children are beginning to wonder if their offspring might not be entitled to greater specialized services as well.

These problems and many others associated with the full implementation of this landmark legislation are treated in a number of publications. Focusing on the larger aspects, such as social and ethical issues, research, and legal matters, are *Shared Responsibility for Handicapped Students: Advocacy and Programming* (1976) edited by Philip H. Mann; Catherine Morsink's "Implementing P.L. 94-142: Challenge of the 1980s," *Education Unlimited* (October 1979); *Special Education in Transition* (1980) edited by Dean C. Corrigan and Kenneth R. Howey; *P.L. 94-142: A Guide for the Education of All Handicapped Children Act* (1979) by Clarence J. Jones and Ted F. Rabold; *Educating the Handicapped: Where We've Been, Where We're Going* (1980) by Mitchell Lazarus; *Educational Handicap, Public Policy, and Social History* (1979) by Seymour B. Sarason and John Doris; and *Foundations of Teacher Preparation: Responses to Public Law 94-142* (1982) edited by Maynard C. Reynolds.

Among works directed specifically at regular classroom teachers are: *Mainstreaming Handicapped Students: A Guide for the Classroom Teacher* (1979) by Ann P. Turnbull and Jane B. Schulz; *Mainstreaming Students With Learning and Behavior Problems* (1981) by Coleen Blankenship and M. Stephen Lilly; and *Teaching Handicapped Students in the Mainstream: Coming Back . . . or Never Leaving*, 2d ed. (1981) by Anne L. Pasanella and Cara B. Volkmor.

Recent research studies include Martin Diebold's "A School-Level Investigation of Predictions of Attitudes About Mainstreaming," *Journal of Special Education* (Fall 1986) and "Willingness of Regular and Special Educators to Teach Students With Handicaps," *Exceptional Children* (October 1987) by Karen Derk Gans. Additional sources include W. N. Bender's "The Case Against Mainstreaming," *Education* (Spring 1985); James J. Gallagher's "New Patterns in Special Education," *Educational Researcher* (June–July 1990); and Lynn Miller's "The Regular Education Initiative and School Reform: Lessons from the Mainstream," *Remedial and Special Education* (May/June 1990).

Mainstreaming presents both moral and practical issues. As Seymour Sarason tells us: "It raises age-old questions: How do we want to live with each other? On what basis should we give priority to one value over another? How far does the majority want to go in accommodating the needs of the minority?"

ISSUE 18

Do "Discipline Programs" Promote Ethical Behavior?

YES: Lee Canter, from "Assertive Discipline—More Than Names on the Board and Marbles in a Jar," *Phi Delta Kappan* (September 1989)

NO: John F. Covaleskie, from "Discipline and Morality: Beyond Rules and Consequences," *The Educational Forum* (Winter 1992)

ISSUE SUMMARY

YES: Lee Canter, developer of the Assertive Discipline program, argues for the value of a positive approach to behavior management.
NO: John F. Covaleskie of Syracuse University criticizes the behavioral approach and claims that it fails to shape character.

Discipline has always been a central problem in formal education. In centuries past the problem was handled by corporal punishment, threats, and other repressive measures. In the twentieth century a number of factors—the emergence of psychology as a dominant influence on schooling, the legal granting of broader rights to the young, the formation of a "youth culture" influenced greatly by the mass media, and the erosion of traditional authority patterns in home, school, and community—have brought new complexities to the concept of discipline.

In the past three decades, the implementation of Skinnerian behaviorism in the instructional and disciplinary procedures of public education has led to the "packaging" of techniques and strategies aimed at the improvement of classroom control, the enhancement of motivation, and the routinization of desirable patterns of student behavior. Just as Carl R. Rogers attacked B. F. Skinner's stimulus-response-reinforcement approach to motivation and self-control as being too "external" and merely expedient (see Issue 3), so have some of today's theorists contended that we must look "inside" the behaving person in order to ground our approach to discipline.

The various contending theories of discipline on the current scene can be placed along a continuum that stretches from "noninterventionists" to "interventionists," with "interactionists" taking up the middle ground position. Noninterventionists (Harris's "I'm O.K. You're O.K." and Gordon's "teacher effectiveness training") rely mainly on observation, questioning, and nondirective statements in an effort to understand the inner workings of student behavior. Interactionists (Dreikurs's "discipline without tears" and Glasser's "schools without failure") also probe with questions, but they add directive statements and engage in the subtle molding of student behavior. Interventionists (Axelrod's "behavior modification" and Canter's "assertive discipline") mold behavior more directly, emphasize positive reinforcement, and sometimes employ threats and physical intervention strategies. A full portrait of these and other current theories of discipline can be found in *Innovative School Discipline* (1985) by John Martin Rich and in *Building Classroom Discipline: From Models to Practice* (1980) by C. M. Charles.

Probably the most widely used and controversial of the various discipline programs is Lee Canter's Assertive Discipline. This approach emphasizes teacher firmness and consistency, the clear communication of behavioral expectations, and an incentive system that rewards positive student performance.

In the pairing presented here, Lee Canter explains the basic procedures for the successful use of Assertive Discipline in the classroom and clears up some misconceptions about his ideas. John F. Covaleskie turns attention to the ends that are served when a given discipline program is employed in the schools. His central criterion is this: Does the approach teach children to make reasoned judgments about what actions are desirable and about how actually to decide to act in those desirable ways?

YES

Lee Canter

ASSERTIVE DISCIPLINE—MORE THAN NAMES ON THE BOARD AND MARBLES IN A JAR

About a year ago I was on an airline flight, seated next to a university professor. When he found out that I had developed the Assertive Discipline program, he said, "Oh, that's where all you do is write the kids' names on the board when they're bad and drop marbles in the jar when they're good."

The university professor's response disturbed me. For some time I've been concerned about a small percentage of educators—this professor apparently among them—who have interpreted my program in a way that makes behavior management sound simplistic. More important, I'm concerned with their misguided emphasis on providing only negative consequences when students misbehave. The key to dealing effectively with student behavior is not negative—but positive—consequences. To clarify my views for *Kappan* readers, I would like to explain the background of the program and address some of the issues that are often raised about Assertive Discipline.

I developed the program about 14 years ago, when I first became aware that teachers were not trained to deal with student behavior. Teachers were taught such concepts as "Don't smile until Christmas" or "If your curriculum is good enough, you will have no behavior problems." Those concepts were out of step with the reality of student behavior in the 1970s.

When I discovered this lack of training, I began to study how effective teachers dealt with student behavior. I found that, above all, the master teachers were assertive; that is, they *taught* students how to behave. They established clear rules for the classroom, they communicated those rules to the students, and they taught the students how to follow them. These effective teachers had also mastered skills in positive reinforcement, and they praised every student at least once a day. Finally, when students chose to break the rules, these teachers used firm and consistent negative consequences—but only as a last resort.

From Lee Canter, "Assertive Discipline—More Than Names on the Board and Marbles in a Jar," *Phi Delta Kappan* (September 1989). Copyright © 1989 by Phi Delta Kappa, Inc. Reprinted by permission.

It troubles me to find my work interpreted as suggesting that teachers need only provide negative consequences—check marks or demerits—when students misbehave. That interpretation is wrong. The key to Assertive Discipline is catching students being good: recognizing and supporting them when they behave appropriately and letting them know you like it, day in and day out.

THE DISCIPLINE PLAN

It is vital for classroom teachers to have a systematic discipline plan that explains exactly what will happen when students choose to misbehave. By telling the students at the beginning of the school year what the consequences will be, teachers insure that all students know what to expect in the classroom. Without a plan, teachers must choose an appropriate consequence at the moment when a student misbehaves. They must stop the lesson, talk to the misbehaving student, and do whatever else the situation requires, while 25 to 30 students look on. That is not an effective way to teach—or to deal with misbehavior.

Most important, without a plan teachers tend to be inconsistent. One day they may ignore students who are talking, yelling, or disrupting the class. The next day they may severely discipline students for the same behaviors. In addition, teachers may respond differently to students from different socioeconomic, ethnic, or racial backgrounds.

An effective discipline plan is applied fairly to all students. Every student who willfully disrupts the classroom and stops the teacher from teaching suffers the same consequence. And a written plan can be sent home to parents, who then know beforehand what the teacher's standards are and what will be done when students choose to misbehave. When a teacher calls a parent, there should be no surprises.

MISBEHAVIOR AND CONSEQUENCES

I suggest that a discipline plan include a maximum of five consequences for misbehavior, but teachers must choose consequences with which they are comfortable. For example, the first time a student breaks a rule, the student is warned. The second infraction brings a 10-minute timeout; the third infraction, a 15-minute timeout. The fourth time a student breaks a rule, the teacher calls the parents; the fifth time, the student goes to the principal.

No teacher should have a plan that is not appropriate for his or her needs and that is not in the best interests of the students. Most important, the consequences should never be psychologically or physically harmful to the students. Students should never be made to stand in front of the class as objects of ridicule or be degraded in any other way. Nor should they be given consequences that are inappropriate for their grade levels. I also feel strongly that corporal punishment should *never* be administered. There are more effective ways of dealing with students than hitting them.

Names and checks on the board are sometimes said to be essential to an Assertive Discipline program, but they are not. I originally suggested this particular practice because I had seen teachers interrupt their lessons to make such negative comments to misbehaving students as, "You talked out again. I've had it. You're impossible. That's 20 minutes after school." I wanted to eliminate the need to stop the lesson and issue reprimands. Writing a student's name on the board would warn the student in a calm, nondegrading manner. It would also provide a record-keeping system for the teacher.

Unfortunately, some parents have misinterpreted the use of names and checks on the board as a way of humiliating students. I now suggest that teachers instead write an offending student's name on a clipboard or in the roll book and say to the student, "You talked out, you disrupted the class, you broke a rule. That's a warning. That's a check."

In addition to parents, some teachers have misinterpreted elements of the Assertive Discipline program. The vast majority of teachers—my staff and I have probably trained close to 750,000 teachers—have used the program to dramatically increase their reliance on positive reinforcement and verbal praise. But a small percentage of teachers have interpreted the program in a negative manner.

There are several reasons for this. First, Assertive Discipline has become a generic term, like Xerox or Kleenex. A number of educators are now conducting training in what they call Assertive Discipline without teaching all the competencies essential to my program. For example, I have heard reports of teachers who were taught that they had only to stand in front of their students, tell them that there were rules and consequences, display a chart listing those rules and consequences, and write the names of misbehaving students on the board. That was it. Those teachers were never introduced to the concept that positive reinforcement is the key to dealing with students. Such programs are not in the best interests of students.

Negative interpretations have also come from burned-out, overwhelmed teachers who feel they do not get the support that they need from parents or administrators and who take out their frustrations on students. Assertive Discipline is not a negative program, but it can be misused by negative teachers. The answer is not to change the program, but to change the teachers. We need to train administrators, mentor teachers, and staff developers to coach negative teachers in the use of positive reinforcement. If these teachers cannot become more positive, they should not be teaching.

POSITIVE DISCIPLINE

I recommend a three-step cycle of behavior management to establish a positive discipline system.

First, whenever teachers want students to follow certain directions, they must *teach* the specific behaviors. Teachers too often assume that students know how they are expected to behave. Teachers first need to establish specific directions for each activity during the day—lectures, small-group work, transitions between activities, and so forth. For each situation, teachers must determine the *exact* behaviors they expect from the students.

For example, teachers may want students to stay in their seats during a lecture, focusing their eyes on the lecturer, clearing their desks of all materials except paper and pencil, raising their hands when they have questions or comments, and waiting to be called on before speaking. Once teachers have determined the specific behaviors for each situation, they must teach the students how to follow the directions. They must first state the directions and, with younger students, write the behaviors on the board or on a flip chart. Then they must model the behaviors, ask the students to restate the directions, question the students to make sure they understand the directions, and immediately engage the students in the activity to make sure that they understand the directions.

Second, after teaching the specific directions, teachers—especially at the elementary level—must use *positive repetition* to reinforce the students when they follow the directions. Typically, teachers give directions to the students and then focus attention only on those students who do *not* obey. ("Bobby, you didn't go back to your seat. Teddy, what's wrong with you? Get back to work.") Instead, teachers should focus on those students who do follow the directions, rephrasing the original directions as a positive comment. For example, "Jason went back to his seat and got right to work."

Third, if a student is still misbehaving after a teacher has taught specific directions and has used positive repetition, only then should the teacher use the negative consequences outlined in his or her Assertive Discipline plan. As a general rule, a teacher shouldn't administer a disciplinary consequence to a student until the teacher has reinforced at least two students for the appropriate behavior. Effective teachers are always positive first. Focusing on negative behavior teaches students that negative behavior gets attention, that the teacher is a negative person, and that the classroom is a negative place.

An effective behavior management program must be built on choice. Students must know beforehand what is expected of them in the classroom, what will happen if they choose to behave, and what will happen if they choose not to behave. Students learn self-discipline and responsible behavior by being given clear, consistent choices. They learn that their actions have an impact and that they themselves control the consequences.

I wish teachers did not need to use negative consequences at all. I wish all students came to school motivated to learn. I wish all parents supported teachers and administrators. But that's not the reality today. Many children do not come to school intrinsically motivated to behave. Their parents have never taken the time or don't have the knowledge or skills to teach them how to behave. Given these circumstances, teachers need to set firm and consistent limits in their classrooms. However, those limits must be fair, and the consequences must be seen as outcomes of behaviors that students have *chosen.*

Students need teachers who can create classroom environments in which teaching and learning can take place. Every student has the right to a learning environment that is free from disruption. Students also need teachers who help them learn how to behave appropriately in school. Many students who are categorized as behavior problems would not be so labeled if their teachers had taught them how to behave appropriately in the classroom and had raised their self-esteem.

WHY ASSERTIVE DISCIPLINE?

The average teacher never receives in-depth, competency-based training in managing the behavior of 30 students. No one teaches teachers how to keep students in their seats long enough for teachers to make good use of the skills they learned in their education classes. In most instances, behavior management is taught through a smorgasbord approach—a little bit of William Glasser, a little bit of Thomas Gordon, a little bit of Rudolf

Dreikurs, a little bit of Lee Canter. The teachers are told to find an approach that works for them.

Such an approach to training teachers in behavior management is analogous to a swimming class in which nonswimmers are briefly introduced—without practice—to the crawl stroke, the breast stroke, the back stroke, and the side stroke; then they are rowed to the middle of a lake, tossed overboard, and told to swim to shore, using whatever stroke works for them. In effect, we're telling teachers to sink or swim, and too many teachers are sinking.

The lack of ability to manage student behavior is one of the key reasons why beginning teachers drop out of teaching. Teachers must be trained thoroughly in classroom management skills. It is not sufficient for them to know how to teach content. They will never get to the content unless they know how to create a positive environment in which students know how to behave.

Assertive Discipline is not a cure-all. It is a starting point. Every teacher should also know how to use counseling skills, how to use group process skills, and how to help students with behavioral deficits learn appropriate classroom behaviors. In addition, classroom management must be part of an educator's continuing professional development. Teachers routinely attend workshops, enroll in college courses, receive feedback from administrators, and take part in regular inservice training to refine their teaching skills. Classroom management skills deserve the same attention. Unfortunately, some educators view training in Assertive Discipline as a one-shot process; they attend a one-day workshop, and that's supposed to take care of their training needs for the rest of their careers.

One day is not enough. It takes a great deal of effort and continuing training for a teacher to master the skills of classroom management. A teacher also needs support from the building administrator. Without an administrator backing a teacher's efforts to improve behavior management, without an administrator to coach and clinically supervise a teacher's behavior management skills, that teacher is not going to receive the necessary feedback and assistance to master those skills.

Parental support for teachers' disciplinary efforts is equally important. Many teachers become frustrated and give up when they don't receive such support. We must train teachers to guarantee the support of parents by teaching teachers how to communicate effectively with parents. In teacher training programs, participants are led to believe that today's parents will act as parents did in the past and give absolute support to the school. That is rarely the case. Today's teachers call parents and are told, "He's your problem at school. You handle it. You're the professional. You take care of him. I don't know what to do. Leave me alone."

RESEARCH AND ASSERTIVE DISCIPLINE

Over the last several years, a number of dissertations, master's theses, and research projects have dealt with Assertive Discipline. The results have consistently shown that teachers dramatically improve student behavior when they use the skills as prescribed. Teachers who use Assertive Discipline reduce the frequency of disruptive behavior in their classrooms, greatly reduce the number of students they refer to administrators, and dramatically increase their students' time-on-task.[1] Other research has demonstrated that student teachers trained in Assertive Discipline are evaluated by their master teachers as more effective in classroom management.[2] Research conducted in school districts in California, Oregon, Ohio, and Arizona has shown that an overwhelming majority of teachers believe that Assertive Discipline helps to improve the climate in the schools and the behavior of students.[3]

No one should be surprised that research has verified the success of the program when teachers use the skills properly. Numerous research studies have shown that teachers need to teach students the specific behaviors that they expect from them. Research also shows that student behavior improves when teachers use positive reinforcement effectively and that the pairing of positive reinforcement with consistent disciplinary consequences effectively motivates students to behave appropriately.[4]

Any behavior management program that is taught to teachers today must have a solid foundation in research. Many so-called "experts" advocate programs that are based solely on their own opinions regarding what constitutes a proper classroom environment. When pressed, many of these experts have no research validating their opinions or perceptions, and many of their programs have never been validated for effectiveness in classrooms. We can't afford to train educators in programs based only on whim or untested theory. We have an obligation to insure that any training program in behavior management be based solidly on techniques that have been validated by research and that have been shown to work in the classroom.

Research has demonstrated that Assertive Discipline works and that it isn't just a quick-fix solution. In school districts in Lennox, California, and Troy, Ohio, teachers who were trained 10 years ago still use the program effectively.[5] The program works because it is based on practices that effective teachers have followed instinctively for a long time. It's not new to have rules in a classroom. It's not new to use positive reinforcement. It's not new to have disciplinary consequences.

Teachers who are effective year after year take the basic Assertive Discipline competencies and mold them to their individual teaching styles. They may stop using certain techniques, such as putting marbles in a jar or writing names on the board. That's fine. I don't want the legacy of Assertive Discipline to be—and I don't want teachers to believe they have to use—names and checks on the board or marbles in a jar. I want teachers to learn that they have to take charge, explain their expectations, be positive with students, and consistently employ both positive reinforcement and negative consequences. These are the skills that form the basis of Assertive Discipline and of any effective program of classroom management.

NOTES

1. Linda H. Mandlebaum et al., "Assertive Discipline: An Effective Behavior Management Program," *Behavioral Disorders Journal*, vol. 8, 1983, pp. 258–64; Carl L. Fereira, "A Positive Approach to Assertive Discipline," Martinez (Calif.) Unified School District, ERIC ED 240 058, 1983; and Sammie McCormack, "Students' Off-Task Behavior and Assertive Discipline" (Doctoral dissertation, University of Oregon, 1985).

2. Susan Smith, "The Effects of Assertive Discipline Training on Student Teachers' Self Concept and Classroom Management Skills" (Doctoral dissertation, University of South Carolina, 1983).

3. Kenneth L. Moffett et al., "Assertive Discipline," *California School Board Journal*, June/July/August 1982, pp. 24–27; Mark Y. Swanson, "Assessment of the Assertive Discipline Program,"

Compton (Calif.) Unified School District, Spring 1984; "Discipline Report," Cartwright (Ariz.) Elementary School District, 10 February 1982; and Confederation of Oregon School Administrators, personal letter, 28 April 1980.

4. Helen Hair et al., "Development of Internal Structure in Elementary Students: A System of Classroom Management and Class Control," ERIC ED 189 067, 1980; Edmund Emmer and Carolyn Everston, "Effective Management: At the Beginning of the School Year in Junior High Classes," Research and Development Center for Teacher Education, University of Texas, Austin, 1980; Marcia Broden et al., "Effects of Teacher Attention on Attending Behavior of Two Boys at Adjacent Desks," *Journal of Applied Behavior Analysis*, vol. 3, 1970, pp. 205–11; Hill Walker et al., "The Use of Normative Peer Data as a Standard for Evaluating Treatment Effects," *Journal of Applied Behavior Analysis*, vol. 37, 1976, pp. 145–55; Jere Brophy, "Classroom Organization and Management," *Elementary School Journal*, vol. 83, 1983, pp. 265–85; Hill Walker et al., "Experiments with Response Cost in Playground and Classroom Settings," Center for Research in Behavioral Education of the Handicapped, University of Oregon, Eugene, 1977; Thomas McLaughlin and John Malaby, "Reducing and Measuring Inappropriate Verbalizations," *Journal of Applied Behavior Analysis*, vol. 5, 1972, pp. 329–33; Charles Madsen et al., "Rules, Praise, and Ignoring: Elements of Elementary Classroom Control," *Journal of Applied Behavior Analysis*, vol. 1, 1968, pp. 139–50; Charles Greenwood et al., "Group Contingencies for Group Consequences in Classroom Management: A Further Analysis," *Journal of Applied Behavior Analysis*, vol. 7, 1974, pp. 413–25; and K. Daniel O'Leary et al., "A Token Reinforcement Program in a Public School: A Replication and Systematic Analysis," *Journal of Applied Behavior Analysis*, vol. 2, 1969, pp. 3–13.

5. Kenneth L. Moffett et al., "Training and Coaching Beginning Teachers: An Antidote to Reality Shock," *Educational Leadership*, February 1987, pp. 34–46; and Bob Murphy, "Troy High School: An Assertive Model," *Miami Valley Sunday News*, Troy, Ohio, 12 March 1989, p. 1.

NO   John F. Covaleskie

DISCIPLINE AND MORALITY: BEYOND RULES AND CONSEQUENCES

For the past two decades, at least, there has been a major concern in American education on the issue of student discipline. During that period, the emphasis has been on behavioral approaches to discipline, which by their nature tend to make discipline largely the responsibility of teachers. The so-called Assertive Discipline has become both the program of choice in many schools and a paradigm of the behavioral approach. Some recent literature reviewing this particular program made clear the extent to which the debate is about means, rather than ends.[1] Rather than endlessly continue the debate about which program best controls student behaviors, we might look at the question from the other end: What is it that we hope to teach children about being good people, and does this mean more than what schools call "discipline"? If we can better define our ends, we might have a better standard by which to evaluate the means to achieve them. This article puts forth a proposal as to the proper ends of education relative to student behavior. Only then can we rationally turn to the question of how best to achieve these ends.

Now what is interesting is that the best recent work on formation of moral character seems agreed on one thing, whatever disagreements there may exist: children do not learn to be moral by learning to obey rules that others make for them. From the fields of psychotherapy,[2] psychology,[3] and philosophy,[4] the current understandings of the formation of moral character involve children learning to think and talk about moral issues in ways that are actively discouraged by programs conceiving of discipline as obedience to authority and rules. What current conceptions of morality help us see is that children grow into morality and ethical thinking, and that they do so by engaging in moral thought and conversation. What helps children become moral is not knowledge of rules, or even obedience to rules, but discussions about the reasons for acting in certain ways. Whether conceived as based in rationality, emotion, or both, morality is not simply obedience to rules.

From John F. Covaleskie, "Discipline and Morality: Beyond Rules and Consequences," *The Educational Forum*, vol. 56, no. 2 (Winter 1992). Copyright © 1992 by Kappa Delta Pi, an international honor society in education. Reprinted by permission.

WHAT COUNTS AS "SUCCESS"?

Given the fact that education should have implications for life, the question can be rephrased. It is not, "What is the best way to control student behavior in schools?" but, "What is the best way to prepare our children to love ethical lives?" Another way of addressing this issue is to ask the opposite question: "What would we consider unsatisfactory?" There are two answers to this last question, one obvious, the other somewhat less so. The obvious answer is that no discipline program would be considered satisfactory if it did not result in children acting responsibly and in accordance with the legitimate rules of behavior established in the school.

I, however, would like to argue the case that there is a more subtle way in which a discipline program can fail. A program that teaches children that they are simply expected to obey rules, even legitimate and duly established rules, fails the children and the larger society, even if it meets the needs of the adults in a school. A discipline program cannot be judged merely by asking whether it does a good job of keeping children out of trouble in school; being a good person is more than that. Children must develop a framework within which they can make good choices about how to act, and we must help them do so.

It is important in this connection to examine the meaning of two central concepts: "good" and "choices." "Good" is used here in the sense of ethical or moral, not in the sense of practical or advantageous. Children must develop a sense of what it means to be a good person—what it means to choose to do the right thing, especially when circum-

stances are such that one is faced with the possibility of doing the wrong thing to one's own advantage, and getting away with it. A good choice can, and often will, place the chooser at a disadvantage, and still be a good choice. Further, learning to be a good person is not the same as learning to obey rules; it is more complex than that.

Obviously, this is no new insight. In the *Nicomachean Ethics*, Aristotle[5] included *phronesis* (practical wisdom) as an essential attribute of the good person. In fact, his definition of a virtuous action was that which a person with practical wisdom would judge to be virtuous. This capacity for judgment was not only necessary for a person to do the right thing, it was the standard by which the right thing was defined. *Phronesis* is closer than obedience to the goal we in schools should have in mind as we help children to form their characters. In choosing how to act in any circumstance, I am making a judgment about what action is the right one to take. Much more often than not, good judgment will dictate behavior that conforms to rules for the situation, but that is not the point. The point is that I must choose and act well even where rules conflict or do not obviously apply.

To illustrate what happens when people do not learn to make and act on these kinds of judgments, we need only consider Milgram's experiment on obedience,[6] in which he discovered that most people would follow a researcher's order to administer what were apparently painful shocks to the alleged "subjects" of a learning experiment. In actuality, these victims were confederates of the researcher, and there was no shock; they were only acting as if in pain. The real purpose of this experiment was to study the behavior of those being told to administer the shocks, and the question was whether they would obey the rules established by the researcher. The results of the experiment were disturbing, to say the least. Average people, chosen at random, would administer, if told to do so by someone in a position of authority (even under no threat of penalty for refusing), what were perceived as painful (even dangerous) shocks to "suffering" victims begging them to stop. Milgram reports that these common people showed real anguish as they administered the shocks—they did not want to do so—but, nevertheless, administer the shocks they did. They followed the rules, and just in doing so, they made a bad moral choice. These were people whose training failed to help them develop effective good judgment. It is instructive to note that many of these individuals appeared to understand that what they were being asked to do was wrong; they lacked confidence in this judgment of their own to translate it into action.

To sum up, any approach to discipline is to be judged a failure not only on the obvious criterion that it fails to establish and affect appropriate standards of behavior, but also if, in establishing such standards, it does so primarily by teaching children to obey rules rather than to make reasoned judgments about what actions are desirable, and about how actually to decide to act in those desirable ways.[7]

Developing good judgment. How can we then help children develop this judgment? It is easy to state, but hard to do: we must teach children that the reason they should not do certain things is that those things are wrong; the reason they should prefer to do other things is that those things are right. We must help them see *why* one thing is wrong as

against another which is right. *Teaching children that X is wrong because there is a rule against X is not the same as teaching them that there is a rule against X because X is wrong, and helping them understand why this is so.* Children should be taught not to steal because it is wrong. They should not be taught not to steal because there is a rule against stealing. Although they certainly need to know that there is such a rule, the rule is not the reason we teach children not to steal. What they need to understand is that *the rule against stealing exists only because stealing is wrong,* and why this is so.

Some help in picturing the pedagogical implications of this comes from Strike,[8] who suggests that the way children develop a moral sense is by using moral language. That is, if we talk with children about the moral implications of their actions, they will be learning to think morally at the same time that they are learning to speak the language of morality.

The standard by which we should be judging "discipline programs" in schools is that of moral responsibility: do our children learn to think, talk, and act morally? The goal is not compliance with rules, but making the choices to live a good life, an ethical life. Further, in order to reach this goal children must learn that certain things are wrong, and should be avoided *for that reason only.* Negative consequences, fear of getting caught, self-advantage, and rules themselves should all yield before the voice of conscience, the internal voice which monitors my actions against the standard of the kind of person I hope to be. This voice of conscience, this sense of right and wrong, is what we must strive to shape in our schools, and this internal voice can best be given shape through external language that models its proper form.

OBJECTIONS CONSIDERED

Implementing this suggestion involves a practical problem of considerable dimension: what (or whose) standards of right and wrong should be taught? I would make three suggestions: (1) this question misconstrues the true nature of moral education, (2) the issue is not, in the long run, relevant, and (3) the difficulty of the task, however great it is, does not excuse us from the effort.

1) The argument against ethics education is usually based on two assumptions: (a) moral education consists merely in telling children what is right or wrong conduct, and (b) the differences of judgment over difficult moral issues make such teaching in public schools inappropriate and/or impossible. What, for example, should we teach children with respect to the rightness or wrongness of capital punishment, abortion, or sexual experimentation? Given the deep divisions within society on these and many other ethical questions, this argument goes, do schools not serve both children and the community better by avoiding discussions of moral and/or ethical behavior? While this argument may seem compelling at first, it fails upon closer examination, since it falsely presumes that moral education must be rules-based, as behavioral approaches to discipline are.

In reality, however, teaching children that there is such a thing as an ethical point of view, and helping them understand what that means, does not mean having an answer for every ethical dispute. This does not entail, or even suggest, that we cannot engage in moral conversation about such issues. Where there are sharp disagreements in society about the moral or ethical stand on an issue (and this merely demonstrates the correctness of the proposition argued earlier, namely, that acting ethically requires the exercise of judgment and that following rules will not help us in life, and should not suffice in school, either), we probably should avoid telling students that X is wrong. We still can, and probably must, make clear the nature of the issues involved that makes, for instance, the abortion choice question a moral dilemma. Similarly, it may just be the job of schools in this regard to help people see that issues of poverty, health care distribution, care for the homeless, or of war and peace are at root moral, not financial or procedural, issues.

On the other hand, most moral issues are not dilemmas; society mostly accepts the idea that it is wrong to steal, barring exceptional circumstances. The fact that there is this agreement is why "Thou shalt not steal" seems so much like a rule which we can follow. The fact that there are exceptions explains why children need to learn moral *reasoning*, not just moral *rules*. Some of our children will be put into conflict even here by the fact that their parents do not believe this, but that must not prevent us from taking the only acceptable ethical stand on that issue: it is wrong to steal, opinions to the contrary notwithstanding.

The same goes for a broad range of socially valuable "civic virtues": e.g., honesty, civic responsibility, and tolerance. The existence of racism in a society may make the teaching of tolerance controversial, even professionally risky; yet the existence of racism is precisely what makes that teaching so necessary. And this teaching must not be rule driven. We do not act tolerantly to others simply by obeying rules—it is more than that; there are no rules that will get us there. It is a matter of whom we choose to be, as individuals and as a society. Further, when we do behave tolerantly, it is not because there are rules that say we should; the rules exist because we should act so. What makes some actions right and others wrong is teachable only by example and discussion, not by dictate and as a set of rules.

2) The second point is that the issue is, in the long run, irrelevant. As they grow, children shaped by rules will discard some of the rules of their childhood while affirming others. Likewise for children raised through moral conversation. Some of what they grow up believing to be right will be denied, while some will be affirmed. What they will carry with them, however, is how they make choices. Will they follow rules, or make careful (and caring) moral judgments? It is like giving children a frame and a canvas upon which they will create themselves— we can shape the canvas, but the actual picture is up to each individual. Since following rules will not suffice in the real world, we had better teach them a better way to make their decisions while we have the opportunity. The specifics do not matter as much as the categories we create for them. Should children make decisions based on the categories of required, prohibited, and permitted, or on those of right, wrong, and neutral? This is not a trivial difference.

3) With regards to the third objection, the difficulty of the task, a simple statement will suffice. If ethically literate adults is the desired goal, and if shaping of ethical beliefs is the only way to get there, then that is what we must try to do, even if doing so is extremely difficult, or we are unsure of how to go about the task.

4) There is a fourth objection to be considered in proposing such an ap-proach to helping children learn ethical behavior, namely, that this way of treating children can result in narrow-minded bigotry and intolerance. A seeming case in point is what Grant graphically showed for Hamilton High School.[9] The students and faculty there had become so certain about their own values in the 1950s and early 60s that it was difficult for them to accept differences in looks, dress, race, religion, or just about anything else.

On the other hand, he also reported that by the 1980s there were no standards of behavior except what was allowed or likely to be gotten away with. There was nothing wrong with cheating, as long as one got away with it. No one had taught these young adults as children that it is wrong to cheat; they only knew that they might be punished if they were caught. The fact that there were no negative consequences for undiscovered cheating meant that it was acceptable to cheat. Grant's conclusion was that schools, in order to function, need a body of agreements that have been negotiated and accepted, and which individuals are expected to accept as a frame of acceptable behavior. He calls the existence of this area of agreement, if it is a healthy one that both allows individuality and establishes ethical boundaries, a "strong positive ethos." It is this positive ethos which we should be striving to create.

The foregoing discussion should make clear the shortcomings in any "discipline" program that sees discipline as something (1) one in authority does to subordinates, or (2) aimed at the control of behavior rather than the shaping of character. It seems clearly the case that this conception of discipline oriented to externalized control is what has driven much educational practice for the past two decades, and that this view deprives our children of the opportunity to learn what it means, and what it takes, to be good people in our society. The lessons of behavioral approaches to discipline are often precisely contrary to what we wish children to learn.

A DIFFERENT STANDARD: A WELL-FORMED CONSCIENCE

Consider an example common enough in a primary classroom: a child, say, a boy, is discovered to have told the teacher, say, a woman, a lie. A teacher trained in a behavior modification program would remind the child that there is a rule against telling lies in her class (let us make the assumption that there is such a rule), and that something will now happen as a consequence of the rule violation. What has the child learned? Perhaps not what we intend. Let us imagine the conversation from the child's point of view. His teacher has reminded him of the rule, and told him that he will now suffer negative consequences as a result of the violation. What the teacher assumes the child is learning is something like, "Don't lie." However, it seems (at least) as plausible that the child is learning something closer to, "Don't get caught lying." After all, the child is not, in fact, receiving negative consequences as a result of lying; he is receiving them only because he got caught. If he had lied better, he would have been *positively* reinforced. He has probably successfully lied on previous occasions, thus learning that there is no *necessary* connection between lying and getting punished. These lessons are not lost on the child. The very best we can hope for is that the child is learning something like, "Don't break rules." More likely, the lesson is, "Don't get caught breaking rules."

Now in certain situations, that is, where there is adequate supervision, these lessons produce very similar results, and children will more often than not tell the truth in such circumstances. However, in other circumstances, which describe most of life, one can often successfully lie. The child who has been taught only by a behavioral approach lacks a moral compass to guide her or him in those circumstances. By definition and philosophical commitment, such approaches attempt to shape behavior only, without regard to "unnecessary" notions like a child's conscience. Having been taught not to lie because of the negative consequences that follow getting caught or positive consequences given for telling the truth, she or he has not the internal voice to help make the right choice when getting caught is unlikely. The discipline here is an external thing, which does not shape the child's actions except when regulated externally.

The question that has been ignored in the current discussion about the most effective or best discipline program is this: "Does it make a difference why students act in desirable ways?" Behaviorists will, if pressed, argue that the answer is no, and this seems wrong. It *does* matter that children are being taught to obey the rules in order to gain externally controlled positive consequences and avoid negative ones. What we want to do with children is to teach them to act morally, not because of the rewards or punishments others will give for good or bad actions, not because it will make their teachers, or others, unhappy, but because it is *wrong* to act immorally, and because they should not wish to be the kind of persons who behave in that way. It is not merely a matter of following rules; it is a matter of knowing the right, wanting to do it, and doing so. It is *caring* about the sort of person *I am*, and recognizing that what I do and who I am are connected. Most often, and in societies that are basically healthy, following rules complies with the requirements of being a good person, but sometimes one must break rules to be good; this is the message of Milgram's experiment. It also highlights the importance of constructing moral conversation in our schools, and teaching our children how to be part of it.

Proper self-esteem. In an effort to protect a child's self-esteem, we often refuse to label a behavior as wrong, as shameful. Does this make sense? What creates the sense of true esteem, if not believing that what I do is, in fact, right and praiseworthy? But actions can only be right and praiseworthy in contrast to that which is wrong and shameful. If one is to have genuine pride in one's behavior, the person must first be capable of feeling shame. Whence comes this legitimate pride except in the message delivered by one's teachers (in the most general sense of this word) that one has acted nobly *in circumstances when one might have acted shamefully?* It is this avoidance of shame that constitutes a valid sense of self-esteem, believing that what one has done is good, is right, and is praiseworthy, *though it might have been otherwise.* Note that, once the individual has developed this sense and awareness, an audience is not necessary.

I feel shame or pride for what I know about myself, not what others know about me. It is this voice of conscience that creates in me the desire, not to obey rules, but to do the right thing, and the awareness of what that means. What matters is not just what we do, but how what we do reflects who we are. Any approach to dealing with children that

explicitly attempts to treat the behavior as separate from the child is cheating the children since it relieves them of the responsibility of feeling shame for behaving shamefully.

This argument in favor of shame requires explanation in today's climate; shame is not synonymous with humiliation, though we often use the terms as though it were. Humiliation is a public shaming of someone, holding the person up to ridicule in the eyes of others. Shame is something else. The precise point of shame is that the child learns to identify his or her own shameful behavior as such. Humiliation need not, and should not, play any part in instructing children in proper behavior. It is likewise true that children should learn to be proud of their good behaviors without being boastful about them. Pride, like shame, has to do with the judgments we pass on ourselves.[10]

IT WILL JUSTIFIABLY BE ARGUED BY BEHAVIorists, as Canter for one does in fact argue,[11] that an ethical approach to behavior is both time consuming and difficult. It takes much longer to obtain desired behavior by shaping thinking than by shaping behavior. However, the force of this argument rests on a false premise: that one makes no attempt to control behavior while working to shape beliefs. Addressing behavior is certainly a necessary condition for teaching children how to behave; it is not, however, sufficient. In addition to learning what to do, children must learn the reasons for so doing. Note that the reasons need to be more than the rewards granted or punishment imposed by others on the basis of behavior.

Because of the inadequacies of behavioral approaches, schools must chart a very difficult course with regard to children's behavior. We must establish the ethical foundations upon which we can agree, and teach children that these will be the bases of judgment about action in the school at all times because of the inherent value we perceive in them, not just because there are rules. We must, of course, also help them learn that these same standards of judgment should apply in their lives outside the school. One way we can do this is by seeing to it that actions that conform to or violate these standards will carry consequences, and adults must be very aware of their own actions relative to these standards as well. However, application of consequences is not enough. Along with rewards and punishments, there must be conversation, not about the rules, but about the standards. The focus, contrary to the teachings of behaviorism, should always be on the person acting and the reasons for actions, not merely the behavior. Our desire should be to help children act responsibly, not just behave manageably.

There is no doubt that this process will be arduous and time consuming. Behavioral approaches, with their more limited goals, are clearly easier and quicker to implement, and are likely to reward the teacher with quick positive reinforcement. However, this also oversimplifies the problem we face as a society. Behavioral approaches teach conformity and compliance, obedient behavior when faced with rules based in authority. Ethical approaches can bring up children who behave well for more substantial reasons. The latter is more difficult and time consuming, but it is also necessary.

REFERENCES

1. Richard Curwin and Allen Mendler, "Packaged Discipline Programs: Let the Buyer Beware," *Educational Leadership* 46 (October 1988): 68–71; Lee Canter, "Let the Educator Beware: A Response to Curwin and Mendler," *Educational Leadership* 46 (October 1988): 71–73; Gary Render, JeNell Padilla, and H. Mark Krank, "What Research Really Shows about Assertive Discipline," *Educational Leadership* 46 (March 1989): 72–75; Sammie McCormack, "Response to Render, Padilla, and Krank: But Practitioners Say It Works!" *Educational Leadership* 46 (March 1989): 77–79; Lee Canter, "Assertive Discipline—More Than Just Names on the Board and Marbles in a Jar," *Phi Delta Kappan* 71 (September 1989): 57–61; Richard Curwin and Allen Mendler, "We Repeat, Let the Buyer Beware: A Response to Canter," *Educational Leadership* 46 (March 1989): 83.

2. Robert Coles, *The Moral Life of Children* (Boston: Houghton Mifflin, 1986).

3. Carol Gilligan, *In a Different Voice: Psychological Theory and Women's Development* (Cambridge, Massachusetts: Harvard University Press, 1982); Lawrence Kohlberg, *The Philosophy of Moral Development* (San Francisco: Harper and Row, 1981).

4. Nel Noddings, *Caring: A Feminine Approach to Ethics and Moral Education* (Berkeley, California: University of California Press, 1984); Kenneth Strike, "Virtuous Speech: An Essay on Moral Learning and Pluralism." (Paper presented at the Schools of Character Forum, Le Moyne College, Syracuse, New York, May 8, 1991).

5. Aristotle, *Nicomachean Ethics*, trans. Terence Irwin (Indianapolis: Hacket, 1985).

6. Stanley Milgram, *Obedience to Authority: An Experimental View* (New York: Harper and Row, 1973).

7. Procedural rules such as, "Hang up your coat," or, "Write your name in the top left hand corner of your page," are not the sort of rules under discussion in this essay. The point is that teachers must understand that there is a basic difference between procedural rules, which are often somewhat arbitrary (though not therefore unreasonable), and those rules of classroom behavior that are not arbitrary but grounded in ethical principles. The former will often appropriately be taught through simple stimulus-response training; the latter should never be.

8. Strike, "Virtuous Speech."

9. Gerald Grant, *The World We Created at Hamilton High* (Cambridge, Massachusetts: Harvard University Press, 1988).

10. See Gabrielle Taylor, *Shame, Pride, and Guilt: The Emotions of Self-Assessment* (Oxford, England: Clarendon Press, 1985), for a fuller exploration.

11. Canter, "Let the Educator Beware."

POSTSCRIPT

Do "Discipline Programs" Promote Ethical Behavior?

"If we continue to follow the dead end of stimulus-response psychology and focus on the symptom rather than the cause," William Glasser contends, "our schools will never be significantly better or more 'disciplined' than they are now." If this is true, then those who hold the position must achieve the theoretical and practical precision that has been a hallmark of behaviorism and assertive discipline programs.

Although the focus of discussion on this issue has been primarily on theoretical aspects, there is a wealth of material available that attempts to translate theory into practical, situational terms. Among the more provocative works are these: R. C. Newell's "Learning to Survive in the Classroom," *American Teacher* (February 1981); "Good, Old-Fashioned Discipline: The Politics of Punitiveness," by Irwin A. Hyman and John D'Alessandro, *Phi Delta Kappan* (September 1984); and "Effective Teacher Techniques: Implications for Better Discipline," by Elizabeth M. Reis, *Clearing House* (April 1988).

The Summer 1987 issue of *Pointer* contains articles on a variety of discipline approaches, as does the January 1988 issue of the *National Association of Secondary School Principals Bulletin*. An article by Lee Canter, "Assertive Discipline and the Search for the Perfect Classroom," appears in the January 1988 issue of *Young Children*. Positive results of Canter's program are reported by Elden R. Barrett and K. Fred Curtis in "The Effects of Assertive Discipline Training on Student Teachers," *Teacher Education and Practice* (Spring–Summer 1986).

Other articles of interest are: Thomas R. McDaniel's "Practicing Positive Reinforcement: Ten Behavioral Management Techniques," *Clearing House* (May 1987); "This 'Step System' of Discipline Helps Kids Improve Their Behavior," by Steve Black and John J. Welsh, *The American School Board Journal* (December 1985); and Larry Bartlett's "Academic Evaluation and Student Discipline Don't Mix: A Critical Review," in the *Journal of Law and Education* (Spring 1987).

The March 1989 issue of *Educational Leadership* offers a special feature on the topic of discipline. Of particular interest is an article on "What Research Really Shows About Assertive Discipline." David Hill's "Order in the Classroom," *Teacher Magazine* (April 1990) draws a provocative portrait of the Canter system.

Two books on the topic are worthy of attention: *Discipline With Dignity* (1989) by Richard L. Curwin and Allen N. Mendler and *The Quality School— Managing Students Without Coercion* (1990) by William Glasser.

ISSUE 19

Are Current Sex Education Programs Lacking in Moral Guidance?

YES: Kevin Ryan, from "Sex, Morals, and Schools," *Theory into Practice* (Summer 1989)

NO: Peter Scales, from "Overcoming Future Barriers to Sexuality Education," *Theory into Practice* (Summer 1989)

ISSUE SUMMARY

YES: Professor of education Kevin Ryan argues for movement toward a firmer moral grounding of sex education programs.
NO: Peter Scales, a leading advocate of sexuality education, feels that current objections to these programs are unwarranted.

As early as the middle of the nineteenth century, English philosopher Herbert Spencer was recommending that sex education be included among the school subjects that are considered essential to the leading of a complete and satisfactory life. He saw the subject as a natural part of preparing for family life that could be grounded firmly in the newly emerging body of scientific knowledge.

There are those who, still today, oppose even narrowly scientific explanations of sexual functioning in the schools. Some people object to the information itself as having a possible corrupting influence. Others contend that clinical information alone, without religiously grounded moral guidance, is misleading. Still others resent the efforts of some educators to infuse sex instruction with values that may be ideologically slanted.

On the larger cultural level, some critics of sex education feel that the recent "sexual revolution" has left many young people adrift without moral moorings and that most of the school efforts fail to counteract this situation. Church or home guidance is deemed preferable by some of these people, while inclusion of ethical considerations in the sex education curriculum is desired by others.

Some central questions are these: Are the schools qualified to handle such subject matter competently? Is there room in the public school curriculum for such studies at a time when performance in basic academic areas is weak? If the answers to these questions are affirmative, many issues stemming from the teaching of sex education need to be addressed, such as: How early should sexuality education begin? By whom should it be taught? Should it be taught separately or as a component of health or biology classes? Is it an appropriate topic for social studies courses? Are some aspects of the topic taboo? How explicit should instructional materials be? What controls on library inclusions are needed? Should parents review or approve course materials? Should parents have the right to exclude their children from such instructional programs? How early should the topic of acquired immunodeficiency syndrome (AIDS) be addressed? Should high schools provide condoms for teenagers?

Indeed, the AIDS epidemic places new urgency on increasing the schools' efforts in the area of sexuality education. A recent Gallup poll shows that 90 percent of respondents are in favor of AIDS education, with 40 percent saying it should begin in the elementary schools. A 1988 report by the Sex Information and Educational Council of the United States, titled *State Update on Sexuality Education and AIDS Education*, shows that 13 states require sexuality education and another 22 have stipulated guidelines for teaching the subject. The range of programs is indeed wide—from full K–12 treatment of the topic to a few hours of instruction on physiological aspects alone.

Although some 80 percent of parents favor sex education in the schools, many feel that values and morals must be included in the instructional program to guide young people in making sex-related decisions. Some parents express concern about the "situational ethics" tone, which some programs seem to espouse, and call for a more direct moral approach.

In the following articles, Kevin Ryan, who is the director of the Center for the Advancement of Ethics and Character at Boston University, contends that sex is not a morally neutral matter and shows how the moral dimension can be infused through the use of an experimental curriculum developed at the center. Peter Scales counters that current comprehensive programs, often run by sexuality educators and health professionals, operate from a firm base of values and ethical concerns.

YES

Kevin Ryan

SEX, MORALS, AND SCHOOLS

Sexuality is an important part of our humanity and an issue that is vital to the survival of the species. It is, therefore, a necessary part of the education we offer to the young. Yet sex has historically been an aspect of human relations shrouded in taboos and rarely talked about openly. Despite changes in this regard, parents who have tried to discuss sex with their children know that it can be an awkward topic.

Sex is controversial today because the authorities in sexual matters have changed. Until this century, many people in this country were guided in what was acceptable sexual practice and what was unacceptable by their religious leaders. Medical doctors have also been a source of advice, often being asked to give talks on sex to high school students. Today, however, authority status seems to be gained by an appearance on a TV talk show or inclusion in the reading rack at the supermarket checkout.

We have undergone a revolution in sexual attitudes and practices in a very short period of time. This change appears to be the result, in part, of our expanded individualism and in part, of easier and improved methods of birth control. Twenty years ago sex before marriage became more acceptable, as did sexual relations between people of the same sex. Many of our prohibitions and inhibitions slipped away, and more and better sex became the goal of many.

Several things have happened since then, however, to give even the most ardent of the apostles of the new sexuality pause. Our family rearing practices have been radically affected. We appear to live in a no-fault divorce climate where it is projected, for instance, that 44 percent of the marriages contracted in 1983 will end in divorce. Since 1970, marriages are down 30 percent and divorces are up 50 percent (Christensen, 1988). We have recently seen the advent of, first, herpes complex B, and now, AIDS.

More to the issue of moral education and sex education, we have the highest levels of teenage sexuality ever recorded in this country. More than one-half of our nation's young people have had sexual intercourse by the time they are 17 (Bennett, 1987, p. 134). In 1980, two professors from Johns

From Kevin Ryan, "Sex, Morals, and Schools," *Theory into Practice*, vol. 28, no. 3 (Summer 1989), pp. 217–220. Copyright © 1989 by the College of Education, Ohio State University. Reprinted by permission.

Hopkins University reported that 49.8 percent of girls between 15 and 19 had premarital sex, compared with 30 percent when they began their study in 1971 (cited in Lickona, 1983, p. 367). Between 1940 and 1985 the rate of out-of-wedlock births to adolescents rose 621 percent (ASCD, 1988, p. 7). In this nation, the sexual landscape for children and adolescents has changed dramatically.

THE MORAL NATURE OF SEX

Teaching the young about sex raises concerns among parents due to its traditional sense of sacredness and taboo, and to the dramatic changes in sexual attitudes and practices. Schools have reacted to this social context by putting more effort and devoting more of students' time-on-task to sex (Kasun, 1979). Critics, however, are contending that our sex education programs are simply feeding the fires of sexual interest and activities among the young (Anchell, 1986; Kasun, 1979). Cuban (1986) states: "Decade after decade . . . statistics have demonstrated the ineffectiveness of such courses in reducing sexual activity, unwanted pregnancy, and venereal disease among teenagers. Before the reformers mindlessly expand school programs aimed at preventing teenage pregnancy, they ought to ask some hard questions" (p. 321). The problem seems to be that while school boards, parents, and teachers know "something is wrong" with this increase in sexual activity among adolescents, they do not approach it as the moral issue it is.

Sexual intercourse is not simply a physical value-free activity. Nor is sexual activity merely a matter of personal taste and choice, although this has been the view among many sex educators. Exemplifying this value-neutral, individualistic approach are the words of a well-known sex educator and author of a sex education curriculum guide for the state of California: 'Right' or 'wrong' in so intimate a matter as sexual behavior is as personal as one's own name and address. No textbook or classroom teacher can teach it" (cited in Cronenwett, 1982, p. 101).

By its very nature, sexual intercourse is moral. It is moral because it is social, involving another person with human dignity and rights. Sex is a mutual giving and mutual taking. It affects body and mind, a person's physical and psychological well-being.

Like all human action, sex is subject to moral judgment. Sexual activities and practices must be open to the question, "What is the right thing to do?" Because sex can have profound consequences for individuals (i.e., birth), it has traditionally been part of a society's rules of behavior, its moral code. Since sex carries the source of a community's existence, it is also natural that it is seen as part of the community's moral code.

All cultures have an overriding mission to endure. The adults in a community are committed to passing on to the young the rules they believe will enable them to endure and to live well. Schools from the time of the Greeks have been seen as one of a society's primary vehicles to pass on to its young its values and moral code (Pratte, 1988; Ryan, 1986). A culture that fails to tell its adolescents these larger facts-of-life and does not think its young have the capacity for sexual self-restraint is one that is giving up the fight.

Nevertheless, as Kasun (1979) and Bennett (1987) point out, the older generation, particularly in our schools, is hesitant to teach sex in its full moral context. A possible reason for this is that sexual morality has traditionally been inter-twined with religious morality and, as Vitz (1986) has demonstrated, our public schools in recent years act as if religion is not part of our cultural life or even our history. It appears that since the moral nature of sex is of concern to many people of traditional religious beliefs, public school educators have shied away from examining the moral dimension of sex in their programs. Certainly, no major de-nomination in our nation's very pluralistic patchwork of churches supports sexual activity among unmarried teenagers. But neither does any responsible group of non-religious people. Most people, religious and non-religious, decry what Jesse Jackson calls, "Babies having babies" (cited in Read, 1988). What, then, keeps sex education programs from taking a strong pro-chastity, pro-abstinence stance?

Our failure to confront the young with moral arguments against engaging in sexual intercourse may be due to adults, including teachers, not wanting to be seen as old-fashioned or out-of-step with views that up until recently have been perceived as progressive and sophisti-cated. In our media-saturated world where sexual images are continually portrayed, attitudes valuing youth and sexual free-dom are easy to acquire. Descriptions like "sexually active" connote vitality and freedom, often leaving the average monog-amous married adult feeling vaguely inert and out-of-step, while chaste single adults may well perceive themselves as relics from our puritan past.

Whatever the reason for teaching sex from a biological and value-free psycho-logical manner, it needs reconsideration. Sex is not a morally neutral matter. The dangers it holds in terms of AIDS, other diseases, and unwanted pregnancy are well known. Eunice Kennedy Shriver (1986), who for several years has been working closely with unwed teenaged mothers, has written about how teenagers want sex dealt with in a value context—values such as self-restraint, compassion-ate understanding of the other, and fidelity. Shriver states:

> Over the years I have discovered that teenagers would rather be given stan-dards than contraceptives. . . . They are thirsting for someone to teach them . . . to tell them that for their own good and the good of society it is not wise for them to have sexual inter-course at 12, 13, 14, or 15 . . . that sex at this age is not necessary for a caring relationship to develop and endure. (p. 7E)

Thus, teenagers as well as adults would welcome having the morality of sex joined with the biological content.

SUGGESTIONS FOR SEX EDUCATION

Since our children will and should come to know and understand sex, it is in everyone's interest that they "get the story right." While it would be comfort-ing to be guided in this by empirically verified procedures, how we conduct sex education must currently rely on good judgment. The following suggestions are offered in the hope that they might con-tribute to sound school policies in this area.

First, sex education should be taught within a moral, though not necessarily religious, context. While teachers should not be moralistic, they should join moral perspectives to the biological informa-tion. They should ensure, as Shriver (1986) and Mast (1986) have urged, that sex be a matter of reflection and moral discourse, and that the biological knowledge and issues are infused with the ethical.

Second, the teacher or the school should not be the lone arbiter of what is taught around this topic. One of a school's goals is to meet the needs of the local community. A sex education course, therefore, should reinforce what the community believes to be correct. It should not be used to separate the young from their families' values. If teachers feel unduly constrained, they should try to educate parents to their views and intentions or, if they fail, find a more accommodating school-community.

Individual parents who are uncomfortable with what their community has decided should be taught may want to find another school for their children. However, allowance has to be made for those parents who object to the school's sexual messages and mores but cannot afford to change schools. Given the many sensitivities around this issue, it is imperative that the public schools and parents find a common moral ground for the sex education programs presented in the schools.

Third, teachers should urge children to talk to their parents about the rightness and wrongness of sexual attitudes and practices. The school could also provide an important service to parents if it shared information with parents on how to talk with their children about these issues. In the same vein, while not teaching the sexual views of a particular religion, the public school could suggest to students an investigation of what their religion has to say about sexual behavior. To teach about religion as a source of knowing and guidance is not a violation of our separation of church and state.

Fourth, the schools should receive the best guidance possible about the biology and morality of sex. The secretary of education and the 50 chief state school officers ought to request a special commission composed of members of the National Academy of Science, other learned associations, and the National Council of Christians and Jews to give guidance to the public schools about what to teach and how to teach it. The state boards of education could then translate these recommendations into educational policy.

Fifth, sex education should not be the sole province of health educators. The question, "What is sex and what should we do with our sexuality?" like other great questions, such as "What is human nature?" and "What is most worth knowing?" does not yield to easy answers. The nature of human sexuality has been the subject of reflection by philosophers, theologians, poets, novelists, sociologists, biologists, and even economists, to name but a few of the groups that have given systematic attention to this topic.

In most American schools today sex education falls to health educators and sometimes physical educators. Their training tends to lean heavily on physiology and psychology. A relatively new discipline, psychology has certainly enriched our understanding of humans, and indeed, of human sexuality. However, psychology has spent much of its brief history jumping from one set of sexual verities to another, and health educators should be cautious about relying on this discipline for guidance.

If health educators continue to be given the major responsibility for sex education, they ought to be educated to draw on several disciplines in their understanding of and teaching about sex. For example, while literature has been largely ignored, much of what we as a human community have learned about sexuality is embedded in our myths, stories, and poems. In literature, sex is more than "the facts of life." It is, rather, a quality of people's lives, charged with energy and meaning, with subtleties and shadings. Literature addresses sexuality in its full complexity of love and jealousy, arousal and rejection, fulfillment and betrayal. Our poems and short stores are "case studies" of what we have learned.

Given this awareness, a group of us at Boston University constructed a literature based curriculum that tries to put the adolescent student's emerging interest in sex in a fuller context than mechanical sexual behavior. Entitled *Loving Well*, this experimental curriculum attempts to engage the student's moral imagination through old and new stories of falling in love, dating, infatuation, romantic betrayal, and the emotional roller coaster of love. Some of the stories and poems involve sexual acts, albeit the descriptions are more suggestive than clinical. However, the sexual situations are framed by lives—lives that must deal with the consequences of these acts, lives that demonstrate how these acts are permeated with ethical considerations. The purpose of the *Loving Well* curriculum, which is currently being tested in classrooms in Massachusetts and Maine, is to get students thinking about their sexuality in this larger context and to discuss the stories and their implications with other students, their teachers, and their parents. While quite preliminary, the initial reactions from students, teachers, and parents have been extremely positive. However, even if effective, we see this curriculum as only one component of a fuller, richer program of sex education.

A final suggestion is that sex education should actively promote sexual abstinence among unmarried teenagers. Sexual abstinence should be presented to the young as an ideal, just as we present honesty as an ideal to be sought after. The self-control involved with sexual abstinence, coupled as it often is with concern for the well-being of another person (i.e., the potentially pregnant teenaged girl or the young man with a venereal disease), can be an important part of character formation for a young person.

But from where does the ideal of sexual abstinence gain its authority? Good sexual attitudes and habits should serve both the individual and the society. Most Americans, regardless of their religious or ethnic affiliation, believe that it is unwise for high school students to be sexually active. A national poll (Leo, 1986) found that two-thirds of our citizens want the schools to "urge teenagers not to have sexual intercourse" and that 76 percent of American adults old enough to have adolescent children considered it "morally wrong for (unmarried) teenagers to have sexual relations."

Thus, it seems reasonable to propose that the schools criticize promiscuity and support sexual abstinence during adolescence. Rather than a value-free approach that advances condoms, abortion, and sexual experimentation, our schools should promote a sex education that not only has the support of the community, but contributes to the development of character and moral maturity.

REFERENCES

Anchell, M. (1986, June 20). Psychoanalysis vs. sex education. *National Review*, 33–61.

Association for Supervision and Curriculum Development (ASCD). (1988). *Moral education in the life of the school*. Alexandria, VA: Author.

Bennett, W. (1987). *Sex and the education of our children*. Washington, DC: U.S. Department of Education.

Christensen, B. (1988, Spring). The costly retreat from marriage. *The Public Interest, 91,* 62.

Cronenwett, S. (1982). Response to symposium on sex and children and adolescents. In E. A. Wynne (Ed.), *Character policy: An emerging issue* (p. 101). Washington, DC: University Press of America.

Cuban, L. (1986). Sex and school reform. *Phi Delta Kappan, 68,* 319–321.

Kasun, J. (1976, Spring). Turning children into sex experts. *The Public Interest, 55,* 3–14.

Leo, J. (1986, November 24). Sex and schools. *Time,* p. 321.

Lickona, T. (1983). *Raising good children.* New York: Bantam.

Mast, C. (1986). *Sex respect.* Bradley, IL: Respect, Inc.

Pratte, R. (1988). *The civil imperative: Examining the need for civic education.* New York: Teachers College Press.

Read, E. W. (1988, March 17). Birth cycle: Teenage pregnancy becomes rite of passage in ghetto. *The Wall Street Journal,* p. 13.

Ryan, K. (1986). The new moral education. *Phi Delta Kappan, 68,* 228–233.

Shriver, E. K. (1986, July 10). Teenage pregnancy: Something can be done. *Philadelphia Inquirer,* p. 7E.

Vitz, P. C. (1986, Fall). The role of religion in public school textbooks. *Religion and Public Education, 13,* 48–56.

NO

Peter Scales

OVERCOMING FUTURE BARRIERS TO SEXUALITY EDUCATION

In the late 1970s, the U.S. Centers for Disease Control embarked on an extensive research effort to understand and improve sexuality education. Part of that effort was funding for the Mathtech research corporation to conduct a national study of the barriers to sexuality education. Based on studying 23 communities' experiences through the 1960s and 1970s, the Mathtech study concluded that (a) administrators' fear of opposition, more than opposition itself, and (b) supporters' inadequate political skills were a central explanation for the widespread lack and/or superficiality of most sexuality education programs in the United States (Scales, 1984).

Some of those barriers have been surmounted. The '80s have seen an expansion of sexuality education, in and out of schools, and more young people seem to be participating in some type of sexuality education. However, the comprehensiveness and timing have not appeared to have changed much from the late '70s. Sonenstein and Pittman (1984) found that perhaps 15 percent of U.S. students experienced a comprehensive sexuality education course in school, as compared with the Mathtech estimate of no more than 10 percent in the late 1970s (Kirby, Alter, & Scales, 1979). This reflects an increase, but is still a distinct minority.

Most differences in when sexuality education is offered may be explained by sexual abuse prevention units in the early grades, as compared to formal sex education in the junior and senior high grades. AIDS prevention efforts do not appear to have taken hold yet below the junior high school level ("Local Districts," 1987). Also, only 10 states require sexuality education today ("Sexuality Education," 1988), as compared to 2 states in 1981 (Kirby & Scales, 1981).

The opposition to sexuality education continues to be a force, most notably in the debate over school based or school linked health clinics, and some old battles are still being fought. For instance, it took until 1987 for Tennessee to pass a law saying it is not a crime to answer relevant questions in sexuality education classes ("Highlights," 1987). However, opponents seem less likely

From Peter Scales, "Overcoming Future Barriers to Sexuality Education," *Theory into Practice*, vol. 28, no. 3 (Summer 1989), pp. 172–176. Copyright © 1989 by the College of Education, Ohio State University. Reprinted by permission.

today to succeed in restricting sexuality education, and supporters seem to have broadened their base.

Those in support had always been the majority, at least since the first Gallup poll on the issue in 1943. The opinion polls today express a popular will to improve and expand sexuality education to a degree unthinkable a generation ago. For example, not only are the usual 80–90 percent in support of comprehensive sexuality education content in the public schools, fully two-thirds of U.S. adults say they think schools should be *required* to establish links with family planning clinics ("Teen Pregnancy," 1986).

In 1988, the theme of the annual meeting of the Society for the Scientific Study of Sex was "sexual literacy." To be sexually literate, the society's program stated, is "to possess the basic sexual information and skills to thrive in a modern world; a comprehensive knowledge of sex and sexuality; the ability to understand alternative sides of a sexual issue; tolerance for ambiguity and paradox; and understanding of the advantages and limitations of different methodologies used in the study of sex" ("Sexual Literacy," 1988). In this broad sense, few would suggest that our nation has become sexually literate.

While barriers to the offering of sexuality education have decreased, many barriers to the effectiveness of sexuality education remain or are likely to appear in the next two decades.[1] If improvement is to occur, the following barriers will have to be overcome.

BARRIER 1. TAKING A NARROW VIEW OF SEXUALITY EDUCATION

In the 1970s, sexuality educators strived to broaden understanding of the field as something more than "sex" education. The focus in many programs had been on reproductive anatomy, or what Gordon (1981) called the "relentless pursuit of the fallopian tubes" (p. 214). To counteract this approach, the term "sexuality" education was emphasized, embracing not just the physical but also the social, emotional, psychological, and spiritual aspects of being human.

Narrowness remains, however, in at least three key ways: (a) overselling the impact of school instruction alone on behavior as contrasted with the impact of broader social actions; (b) basing judgments of sexuality education only on its measurable impact; and (c) taking a "back to the basics" approach to sexuality education.

Overselling sexuality education's impact. The impact of school curriculum on teenage pregnancy and AIDS tends to be oversold, particularly in light of the small part sexuality education courses play in the everyday life of students. Teen pregnancy reduction can occur, but reaching this goal requires going beyond the school curriculum.

School based health clinics, comprehensive programs combining dropout prevention, job opportunities, recreation, and other components, and mentor programs with adults and older youth helping younger persons all have been shown to have better impact on pregnancy reduction than sexuality education alone, although sexuality education is almost always a component in these multifaceted efforts.[2] New Jersey's commissioner of human resources notes that their $6 million pilot investment in comprehensive "youth services in the schools" programs was made because the "boundaries between education and human services don't work anymore" (Sullivan, 1988, p. A23).

Sexuality education courses can make a difference, but their impact is limited. Regarding teen pregnancy prevention, for example, the impact seems to occur through promoting greater contraceptive use among those who would be having sexual intercourse anyway, rather than by reducing sexual activity rates (Kirby, 1985). Given that all of schooling takes up just 8 percent of a person's life by age 18 (Finn, 1986), and the most comprehensive sexuality education programs take up just a fraction of that, the impact of school curriculum alone should not be oversold.

The "measurement" factor. Justifying sexuality education only on the basis of its measurable "impact" instead of its intrinsic value is a second type of narrowness. This is a more subtle barrier because of the emphasis the education reform movement of the last several years has placed on "results" in the form of higher test scores, readiness of youth for the workforce, and other instrumental impacts. In contrast, sexuality education may deserve a prominent place in the curriculum because we define such knowledge as an essential part of being fully human.

A broader barrier to truly comprehensive sexuality education may be the absence of a genuinely "liberal" ethic for education, in the non-political sense of the word. Such an ethic would support education for the sake of well-roundedness, a belief that, apart from what economic purpose they serve, certain areas of human experience and knowledge must comprise the common understanding of people in our society. In the debate about what it means to be educated, we must include an answer to a new fundamental question: What place do human sexuality and gender issues have within that common understanding of "being educated"?

The "back-to-the-basics" approach. Thinking about educational excellence as "back to the basics" is a third type of narrowness, which needs to be replaced with a "forward to the basics" framework (Scales, 1987a). A new set of "basics" is required for the future demands young people will face as they deal with collisions of emerging technology, enduring values, and changing national and world politics. AIDS, surrogate parenthood, global population pressures, and myriad other issues involving sexuality and family concerns will require citizens with well-developed critical thinking skills.

These skills should include the ability to challenge one's own assumptions, set priorities, make difficult choices among competing values, negotiate differing points of view, evaluate information brought to bear on a question, and communicate clearly and effectively. All young people need these skills for the future, not only those who go on to college. Instead of toughening standards and focusing on the college bound, a genuine reconstruction of the curriculum is needed based on rethinking the basics for the future of all children.

BARRIER 2. FAILURE TO UNDERSTAND THE IMPORTANCE OF SELF-EFFICACY

For decades, sexuality educators have held that self-esteem is a key element in behavioral change, and thus must be a key goal in sexuality education curricula. Numerous curriculum guides contain exercises teachers are supposed to use to increase students' self-esteem.[3] Mostly, however, self-esteem in this context has referred to the self-worth part of the construct, rather than what researchers believe may be a more relevant component for behavioral change, the self-efficacy aspect.

Briefly, self-efficacy refers to an individual's perception that he or she is able to do or accomplish what is desired or expected. It has to do with the sense that one can make things happen. Theorists believe that a better understanding of self-efficacy can help educators promote decisions to use contraception or avoid unprotected intercourse (Lawrance & McLeroy, 1986; Rosenstock, Strecher, & Brecher, 1988).

A problem is that neither self-worth nor self-efficacy can really be *taught*, as may be inferred from the generally disappointing results of evaluations showing little increase in self-esteem from a sexuality education program (Kirby, 1985; cf. with the contrasting construct of "sexual self-concept" in Winter, 1988). Self-worth can perhaps be nurtured through self-talk and cheerleading. Years ago, I chanted "I am somebody" along with hundreds of others at a national conference for teenagers in Atlanta, led by Jesse Jackson. I have no doubt that saying "I am somebody" helps. But it doesn't instantly give people the sense that they can make things happen in the world.

Social action must be part of the equation. Perhaps the best we as educators, helpers, and policymakers can do is to maintain the conditions in which that personal sense of self-efficacy can flourish. The sense that we can make things happen doesn't come from slogans, no matter how helpful they are to self-image. It comes only from making things happen.

BARRIER 3. FAILURE TO RESOLVE THE ROLE OF PUBLIC SCHOOLS AS "SURROGATE PARENTS"

As Dryfoos and Klerman (1988) point out, the movement to use schools as "surrogate parents" is burgeoning as schools seek help with this role. Principals in Alaska use the term "second responsibility" to describe the schools' increasing responsibility for the social, physical, and emotional well-being of children. We must acknowledge, however, that all of us—not just the schools—have responsibility for the society we live in.

To expect "the schools" to miraculously solve societal problems without a thorough rethinking of the roles families and other institutions play in the development of our young, and how we invest in those families and institutions, is ludicrous. We need to move beyond this narrow view of the schools' role. To do this, we can restructure the curriculum, as discussed earlier, and improve young people's understanding of common social needs by addressing the sexism and racism that characterize much sexuality education today.

For example, Fine (1988) calls for greater attention beyond gender roles to a "discourse on desire." Fine asks whether our focus on education through fear (in this case, fear of pregnancy) is ideologically perpetuating females as "the potential victim of male sexuality." In this setting, she says, "there is little possibility" of anyone developing "a critique of gender or sexual arrangements" (p. 31). How does the absence of that critique affect our ability to lessen interpersonal violence and promote broader equality between the sexes? Does the focus and language of current sexuality education merely reinforce the victimization of females and prevent growth in self-worth and self-efficacy for many young women, especially low-income women?

This kind of discussion in sexuality education goes beyond preventing pregnancy and points toward a more fundamental examination of human rights and human potential. Perhaps the continuing need for such discussion is best illustrated by the results of a 1987 Rhode Island survey of 1,700 sixth–ninth graders. About 25 percent of the boys and 17 percent of the girls thought it was acceptable for a man to force a woman to have sex if he had spent money on her; and an astonishing 65 percent of the boys and 57 percent of the girls said such rape was acceptable if a couple had been dating for more than 6 months ("Youths in Study," 1988).

We need to call for social action as well as education. While AIDS captures our caring and our headlines, and is a life and death issue, less dramatic events consign millions of people to a slower, no less anguished death. Racism may be at the core here, for minorities are disproportionately the victims in our society, whether we talk about poverty, rates of violence, teenage parenthood, dropping out of school, or alcohol and other drug abuse (Scales, 1988).

BARRIER 4. AIDS AND THE DECLINE OF PLURALISM

Kelly (1987) notes that the anti-sexuality messages associated with AIDS prevention may already be producing, as fallout, a decline in our national acceptance of a pluralism of values that has been a fundamental tenet of modern sex education and democracy. In its extreme, this decline of pluralism can lead to (and

from some reports [Greer, 1986; Kin, 1988] has already led to) an increase in discrimination as the debate over personal liberty and public safety prompts some people to accept apparently easy answers to these complex dilemmas.

How this personal liberty versus public safety dilemma is handled will have a deep impact on many levels. The President's AIDS Commission understood this and enunciated clearly that non-discrimination is the cornerstone of any effective and ethical approach to AIDS in our democratic society. However, former President Reagan's rejection of this anti-discrimination language killed any legislative attempts to reduce AIDS discrimination in 1988 ("Presidential Rejection," 1988).

On a less noticeable level to many, but equally pernicious in its ultimate impact, the decline of pluralism will end up expressing itself in broader censorship and restrictions on freedom of speech. This danger can be expressed in subtle and sometimes not so subtle ways. For example, Sen. Alan Simpson (R-WY) was quoted as being sore at the "thousands of creative staff people" who are "cooking them [issues] up . . . all of it cranked up with special interest groups" (Lovison, 1988, p. 40). Yet, listening to that cacophony of special interest groups, not being irritated by them but welcoming them and reflecting on their messages, is part of the responsibility of governance. After all, we all belong to at least one "special interest group."

Each of us, liberal or conservative, must build honest, guiding values that are strong but still flexible enough to be open to reflection and change. If we honor this democratic process, we will find the right answers to vexing questions. This starts with a simple enough proposition; that, in a democracy, ideas, values, and people are the same. Banning an idea and discriminating against a person are just different sides of the same coin. It is only a small step from going after Anne Frank's diary to going after Anne Frank.

BARRIER 5. INADEQUATE POLITICAL SKILLS

Political savvy has improved among sexuality education advocates. Like children's advocates more generally, they are more aggressive today than 10 years ago. However, political skills still need to be developed in the following areas: (a) translating beliefs into budgets, (b) setting the right agenda, and (c) speaking for ourselves.

As former Centers for Disease Control leader Ogden (1986) wrote, the political battle is about resource allocation. On the most basic economic level, we've only just begun to translate our beliefs into budgets. Through our budgets, we express our public policy values—a different type of "values" than the sex education community has historically focused on. For example, just one Stealth bomber costs about three times as much as our entire federal family planning program (the Stealth is variously put at between $380–450 million each, while Title X stands at $138 million for fiscal year 1989 ["Appropriations," 1988]).

Seeing budgets reflect advocates' beliefs involves avoiding the wrong agenda. The wrong agenda is having just more sexuality education, or earlier, or with better trained teachers. The right agenda, on the other hand, focuses on all the issues discussed in this article, and places sexuality education into a more realistic perspective.

Such an agenda must be based on (a) a broad head start for *all* children; (b) action to lessen poverty and welfare dependence through policies that empower people; (c) greater attention to the life skills needs of the 70 percent of children who will not get a college degree; and (d) expanded opportunities for young people to become better linked with their communities through service and voluntarism, among other principles (Hamburg, 1987; Scales, 1988; Schorr & Schorr, 1988; Weckstein, 1988).

All those things achieve the goal sexuality educators have had for years: to promote healthy, capable people who have purpose, high expectations, and lots of support. These people are more likely to avoid teen pregnancy, substance abuse, suicide, and other problems.

Finally, sexuality education advocates must not allow others to say what advocates believe. To do so is to be "reactive," always being in a position of saying "no, wait a minute, what we really mean is . . ." or "no, we didn't mean that." We should not let others say what we believe in, what we stand for. We should say it ourselves. That is our first—and our final—responsibility.

NOTES

1. An update on the extent of sex education and obstacles to providing it was released just prior to publication of this article. The Alan Guttmacher Institute study of 4,200 junior and senior high teachers, superintendents of 162 of the nation's largest school districts, and all state education agencies found some improvement in the scope of sexuality education, but not dramatic improvement, so numerous inadequacies and barriers remain, including those selected for discussion here (*Risk and Responsibility*, 1989).

2. See reviews in Scales, 1987b; Scales, 1988, as well as a program example in Carrera and Dempsey, 1988, and an example of a successful community "saturation" model in Vincent, Clearie, & Schluchter, 1987).

3. Two widely used examples are "K–12 Family Life Education Curriculum" (1987) and "Family Life Education" (1980).

REFERENCES

Appropriations Fiscal 89: Labor, HHS, Education & HUD. (1988). *Youth Policy, 10*(9), 47.

Carrera, M., & Dempsey, P. (1988). Restructuring public policy priorities in teenage pregnancy. *SIECUS Report, 16*(3), 6–9.

Dryfoos, J. G., & Klerman, L. V. (1988). School-based clinics: Their role in helping students meet the 1990 objectives. *Health Education Quarterly, 15,* 71–80.

Family life education: Curriculum guide. (1980). Santa Cruz, CA: Network Publications.

Fine, M. (1988). Sexuality, schooling, and adolescent females: The missing discourse of desire. *Harvard Educational Review, 58,* 29–53.

Finn, C. (1986). Educational excellence: Eight elements. *Foundations News, 27*(2), 40–45.

Gordon, S. (1981). The case for a moral sex education in the schools. *Journal of School Health, 51,* 214–218.

Greer, W. R. (1986, November 23). Violence against homosexuals rising, groups say in seeking protections. *New York Times,* p. 15.

Hamburg, D. (1987). *Fundamental building blocks of life.* New York: Carnegie Corporation (president's annual essay).

Highlights of state-level victories for children, 1987. (1987). *Children's Defense Fund Reports, 9*(6), 3–8.

K–12 family life education curriculum (1987). Burlington, VT: Planned Parenthood of Northern New England.

Kelly, G. (1987). On being attacked by sex education foes. *Journal of Sex Education and Therapy, 13*(2), 3–4.

Kim, J. (1988, July 3). Are homosexuals facing an ever more hostile world? *New York Times,* p. E16.

Kirby, D. (1985). The effects of selected sexuality education programs: Toward a more realistic view. *Journal of School Health, 11,* 28–37.

Kirby, D., Alter, J., & Scales, P. (1979). *An analysis of U.S. sex education programs and evaluation methods.* Springfield, VA: National Technical Information Service.

Kirby, D., & Scales, P. (1981). State guidelines for sex education instruction in the public schools. *Family Relations, 30,* 229–237.

Lawrance, L., & McLeroy, K. R. (1986). Self-efficacy and health education. *Journal of School Health, 56,* 317–321.

Local districts active in AIDS education. (1987). *Family Life Educator, 5*(4), 4–12.

Lovison, D. (1988). State legislatures: The proving ground for national leadership. *State Legislatures, 14*(6), 40–44.

Ogden, H. (1986). The politics of health education: Do we constrain ourselves? *Health Education Quarterly, 13,* 1–7.

Presidential rejection of AIDS anti-bias law dashes hopes for action in 100th Congress. (1988). *The Nation's Health, 18*(9), 4.

Risk and responsibility: Teaching sex education in American schools today. (1989). New York: Alan Guttmacher Institute.

Rosenstock, I. M., Strecher, V. J., & Brecher, M. H. (1988). Social learning and the health belief model. *Health Education Quarterly, 15*(2), 175–184.

Scales, P. (1984). *The front lines of sexuality education: A guide to building and maintaining community support.* Santa Cruz, CA: Network Publications.

Scales, P. (1987a). Forward to the basics: Life skills education for today's youth. *Family Life Educator, 5*(3), 4–9.

Scales, P. (1987b). How we can prevent teenage pregnancy (and why it's not the real problem). *Journal of Sex Education and Therapy, 13*(1), 12–15.

Scales, P. (1988). An agenda for investing in children and youth. *Youth Policy, 10*(4), 3–7.

Schorr, L., & Schorr, D. (1988). *Within our reach: Breaking the cycle of disadvantage.* New York: Anchor/Doubleday.

Sexual literacy 88. (1988). Mount Vernon, IA: Society for the Scientific Study of Sex. (November 1988 annual meeting program.)

Sexuality education. (1988). New York: Planned Parenthood Federation of America Fact Sheet.

Sonenstein, F. L., & Pittman, K. J. (1984). The availability of sex education in large city school districts. *Family Planning Perspectives, 16,* 19–25.

Sullivan, J. (1988, January 10). 29 Jersey schools will offer program to aid troubled youths. *New York Times,* p. A23.

Teen pregnancy: Over one million teens become pregnant each year. (1986). *Children and Teens Today, 6*(7), 5–6.

Vincent, M. L., Clearie, A. F., & Schluchter, M. D. (1987). Reducing adolescent pregnancy through school and community-based education. *Journal of the American Medical Association, 257*(24), 3382–3386.

Weckstein, P. (1988). Youth, education and the economy. *Youth Policy, 10*(6), 4–24.

Winter, L. (1988). The role of sexual self-concept in the use of contraception. *Family Planning Perspectives, 20*(3), 123–127.

Youths in study say rape acceptable in some instances. (1988). *The Network, 3*(3), 3. (Newsletter of the North Carolina Coalition on Adolescent Pregnancy).

POSTSCRIPT

Are Current Sex Education Programs Lacking in Moral Guidance?

Protests against sex education practices in the public schools often originate through local efforts on the part of a group of parents who resent intrusions by the schools into what they consider to be very private aspects of life. The demarcation of appropriate provinces of parental and school influence has been difficult to draw—and probably always will be. As long as the schools only *offer* instruction in human sexuality without demanding that all students participate, parental protests of this sort would seem to be unjustified. When sexual topics are infused throughout the required curriculum, the problem is compounded.

Joseph Fay and Sol Gordon treat this problem in "Moral Sexuality Education and Democratic Values," *Theory into Practice* (Summer 1989), in which they explore the differences between a *moral* approach and a *moralistic* approach to human sexuality. They state that, while one cannot escape the fact that values are a major component of sexuality education, the moralistic "just say no" strategy is simplistic and ineffective in that it fails to "appreciate the complexity of sexuality and the many factors that may influence a young person's decision to become sexually active."

The Summer 1989 issue of *Theory into Practice* has additional valuable material, namely "Sexuality Education in the U.S.: What It Is, What It Is Meant To Be," by Ann Welbourne-Moglia and Ronald J. Moglia, and "AIDS and Sexuality Education," by Debra W. Haffner, the executive director of the Sex Information and Education Council of the United States (SIECUS). Questions regarding the content of AIDS instruction and the rights of HIV-infected children have been addressed recently. Some important views can be found in "AIDS: Students in Glass Houses," by Perry A. Zirkel, *Phi Delta Kappan* (April 1989); "The Legacy of Ryan White for AIDS Education," by Stephen R. Sroka, *Education Week* (May 23, 1990); and "The Social Dimensions of AIDS," by Harvey V. Fineberg, *Scientific American* (October 1988).

Among relevant publications are D. L. Kirp's book *Learning By Heart: AIDS and Schoolchildren in America's Communities* (1989); the Children's Defense Fund's *A Vision for America's Future* (1989); and "A Battle Lost," by Madelon Zady and Kenneth Cuckworth, *The American School Board Journal* (February 1991).

In the last analysis, this issue must be resolved in the context of the purposes of education. If schooling is designed to address the needs of the "whole person," then sex education, including the problems of human sexuality, morality, and love, would seem to be of central importance.

ISSUE 20

Should Schools of Education Be Abolished?

YES: Rita Kramer, from *Ed School Follies: The Miseducation of America's Teachers* (Free Press, 1991)

NO: Donald J. Stedman, from "Re-inventing the Schools of education: A Marshall Plan for Teacher Education," *Vital Speeches of the Day* (April 15, 1991)

ISSUE SUMMARY

YES: Researcher Rita Kramer reports on her nationwide observations of teacher training institutions, concluding that they are not doing what they should do.
NO: School of education dean Donald J. Stedman feels that these programs are necessary and can be retooled to reach maximum effectiveness.

Critical commentary on the manner in which teachers are prepared for professional service has been rife in recent decades, reaching a crescendo in the past 10 years. In 1963 James B. Conant's *The Education of American Teachers* and James D. Koerner's *The Miseducation of American Teachers* stirred professional and public debate across the nation. Conant called for deeper academic training and a broader liberal arts base for aspiring teachers. Koerner called for the elimination of all education courses from teacher preparation programs.

In the 1980s a number of powerful forces within the profession pressed for reforms. In 1985 the Carnegie Forum released its agenda for improvements, and the American Association of Colleges of Teacher Education published *A Call for Change in Teacher Education*. Of greater impact was the Holmes Group's *Tomorrow's Teachers*, released in 1986, which advocated stronger liberal arts and academic major preparation and the moving of education courses from the undergraduate to the graduate level. In 1987 the National Board of Professional Standards was formed, offering the prospect of a higher level of certification and status enhancement for the profession. An interesting commentary on these reform movements may be found in William R. Johnson's "Empowering Practitioners: Holmes, Carnegie, and the Lessons of History," *History of Education Quarterly* (Summer 1987).

While schools of education are upgrading their standards and expectations, teacher shortages are forcing states and localities to devise alternative certification programs. Such programs greatly reduce the number of education courses required and rely more on on-the-job training. As Emily Comstock DiMartino states, in "Teacher Education for the Twenty-first Century," *Education* (Spring 1991), "This is a very unusual time in teacher education."

John I. Goodlad studied the education of educators in a representative sample of colleges and universities in the late 1980s. His research resulted in a book, *Teachers for Our Nation's Schools* (1990), which offers a variety of recommendations based on some 1,800 hours of interviews. Among the ideas presented are these: the creation of an autonomous "center of pedagogy" for teacher preparation, the formation of school/university partnerships, and the collaborative establishment of professional development schools. These structures would not necessarily operate within the context of the schools of education that are currently under fire. Goodlad expresses the fear that "large numbers of people will continue to equate these institutions with teacher education and assume erroneously that drastic action against them will automatically take care of the problems of teacher education."

One of the people calling for drastic action against schools of education is Rita Kramer, author of *Ed School Follies: The Miseducation of America's Teachers* (1991). Kramer spent a year visiting the schools that prepare tomorrow's teachers and found an ideological sameness that places the promotion of self-esteem in young people above the fostering of the pursuit of knowledge, the protecting of poor students above the inspiring of good students, and making sure everyone gets a passing grade above producing individuals who are capable of serious effort and mastery of knowledge.

In the selection from her book that follows, Kramer makes the case that teacher-training institutions in the United States are "factories" that process material from the bottom of the heap and turn out "experts" in techniques whose knowledge of science and the liberal arts is "practically nonexistent." In opposition, Donald J. Stedman, a dean of one of the schools attacked by Kramer, presents the case for internal renewal of teacher preparation programs, drawing on reforms suggested in the past decade.

YES

Rita Kramer

ED SCHOOL FOLLIES: THE MISEDUCATION OF AMERICA'S TEACHERS

Schools of education as such are only about 150 years old. In 1839 Horace Mann established the first of the state institutions to train teachers for the nation's common schools by acquainting them with the principles or "norms" of classroom instruction. These single-purpose institutions devoted to vocational practice, which came to be known as "normal" schools, were largely staffed by faculty with teaching experience but no academic credentials. Those they enrolled, the majority of them women, were taking what amounted to a step upward on the socioeconomic ladder.

In the early years of this century, the normal schools began to evolve into four-year teachers' colleges, which could grant degrees enabling their graduates to teach not just in the elementary grades but in the increasingly important high schools. Eventually they became general purpose state colleges and universities, part of the expanding system of public institutions of higher education that gained momentum in the years following World War II, when the federal government and state legislatures appropriated unprecedented sums for the education of returning veterans. As a result, an apprenticeship model was replaced by that of professional training and scholarship, and to the preparation of classroom practitioners was added that of educational bureaucrats.

The quest for academic status and acceptance as an equal of the other professional faculties such as law and medicine led to the abandonment on many college and university campuses of the connection with the lowly women who taught children in elementary classrooms.[1] Those who are trained in the vocations of law and medicine profess to know more than their clients about their fields and their clients' needs; they work independently and not under bureaucratic control; and they possess a fixed body of specific knowledge. In contrast, teachers are directed in their daily work by political bodies outside of their field, and their training institutions have no agreed-on disciplinary content. This may help to explain why, as Glazer puts it, "They never seem to be long secure in their adoption of any curriculum and mode of training, and they undertake 'radical revolutions' every decade or so." Professors were too busy inventing a discipline of education to concern themselves with the present realities of the public schools. That was left to the less elite—and less selective—institutions. And even at those, more and more courses in theory began to supplement practice teaching under the influence of the graduate school culture, with its emphasis on the scientific study of education rather than on the practical training of teachers.

Today graduate schools and departments of education exist alongside the other professional faculties like law and medicine, business, and engineering in the large prestigious research-oriented universities, both private and public, from which their influence emanates. Harvard's and Berkeley's schools of education are not in the business of training classroom teachers. More devoted to research, grantsmanship, publication, and the other trappings of scholarship that define academic pursuit than to teacher training, they produce a leadership cadre for the educational establishment: professors and deans of other education faculties, high-level administrators, superintendents, principals— all those whose careers in education lie outside the classroom. Their eye is on policy and theory, not practice, but the theories they generate—their interpretations of their findings on how children learn and how teachers should teach— influence what is taught in teacher-training programs and thus eventually in the nation's classrooms.

There are some 150 graduate schools of education in the United States today,

comprising less than 10 percent of the thirteen hundred institutions—from small private colleges with religious affiliations to major state campuses—that prepare teachers. The influence of the most prestigious dozen or so of the graduate schools is enormous. Their deans and their alumni elsewhere in the education establishment sit on—and often chair— the boards and commissions empaneled by government and foundations to pronounce on matters affecting the schools. Those pronouncements then define the direction of policy in the years until another blue-ribbon panel issues another report explaining why matters haven't improved much since the last one.

AS NORMAL SCHOOLS EVOLVED INTO STATE teachers colleges and eventually became absorbed into university graduate schools of education, there remained a number of colleges of education, both on private campuses and publicly supported ones, that provided teacher-training programs for undergraduates. Notoriously nonselective, they offered three or four years of concentration on pedagogy to students barely out of high school, whose general education was slighted while they prepared to devote themselves to the education of others. On the one hand, graduate schools were producing specialists in such matters as the psychology and philosophy of education while, on the other, undergraduate programs were turning out classroom teachers with minimal background in the subjects they were destined to teach. All of them knew more about how to teach than what to teach.[2]

By the close of the 1970s, most of the country's teachers were coming not from the education schools and departments of liberal arts colleges and elite universities but from the upgraded state teachers' colleges, less well known, less selective, and less demanding. They had already come under attack in numerous works two of whose titles told the story: *Educational Wastelands* and *The Miseducation of American Teachers*. Gradually, the idea began to take hold among critics that undergraduate teacher education should be abolished altogether and replaced with a liberal arts education followed by a fifth year of education courses and practice teaching leading to a master's degree in teaching. A year of internship in the schools would precede taking on full classroom responsibility. This was the recommendation of both of the much-publicized reports issued in 1988, that of the Holmes Group of deans of leading graduate schools of education in research universities and that of the Carnegie Corporation's Task Force on Teaching as a Profession, a group of business leaders and government, union, and school officials.[3]

Both groups saw the move to place all teacher education at the graduate level as a step toward improving the quality of teaching. Teachers would be professionals if they were certified only after graduate professional study. Professional education would replace vocational training and people who knew something they had studied as undergraduates would turn to the matter of how to teach it in graduate school.

Would this bring better people into the classroom? There were those, like Peabody College's Dean Willis D. Hawley, who disagreed with the Holmes and Carnegie reports' recommendations and maintained that a solid liberal arts background could be integrated with course work on learning theory and teaching methods while at the same time getting future teachers into the classroom much earlier in their careers. And there were still others who sought to circumvent the existing systems of teacher training altogether—both graduate and undergraduate—for alternative routes.

Since the federal government's move into the education scene in the late 1950s and subsequent legislation, a vast education industry has proliferated in response to the availability of funds for mandated programs addressed to problems of racial integration, the disadvantaged, education of the handicapped and of the non-English speaking, and so on. Government-funded research projects are ubiquitous on campuses and in consulting firms all over the country. Publications abound, with reports and surveys filling data banks and spilling over library shelves.

As federal money was becoming available to those in the education field, another change was being put into place. The "new left" social scientists who came on the scene in the late 1960s began to reinterpret American history and sociology from a preponderantly Marxist point of view, and nowhere were the revisionists more radical than in the field of schooling. The books by Kozol, Goodman, Illich, and others became best sellers and their ideas about the relationship between school and society, teacher and pupil, permeated the ed school world, both in terms of what was taught and how research was designed, carried out, and interpreted.

With a few exceptions, such as Teachers College of Columbia University and the College of Education at Michigan State University, the leading institutions in the field of education largely shy away from identification with the preparation of the elementary school teaching force. They are more intent on proving that education is an academic discipline with its own subject matter worthy of a place alongside the other university schools and departments. To that end they emphasize graduate education, research, and publication. The training of primary school teachers thus devolves upon the second-tier institutions, from small private colleges to large state universities, less selective in admissions and less demanding of those they admit. . . .

WHEREVER I WENT IN MY YEAR OF CRISS-crossing the country from one college or university to another, whether in public institutions or on private campuses, in urban centers or rural areas, I found a striking degree of conformity about what is considered to be the business of schools and the job of teachers. Everywhere I visited, in new concrete structures and old stone halls of ivy, among undergraduates or older students, I heard the same things over and over again. And failed to hear others.

Everywhere, I found idealistic people eager to do good. And everywhere, I found them being told that the way to do good was to prepare themselves to cure a sick society. To become therapists, as it were, specializing in the pathology of education. Almost nowhere did I find teachers of teachers whose emphasis was on the measurable learning of real knowledge.

Hardly anywhere did I find a sense that any kind of knowledge is valuable in itself or more valuable than any other, a fact which ceased to surprise me once it became clear that among teacher-educators today, the goal of schooling is not considered to be instructional, let alone intellectual, but political. The aim is not to produce individuals capable of effort and mastery, but to make sure everyone gets a passing grade. The school is to be remade into a republic of feelings—as distinct from a republic of learning—where everyone can feel he deserves an *A*.

In order to create a more just society, future teachers are being told, they must focus on the handicapped of all kinds—those who have the greatest difficulties in learning, whether because of physical problems or emotional ones, congenital conditions or those caused by lack of stimulation in the family or lack of structure in the home—in order to have everyone come out equal in the end. What matters is not to teach any particular subject or skill, not to preserve past accomplishments or stimulate future achievements, but to give to all that stamp of approval that will make them "feel good about themselves." Self-esteem has replaced understanding as the goal of education.

Thus the education of teachers has not only been politicized; it has been reoriented toward what is euphemistically called "special education." The ed school culture today is dominated by the diagnosis of learning pathologies and the development of learning therapies—methods for dealing with, if not actually teaching anything to, the various kinds of children with learning difficulties. It is no longer acceptable to think in terms of different systems for different kinds of students of differing degrees of ability and motivation, since it is no longer learning that is at the center of the educational enterprise but, increasingly, the promotion of "equity."

Where the goal of the teacher is to promote self-esteem in everyone in equal measure, performance will no longer count for much. Nor will it seem to matter much what is taught. What is coming increasingly to fill the time and occupy the attention of those being trained to teach are those "instructional strategies" that will enable them to cope with the various kinds of handicapped students they must be prepared to pass along through the same system, without suggesting that they may not be performing at the same level as the more able students. What happens to those more capable or motivated students is hardly anyone's concern.

Where the purpose of the educational system is to promote "self-esteem" regardless of actual accomplishment, substitutes for accomplishment must be found. In the current political climate the chief substitute for measurable individual achievement has become emphasis on the (superior) characteristics of the racial or ethnic subgroup to which one belongs. As a result, the emphasis is shifted from the common values of the larger society to identification with the special interests—and perceived grievances—of this or that racial or ethnic group. And membership in a particular group becomes a more important qualification for teaching than expertise or experience. Thus the ubiquitous concern in teacher education for more "minority teachers" rather than for more good teachers of science, math, history, or literature, no matter who they are or where they come from.

As separatism is emphasized and content trivialized, accountability is ignored. Testing, in the ed school world, is almost as bad as "tracking." No one wants to know the actual results of these policies—whether they really help poor students, how they affect the bright and the gifted. The ed school establishment is more concerned with politics—both academic and ideological—than with learning.

Since what matters is not whether or not anyone has learned anything, but that no one fail to pass, the threshold is lowered as required for almost anyone to get by—in the schooling of teachers as well as in the schools in which they will teach. After all, special methods, not specific subject matter, is what they will be expected to demonstrate.

Meanwhile, any criticism of this state of affairs is met with the charge of elitism or, worse still, racism. No one in the ed school universe dares publicly to advocate a curriculum that resists the "cooperative learning," the "multicultural" and "global" approach that is often a thinly disguised rejection of individualistic democratic values and institutions and of the very idea that underneath all our variety of backgrounds we Americans have been and should continue to become one nation, one culture. That aim and, in fact, any knowledge or appreciation of that common culture and the institutions from which it derives, I found to be conspicuously absent in the places that prepare men and women to teach in our country's public schools today.

THE ONLY WAY TO HAVE BETTER SCHOOLS is to get better teachers. We will never improve schooling, no matter how many reports by commissions, panels, and committees prescribe whatever changes in how the schools are structured or how reading or math is taught, until we improve teacher education. What we have today are teacher-producing factories that process material from the bottom of the heap and turn out models that perform, but not well enough. What we need is to sacrifice quantity for quality, both in the institutions that educate teachers and their graduates. The institutions should be essentially academic, and their graduates should be judged by how much they know, not just how much they care.

If we expect to attract better applicants, they will have to be able to look forward to being paid well; to being given a measure of independence from administrators, politicians, and special-interest groups; and to being able to advance in their profession according to their achievement in a more narrowly defined job. That means as teachers of reading and writing skills, of history, science, math, literature—not as social workers, baby-sitters, policemen, diagnosticians, drug counselors, psychotherapists. They will have to be able to anticipate the challenge presented by gifted students, and not be expected to devote most of their attention and efforts to remediation for the slow, the weak, the apathetic, the hostile. That does *not* mean we give up trying to educate those pupils, it only means we stop trying to do so at the expense of those who can and want to learn and give teachers the opportunity of helping them do it.

But we will never have better teachers until the quality of education at our colleges and universities improves, providing better educated candidates for teaching as for all else. More exacting college and university entrance requirements would necessitate higher standards for high schools in order to meet them, and eventually for elementary schools, which would have to provide literacy and numeracy, in order to prepare for high school. Better schools and better teachers are inextricable. As long as colleges accept high school graduates only 30 percent of whom have had four years of English and three years each of math, science, and social studies, their degrees will mean little. A more exacting core curriculum in our high schools is

indispensable for the preparation of those who would be teachers. That means no longer automatically passing students from one elementary grade to the next regardless of performance in order to bolster their self-esteem. It means our college and university students would no longer be learning things they should have learned in high school—and sometimes even before that.

At present, our teacher-training institutions, the schools, colleges, and departments of education on campuses across the country, are producing for the classrooms of America experts in methods of teaching with nothing to apply those methods to. Their technique is abundant, their knowledge practically nonexistent. A mastery of instructional strategies, an emphasis on educational psychology, a familiarity with pedagogical philosophies have gradually taken the place of a knowledge of history, literature, science, and mathematics. Little wonder then that in so many of our high schools those subjects have given way to courses in film-making, driver education, and marriage and family living. Neither possessing nor respecting knowledge themselves, how can teachers imbue their students with any enthusiasm for it? Nowhere in America today is intellectual life deader than in our schools—unless it is in our schools of education.

Next to the media in general and television in particular, our schools of education are the greatest contributor to the "dumbing down" of America. They have been transformed into agencies for social change, mandated to achieve equality at all costs, an equality not of opportunity but of outcome. No one can be tested because no one must fail.

At the same time they denigrate the history of the institutions that made us the nation that we are, a nation that they must surely notice people want to come to from all over the world and that few leave voluntarily for other parts. While faced with educating the waves of immigrants who persist in wanting to come and live here, they misprize the Western civilization that defined our political institutions and the cultural ideas and artifacts it gave rise to. They have moved from the ideal of integration back to separatism. They have replaced a civic ethos with an emphasis on one's special racial, ethnic, or linguistic group or on one's self, on "multicultural" and bilingual education and "self-esteem." They demean the immigrant and the poor by saying they can't become part of what has gone before and enriched others, can't appreciate the accumulated wisdom of the past, that we have to ask less of them, bend the rules for them, if they are to enter the mainstream. They are too impatient or have too little confidence in them to encourage the underachieving to work to better their situations while educating the next generation for further success. And ultimately they leave them hopeless in the face of the disappearance of the family structure that nourished such patterns in previous generations.

We have set aside equality of opportunity—the idea of opening doors to anyone—and replaced it with equality of results. Everyone has to pass, to be promoted, to enter college, to get a degree. And so a degree has come to mean little more than that one is alive and has applied for one.

That is why alternative certification programs are no panacea for the ills that affect our schools. The good news about these programs is that they provide a way to circumvent the unnecessary baggage imposed by the ed school curriculum, leaving room for substantive learning instead. The bad news is that the people coming out of these programs are only as good as the education they themselves have had—which brings us back full circle to the cumulative inadequacies of an educational system whose erosion of standards has left the average college degree meaning very little and the average college graduate not particularly rich in substantive learning.

Another solution that has been proposed for the problem of quality control of teachers is a national proficiency examination designed to function like the national board exams in medicine and the bar exams in law, a somewhat questionable analogy, since teaching is not a profession with its own specific body of knowledge. The idea is to establish uniform criteria for selection, training, and placing of qualified teachers by means of standard assessment measures for entrance, during, and at the end of their academic and "clinical" preparation. This, it is said, would make teaching a more selective occupation and provide a rationale for higher salaries and career advancement based on proven ability rather than automatic seniority.

Is the attempt to "professionalize" the already overbureaucratized and unionized teaching occupation a good idea? If we have learned anything from the social history of this country in the last half-century, it is that policies and programs often have unforeseen and unintended results. It is possible that legislating standards for teachers will attract some who are better qualified; at the same time it might discourage those maverick adults from outside the system who would like to teach and would be good at it but are unwilling to go through the process of meeting arcane and time-consuming certification requirements. Why make it harder for talented and knowledgeable individuals to be absorbed into the system by extending those requirements on a national basis? Why not let local school districts respond to their needs as they arise? This could be done using their own selection criteria and procedures for on-the-job appraisals.

Everything they need to know about how to teach could be learned by intelligent people in a single summer of well-planned instruction. As it now stands, only individuals with three years of teaching experience are eligible to take the tests for board certification, which virtually closes the door to those outside the existing ed school–state certification route. What is needed is a truly independent board, independent both of the educational bureaucrats and the government. Its members ought to be liberal educators, not union officials, and its money ought to come from the private sphere rather than legislatively dictated federal funds.

We have impoverished ourselves as a nation by failing to nurture a liberally well-educated citizenry that includes a scientifically and technologically literate labor force. To do so we would have to put in place a curriculum that begins in the earliest grades to teach children history and literature, mathematics and science, music and foreign languages. And to do that we would need to see to it that all teachers have a solid liberal education that includes all of the above.

The graduates of those institutions which educate teachers are a long way from fitting that description today.

NOTES

1. An interesting discussion of the characteristics of the various professions and their respec-
tive training institutions is Nathan Glazer's "The Schools of the Minor Professions," in *Minerva*, Vol. XII, No. 3, July 1974 (London).

2. For a general overview of this topic, see Geraldine Joncich Clifford and James W. Guthrie, *Ed School: A Brief for the Professional Education* (Chicago: University of Chicago Press, 1988). See also Harry Judge, *American Graduate Schools of Education: A View from Abroad* (New York: Ford Foundation: 1982).

3. Holmes Group, *Tomorrow's Teachers: A Report of the Holmes Group* (East Lansing, Mich.: Holmes Group, 1986); Carnegie Task Force on Teaching as a Profession, *A Nation Prepared: Teachers for the 21st Century* (New York: Carnegie Forum on Education and the Economy, 1986).

NO

Donald J. Stedman

RE-INVENTING THE SCHOOLS
OF EDUCATION

Few educational organizations have endured so prolonged a period of stress, analysis, reorganization, derision, and sometimes despair as the Schools of Education in the United States over the past twenty years.

Faced constantly with low budgets, demands for high productivity on and off the campus, constant revision of standards, and linked regularly with the difficulties and problems of the public schools, the Schools of Education have barely survived the eighties to face yet additional waves of reform in the nineties. Little wonder that new leadership for the Schools is hard to come by, that admissions flourish most when the scholarships for education students are higher than those for students in other "helping professions," and that faculty morale may be at its lowest ebb since pre-sputnik years.

In times of trial, teacher education often has been the institutional "cash cow," the easy ride for the football team, and the dog to kick when the university has failed in its relations with the surrounding community. With all the talk about reform, all the press for higher teacher salaries, all the rhetoric about education and economic growth, the Schools of Education (the engines of the education economy) have been pressured to perform without new investment in basic resources, without basic attention to the need for new knowledge production, and without regard to the urgent need for reshaping, or perhaps re-inventing, a new School of Education that will help serve the needs of a profoundly changing public school system racing to track fundamental shifts in the American family and society.

Revitalizing the old School will not be enough, simply retooling the old faculty will not be sufficient, rehabilitating the old curriculum is not appropriate. There will be no substitute for a professional School of Education on the campus of the university but its role, function, and organization must be re-invented to undergird the next great leap forward in American education and to sustain new initiatives with a balanced program of effective professional education, research and development, and public service. The question is how?

From Donald J. Stedman, "Re-inventing the Schools of Education: A Marshall Plan for Teacher Education," *Vital Speeches of the Day*, vol. 57, no. 13 (April 15, 1991). Copyright © 1991 by Donald J. Stedman. Reprinted by permission.

Some thoughtful propositions have been put forward, notably John Goodlad's recent work, but none has yet set out the basic reformation that the professional School of Education must undergo. Even though it is not completely clear what the best options are, the general directions are clear. And, universities that ignore the signals and do not rearrange their schools and colleges of education run the certain risk of forfeiting their role in the education reform movement by the mid-90s. For the university to be a salient part of reform, it must be clear about its role in the effort to strengthen the public schools. For their part, the public schools must also make certain commitments for the university to be effective in its response to the course charted for reform of the public schools.

It is unproductive to blame Schools of Education for failure to adequately respond to the calls for help in educational reform. The worst strategy would be to abolish *all* Schools of Education as some would have us do. It is dramatic to say so but it is no solution, just as it is no solution to simply abandon the public schools in favor of home-based education, total free-market choice, or other calls for de-institutionalization currently being considered.

When there is economic recession and turmoil in the business community, we do not seek to abolish the Schools of Business. When there is trouble in the cost and delivery of health care, we do not call for the destruction of the Schools of Medicine. When our social fabric creaks and our welfare system falters, we do not blame the Schools of Social Work.

Neither then is it proper to advocate abolition of our Schools of Education when the needs of our public schools are at their zenith. Instead, we should restructure, renew, and reaffirm the professional Schools of Education to bolster our public education system and to work in partnership with the public schools and state and local government.

What is required is (1) to center on the essential components of a successful system of education, (2) to characterize the proper role of the university in mounting actions to strengthen the public schools, and (3) to restructure the present day School of Education to assure that the teacher preparation, professional development, and research and technical assistance needs of the public schools is the most effective operation possible. This will require more flexibility and a more useful system of accountability than is now the case.

ESSENTIAL COMPONENTS OF A SUCCESSFUL EDUCATION SYSTEM

The developing scheme of essential components of a successful school system emerging from the seminars of the Business Roundtable and the National Governors Association are providing guidelines for schools and universities. These components include the following:

1. A commitment to the following operating assumptions that:

a. virtually all students can learn at high levels.

b. we know how to teach all students successfully.

c. curriculum content (in the schools) must reflect high expectations of the students.

2. The education system must be outcome- or performance-based.

3. Assessment strategies must change.

4. School success must be rewarded and school failures must be sanctioned.

5. School-based staff must have a major role in shaping instructional strategies.

6. Staff development in the schools must be regular, available and directed toward assuring that teachers and administration have the capacity to administer and to teach effectively.

7. Pre-school programs must be made available to all children, particularly children at risk.

8. Health, social and other support services must be provided sufficient to reduce barriers to learning and to provide all children with a healthy start in life.

9. Technology must be made available to provide critically important access to learning.

THE ROLE OF THE UNIVERSITY

The university, in turn, must also adopt a clear understanding of its role in strengthening the public schools. It must acknowledge that:

1. The economic, social and cultural development of a state are determined primarily by the quality and effectiveness of its public schools.

2. The principal contribution of higher education toward strengthening the public schools is the preparation of teachers and school leadership and that it is a central priority for university operations.

3. The preparation of teachers and school leadership is a campus-wide responsibility, not simply the responsibility or domain of the Department or School of Education.

4. The preparation and continuing professional development of teachers and school leadership are best carried out through authentic partnerships among colleges, public schools, businesses, and local agencies.

5. The essential ingredients of an effective teacher education program are:

. . . A strong program in the Arts and Sciences.

. . . Effective clinical training, including well planned and close supervision in classroom and school settings in partnership with selected school systems.

. . . An intellectually energetic and experienced teacher education faculty to select, prepare, and support prospective teachers and school leadership.

6. To be effective, colleges and teacher education programs require strong legislative support and the support and involvement of the business and corporate community.

7. The improvement of teacher education programs requires long-term support and regular and periodic review and revision by external agencies.

8. The Chief Executive Officers (Presidents or Chancellors), Chief Academic Officers, and Boards of Trustees of colleges or universities preparing teachers must be directly involved in and supportive of school-college partnerships, campus-business relationships, and the operations and accreditation of teacher education programs.

9. There must be broad public support for, and a high value placed on, education for colleges and universities and the public schools to function effectively.

RE-INVENTING THE SCHOOL OF EDUCATION

If the present day professional School of Education is to aid in the fulfillment of the essential components of a successful school system and assist the university in fulfilling its role, then it must be re-invented. The reasons are simple. Public school-based reform has taken place so rapidly and so sporadically that the capacity of most Schools of Education to be responsive to the public schools nearly has been lost.

In very large measure, it is the credentialing process that has driven academic programs to scattershot and overly specialized program productivity. The result has been to severely dilute, if not actually to lose, the fundamental ability of universities to educate teachers as true professionals and to acknowledge their status as professionals in their own classrooms. True empowerment for teachers is to educate them so highly and to prepare them for such a high level of professional competence in teaching, so completely, that they will command respect and exude effectiveness. Empowerment simply to share in the decision-making in the administrative operations of schools is a shallow undertaking and only creates further confusion in the schools. To empower teachers and to produce and sustain effective teachers and school administrators, the Schools of Education must (1) focus on the production of more generally educated products, (2) assist school systems in the development of the capacity to specialize beginning teachers, (3) help coordinate professional development programs and produce professional development program specialists, (4) devise a system of technical assistance that will transfer useful research products and best practices that will inform the policy of the governance structures of the public schools and improve curriculum, instruction, and teaching in the schools, and (5) be set free from the restraints of the credentialing bureaucracy and the elaborate program approval procedures that restrict flexibility and responsive program change.

PROPOSED RESTRUCTURING OF SCHOOLS OF EDUCATION

The present day professional school, driven to high productivity to meet the demand and distribution problems of the public schools, has become a rigid system, compliant with the bureaucratic structures of the quality assurance process and incapable of the flexible productivity required by fast-changing public schools. Attempts to overcome this rigidity have been to modify certification procedures rather than to rearrange the production process. Schools of Education that pursue this rigid standard system of preparing professional personnel are doomed to the scrap heap. Those that can restructure themselves to a flexible system will not only survive, they will help make a difference. The new lean and flexible look is characterized by:

1. Active recruitment of prospective teachers and school administrators.

2. Involvement of teachers and students in the curriculum design phase and in the evaluation of graduates.

3. Effective preparation of small groups of students trained in cohorts, *and*

4. Interdisciplinary and team faculty teaching, research, and consultation to the public schools.

To achieve this restructuring and to gain the flexibility needed, greater emphasis must be placed on (1) performance-based teacher evaluation systems and (2) external sources of program review. Specifically, state level program approval procedures should consist of assessment of the performance of graduates of teacher education programs to decide on approval and continuation of such programs, and current procedures should be abolished. In addition, all teacher education programs should be required to meet the new standards of the National Council for Accreditation of Teacher Education (NCATE) as an eligibility requirement to seek and to maintain state level program approval. This combination of national accreditation coupled with outcomes assessment at the state level would provide for an improved system of quality assurance and create more flexible and responsive teacher education programs. It would also reduce the number of teacher education programs now operating, many of which are marginal, and would probably lead to regional consortia of interinstitutional teacher education programs operating more effective, less costly, and more innovative programs.

In this context "alternative routes" into the profession could be planned, organized, and supported by university and schools alike, not by tinkering with certification policies, creating unattended back doors and bypasses, but by relating the personnel needs of the schools to the production process and basing success on the performance of the graduates, not on its inventory of courses, competencies, or the number of door knobs in the library.

All of this will require more research and development and a greater federal and state investment in restructuring and strengthening teacher education. What is needed is a modern day "Marshall Plan" for teacher education programs and the will to step out and take charge of a situation that will continue to deteriorate without bold action.

POSTSCRIPT

Should Schools of Education Be Abolished?

The 1990s are certain to produce some dramatic changes in the way teachers are educated. A number of colleges and universities have already abandoned their undergraduate teacher-training programs and have followed the Holmes Group's impetus to design new graduate-level certification programs. New guidelines by the National Council for the Accreditation of Teacher Education (NCATE), released in 1990, are prompting numerous internal reforms in current programs.

Many sources of advice are available to those who are rethinking the process of professional preparation and development. Among these are *Ed School: A Brief for Professional Education* (1988) by Geraldine J. Clifford and James W. Guthrie; Jurgen Herbst's *And Sadly Teach: Teacher Education and Professionalization in American Culture* (1989); Alan R. Tom's *How Should Teachers Be Educated?* (1987); Gene I. Maeroff's *The Empowerment of Teachers* (1988); *What Teachers Need to Know* (1990) by David D. Dill et al.; T. L. Good's *Building the Knowledge Base of Teaching* (1990); and *Teacher Education and the Social Conditions of Schooling* (1991) by Daniel P. Liston and Kenneth M. Zeichner.

Numerous articles on the topic may be found in the *Journal of Teacher Education*, the *Teacher Education Quarterly*, and the *Journal of Education for Teaching*. The November 1990 issue of *Phi Delta Kappan* features eight relevant articles, including "Policies for Reforming Teacher Education," by Arthur E. Wise. Two other *Phi Delta Kappan* articles are worthy of note: Pearl R. Kane's "Just Ask Liberal Arts Grads to Teach" (May 1990) and Mary K. Kennedy's "Policy Issues in Teacher Education" (May 1991).

Jacques Barzun, in his book *Begin Here: The Forgotten Conditions of Teaching and Learning* (1991), joins Rita Kramer's crusade against education courses. According to Barzun, "The present shortage of teachers, which has brought about the admission of college graduates *without* indoctrination in 'methods,' is an opportunity not to be missed. Liberal arts majors, if their courses were truly liberal, will be free of crippling ideas about how to teach. They will know their subject, they will think about *it* and not some 'strategy,' they will not believe the absurd dogma that there is no transfer of learning ability from one subject to another." This sort of criticism is certainly not new but must be dealt with as teacher educators repave the road into the profession.

CONTRIBUTORS
TO THIS VOLUME

EDITOR

JAMES WM. NOLL is an associate professor in the College of Education at the University of Maryland in College Park, Maryland, and a member of the American Educational Studies Association, the National Society for the Study of Education, the Association for Supervision and Curriculum Development, and the World Future Society. He received a B.A. in English from the University of Wisconsin, an M.S. in educational administration from the University of Wisconsin, and a Ph.D. in the philosophy of education from the University of Chicago. His articles have appeared in several education journals, and he is the coeditor, with Sam P. Kelly, of *Foundations of Education in America: An Anthology of Major Thought and Significant Actions* (Harper & Row, 1970). He has also served on the editorial boards for The Dushkin Publishing Group's *Annual Editions: Education* and *Computer Studies: Computers in Education* for many years.

STAFF

Marguerite L. Egan   Program Manager
Brenda S. Filley   Production Manager
Whit Vye   Designer
Libra Ann Cusack   Typesetting Supervisor
Juliana Arbo   Typesetter
David Brackley   Copy Editor
David Dean   Administrative Assistant
Diane Barker   Editorial Assistant

AUTHORS

MORTIMER J. ADLER is the director of the Institute for Philosophical Research in Chicago, Illinois, and the chairman of the board of editors for *Encyclopaedia Britannica*. He is the author of *A Guidebook to Learning: For a Lifelong Pursuit of Wisdom* (Macmillan, 1986) and *Reforming Education: The Opening of the American Mind* (Macmillan, 1988).

MOLEFI KETE ASANTE is a professor in and the chairman of the Department of African American Studies at Temple University in Philadelphia, Pennsylvania. A leading proponent of the Afrocentric philosophy, he is the author of 33 books, including *Afrocentricity: The Theory of Social Change*, 2d ed. (Africa World, 1990).

JAMES A. BANKS is a professor of education at the University of Washington in Seattle, Washington.

R. FREEMAN BUTTS is the William F. Russell Professor Emeritus in the Foundations of Education at Columbia University's Teachers College and a principal contributor to CJVITAS, a Framework for Civic Education. His publications include *The Civic Mission in Educational Reform: Perspectives for the Public and the Profession* (Hoover Institute Press, 1989).

LEE CANTER is president of Lee Canter and Associates in Santa Monica, California, and the developer of the Assertive Discipline program. His publications include *Assertive Discipline: A Take-Charge Approach for Today's Educator* (Canter & Associates, 1976), coauthored with Marlene Canter, and *Assertive Discipline for Parents* (Canter & Associates, 1982).

JOHN E. CHUBB, a partner in the Edison Project in Knoxville, Tennessee, is a senior fellow in the Governmental Studies Program at the Brookings Institution. His publications include *Can the Government Govern?* (Brookings Institution, 1989), coauthored with Paul E. Peterson, and *Politics, Markets, and America's Schools* (Brookings Institution, 1990), coauthored with Terry M. Moe.

EVANS CLINCHY is a senior field associate at the Institute for Responsive Education in Boston, Massachusetts. He is the coauthor, with Timothy W. Young, of *Choice in Public Education* (Teachers College Press, 1992).

ROBERT L. CORD is a professor of political science and the University Distinguished Professor at Northeastern University in Boston, Massachusetts. He is the author of several books and articles about the U.S. Constitution, including *Separation of Church and State: Historical Fact and Current Fiction* (Baker Book House, 1988), which has been cited in numerous constitutional law books and in the opinions of U.S. Supreme Court justices for "church and state" cases.

DEAN C. CORRIGAN is a professor of educational administration at Texas A&M University in College

Station, Texas. He also teaches courses in the politics of education and leadership in interprofessional education, and he has the distinction of being the first holder of the university's Ruth Harrington Chair in the Department of Educational Leadership.

JOHN F. COVALESKIE is a doctoral candidate of the cultural foundation of education and curriculum in the School of Education at Syracuse University in Syracuse, New York.

LARRY CUBAN is a professor of education and the associate dean of the School of Education at Stanford University in Stanford, California. A member of the board of editorial consultants for *Phi Delta Kappan,* he is the author of *How Teachers Taught: Constancy and Change in American Classrooms, 1890–1980* (Longman, 1984).

JOHN DEWEY (1859–1952) was a philosopher and a leader in the field of education. He emphasized the importance of "learning by doing," and his writing and teachings profoundly affected such diverse fields as philosophy, educational theory, psychology, law, and political science. His many works include *The School and Society* (1899), *Democracy and Education* (1916), and *Experience and Education* (1938).

DENIS P. DOYLE, an education consultant, speaker, and author, is a senior research fellow of the Hudson Institute. He is a member of the National Education Commission on Time and Learning and a former

director of education policy studies and human capital studies at the American Enterprise Institute. He is the author or coauthor of four books and numerous articles on education, including *Excellence in Education: The States Take Charge* (American Enterprise Institute, 1985), co-authored with Terry W. Hartle.

CLIFTON FADIMAN is a writer, editor, and radio and television performer whose articles have appeared in numerous magazines. He has been a member of the board of editors for *Encyclopaedia Britannica* since 1959, and he served as an editorial consultant to the Encyclopaedia Britannica Education Corporation from 1963 to 1970.

FRANCES C. FOWLER is an assistant professor in the Department of Educational Leadership at Miami University in Oxford, Ohio. She received a B.A. from Cornell University, an M.A. from the University of Illinois, and a Ph.D. from the University of Tennessee. Her research interests include educational policy analysis and comparative educational policy.

DAVID GUTERSON is an English teacher at Bainbridge High School in Bainbridge Island, Washington. His publications include *The Country Ahead of Us, the Country Behind* (Harper & Row, 1989).

E. D. HIRSCH, JR., is the Linden Kent Professor of English at the University of Virginia in Charlottesville, Virginia, and a member of the board of directors of the Foundations of Literacy Project. His publications include *The Aims of Interpretation* (University of Chicago Press, 1976) and *Cultural Literacy: What Every American Needs to Know* (Houghton Mifflin, 1987). He received a Ph.D. in English from Yale University in 1957.

JOHN HOLT (1923–1985) was an educator and a critic of public schooling. He authored several influential books on education, including *How Children Fail* (Pittman, 1964), *Escape from Childhood* (E. P. Dutton, 1974), and *Instead of Education: Ways to Help People Do Things Better* (Holt Associates, 1976).

ROBERT M. HUTCHINS (1879–1977) was a chancellor of the University of Chicago, a cocompiler of Encyclopaedia Britannica, Inc.'s *The Great Books of the Western World*, and a director of the Center for the Study of Democratic Institutions.

LAWRENCE KOHLBERG (1927–1987) was a professor of education and a director of the Center for Moral Education at Harvard University. He wrote many articles based on his research into the relationship between cognitive growth and ethicality, and he compiled a two-volume collection of essays on moral development that is now considered a classic.

JONATHAN KOZOL, a graduate of Harvard University and a former teacher, is a writer and social commentator who writes on the problems of the American public education system. His publications include *Death at an Early Age* (Plume Books, 1968), which was the winner of the National Book Award in 1968, and *Savage Inequalities: Children in America's Schools* (Harper-Perennial, 1991).

RITA KRAMER is a free-lance writer, editor, and researcher. Her publications include *At a Tender Age: Violent Youth and Juvenile Justice* (Henry Holt, 1988).

DONALDO MACEDO is an associate professor of linguistics in the Department of Bilingual and English as a Second Language Studies at the University of Massachusetts–Boston.

FLORETTA DUKES McKENZIE, a former superintendent of public schools for Washington, D.C., is the president of the McKenzie Group and a limited partner of Hogan and Hartson, both in Washington, D.C.

TERRY M. MOE is a professor of political science at Stanford University in Stanford, California, where he has been teaching since 1981. He has written extensively on a variety of topics, including public bureaucracy, the presidency, and the education system, and his book *Politics, Markets, and America's Schools* (Brookings Institution, 1990), coauthored with John E. Chubb, has received national attention for its institutional critique of the American school system and its market-based proposal for sweeping institutional change.

GEOFFREY MORRIS is an executive editor of *National Review* magazine, where he writes regularly about education, politics, and other issues.

CHARLES NEVI is the executive director of curriculum and instruction for the Puyallup School District in Puyallup, Washington. He received an Ed.D. from Seattle University.

JEANNIE OAKES is a professor of education in the Graduate School of Education at the University of California, Los Angeles. She is the author of *Keeping Track: How Schools Structure Inequality* (Yale University Press, 1985), which was chosen as one of the "Ten Most Read Books of 1985" by *The American School Board Journal,* and the coauthor, with Martin Lipton, of *Making the Best of Schools: A Handbook for Parents, Teachers, and Policymakers* (Yale University Press, 1990).

SUSAN OHANIAN, a former teacher, is a free-lance writer whose interests focus on schools and the people in them. Her publications include *The Language of a Teacher* (Boynton/Cook/Heinemann, 1993).

DONALD A. RAKESTRAW is an assistant professor in the Department of History at Georgia Southern College in Statesboro, Georgia.

JENNIE F. RAKESTRAW is an assistant professor in the Department of Early Childhood Education and Reading at Georgia Southern College in Statesboro, Georgia.

DIANE RAVITCH is an adjunct professor of history and education at Columbia University's Teachers College in New York City. Her publications include *Troubled Crusade: American Education, 1945–1980* (Basic Books, 1983).

CARL R. ROGERS (1902–1987) was a noted psychologist and educator who taught at the University of Chicago and at the University of Wisconsin–Madison. He introduced the client-directed approach to psychotherapy in 1942, stressing the importance of a personal doctor-patient relationship, and he was the first psychologist to record and transcribe therapy sessions verbatim, a practice now standard with psychotherapy. His publications include *On Becoming a Person* (Houghton Mifflin, 1972).

KEVIN RYAN is the director of the Center for the Advancement of Ethics and Character at Boston University in Boston, Massachusetts. He has been an instructor in teacher education for 30 years.

PETER SCALES is the director of national initiatives for the Center for Early Adolescence in the School of Medicine at the University of North Carolina at Chapel Hill, where he is also an associate professor in the School of Social Work. He has been the director of education for the Planned Parenthood Federation of America and a research director of Syracuse University's Institute for Family Research and Education. He has published more than 100 articles, essays, and books, and he serves on the editorial boards of *Child Welfare* and the *Middle School Journal.*

ARTHUR M. SCHLESINGER, JR., is the Albert Schweitzer Professor of the Humanities at the City University of New York. His publications include *The Disuniting of America: Reflections on a Multicultural Society* (W. W. Norton, 1992).

PETER SCHRAG is the editorial page editor of *The Sacramento Bee*.

RUTH SIDEL is a professor of sociology at the Hunter College of the City University of New York. She received an M.S. in social work from Boston University and a Ph.D. in sociology from Union Graduate School. Her publications include *On Her Own: Growing Up in the Shadow of the American Dream* (Viking Penguin, 1990).

B. F. SKINNER (1904–1990), noted psychologist and an influential exponent of behaviorism, was the holder of the William James Chair in the Department of Psychology at Harvard University. His major works include *Behavior of Organisms* (1938), *About Behaviorism* (Random House, 1976), and *Reflections on Behaviorism and Society* (Random House, 1978).

DONALD J. STEDMAN is a professor in and the dean of the School of Education at the University of North Carolina at Chapel Hill. He has taught at Vanderbilt University and at Duke University, and at one time he was the associate director of the Joseph P. Kennedy, Jr., Foundation in Washington, D.C., where he served as a special assistant to then-president John F. Kennedy, acting as coordinator of the first White House Conference on Mental Retardation.

PAUL WOODRING is the Distinguished Service Professor Emeritus at Western Washington University in Bellingham, Washington. He began teaching in 1927 and has taught at all levels of education, from elementary school to college and graduate school. He received a Ph.D. in psychology from Ohio State University, and he is the author of 10 books and more than 300 editorials, articles, and book reviews on education.

EDWARD A. WYNNE is a professor in the College of Education at the University of Illinois at Chicago. He is the author of numerous books and articles on character and education, including *Looking at Schools: Good, Bad, and Indifferent* (Lexington Books, 1980).

INDEX